COLLECTED ESSAYS IN LAW

Regulation, Crime, Freedom

The Collected Essays in Law Series
General Editor: Tom D. Campbell

Law's Premises, Law's Promise:
Jurisprudence after Wittgenstein

Thomas Morawetz

ISBN: 0 7546 2013 1

Constitutional Interpretation

Frederick Schauer

ISBN: 0 7546 2039 5

The Jurisprudence of Law's Form and Substance

Robert S. Summers

ISBN: 0 7546 2024 7

Legal Rules and Legal Reasoning

Larry Alexander

ISBN: 0 7546 2004 2

John Braithwaite

Regulation, Crime, Freedom

Ashgate

DARTMOUTH

Aldershot • Burlington USA • Singapore • Sydney

Published by
Dartmouth Publishing Company Limited
Ashgate Publishing Limited
Gower House
Croft Road
Aldershot
Hampshire GU11 3HR
England

Ashgate Publishing Company
131 Main Street
Burlington
Vermont 05401
USA

Ashgate website: http://www.ashgate.com

British Library Cataloguing in Publication Data
Braithwaite, John, 1951–
    Regulation, Crime, Freedom. –
    (Collected Essays in Law)
    1. Criminology. 2. Equality. 3. Free will and determinism.
    I. Title
    364

US Library of Congress Cataloging-in-Publication Data
Braithwaite, John
    Regulation, Crime, Freedom / John Braithwaite.
        p.   cm. – (Collected Essays in Law 2)
    Articles originally published 1975–1997.
    Includes bibliographical references and index.
    1. Crime Prevention. 2. Rules of Law. 3. Equality. 4. Liberty.
    5. Reparation. Social Movements. I. Title II. Series
    HV7431.B695 2000
    364.4 21– dc21   99–039395

ISBN 0 7546 2005 0

Printed in Great Britain by
Antony Rowe Ltd, Chippenham, Wiltshire

Contents

John Braithwaite is a Professor in the Research School of Social Sciences, Australian National University. He has been Head of Law there and coordinated interdisciplinary networks – Reshaping Australian Institutions (1992–96) and the Regulatory Institutions Network (RegNet). He has been active in social movement politics, representing community groups on the Economic Planning Advisory Council Chaired by the Prime Minister of Australia between 1983–87. Between 1985 and 1995 he was a part-time Commissioner with the Trade Practices Commission.

Series Editor's Preface

Collected Essays in Law makes available some of the most important work of scholars who have made a major contribution to the study of law. Each volume brings together a selection of writings by a leading authority on a particular subject. The series gives authors an opportunity to present and comment on what they regard as their most important work in a specific area. Within their chosen subject area, the collections aim to give a comprehensive coverage of the authors' research. Care is taken to include essays and articles which are less readily accessible and to give the reader a picture of the development of the authors' work and an indication of research in progress.

The initial volumes in the series include collections by Professors Frederick Schauer (Harvard), *Constitutional Interpretation*, John Braithwaite (ANU), *Regulation, Crime and Freedom*, Tom Morawetz, *Law's Premises, Law's Promise*, Robert Summers (Cornell), *Law's Form and Substance*, and Larry Alexander (San Diego), *Legal Rules and Legal Reasoning*. These collections set a high standard for future volumes in the series and I am most grateful to all of these distinguished authors for being in at the start of what it is hoped will become a rich and varied repository of the achievements of contemporary legal scholarship

Acknowledgements

My thanks to Tom Campbell, editor of the Dartmouth series of Collected Essays in Law for the encouragement to put together this collection and to Alison Pilger for practical help to make it happen. Particular thanks are due to my partner in all things, Valerie Braithwaite, and my friends, Brent Fisse and Stephen Mugford, for permission to reprint works co-authored with them. Indeed, I owe a huge debt to all my co-authors. I doubt if many scholars have learnt as much from co-authors. In my writing I have enjoyed straying beyond my competence, but only after being emboldened by co-authors who were extraordinarily competent in the fields I invaded. A similar debt is owed to my PhD students who have brought competencies to our various shared enterprises that were lacking in me. Acknowledgment is also due to the publishers listed in the Table of Contents for their permissions to reprint.

Finally, I thank the institutions where I worked as these pieces were written for the many ways they sustained me and nurtured my intellectual citizenship. I am glad I worked at every one of them. In 1969 I started as an undergraduate at the University of Queensland. John Western and Paul Wilson, in particular stuck by me even though my academic record was not impressive; among other things, I failed to obtain a pass in first year sociology and in mathematics honours and obtained only a second class honours in anthropology and sociology. I finished up at the University of Queensland in 1978 after periods as a research assistant, PhD student and lecturer. The subsequent employers I wish to thank are Griffith University (1975–77), the Australian Institute of Criminology (1978–82), the University of California, Irvine (1979), the Australian Federation of Consumer Organizations (1982–84), the American Bar Foundation (1988, 1990) and the Australian National University (since 1984). While the debts I owe to all of them are genuinely deep, the deepest is to the Australian National University and the wonderful group of colleagues and support staff of the Research School of Social Sciences.

Introduction

Regulation, Communities and Freedom

Substantively, there have been two main foci of my work – crime and business regulation. An early interest in corporate crime led to a broader concern with strategies of business regulation. This in turn fed back to the study of regulatory approaches to preventing crime. It is hard to study these phenomena without questioning what should be regulated, what should be criminalized, and how? So my work has always been explicit in its commitment to integrating explanatory and normative theory.

Its ambition has been to contribute toward a vision of how to regulate more justly. Its audience is only secondarily policy makers in the state and business. Beyond the academy, its audience has been much more centrally the social movements in which I have been active – the consumer, environment, development and labour movements and the social movement for restorative justice – and those with which I have been a sympathizer and fellow traveller – the women's, human rights, indigenous peoples', older person's, gay and lesbian, peace, disabilities, and animal welfare movements. We will see that this vision of how to regulate more justly is about liberty, equality, fraternity and sorority, about how to give concrete institutional meaning to republican ideals that are informed by an empirical understanding of how the world actually works.

Inequality was the early concern as an explanation of non-compliance with the law and as something to struggle against. A second concern was freedom. In a number of papers freedom is found to be important to the explanation of crime. An analysis of homicide rates in 31 nations found the Freedom House Political Freedom Index to be the strongest predictor of homicide in the study (Chapter 2). Freer societies and more egalitarian societies had lower homicide rates. Another essay sets out to explain how a republican separation of powers is a central idea of institutional design because it simultaneously advances freedom and prevents crimes of the powerful (Chapter 12). Chapter 4 conceives of unfreedom as one dimension of inequality – a society where some dominate and others lose their freedom by having their choices dominated – an inequality that contributes to crime. In *Crime, Shame and Reintegration* (Braithwaite, 1989) I argued that a low crime society will be strong on rights and strong on responsibilities, and especially strong on responsibilities to disapprove when the rights of others are crushed. In these senses, a low crime society is characterised by active community engagement with defending the institutions of freedom. Freedom, equality and community thus end up as both the key explanatory variables and the central normative ideals.

Republican Freedom

A turning point in my career was the collaboration with Philip Pettit that produced *Not Just Deserts: A Republican Theory of Criminal Justice* (Braithwaite and Pettit, 1990). This integrated normative concerns with freedom and equality. In that book we argued for a republican conception of freedom, which we called dominion. Pettit (1997) subsequently called this freedom as non-domination, which I also prefer to dominion. Republican freedom on this view requires more than the good fortune of averting interference with one's choices. It requires guarantees that one will not even be exposed to the possibility of arbitrary interference by an unregulated power. Such assurance is not possible without strong communities that mobilize disapproval against those who trample the rights of others and without a high degree of structural equality. So republican freedom requires liberty, equality and plural communities. Because the poor are bound to have their choices dominated, freedom as non-domination will not be secured in a society with high levels of structural inequality. Concentrations of power tend to fight back to reinstitute domination (Braithwaite, 1999). The greater the inequality of wealth and power in a society , the lesser will be the freedom as non-domination in that society. Hence, freedom as non-domination requires ceaseless social democratic struggle for greater equality of outcomes. Equality before the law and equality of opportunity are important but utterly insufficient.

Criminal justice systems and other regulatory institutions, according to Braithwaite and Pettit (1990), ought to be designed to maximize freedom as non-domination. The loss of freedom as non-domination when a felon is locked up must be balanced against what is delivered to crime victims (and the community generally) in enhanced freedom as non-domination. From this framework we derive the need for upper constraints on how much punishment the state or community can impose for a particular kind of crime and the need to abolish all lower constraints that require minimum levels of punishment. We argue for iteratively winding back levels of punishment until clear evidence emerges of increased crime or other threats to freedom as a result of the decline in the level of punishment.

This means that the view of equality is very different from that of liberal just deserts theorists. Equal punishment for equal wrongs is not important for its own sake from this republican perspective. If a policy of equal punishment for equal wrongs reduces freedom as non-domination in the society, and Braithwaite and Pettit (1990) argue that it does, then this is a bad kind of equality. Equal justice for victims and equal justice in the punishment of offenders are fundamentally incompatible goals. Equal consideration for victims requires that a victim be heeded if they wish to heal themselves through the grace of granting mercy to an offender, as they often do in restorative justice processes. Restorative justice processes come up with a practical way of balancing the justice claims of offenders and victims that can be defended in terms of freedom as non-domination. Both victims and offenders are guaranteed a certain level of security against domination. Victims are assured that their wishes will be heard and debated and that offers will be made to repair the harm they have suffered insofar as it is possible to do so. Offenders are guaranteed that they cannot be punished above a statutory maximum level of punishment for a given offence.

My work therefore involves an iterated adjustment of concepts like inequality, freedom and shame from explanatory theory and normative theories of the same concepts as they can be applied in real-world praxis (Parker, 1999). So we have an explanatory account of how inequality increases crime, a normative account of equality as a republican ideal and a sociologically possible practice for realising a certain kind of equality – restorative justice as an alternative to retributive justice, equitable tax policies. Over time the explanatory and normative accounts of inequality that can be realised in practice are mutually adjusted. An integrated normative-explanatory theory of crime then becomes possible. This is my project with concepts like inequality, freedom, shame and the separation of powers. It is motivated by the view that pursuing normative theories that are disconnected from testable explanatory theories has barren consequences. The result is prescriptions that can only be realised in some sociologically impossible world. Equal punishment for equal wrongs is a good example of an impossibilist normative theory that has disastrous consequences in a world where it is always possible to punish the poor and the powerless but rarely the rich and powerful.

The republican vision therefore clarifies our perception of how crime hurts and how justice might heal. Empirically, its research program shows that punishment adds extra hurt into a world with deeply structured inequity. Normatively, it illuminates an ideal of justice about healing as an alternative to hurting.

Dimensions of Inequality

The first essay in this collection was written while I was a student. It conceives schools as having destructive features because they are 'the mouse race that prepares us for the rat race'. Schools vary in the depths to which they sink in structuring inequality into their outcomes. Ipswich Central Boys' State School, which I attended, ranked students from the top at the left back row to the bottom at the right front row ('where it is easier to reach you with my ruler' as some teachers were fond of saying). This was affirming for those who sat in the back but degrading for the dunces in the front row. Better schools motivate children to strive to improve on their own past performance more than compete against others (though to a certain degree the latter is inevitable). What Knight (1985: 266–70) later called 'redemptive schooling' is the egalitarian ideal explored in this essay – schooling that emphasises learning through strengths, where every child is assumed to have strengths, where 'everyone can be someone'.

'The Effect of Income Inequality and Social Democracy on Homicide' (co-authored with Valerie Braithwaite) explored the suspicion that decent social democratic government – giving priority to freedom and equality – was likely to deliver lower crime rates. Among 31 nations, we did indeed find that less equal societies suffered more homicide, societies with stronger social democratic representation in their legislatures and greater political freedoms suffered less homicide. Many subsequent studies controlled for more variables than we did in this early effort and affirmed the homicide-inequality association cross-nationally and across cities within nations. The effect of freedom and social democracy on homicide unfortunately was ignored in this subsequent research.

Corporate crime is a natural topic for an egalitarian social democrat. One book on safety in coal mines was directly motivated by my involvement in the labour movement in Ipswich, then a coal mining town. One disaster took the lives of mates I loved and I resolved to write an angry book on the need to deter unsafe practices in mines. It turned out not to be a punitive book (Braithwaite, 1985) because I came to the view from my empirical studies that punitiveness is often a counterproductive regulatory strategy. By 1985 pursuit of punishment for corporate criminals commensurate to the punishment meted out to blue collar criminals seemed to me a strategy contrary to the interests of blue collar victims of corporate crime.

'Inegalitarian Consequences of Egalitarian Reforms to Control Corporate Crime' (Chapter 3) was a first step toward this realisation. It was also a step toward seeing the problem as one of transnational rather than national regulation. The argument was that as reform governments enacted more laws to crack down on corporate crime (as they had been doing in the 1970s) the law became more complex, thereby favouring more formal and rational organizations. The increased complexity increases costs of investigation and conviction to the point where action can only be taken against the gravest injustices. Transnational corporations responded by shifting their gravest injustices to the Third World. Injustice increased both nationally and internationally as a result of playing legal cat and mouse with corporate power.

'Poverty, Power, White-Collar Crime and the Paradoxes of Criminological Theory' (Chapter 4) weaves together a consideration of a number of different dimensions of inequality. It seeks to show that widening inequality increases both crimes of the powerless and crimes of the powerful, crime in the streets and crime in the suites. The final paper in Part I, 'Inequality and Republican Criminology' is as optimistic as 'Inegalitarian Consequences of Egalitarian Reforms' is pessimistic. It argues that our most serious crime problems are those we are in the best position to prevent. Social movements with egalitarian criminal justice agendas (like the women's movement) are the key actors with this preventive power. The fundamental reason is that patterns of shaming are structured by relations of power; yet these patterns are vulnerable to social movement politics. Shaming is one of the few potent tools available to the weak and it can be extremely potent.

Responsive Regulation

'Preventive Law and Managerial Auditing' (Chapter 6) sets out in practical terms what corporations must do if they want effective internal compliance systems. That piece was co-authored with Brent Fisse, who was the first of three co-authors who taught me new skills during the 1980s (see Fisse and Braithwaite, 1983, 1993). The others were Ian Ayres and Peter Grabosky. Grabosky and I came up with the label 'Benign Big Gun' to describe a number of Australian business regulatory agencies who managed to 'speak softly while carrying a big stick' (Grabosky and Braithwaite, 1986). Grabosky led me into the most systematic empirical study of business regulatory strategy in one country ever undertaken – involving the 96 most significant business regulatory agencies in Australia. 'Convergence in Models of Regulatory Strategy' (Chapter 7) was the first place where I developed the idea of the Benign Big Gun into a normative ideal – a move from explanatory to normative theory consummated with Ian Ayres in *Responsive Regulation* (Ayres and Braithwaite, 1992).

Responsive regulation was taken back into criminology in a piece called 'Beyond Positivism: Learning from Contextual Integrated Strategies' (Chapter 8). Reflexivity, systemic wisdom and enforcement strategy that is dynamic rather than passive were the key elements of this regulatory approach to crime prevention. By this point, crime had become just another regulatory problem for me: the regulation and criminal justice research agendas had collapsed into each other, relying on similar methods, normative theories and regulatory tactics. 'Transnational Regulation of the Pharmaceutical Industry' (Chapter 9) argued that the pharmaceutical industry has been characterized by high rates of corporate crime, low levels of criminal enforcement, yet considerable improvement in safety and ethical standards. The improvements have been accomplished by a web of rather global controls, many of them informal – such as professional standards and social movement activism. Each strand in the web of controls is weak; yet the entire fabric of the web can be strong. Equal enforcement of national criminal laws thus comes to be seen as an antiquated remedy when what is needed to secure freedom as non-domination is global ratcheting up of regulatory standards. Tightening the knots that hold a web of controls together. And this might be achieved through the strength of weak (and informal) sanctions. My next book, *Global Business Regulation* (with Peter Drahos), develops this theme systematically and globally across the entire range of regulatory regimes that I studied in the national arena with Grabosky.

Republican Legal Institutions

The rule of law is central to republican normative theory. Without the rule of law, arbitrary power is unchecked, freedom as non-domination at risk. But what kind of rule of law? 'The Politics of Legalism: Rules Versus Standards in Nursing-Home Regulation' (Chapter 10) demonstrates a need to examine empirically our presumptions about the rule of law. It shows (and shows why) vague nursing home standards result in more consistent legal interpretation than precise rules. The analysis is a republican one because it finds the greater consistency of vague Australian standards to be about the quality of a regulatory dialogue in which there is empowerment of the voices of (normally silenced) stakeholders.

'Community Values and Australian Jurisprudence' (Chapter 11) tackles the question of strict legalism versus more purposive legal interpretation at the level of appellate courts, moving up from the street level enforcement considered in the previous essay. Legal interpretation is found to be impossible without reference to community standards that are often not codified in the law. At the same time arbitrary invocation of the attitudes of judges (often under cover of an appeal to community values) is a threat to the rule of law and therefore to republican freedom. A standard distinction from social psychology is made between attitudes and values. It is argued that judges should never argue from community attitudes when the law is silent. Reasoning from values inherent in the law itself and community values on which there is a strong consensus is found to be more acceptable. Better still to require judges to reason from a specific set of values and rights referred to in a Bill of Values and Rights when statute and common law are insufficient on their own to supply answers. In Australia, since this was written, the debate has been not on a Bill of Values and Rights, but on whether and how values should be written into the Preamble of a Constitution for a new Australian Republic. The final essay in this section is on separations of private and public powers (Chapter 12). It involves a radical rethinking of the separation of powers doctrine for a world in which freedom is more under threat from the domination of private than public power. Along the way, it seeks to reframe deterrence theory for deterring the abuse of power.

Restorative Justice

In Part IV republican normative theory and the explanatory theory of reintegrative shaming are used to lay foundations for restorative justice as an alternative to retributive justice. 'Shame and Modernity'(Chapter 13) confronts the worry that we live in a shameless society, that the theory of reintegrative shaming is relevant only to a world of Jeffersonian rural republicanism. 'Conditions of Successful Reintegration Ceremonies' (with Stephen Mugford) describes the nuts and bolts of how restorative justice conferences make it possible to move criminal justice practices away from stigmatization toward reintegration. 'Restorative Justice and a Better Future' (Chapter 15) articulates a culturally plural vision for restorative justice. It is about:

> Helping indigenous community justice to learn from the virtues of liberal statism – procedural fairness, rights, protecting the vulnerable from domination; and

> Helping liberal state justice to learn from indigenous community justice – learning the restorative community alternatives to individualism.

Summarizing the Themes

Ten points will suffice for summarizing the threads that are interwoven through the essays in this collection:

1. The categories of normative theory can be adjusted to accommodate concepts that have real world explanatory power; explanatory theory concepts can be adjusted so they connect to a vision for a more decent society. This contrasts with the statist temptations to which criminology has often succumbed – explaining that assists the creation of more perfect systems of domination. Normative and explanatory theory are both enriched by a principled commitment to mutual adjustment of their categories.

2. Domination explains crime. Freedom as non-domination is a richer conception of freedom as a normative ideal than freedom as non-interference. This republican freedom explains crime and redefines the kind of regulatory order we might want in contemporary societies.

3. Inequalities based on wealth, power, school failure, race, gender and on

freedom itself explain crime. Normatively, freedom as non-domination requires constant struggle to peg back all these forms of inequality.

4. The rule of law – not abolitionism or deregulation, but taking crime and regulatory law seriously – is necessary for crime prevention. The rule of law is also necessary for the preservation of freedom as non-domination on other fronts. It is therefore a central normative ideal.

5. The separation of powers is another central ideal because it is integral to business regulatory effectiveness, crime prevention and freedom as non-domination.

6. Shaming is a great evil when it is stigmatizing: it causes non-compliance with the law and degrades those it touches. Reintegrative shaming, disapproval of the act while showing love or respect for the actor, improves compliance with the law; it is a normative ideal only when reintegrative shaming enhances freedom as non-domination.

7. Social movement politics is fundamental to shaping the effectiveness of regulation, the character of freedom as non-domination and the possibilities for reintegrative shaming of wrongdoing.

8. Restorative justice is a superior path than retributive justice because it has the potential to be more procedurally fair, more protective of freedom as non-domination and build compliance with the law.

9. Restorative justice is emerging as a social movement that can transform the criminal justice system and our institutions of regulation generally. This is because citizens find they like putting the problem rather than the wrongdoer in the centre of a circle of stakeholders, they prefer the experience of healing over hurting, they connect to values of prevention, community caring, community participation, community learning, respectful dialogue, making amends, apology, and forgiveness. The more intractable the regulatory problem, the deeper the evil, the more true this becomes. Like St. Paul, those who engage with restorative justice learn that 'where sin abounded, grace did much more abound'. Aug San Suu Kyi, the Dalai Lama, Mandela, Tutu, Ghandi all manifest how the greater the evil of the crime, the greater the opportunity for grace to inspire a transformative will to resist tyranny with compassion.

10. A particularly attractive feature of restorative justice is its emphasis on deliberation as a regulative ideal. High quality deliberation not only enriches democracy; it also provides the safeguard of helping to reveal our mistakes, including the possibility that my points 1–9 are mistaken.

For the future, a marriage of rigorous, methodologically plural regulatory science to social movement politics seems more productive than the past of narrow, normatively muted, criminal science wed to the punitive state. The social movement for restorative justice is an exciting focus for that scholarship, one with an inspiring vision for a freer future. But so are older social movements such as the human rights, environment, womens' movement, and many others where law, social science and politics might be fused for a regulation that advances freedom as non-domination.

References

Ayres, Ian and John Braithwaite, *Responsive Regulation: Transcending the Deregulation Debate* (New York: Oxford University Press, 1992).

Braithwaite, John, *Inequality, Crime and Public Policy* (London: Routledge and Kegan Paul, 1979).

Braithwaite, John, *To Punish or Persuade: Enforcement of Coal Mine Safety* (Albany: State University of New York Press, 1985).

Braithwaite, John, *Crime, Shame and Reintegration* (Melbourne: Cambridge University Press, 1989).

Braithwaite, John, 'Republican Theory, the Good Society and Crime Control,' ed. S. Karstedt and K. Bussman, *Social Dynamics and the Regulatory Order in Modern Society* (1999).

Braithwaite, John and Philip Pettit, *Not Just Deserts: A Republican Theory of Criminal Justice* (Oxford: Oxford University Press, 1990).

Fisse, Brent and John Braithwaite, *The Impact of Publicity on Corporate Offenders* (Albany: State University of New York Press, 1983).

Fisse, Brent and John Braithwaite, *Corporations, Crime and Accountability* (Albany: State University of New York Press, 1993).

Grabosky, Peter and John Braithwaite, *Of Manners Gentle: Enforcement Strategies of Australian Business Regulatory Agencies* (Melbourne: Oxford University Press, 1986).

Knight, Tony, 'Schools and Delinquency,', ed. A. Borowski and J.M. Murray, *Juvenile Delinquency in Australia* (Melbourne: Methuen 1985).

Parker, Christine, *Just Lawyers* (Oxford: Oxford University Press, 1999).

Pettit, Philip, *Republicanism* (Oxford: Clarendon Press, 1997).

PART I

Dimensions of Inequality

[1]
Competitiveness in Schools and Delinquency

Some theories to explain the relationship between school failure and delinquency are examined. It is argued that it is the condition of status deprivation through being given a low rank on the status hierarchy of the school that leads to delinquency. Policies of equality of opportunity achieve a reordering of children on the hierarchy, but leave the hierarchy itself intact. Delinquency may be part of a more general pathology which arises from competitiveness in schools.

Two of the best supported hypotheses in delinquency research are that children who fail at school are likely to become seriously delinquent,[1] and that lower class children have high delinquency rates.[2] Albert Cohen has built a theory of delinquency around these two propositions.[3]

Lower class children, says Cohen, fail at school because they are culturally and intellectually deprived, and because the middle class status system of the school is foreign to their lower class socialization. Their failure and humiliation make them so bitter that they react against everything that the school stands for. This reaction formation consists of the adoption of values which are the exact inverse of the middle class values of the school. They exhibit contempt instead of respect for property and authority, immediate impulse gratification instead of impulse control, apathy instead of ambition, toughness instead of control of aggression, and so on. The lower class delinquent's conduct is right by the standards of his subculture precisely because it is wrong by the standards of the school. Cohen sees the delinquent subculture as a solution to the status problem of the lower class youth. Denied status in the respectable society, the delinquent subculture provides him with criteria of status which he can achieve. Many policy makers have inferred from Cohen's theory that an effective way to reduce delinquency is to provide greater educational opportunities for lower class children. For example, many of the equality of opportunity programmes in the

108

United States 'War on Poverty' were partly motivated by a desire to reduce crime.

However, such inferences may not be justified. The status system of the school approximates a hierarchy, with all children being given a ranking. But if some children are helped up from the bottom of the hierarchy, their place will still be taken over by other children. Thus educational opportunities for lower class children only achieve a re-ordering of children in the hierarchy. But it is the hierarchy itself, and the condition of being at the bottom of it, which are believed to create delinquency. Equality of opportunity does not change the number of children who end up in that condition. For example, improving educational opportunities for aborigines will not change the fact that someone will come bottom of the class—except that he may be white instead of black. To reduce delinquency schools must be made less competitive, so that no one (black or white) is confronted with the stigma of coming bottom of the class.

Furthermore, rather than reduce delinquency, it may be that equality of opportunity will actually increase it. Stinchcombe found that middle class children who failed at school were greater discipline problems than lower class failures.[4] Since lower class failures have low expectations for success, the discrepancy between expectations and actual performance is less than for middle class failures. This theory predicts that a reordering of children in the status hierarchy of the school, so that more middle class children end up near the bottom, will increase the overall delinquency rate.

Desirable though equality of opportunity may be on grounds of social justice, it is no solution to delinquency. Efforts at delinquency reduction would be better directed at reducing the competitiveness of schools so that no children are shattered and embittered through coming off worst in the competitive hierarchy. Many Australian schools are moving towards competition against the individual's own past performance instead of against the performance of other children. Under the ipsative model all children 'succeed' and none 'fail', since all improve their own past performance.

Schools can function successfully by motivating children to achieve goals of absolute worth rather than by motivating children to do relatively better than other children.[5] By focusing attention on the competitive system rather than on the goal itself, schools socialize children to uncritically accept the goals which are striven for in the competitive systems of the wider society.

Delinquency should not be the only pathology considered in an analysis of competition in schools. Various behavioural and emotional problems of adolescence may be related to outright failure at school, worry about the possibility of failure, or not achieving the success either expected or aspired to. For example, a recent survey by the New South Wales Department of Health found a strong association between school failure and smoking.[6] Perhaps reducing the competitive order of our schools may be as effective an attack on lung cancer as anti-smoking campaigns!

A counter to the above arguments arises in the theorizing of Stinchcombe:

> Whenever present activity fails to make sense by being clearly connected to future increments in status, the student tends to become expressively alienated and rebellious. The student who grasps a clear connection between current activity and future status tends to regard school authority as legitimate, and to obey.[7]

If Stinchcombe is right a competitive school system, which is continually comparing performances in order to determine who is most worthy of access to high status occupations, will command greatest conformity. Note however that this is conformity to norms while at school, and does not include conformity to norms when outside of the school grounds.

Assuming that Stinchcombe's hypothesis is correct, and assuming that it is acceptable to base the legitimacy of the school's authority on power over the future of its students, conformity can be achieved without continually confronting poor students with their failure. Surely competitive tests need only be sufficiently regular to ensure reasonably accurate measurement of performance for employment purposes, and results of such tests need not be made public knowledge. Moreover, Stinchcombe's hypothesis can be no justification for a competitive primary school system. Primary school results bear no relation to future increments in status except in so far as they indicate the likelihood of good secondary school performance. This is just as true for ipsative results as it is for competitive results.

Finally, the competitive system in schools may well reinforce competitiveness in the personalities of its students. These competitive personalities go out into the wider society, and thus competitive arrangements in the wider society are perpetuated. In the same way that juvenile delinquency is generated by failure in the school's competitive system, so is adult crime generated by failure in the competitive system of the wider society.[8] Other forms of social pathology such as suicide,[9] alcoholism,[10] dangerous driving,[11] and mental illness[12] are associated with failure in the competitive system of the wider society. Moreover, much social pathology, while not associated with failure in the competitive system, is associated with the pressure of keeping up in the

110

competitive system. Witness the classic case of the successful business-man plagued by an ulcer.

If the school is the mouse race that prepares us for the rat race, then a solution to the social pathology of the rat race may lie within the school.

REFERENCES

1. Lunden, W. A., *Statistics on Delinquents and Delinquency*, Springfield, Illinois: Charles C. Thomas, 1964. W. C. Kvaraceus, *Juvenile Delinquency and the School*, New York: World Book Co., 1945. W. E. Schafer and K. Polk, Delinquency and the Schools, in President's Commission on Law Enforcement and the Administration of Justice, *Task Force Report, Juvenile Delinquency and Youth Crime*, Washington D.C.: Government Printer, 1967, pp. 222-277. A. L. Rhodes and A. J. Reiss, Apathy, Truancy and Delinquency as Adaptations in School, *Social Forces*, 1969, 48, pp. 12-22. F. Mugishima and Y. Matsumoto, An Analysis of Delinquent Differentiation Related to Boy's Social Origin and Educational Attainment, *Report of the Japanese Research Institute of Police Science*, 1973, 14 (1).
2. Reiss, A. J., and A. L. Rhodes, The Distribution of Juvenile Delinquency in the Social Class Structure, *American Sociological Review*, 1961, 26, pp. 720-732. Y. Matsumoto, The Distribution of Juvenile Delinquency in the Social Class Structure: A Comparative Analysis of Delinquency Between Tokyo and Nashville, *Japanese Sociological Review*, 1970, 20, pp. 2-18. W. Bytheway and D. May, On Fitting the 'Facts' of Social Class and Criminal Behaviour, *Sociological Review*, 1971, 19, pp. 585-607.
3. Cohen, A. K., *Delinquent Boys*, London: Routledge and Kegan Paul, 1956.
4. Stinchcombe, A., *Rebellion in a High School*, Chicago: Quadrangle, 1964.
5. See, for example, P. Adams, L. Berg, N. Berger, M. Duane, A. S. Neill and R. Ollendorff, *Children's Rights: Towards the Liberation of the Child*, London: Elek Books, 1971.
6. *Brisbane Telegraph*, 4 November 1973, p. 22.
7. Stinchcombe, *op. cit.*
8. The President's Commission on Law Enforcement and Administration of Justice, *The Challenge of Crime in a Free Society*, Washington D.C.: Government Printer, 1967, pp. 43-49.
9. Kessell, N., Self-Poisoning, in E. S. Schneidman (ed.), *Essays in Self-Destruction*, New York: Science House, 1967, pp. 345-372.
10. Calahan, D., *Problem Drinkers*, San Francisco: Jossey-Bass, 1970, Chapter 4.
11. Willett, T. C., *Drivers After Sentence*, London, Heinemann, 1973.
12. Freeman, H. E., and J. M. Giovannoni, Social Psychology of Mental Health, in G. Lindsey and E. Aronson, *Handbook of Social Psychology*, 2nd edition, Vol. 5, pp. 678-681.

[2]

The Effect of Income Inequality and Social Democracy on Homicide

BRADY (1975, p. 76) expressed extreme confidence in the existence within the criminological research community of a consensus over the efficacy of reducing inequality as a solution to crime when he said: ". . . poverty, discrimination, and human exploitation. Nearly all brands of criminologists will now argue that these conditions are the underlying causes of crime." While all criminologists are familiar with many of the arguments which have been advanced to support the contention that a more equal society would be a society in which there would be less crime, Brady is mistaken to assume that most criminologists accept them. Indeed there is still dispute as to whether inequality is a correlate of crime, let alone a cause.

In a previous work Braithwaite (1979) has reviewed the theory and empirical evidence bearing upon the question of whether a more equal society might be a society in which there was less crime. One of the several levels of analysis in attempting to reach an answer to that question was the international comparison. Homicide data on only 20 nations for a one-year period were analysed in that work. The purpose of the present paper is to undertake a more elaborate cross-national comparison of inequality and crime on a larger sample of countries with data covering a longer time period. The larger sample will permit the introduction of more controls for extraneous variables.

As was argued in the previous work, homicide is the only crime category for which there is an acceptable level of uniformity among nations. Cross-national comparisons such as those by Krohn (1976) and McDonald (1976) which compare nations on levels of property crime from police statistics are sure to provide misleading conclusions. Homicide, in contrast, has higher levels of reportability, seriousness, and uniformity of interpretation than any other crime category.

The Homicide Measure

There are considerable risks in adopting an official homicide rate for one year as an estimate of true homicide rate. To enhance the reliability of the present data, homicide rates were averaged over a 20-year period from 1955 to 1974 inclusive. The source of the data was Interpol's *International Crime Statistics*. Nations were only included in the analysis if data were available for at least half the years within the time period, or if a complete data set were available from the time the nation was formed as an independent entity. For the 31 countries included in the final analysis reported in this paper homicide data were available for an average of 16 years. These 31 countries are listed in Appendix A.

Several countries which met the overall requirements of data availability were excluded from the investigation because of inexplicably wild variations in homicide rates. To take the most extreme example, Spain showed rates of $0 \cdot 32$ and $0 \cdot 41$ per 100,000 in 1955 and 1956 respectively, which jumped to $80 \cdot 01$ in 1959 and $78 \cdot 69$ in 1960. The two most likely sources of gross error are charges in the policy regarding the inclusion of unlawful killing through the use of a motor vehicle and the inclusion of deaths resulting from warfare, either civil or external. While it is hoped that data incorporating these sources of error have been excluded, it is clearly impossible to have sufficient familiarity with each nation's crime statistics to be absolutely confident of this in every case.

Inequality Measures

Correlations between a number of readily available indices of income inequality and homicide were calculated. These were Lydall's (1968) three indices of the ratios of the fifth, tenth, and seventy-fifth percentiles to the fiftieth percentile of the earnings distribution (P_5, P_{10} and P_{75}). P_5 and P_{10} are measures of the gap between the rich and the average income earner, P_{75} a measure of the gap between the poor and the average income earner. Another Lydall index is the bricklayers' differential, which is the hourly wage rate in 1964 for adult labourers in building expressed as a percentage of rates for bricklayers. Clearly the latter is an index of inequality within the bottom tail of the income distribution only.

The next two indices are based on Taylor and Hudson's (1972) examination of intersectoral income inequality. These measures are concerned with inequality among approximate average levels of income in eight different sectors of industry—agriculture, forestry, hunting and fishery; mining and quarrying; manufacturing; construction; electricity, gas, water, and sanitary services; commerce (wholesale and retail trade, banking, insurance and real estate); and transportation, storage, and communication and services. The first Taylor and Hudson index is the Gini coefficient of intersectoral income inequality—an overall index of how equally income is dispersed among the eight sectors. Such an index clearly understates the level of inequality since inequality within industry sectors is ignored. Similarly with Taylor and Hudson's second intersectoral index—the size of the smallest sectors of the population with half of the total income. Clearly, however, a society in which a very small proportion of the population receives half of the total national income would be an unequal society.

Wages and salaries are not the only sources of inequality of wealth. Social security expenditure is explicitly intended to have a redistributive effect. Hence, the United States Social Security Administration's (1965) index of percentage of the gross national product spent on social security was included as an inequality measure. Land is another important basis of inequality, especially in less developed countries. The two indices used were Taylor and Hudson's (1972) Gini index of inequality in the distribution of land and smallest number of farms with half the total acreage.

46

THE EFFECT OF INCOME INEQUALITY AND SOCIAL DEMOCRACY ON HOMICIDE

TABLE 1

Correlation of various indices of inequality
with average homicide rates 1955–1974

	r	Number of countries on which correlation is based
P₅ (Ratio of 5th to 50th percentile)	0·774*	17
P₁₀ (Ratio of 10th to 50th percentile)	0·774*	17
P₇₅ (Ratio of 75th to 50th percentile)	−0·505*	15
Bricklayers' differential	−0·210	14
Gini for intersectoral income inequality	0·623*	31
Size of smallest sectors with half total income	−0·547*	31
Per cent. of GNP on social security	−0·480*	28
Gini for land	−0·100	29
Smallest number of farms with half acreage	−0·016	25

* Significant at 0·05 level.

It can be seen that most of the variables in Table 1 have strong and statistically significant correlations with homicide. All of the correlations except Gini for land are in the direction of greater inequality being associated with higher homicide rates. Clearly inequality in the distribution of land is not a good predictor of homicide levels. The strongest correlations are with Lydall's two indices of the earnings gap between the rich and the average income earner (P_5 and P_{10}). The next best correlate is Gini for intersectoral income inequality. Because adequate data on both intersectoral income inequality and homicide are available for 31 countries, this variable, rather than P_5 or P_{10}, has been chosen as the focus for further investigation.

Correlation of Intersectoral Income Inequality with Other Inequality Measures
Before proceeding to examine the effect of intersectoral income inequality on homicide after controlling for important extraneous variables it is necessary to test the validity of the variable as a measure of inequality. In Table 2 the correlations of intersectoral inequality with other inequality measures are listed.

TABLE 2

Correlation of intersectoral income inequality
with alternative measures inequality

	r	Number of countries on which correlation is based
P₅ (Ratio of 5th to 50th percentile)	0·776*	15
P₁₀ (Ratio of 10th to 50th percentile)	0·769*	15
P₇₅ (Ratio of 75th to 50th percentile)	−0·444*	14
Bricklayers' differential	−0·394	12
Size of smallest sectors with half total income	−0·989*	31
% of GNP on social security	−0·529*	23
Gini for land	0·170	24
Smallest number of farms with half acreage	−0·110	20

* Significant at 0·05 level.

All correlations in Table 2 are in the direction necessary for the validation of intersectoral income inequality, although the correlations with the two indices of inequality in the distribution of land are very low indeed. The strong correlation with the earnings based indices gives some confidence that intersectoral income inequality might be a valid index of overall earnings inequality even though it neglects intra-sector dispersion.

The Meaninglessness of Statistical Significance

The correlation of 0.623 between intersectoral income inequality and homicide is statistically significant at the 0.001 level. In the context of the present research, however, statistical significance is a meaningless concept. Significance tests assume a random sample of an infinite population. Here we have a systematically non-random sample of a finite population. Thirty-one of the approximately 200 countries in the world are included in this study. It would be dishonest to say that we are dealing with a population rather than a sample—the population of all countries for which both adequate homicide and income inequality data are available. To make such a claim would be to play semantic games. Whatever the group of 31 countries is called, the correlations are best treated as descriptive rather than inferential statistics. Similarly with the multiple regression analyses reported in the next section. The total variance explained by the regression equation is meaningful as a description of the exact amount of variance which can be explained by the predictors in the 31 countries of the world from which accurate statistical records can be obtained. Significance tests for each predictor are provided. While only the statistically naive reader would pay attention to these F-tests, they are included lest some critic chooses to castigate us for concealing the non-significance of some of our findings.

The Income Inequality Regressions

The most difficult question to answer for researchers operating at a cross-national level of analysis is whether or not the correlation they have established is spurious. It might be, for example, that developed countries have lower levels of both inequality and homicide than developing countries, and that this is why there appears to be a relationship between income inequality and homicide. Multiple regression is the technique which has been used to handle this problem. The first regression model includes as predictors extraneous variables which it is suspected might show the correlation between inequality and homicide to be spurious. Inequality is then added to this group of predictors (the control variables) so that it can be ascertained whether inequality explains any variance in homicide rates over and above that explained by the control variables.

Unfortunately, on so small a number of cases as 31 the entry of too large a number of predictors into the regression results in an abuse of the assumptions of the multiple regression model. The number of predictors for any one regression in the present analysis was limited to four. The task is then to select those few variables which are most likely to explain away the relationship between inequality and homicide. Since there is little by way of theory

THE EFFECT OF INCOME INEQUALITY AND SOCIAL DEMOCRACY ON HOMICIDE

to guide such a choice, the decision was made on empirical grounds. A number of variables from a variety of sources were thrown into a correlation matrix with intersectoral income inequality and homicide. The variables included protein grams *per capita* (Taylor and Hudson, 1972), the Freedom House political freedom index, an ethnic fractionalisation index (Taylor and Hudson, 1972), Gross Domestic Product *per capita*, Gross National Product *per capita*, Gross National Product growth between 1950 and 1965, concentration of population (an urbanisation measure), type of political system, and a freedom of the press index. The first three of the above variables showed the strongest correlations with homicide and so were chosen to be entered as control variables in the regression model.

The first problem for the regression analysis is that the plot of homicide rate against income inequality is not quite linear. Homicide rate is a positively accelerated function of income inequality. While a curvilinear regression might have explained somewhat more variance, it was decided to opt for the simplicity of a linear model.

There is a high degree of multicollinearity among the three predictors and intersectoral income inequality. Countries with few protein grams *per capita* have both high homicide rates and high income inequality, the correlation between the latter and protein grams *per capita* being —0.686. Nations which rate poorly on the 100-point political freedom index are high on both homicide and inequality, the inequality-freedom correlation being —0.621. The multicollinearity problem is not so severe with ethnic fractionalisation, which correlates only 0.148 with income inequality. Multicollinearity among predictors has two consequences. First, it results in the size of the regression coefficients being arbitrary. This is of little concern for the purposes of this analysis, since there is no intrinsic interest in either the size of regression coefficients or in the form of the regression equation. Secondly, the high correlations of income inequality with the control variables mean that a highly conservative test has been undertaken of whether income inequality can explain homicide rates. For example, to partial out the large amount of variance shared between income inequality and political freedom is to assume implicitly that it is lack of political freedom which causes both high homicide rates and high levels of income inequality. While that might be partly true, it might also be true that part of the shared variance is explicable in terms of income inequality causing both high homicide rates and lack of political freedom. The model, erring on the side of under-estimating the effect of income inequality, explicitly excludes the latter possibility.

It can be seen from Table 3 that the four predictors explain the extremely high proportion of 68·7 per cent. of the variance in homicide rates. With intersectoral income inequality forced to be entered last into the step-wise model, it explains only 1·3 per cent. of additional variance over and above that explained by the control variables. This is perhaps not surprising given that a rather massive 67·4 per cent. of the variance had already been partialled out by the other three predictors, leaving only a relatively small proportion of the variance available for explanation.

TABLE 3

*Summary table for step-wise multiple regression to predict homicide rate in
31 countries with intersectoral income inequality entered last*

	Beta	R^2	R^2 change	F
Protein grams per capita	−0·259	0·505	0·505	1·952
Political freedom	−0·377	0·619	0·114	5·483*
Ethnic fractionalisation	0·274	0·674	0·055	4·414*
Intersectoral income inequality	0·170	0·687	0·013	0·922

* F significant at 0·05 level.

The emergence of protein grams *per capita* as the best predictor of homicide is most interesting in the context of the present analysis. A low level of protein grams *per capita* could be interpreted as indicative of a wide gulf between the poor and the remainder of the population—that is, of income inequality. It is the existence of extremely poor people living in conditions of hunger which drag down the average level of protein grams *per capita*, and such extremes of privation are most likely to occur in nations with wide disparities of wealth. Consistent with such an hypothesis, protein grams *per capita* has a higher correlation with intersectoral income inequality (−0·686) than with either of the other two predictors. Moreover, its correlation with Gross Domestic Product *per capita* is slightly lower (−0·637) than its correlation with income inequality. Protein grams *per capita* might be just as much (or more) a measure of inequality of wealth as of aggregate level of wealth. It was therefore decided to repeat the regression analysis replacing protein grams *per capita* with a predictor which is unequivocally a measure of aggregate wealth rather than inequality of wealth—GDP *per capita*. Gross Domestic Product *per capita* was in fact the next strongest correlate of homicide after the three control variables included in the regression above.

TABLE 4

*Summary table for second step-wise multiple regression to predict homicide rate in
31 countries with intersectoral income inequality entered last*

	Beta	R^2	R^2 Change	F
Political freedom	−0·576	0·494	0·494	9·429*
Ethnic fractionalisation	0·323	0·605	0·111	6·832*
GDP per capita	0·239	0·609	0·004	1·618
Intersectoral income inequality	0·370	0·683	0·074	5·126*

* F significant at 0·05 level.

It can be seen from Table 4 that replacing protein grams *per capita* with GDP *per capita* produces virtually no change in the total amount of variance explained by the model (68·3 per cent.), but increases substantially the residual variance explained by income inequality. Income inequality explains a respectable 7·4 per cent. of the variance in homicide rates even after more than 60 per cent. of the variance has been partialled out by the control variables. Given that two of the control variables correlate −0·621

THE EFFECT OF INCOME INEQUALITY AND SOCIAL DEMOCRACY ON HOMICIDE

and −0·637 with income inequality, it is via a very conservative test that this regression provides confirmation of the potency of income inequality as a predictor of homicide rates for these 31 countries.

Social Democracy and Homicide Rates

If earnings equality is associated with low homicide rates, then a central question becomes whether countries with strong parliamentary representation of social democratic parties which are committed to equalising wealth have low homicide rates. If inequality causes crime, then parties committed to reducing inequality should reduce crime. Some confidence in such an hypothesis is generated by Hewitt's (1977) finding that the " average post-war legislative strength of Socialist parties 1945–65 " was strongly positively associated with the equality of the class system in 25 countries. Hewitt's legislative strength of socialist parties variable, based on average percentage of the vote obtained by socialist parties in elections, has been taken over into the present analysis. The variable does not in fact measure the strength of " socialist " parties, but rather social democratic parties. China, Cuba, and the Soviet block countries are not included because of the absence of elections with more than one party. To be counted as a socialist party, it had to be in a list provided by the General Secretary of the Socialist International. This list included some very moderately radical egalitarian parties such as the Labour Parties of Britain, Australia and New Zealand, but excluded all of the major parties in the United States and Canada.

For the 19 countries for which both data on the average post-war strength of socialist parties and intersectoral income inequality were available the correlation between the two was −0·416. The correlation between average post-war strength of socialist parties and homicide rate was −0·365 for the 20 nations on which the data were adequate. The latter coefficient is significant at the 0·05 level but not at the 0·01 level. Tables 5 and 6 summarise the results of the application to legislative strength of socialist parties of the same regression models which were applied to income inequality.

On the smaller sample of 20 nations in the legislative strength of socialist parties' regressions, protein grams *per capita* emerges as a much stronger correlate of homicide rate than any other variable and GDP *per capita*

TABLE 5

Summary table for step-wise multiple regression to predict homicide rate in 20 countries with average post-war legislative strength of socialist parties 1945–1965 entered last

	Beta	R^2	R^2 Change	F
Protein grams per capita	−0·618	0·318	0·318	13·217*
Ethnic fractionalisation	0·522	0·602	0·284	8·892*
Political freedom	−0·233	0·648	0·046	1·979
Legislative strength of socialist parties	−0·167	0·673	0·025	0·969

* F significant at 0·05 level.

TABLE 6

Summary table for second step-wise multiple regression to predict homicide rate in
20 countries with average post-war legislative strength of
socialist parties 1945–1965 entered last

	Beta	R^2	R^2 Change	
Ethnic fractionalisation	0·459	0·146	0·146	3·296
GDP per capita	−0·254	0·271	0·125	0·932
Political freedom	−0·269	0·323	0·052	1·228
Legislative strength of socialist parties	−0·262	0·384	0·061	1·295

becomes only a very weak correlate of homicide (−0·158). Consequently, when GDP *per capita* replaces protein grams *per capita* in the second regression the total variance explained drops from 67·3 per cent. to 38·4 per cent. After partialling out the variance explained by the control variables, legislative strength of socialist parties explains 2·5 per cent. of the variance in the first analysis and 6·1 per cent. in the second.

Summary

Multiple regression analysis has been used as a descriptive statistic to test the hypothesis that inequality is a correlate of homicide rates cross-nationally. First-order correlations between homicide and a number of inequality indices, except inequality in the distribution of land, were strong. Even after simultaneously controlling for the effects of the strongest available correlates of international homicide rates, intersectoral income inequality still explained notable amounts of variance in homicide levels for 31 countries.

It was also hypothesised that the legislative strength of social democratic parties would be a correlate of cross-national homicide rates. This was supported, although the correlation was not as strong as with income inequality. The legislative strength of social democratic parties data was also not as compelling as that for income inequality because it was based on only 20 countries, and because, even though as much as 6·1 per cent. of the variance in a step-wise procedure could be explained by the legislative strength of social democrats, this was after only 33·3 per cent. of the variance had been partialled out by the control variables.

On their own data of this kind do not constitute a convincing case for the proposition that a more equal society would be a society in which there would be less homicide. Intersectoral income inequality, even though it has been partially validated in this article, is a crude index which ignores inequities in the distribution of wealth within industry sectors. Moreover, the homicide data, even though the best available for the time period, are fraught with many sources of error. What is true of homicide might not be true of the other types of crime which are unmeasurable at the cross-national level of analysis.

Nevertheless, this study does not stand on its own. Its findings are consistent with those of Krohn (1976), McDonald (1976) and Braithwaite

THE EFFECT OF INCOME INEQUALITY AND SOCIAL DEMOCRACY ON HOMICIDE

(1979) that with respect to cross-national comparisons of homicide rates inequality and crime are associated. More importantly, international comparisons form the least explored and most difficult fragment of the vast body of evidence on the relationship between inequality of wealth and crime which has been reviewed by Braithwaite (1979). Increasingly, this corpus of empirical findings is suggestively pointing to the conclusion that a more equal society might be one in which there is less homicide.

REFERENCES

BRADY, J. P. (1975). "The Talking Stone: Evolution and Action of People's Criminology." *The Insurgent Sociologist*, **5**, 76.

BRAITHWAITE, J. (1979). *Inequality, Crime, and Public Policy*. London and Boston: Routledge and Kegan Paul.

HEWITT, C. (1977). "The Effect of Political Democracy and Social Democracy on Equality in Industrial Societies: A Cross-National Comparison." *American Sociological Review*, **42**, 450–464.

KROHN, M. D. (1976). "Inequality, Unemployment and Crime: A Cross-National Analysis." *Sociological Quarterly*, **17**, 303–313.

LYDALL, H. (1968). *The Structure of Earnings*. Oxford: Clarendon Press.

McDONALD, L. (1976). *The Sociology of Law and Order*. Boulder, Colorado; Westview Press, Chap. 5.

TAYLOR, C. L. and HUDSON, M. C. (1972). *World Handbook of Political and Social Indicators*, 2nd Edition. New Haven: Yale University Press.

UNITED STATES SOCIAL SECURITY ADMINISTRATION (1965). *International Comparisons of Ratios of Social Security Expenditures to Gross National Product*. Research and Statistics Note No. 5. Washington, D.C.: U.S. Government Printing Office.

APPENDIX

List of 31 Nations Included in Intersectoral Income Analyses in Tables 3 and 4

Australia
Austria
Canada
Cyprus
Denmark
England and Wales
Finland
France
Federal Republic of Germany
India
Iraq
Eire
Israel
Italy
Jamaica

Japan
Jordan
Republic of Korea
Luxembourg
Netherlands
Norway
Peru
Phillipines
Scotland
Thailand
Trinidad and Tobago
Turkey
United Arab Republic (Egypt)
Venezuela
United States

[3]
Inegalitarian Consequences of Egalitarian Reforms to Control Corporate Crime

INTRODUCTION

In some ways Watergate had a greater impact on the domestic affairs of other countries than it did on those of the United States. The United States had a growing government apparatus for the control of white-collar crime prior to Watergate, whereas in many countries, including Australia,[1] a significant effort to control white-collar crime emerged for the first time with the post-Watergate attitude toward the abuse of power.[2] It has been the social democratic parties of the capitalist democracies that have been at the forefront of campaigns to crack down on white-collar crime.[3] The last Labor Attorney General in the Australian national government took that position proclaiming he would change the focus of consumer affairs legislation from *caveat emptor* to *caveat vendor*. Social democrats assume that they are acting in the interests of their working class constituency by supporting legal controls on white-collar crime. Such controls are seen as an attempt to protect the powerless from the depredations of the powerful.

Often, however, these measures prove counterproductive. The corporate affairs commissions which the social democratic politicians so strongly supported, and which the conservatives equally vehemently opposed, frequently fall into a role in modern capitalism that is more concerned with protecting the corporation from crimes perpetrated by its employees or its creditors than with protecting employees and consumers from being victimized by the corporation.[4] In all developed

---

1. State governments in Australia all manifested utter neglect of white-collar crime until the New South Wales Labor government elected in 1976 began a series of initiatives. Federal trade practices and consumer protection activism was also dormant until the Labor government's strengthening of the Trade Practices Act in 1974. *See* A. HOPKINS, CRIME, LAW AND BUSINESS: THE SOCIOLOGICAL SOURCES OF AUSTRALIAN MONOPOLY LAW (1978).

2. The 1975 United Nations Congress on the Prevention of Crime and Treatment of Offenders was the first in which one of the five agenda topics focused on white-collar crime.

3. In the United States, which has no significant social democratic party, it is probably true to say that the liberal sections of the Democratic Party have been most vocal in directing fire and thunder at white-collar criminals. Key figures in this movement have been Senator Kennedy and Congressman Conyers.

4. Arguably the United States has been an exception to this pattern, in that the concern to protect industry from white-collar criminals has been matched by a com-

countries we find that business interests have succeeded in making computer crime—a form of crime in which it is usually a corporation that is the victim [5]—one major preoccupation of the effort to control white-collar crime. The effect of the widespread use of public money to catch computer criminals is, in aggregate, to redistribute wealth from the average taxpayer to the companies that are saved from computer crime victimization.[6] It is conceivable that some social democratic politicians would adopt the attitude that corporations can afford to protect themselves from computer criminals if they were confronted with the reality of how the resources from their war against white-collar crime were being spent.

Most readers undoubtedly have been exposed to the above argument about how a campaign motivated by egalitarian sentiments can in practice have redistributive effects which are inegalitarian. This paper attempts to develop somewhat more sophisticated arguments to show how the nature of law is such that egalitarian attempts to control crimes of corporations can have the consequence of worsening both intranational and international inequality.[7] It will be argued that this occurs because such egalitarian efforts at control often increase the complexity of law and because it is large organizations rather than powerless individuals that can effectively exploit legal complexity. Law in some small way can shift the balance of power. So when the expression "inegalitarian consequences" is used, it can mean widening inequities in the distribution of wealth, or fostering greater inequality in certain types of suffering against which the law is designed to be a protection (e.g. occupational disease). The inequality can be between rich and poor individuals, or between powerful organizations and powerless individuals. All of these types of inequality have been concerns of the social democratic reformers.

mitment to agencies such as the Occupational Safety and Health Administration and the Food and Drug Administration whose charter is clearly the protection of workers and consumers. Possibly this is because the United States is the only country in the world where consumer movements have achieved anywhere near the level of effectiveness of corporate lobbyists.

5. D. PARKER, CRIME BY COMPUTER (1976).

6. Galbraith has confessed that "In *The Affluent Society* I dealt with the starvation of the public services as though all services were alike. I did not see that this deprivation was great where public needs were involved, nonexistent where powerful industry pressed its requirements on the state." J. GALBRAITH, ECONOMICS AND THE PUBLIC PURPOSE, viii (1973).

7. In this paper, therefore, the concern will not be with "white-collar crime," as defined in the most influential formulations of either E. SUTHERLAND, WHITE-COLLAR CRIME (1949) or H. EDELHERTZ, THE NATURE, IMPACT AND PROSECUTION OF WHITE-COLLAR CRIME (1970), but with that subset of white-collar crime called corporate crime—law violations perpetrated by corporations or by corporate officers acting on behalf of the corporation. The paper is not concerned with criminal law in a narrow sense, but adopts a definition of corporate crime which includes civil as well as criminal violations.

The paper will go on to argue that there are certain reasons why only a small number of notably severe abuses by powerful corporations are selected for effective legal control in developed countries. One of the strategies which is then adopted by transnational corporations is to shift the abuses to the Third World. Hence, legal controls may have, for most purposes, strengthened the hand of those powerful organizations which can exploit legal complexity; while, for a few purposes, such controls protected powerless individuals in developed countries at the expense of even more powerless individuals in the Third World. Finally, it will be argued that such a theory does not have general applicability, and some attempt is made to specify the conditions under which it does apply. Before developing the theory, it is necessary to establish two propositions which underpin it. The first is that corporate crime in the 1980's cannot fully be understood by analyses which restrict their focus within one set of national boundaries; an international perspective is essential. The second proposition is that the effectiveness of legal controls depends upon the diffuseness or concentration of the interests which will be affected by the laws. Because a corporation tends to have a stronger interest in laws regulating its behavior than an individual whom such laws are designed to protect, such laws will inevitably tend to be ineffective.

I. CORPORATE CRIME AND THE INTERNATIONALIZATION OF CAPITAL

It is projected that within the present decade seventy-five per cent of world trade and production will be controlled by three hundred or fewer transnational corporations.[8] Even at the beginning of the last decade, thirty-two transnational corporations[9] had annual sales greater than the gross national products of South Vietnam, Libya, or Saudi Arabia.[10] The internationalization of capital combined with the internationalization of communications (jet travel, telecommunications, satellites, etc.) is making the world a global village, albeit a divided one. The most critical legal problems, therefore, inevitably acquire an international character. When the *Torrey Canyon* was wrecked, causing coastal damage to both Britain and France, it was carrying

8. Note, *Control of Multinational Corporations' Foreign Activities,* 15 WASH-BURN L.J. 435 (1976).

9. General Motors, Standard Oil (N.J.), Ford, Royal Dutch/Shell Group, General Electric, International Business Machines, Mobil Oil, Chrysler, Unilever, International Telephone and Telegraph, Texaco, Gulf Oil, Western Electric, United States Steel, Volkswagen, Westinghouse, Standard Oil (Calif.), Philips, British Petroleum, Ling-Temp-Vought, Standard Oil (Ind.), Boeing, Dupont, ICI, British Steel, General Telephone and Electronics, Nippon Steel, Hitachi, Radio Corporation of America, Goodyear, and Siemens.

10. L. BROWN, THE INDEPENDENCE OF NATIONS (1972).

117,000 tons of oil from Kuwait, was Liberian registered, American owned and chartered, sailed by an Italian captain and crew, grounded in international waters, contracted to a Dutch company for salvage, and destroyed by rockets of the British navy and air force.

The law, however, has not changed to reflect the increasingly international character of legal problems. One of the fundamental realities about law is that it is too slow-moving to keep up with rapidly changing technological and economic realities.[11] Legal institutions are designed to be stable and predictable, while economic institutions are designed to be rapidly adaptable to changing market conditions. Many scholars have pointed out that the law, lagging behind the corporatism of late capitalist development, remains fixed at the level of individualism.[12] In addition to being constrained by the datedness of its content, the effectiveness of law is also compromised by outmoded jurisdictional limitations. For example, Australia, a federation of six state governments, will for the first time in the 1980's confront the reality that most companies are no longer confined within the borders of one state with the establishment of the National Companies and Securities Commission.[13] This is at a time when the new structural reality is not interstate, but international.

The internationalization of capital has changed the very nature of corporate crime, but few scholars have attempted to study these changes.[14] Gross has implied that what is now needed is an interactionist analysis of relationships between people at corporate headquarters and managers at the periphery.[15] He observes that when subsidiaries run afoul of local laws, headquarters may disclaim responsibility, plead ignorance of local laws, or even make a virtue of a policy of allowing branches "autonomy":

> Headquarters may insist that their subsidiaries meet certain profit (or other) goals, while at the same time making it

---

11. See C. STONE, WHERE THE LAW ENDS: THE SOCIAL CONTROL OF CORPORATE BEHAVIOR (1975).

12. Unfortunately, almost all legal systems in the world have evolved to deal with the crimes of private individuals rather than those of complex organizations. *See, e.g., id.*; M. TIGAR & M. LEVY, LAW AND THE RISE OF CAPITALISM (1977); Fisse, *The Social Policy of Corporate Criminal Responsibility*, 6 ADEL. L. REV. 361 (1978); Kamenka, *Beyond Bourgeois Individualism: The Contemporary Crisis in Law and Legal Ideology*, in FEUDALISM, CAPITALISM AND BEYOND (E. Kamenka & R. Neale eds., 1975).

13. The United States does not seem to have a notably superior record in rapidly moving towards federal jurisdiction over patently interstate corporate activities. Compaigns for federal chartering of corporations seem to continue to fall on deaf ears. *See* Young, *Federal Corporate Law, Federalism, and the Federal Courts*, 41 L. & CONTEMP. PROBS. 146 (1977).

14. The work which Edelhertz is beginning to mount in this area will hopefully begin to remedy this deficiency. *See* EDELHERTZ, *supra*, note 7.

15. Gross, *Organizations as Criminal Actors*, in TWO FACES OF DEVIANCE: CRIMES OF THE POWERLESS AND POWERFUL 209 (P. Wilson & J. Braithwaite eds. 1978).

clear that headquarters can hardly be intimately acquainted with the laws of foreign countries. Hence, under the guise of "local autonomy" (which may be hailed as "throwing off the shackles of colonialism" by local enthusiasts), the subsidiary may be forced to engage in crime for which *they will be held responsible by their governments.* Meanwhile, headquarters (in New York, Tokyo, or Rotterdam), while hardly pleased with the result (loss of income), nevertheless escapes criminal prosecution. The enormous chaos created by Lockheed bribe payments to Japanese government officials nearly brought the government down, but at Lockheed headquarters in the U.S., the company was able to escape criminal liability.[16]

It is not difficult to understand how it might be rational for a transnational corporation to set goals for its subsidiaries that can only be achieved through law-bending or law-breaking. Corporate headquarters might be quite happy to act as an insurer, bearing the risk of any penalties that might be incurred by its subsidiaries throughout the world in the (correct) belief that every loss resulting from corporate crime will be more than offset by many illegal gains in other parts of the world.

While Gross' observations are important, there is a more basic distinction between transnational corporate crime and traditional white-collar offenses. I shall now attempt to argue that the way the transnational corporation deals with legal constraints is qualitatively different from most localized forms of white-collar crime in that the transnational's predominant strategy is law evasion rather than law violation.[17] Tax evasion is a useful paradigm for understanding transnational corporate crime. It is common knowledge that both individuals and companies frequently transfer income to tax havens outside of the national borders of the country in which they operate so as to avoid tax.[18] Related to this is the ubiquitous phenomenon of the transnational subsidiary in a low-tax country selling goods at a grossly excessive price to another subsidiary of the same transnational located in a high-tax country. This decreases the profits recorded in the high-tax country and concomitantly increases profits for the low tax subsidiary. Such shifting around of profits obviously may be quite legal from the perspective of each set of national laws. Equally obviously, these activities are frequently accompanied by a variety of devices for fraudulently misrepresenting profits. Our concern here is

---

16. *Id.*

17. *See also* Braithwaite, *Transnational Corporations and Corruption: Toward Some International Solutions,* 7 INT'L J. Soc. L. 125 (1979).

18. *See* J. NEWTON, TAX HAVENS 2 (1977).

not with the legality or illegality of the avoidance-evasion strategies; [19] rather, it is with the way that the transnational plays off one set of laws against another to its own advantage and to the long-term disadvantage of both host countries. Each nation must then choose between the lesser of two evils—either to set lower company tax rates or risk having less company profits to tax.[20]

The tax evasion example clearly illustrates how the transnational corporation exploits differences in national laws to find the line of least resistance to achieving its ends. Another paradigmatic area where there are vast differences in the severity of legislation that restricts the activities of transnationals is the policing of new drug releases. Developed nations critically evaluate the results of exhaustive experimentation on animals and then humans before allowing a new drug to be marketed and usually conduct independent tests as well. Most Third World countries cannot afford to employ pharmacologists and toxicologists to check the accuracy of claims made by drug companies, nor even the bureaucrats to police the sale of untested drugs. It may therefore be rational for the transnational to initially market a risky drug in a Third World country. This was the case with the development of the contraceptive pill in the 1950's and 1960's where primarily Puerto Rican and Mexican women were used as the guinea pigs.[21] If people die, or suffer serious side effects, then at least the company has made a small amount of money while the going was good, and it has saved money on expensive laboratory testing of the drug. If people suffer few side effects from the drug, then the clinical trials from Third World countries can be used to justify entry into countries with somewhat more stringent regulations. In other situations, a reversed law evasion strategy may be appropriate. A product might be developed in the United States for the domestic market, then dumped on the Third World market when rejected as unsafe by an American regulatory agency.[22]

---

19. Clearly, the legality of the strategies is for most purposes a crucial question, but here the point being made is that the existence of multiple legal systems makes the importance of the position taken by any one system a constraint of limited relevance.

20. *See* Laver, *Intergovernmental Policy on Multinational Corporations: A Simple Model of Tax Bargaining,* 5 Eur. J. Political Research 363 (1977).

21. The problem of international law evasion in the pharmaceutical industry will be dealt with extensively in a book on corporate crime in the pharmaceutical industry which I am writing at the moment.

22. For various examples of dumping by United States companies, *see* Dowie, *The Corporate Crime of the Century,* Mother Jones, November, 1979. It is not only Third World consumers who are the victims of American dumps. Australia has suffered from more than one dumping of infant pacifiers which faced rejection by the Consumer Product Safety Commission. *See id.* at 35, for a discussion of dumping in Australia of 120,000 unsafe teething rings.

Another classic example of the transnational law evasion paradigm is the company which evades tough pollution control laws in a developed country by shifting capital investments in the highly pollutive aspects of its operations to a developing country that has less stringent regulations. Barnet and Müller have discussed this phenomenon:

> For "very high polluting plants such as nonferrous metals smelting and refining operations," Welles's research suggests, "pollution havens" in the underdeveloped world are going to provide an answer. (In Mexico City's English-language newspaper the State of Mexico advertises for polluters: "RE-LAX. WE'VE ALREADY PREPARED THE GROUND FOR YOU. If you are thinking of fleeing from the capital because the new laws for the prevention and control of environmental pollution affect your plant, you can count on us." The use of "pollution havens" is already well advanced. There are dozens of refineries along the 1,700 mile Caribbean coast. One petrochemical complex on the south coast of Puerto Rico belches smoke clouds as far as 90 miles away. The lovely island of St. Croix, according to the president of the Caribbean Conservation Association, "now gets oil spills two to three times a week.") [23]

Barnet and Müller have been the most influential proponents of the view that Third World countries more often than not suffer a net financial disadvantage from investment by transnational corporations. This is because transnationals supplant indigenous companies, attract both local and international loan financing away from local business, avoid taxes through transfer pricing, precipitate exchange rate crises, repatriate rather than reinvest profits, and engage in other practices which maintain dependence and inhibit the self-sustaining growth of Third World economies. Defenders of transnationals, on the other hand, point out that foreign investment in the Third World creates jobs, generates tax revenues, and improves balances of payments. The debate leads nowhere.

Obviously, some types of investment provide an aggregate benefit to the host economy and others impose a net cost. In cases where there is a financial benefit, it may be that the Third World country is acting in the interests of its citizens by tolerating the non-financial cost (*e.g.* pollution). This is not necessarily to say that the harm to the Third World from the redistribution of pollution will be counterbalanced by greater financial equity between developed and Third World economies. The financial benefits to the Third World will in a large proportion of cases be exceeded by the benefits to the developed

---

23. R. BARNET & R. MÜLLER, GLOBAL REACH: THE POWER OF THE MULTINATIONAL CORPORATIONS 344-45 (1975).

economy resulting from expanded markets. Hence, while the impact of international law evasion on the distribution of exploitative industrial practices is clear, its impact on the international distribution of wealth is a separate issue which can only be resolved through case-by-case investigation.

An important thing to understand about international law evasion activities is that, in addition to fostering international inequality by saddling the Third World with the most exploitative industries, they also foster intranational inequality between powerful corporations and powerless individuals in every nation of the world. The most important consequence of a pattern of international law evasion is not that workers or consumers will be victimized in the country where the transnational does finally decide to invest, but that all other countries become afraid to act against transnationals to protect its people lest an exodus of capital be precipitated.[24] Standards everywhere become depressed in response to the fear of capital flight.

II. The Diffuseness of Interests

It is a commonplace observation that while the benefit from a company violation such as price fixing is concentrated in the hands of the company, the cost is dispersed over a large number of victims.[25] Thus, while it might not be worthwhile for the individual consumer to sue a company that has illegally overcharged several dollars for a product,[26] the same case might be worth millions of dollars to the company, which is therefore willing to employ the best lawyers to defend what could be the lifeblood of its success.[27] The diffuseness

---

24. Developed as well as Third World countries are caught up in these threats of capital flight. See, for example, a piece on threats by U.S. finance capital to withdraw from the Australian market unless there is a loosening of the regulatory stringency of the Australian Insurance Commissioner. The Weekend Australian, Apr. 7-8, 1979.

25. See A. Bequai, White-Collar Crime: A 20th Century Crisis (1978). M. Clinard, P. Yeager, J. Brissette, D. Petrashek, & E. Harries, Illegal Corporate Behavior (1979).

26. In some jurisdictions, of course, there is the possibility of class actions. See Cappelletti, *Vindicating the Public Interest Through the Courts: A Comparativist's Contribution*, 25 Buffalo L. Rev. 643 (1976); Chayes, *The Role of the Judge in Public Law Litigation*, 89 Harv. L. Rev. 1281 (1976); Miller, *Of Frankenstein Monsters and Shining Knights: Myth, Reality, and The "Class Action Problem,"* 92 Harv. L. Rev. 664 (1979); Simon, *Class Actions: Useful Tool or Engine of Destruction*, 55 F.R.D. 375 (1973); *Developments in the Law, Class Actions*, 89 Harv. L. Rev. 1318 (1976); *Class Actions*, Australian Law Reform Commission Discussion Paper No. 11 (1979).

27. Vice President Mondale, in an address to the Second Judicial Circuit Conference on September 10, 1977 indicated that he saw the diffuseness of interests reality as a most pressing concern for reformers: "Nothing is more destructive to a sense of justice than the widespread belief that it is much more risky for an ordinary citizen to take $5 from one person at the point of a gun than it is for a corporation to take $5 each from a million customers at the point of a pen."

of interests argument applies to most areas of corporate crime. Even a factory which is being asked to spend money to control the emission of a carcinogen is likely to be more protective of its interests than an individual who is threatened with the more serious consequence of cancer. This is because, whereas the expense to the company is certain, the risk of cancer to the individual may be only one in 10,000.

The government, like the individual consumer, has only diffuse interests in matters that are of great interest to its potential corporate adversaries. Corporate affairs and consumer affairs departments see so many corporate violations that are adversely affecting the interests of the community that any one of them represents only a tiny fraction of their concerns. We therefore end up with a confrontation between a government, which is prepared to devote only a small fraction of its resources to any one act of litigation, and a company, which may well be prepared to expend every resource available in what it regards as a legal fight to the death.[28] In such circumstances the company would be expected to win, but what in reality usually happens is that the government realizes the futility of an all-out legal battle over a matter involving the company's vital interests, so it either abandons the fight or uses whatever pressure it can muster in out-of-court negotiations. Civil servants who push on with such litigation may be rapped over the knuckles for involving the government in the expense of court cases which run for months or years.[29]

In almost all circumstances, therefore, large corporations engaged in economic crimes have considerable advantages over their potential legal adversaries. Large corporations usually have a concentrated interest in litigation affecting them, as well as the resources to fight. On the other hand, the governments of developed countries have only a diffuse interest in such litigation, though they do have the resources necessary to fight. Individuals (and often small companies) who are the victims of corporate crime typically have only a diffuse interest,

---

28. Many authors have discussed the practical problems of governments in using law to control corporate crime. *See* EDELHERTZ, *supra* note 7; M. GREEN, THE CLOSED ENTERPRISE SYSTEM 162 (1972); R. NADER, M. GREEN AND J. SELIGMAN, TAMING THE GIANT CORPORATION 33-61 (1976); STONE, *supra* note 11; Braithwaite, *supra* note 17; Kadish, *Some Observations on the Use of Criminal Sanctions in Enforcing Economic Regulations*, 30 U. CHI. L. REV. 423, 426 (1963); Levin, *Crimes Against Employees: Substantive Criminal Sanctions Under the Occupational Safety and Health Act*, 14 AM. CRIM. L. REV. 717, 736-37 (1977); Ogren, *The Ineffectiveness of the Criminal Sanction in Fraud and Corruption Cases: Losing the Battle Against White-Collar Crime*, 11 AM. CRIM. L. REV. 959, 961-75 (1973); *Developments in the Law, Corporate Crime: Regulating Corporate Behavior Through Criminal Sanctions*, 92 HARV. L. REV. 1227, 1243-61 (1979); Comment, *Increasing Community Control Over Corporate Crime—A Problem in the Law of Sanctions*, 71 YALE L.J. 280, 293 (1961).

29. *See* S. WEAVER, THE DECISION TO PROSECUTE: ORGANIZATION AND PUBLIC POLICY IN THE ANTITRUST DIVISION (1977).

and also lack the resources to fight. Finally, in many ways, the governments of Third World countries are in the same situation as individuals in developed countries—they have a diffuse, though real, interest in corporate crime, but insufficient resources to undertake litigation against a transnational. The typical result is that no one challenges many of the crimes perpetrated by transnational corporations.

III. MAKING THE GAME MORE COMPLEX FAVORS THOSE WITH MOST RESOURCES AND LEAST DIFFUSE INTERESTS

Now the point has been reached where it can be argued that even though efforts to expand laws limiting companies arise from the most egalitarian of ideals, they may produce the most inegalitarian of consequences both nationally and internationally. A first lead to how such a paradox is possible comes from work by Sutton and Wild [30] which applies Weber's [31] theories to company law. [32] Sutton and Wild point out that when reformist politicians enact laws to crack down on corporate criminals, one consequence is that they make the whole web of relevant law more complex. The proliferation of laws results in a proliferation of loopholes over which legal argument is possible and in increased costs of litigation to the extent that the law does become more complex. "The more precise a rule is, the more likely it is to open up loopholes—to permit by implication conduct that the rule was intended to forbid." [33]

Moreover, as Sutton and Wild observe, "[t]he more formal and complex the body of law becomes, the more it will operate in favour of formal, rational bureaucratic groups such as corporations. In one sense, therefore, 'law' and 'justice' may be fundamentally irreconcilable." [34] One important aspect of the formality of Western law is its predictability. That predictability is achieved by the doctrine of stare decisis—the precept that courts are bound by their own precedents and lower courts by the precedents of higher courts. This predictability is of much more value to the corporation lawyers who advise their clients on how to carefully circumvent the law than it is to the consumer who is quite oblivious to legal precedent. This idea is no more than a specific illustration of Ehrlich's general contention that "[t]he more the rich and the poor are dealt with according to the same legal

---

30. Sutton & Wild, *Corporate Crime and Social Structure,* in Wilson and Braithwaite, *supra* note 15, at 177.
31. *See* Weber's work in legal codification in M. WEBER, ON LAW IN ECONOMY AND SOCIETY (1954).
32. Sutton and Wild's discussion primarily relates to the New South Wales Companies Act, Securities Industry Act, and Crimes Act.
33. R. POSNER, ECONOMIC ANALYSIS OF LAW 425 (1977).
34. Sutton & Wild, *supra* note 30, at 195.

propositions, the more the advantage of the rich is increased." [35] Or, as Galanter has more colorfully expressed it, "[t]he sailor overboard and the shark are both swimmers, but only one is in the swimming business." [36] Hence, the argument is that the more laws we have, irrespective of their content, the more the premeditated and rational decisions of corporations can turn the web of law to their advantage and to the disadvantage of "irrational" consumers and workers. [37]

This does not mean that it is impossible to enact particular laws which plug loopholes or simplify the law in some way. The distinction which must be grasped is that between the structure of law as a totality and the content of individual laws. An appropriate analogy is with organizations becoming larger and more bureaucratic as a consequence. It could be said that organizations need not inevitably become more bureaucratic as a result of having more people if the new people are committed to fighting bureaucracy. An organization might decide to appoint new managers who are strongly opposed to red tape. Each of these new managers, however, will require secretaries, clerks, research assistants, and other support staff who may not be as committed to cutting red tape as the manager. Irrespective of the nature of the individuals added to organizations, by the very fact of increasing the size of the organization the structural imperatives of bureaucratization are encouraged.

The enactment of laws to regulate corporate misbehavior is a good way of salving social democratic consciences. But the reformers soon find that enactment is easier than enforcement. Enthusiasm for the crack-down on white-collar crime rapidly wanes when the first prosecution under the new laws occupies a hundred days in court. This is exacerbated, of course, if the prosecution is unsuccessful. Government lawyers, who must in many ways be general practitioners, frequently cannot compete with corporation lawyers who spend their lives finding out everything there is to know about a narrowly de-limited area of, for example, tax loopholes. In time, the legislation falls into disuse, but it remains on the statute books to render the body of law more complex. [38]

---

35. E. Ehrlich, Fundamental Principles of the Sociology of Law 238 (1936).

36. Galanter, *Why the "Haves" Come Out Ahead: Speculations on the Limits of Legal Change,* 9 Law & Soc'y Rev. 363 (1975).

37. See, for example, Wanner's evidence that corporate plaintiffs in a sample of 7,900 civil cases win more, settle less, and lose less than individual plaintiffs. Wanner, *The Public Ordering of Private Relations Part I: Initiating Civil Cases in Urban Trial Courts,* 8 Law & Soc'y Rev. 421 (1974); Wanner, *The Public Ordering of Private Relations Part II: Winning Civil Cases in Urban Trial Courts,* 9 Law & Soc'y Rev. 293 (1974).

38. Of course there are many more general arguments about the undesirability of laws which are difficult and costly to enforce either because of their nature or

Of course, such legislation is most likely to be enforced in situations where the government perceives the corporation as doing relatively great harm to the nation or its citizens.   When the government uses or threatens to use the full force of its dormant laws against a transnational, a common response is for the transnational to shift its activities to a more permissive country.   In recent years, for example, there has been growing concern on the part of unions and governments in Western nations at the high mortality rates from cancer and asbestosis of workers who are exposed to high concentrations of asbestos dust.[39]   This concern has resulted in pressure for the enforcement of widely violated safety standards.[40]   In turn, these pressures have led asbestos users to relocate their operations in Third World countries.[41]

What is being suggested, then, is that it is only when cases of quite serious exploitation are brought to its attention that the Western government will enforce its otherwise largely unused legislation controlling companies.   In such circumstances, if the Western government is determined to crack down on the transnational, then the transnational is likely to transfer its investment to a capital-starved Third World country.   Unlike the developed economy, the Third World country's economy lacks indigenous means of capital formation, and its government is appropriately obsessed with the need to provide a favorable climate for foreign investment.   It may lack the capacity to say no.   A Third World country may even accept patently unbeneficial and exploitative industries in order to protect its reputation as a stable locus for foreign capital.   The transnational finds that in the Third World country it is not plagued by corporate affairs investigators, pollution control officers, consumer affairs advocates, health department officials, or industrial safety inspectors.   There is simply not the money for the government to be able to employ such people.

because of who they are designed to control.   Laws which become dormant are a waste of the legislature's scarce time, undermine confidence in the power of legal sanctions, and foster disrespect for law and the legislature.   On the other hand, there are dangers in arguing for the repeal of disused laws without asking the question: Is repeal likely to lead in the long term to a weakening of the moral condemnation of such conduct?   *See* Cross, *Unmaking Criminal Laws*, 3 MELB. U.L. REV. 415, 415-21 (1962).

39. *See* P. EPSTEIN, THE POLITICS OF CANCER (1979).   For a discussion of the way transnationals buy off union acquiescence with threats of shifting capital investment, *see* Kassalow, *Aspects of Labour Relations in Multinational Companies: An Overview of Three Asian Countries,* 117 INT'L LABOUR REV. 273 (1978).

40. In one Australian mine, asbestos dust concentrations were found to exceed the Australian safety standard by a factor of 30.   Broadband, Australian Broadcasting Commission current affairs radio program, Sept. 29, 1977.

41. It is interesting to note that the largest manufacturer of asbestos products in Australia, the highly profitable James Hardie Company, has recently spent many millions of dollars in relocating some of its asbestos operations in Indonesia—a country not noted for the stringency with which it enforces safety regulations to protect workers.

FIGURE 1

SUMMARY SCHEMA FOR A THEORY OF HOW REFORMS TO CONTROL CORPORATE CRIME CAN INCREASE INTRA AND INTERNATIONAL INEQUALITY

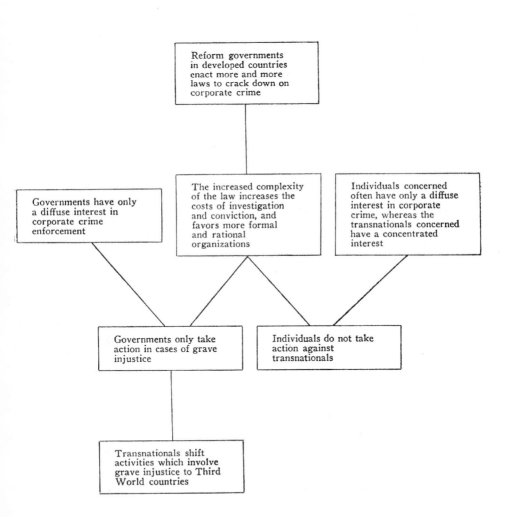

It may be, therefore, that there is a two-fold irony to the activities of egalitarian legal reformers in developed countries who crusade for new laws to crack down on corporate crime. First, the enactment of these (largely unusued) laws increases the complexity of the body of law, and thereby favors the formal and rational large corporations with their specialized departments full of legal experts over the less directed consumers and workers. Second, one upshot of the (infrequent) threats by developed governments of prosecution under such laws is to spur a transfer of the most obviously exploitative of transnational operations to the Third World. Therefore, some attempts to control corporate crime might paradoxically foster both intra and international inequality.

IV. Setting Limits to the Argument

The scenario summarized in Figure 1, however, does not represent a theory which has universal applicability to attempts to use law for the control of corporate crime. Indeed, most such reforms probably do not have paradoxically inegalitarian effects. Even Sutton and Wild in a recent paper accept this. They argue that greater codification and systematization of the rules defining what constitutes a "true and fair" keeping of company accounts is necessary for effective control of corporate accounting abuses.[42] To make it clear that I am modest about the breadth of applicability of the arguments represented by Figure 1, I shall suggest some areas where they patently do not apply.

Consider tax evasion. It hardly needs to be argued that the more complex tax law becomes, the more that body of law can be turned to advantage by the tax specialists of large corporations.[43] Hence, the intranational part of the argument seems applicable. But a consideration of the international aspect of the argument leads to the conclusion that the facts do not fit at all. If the United States government were to become extraordinarily tough and effective in the application of its corporate tax laws, then transnationals would shift more of their taxable income offshore. Some of it would go to Third World countries; much would go to tax havens. The effect would then be an egalitarian shift of income from a more affluent nation (the United States) to a number of less affluent nations. Of course, this conclusion must be

---

42. Sutton & Wild, *Companies, the Law and Professions: A Sociological View,* in Legislation and Society in Australia (R. Tomasic ed.) (1979).

43. In many developed countries, including the United States, governments have established committees to consider ways of simplifying tax laws in part because of assumptions about the way that the wealthy exploit this complexity. Hickman, *Federal Tax Regulations—The Need to Expedite and Simplify,* 30 Nat'l Tax J. 313, 313-14 (1975); *Simplification Symposium,* 34 Tax L. Rev. 1-77 (1978).

qualified by pointing out that the reality of international tax evasion makes all Third World countries wary of using taxation to effect a substantial redistribution of wealth from American companies to their own citizens.

There can be cases where an international law evasion strategy does shift exploitative activities to the Third World but where, on balance, the strategy could not be said to produce inegalitarian consequences. A Japanese transnational that relocates a plant from polluted Tokyo to a Third World pollution haven in some circumstances could be said to be equalizing the effects of pollution, indeed even lessening its impact through a policy of dispersion. This is not the case, though, if the lesser stringency of regulation in the pollution haven is sufficient to offset the limited benefits (in global terms) of dispersion. Nevertheless, if the industry is one which genuinely does benefit the Third World country, the social democrat might not regard the law evasion as producing inegalitarian effects. Again, it must be emphasized that each example must be weighed on its own merits. It would be foolish to consider any single illustration, no matter how clearly it supports either Figure 1 or a converse formulation, as an explanation of general applicability. To consider but one complication, a justification for exploiting pollution havens in terms of sharing the burden of pollution equally between the heavily industrialized and underdeveloped countries ignores the fact that the impact of any health deficit will be greater in a poor country with inadequate health care services.[44]

Consider a different example, one where the international side of the argument applies, but the intranational side does not: laws regulating the safe manufacture of drugs. Tough United States laws on drug quality result in considerable dumping of drugs that fail to meet domestic standards on the Third World. In addition, these laws are a factor in decisions by American pharmaceutical companies to locate manufacturing plants offshore, in countries such as Guatemala which effectively have no government regulation.[45] Thus, the international part of the argument holds up. Experience with the regulation of pharmaceuticals in the United States, however, contradicts the intranational part of the argument. The nature of laws delineating proper manufacturing practices for drugs is such that they generally have clear specificity of meaning and do not in any practical sense add to the complexity of law. It is difficult, for example, to see how a new

44. There is also the moral argument that Third World countries do not benefit equally from the world's pollutive industries, so why should they equally share the social cost?

45. This matter will also be discussed in more detail in my forthcoming book on the pharmaceutical industry.

law requiring drug manufacturers to do a certain sterility test on all batches of drugs can be used to advantage by drug company lawyers. Such laws do not tend to open up new areas of legal argument, modify existing precedents, or require other laws to be enacted to 'cover their loopholes. In practice, company lawyers find it difficult to use the doctrines implicit in one part of the drug safety laws as justification for actions that evade other parts of the same body of law.[46] Thus, the only effect of the new laws seems to be to relieve government lawyers of the burden of proving such vague charges as "failure to implement adequate quality control measures."

It is essential, then, that social democrats who want to direct fire and thunder at corporate criminals ask themselves whether they are setting up the kind of inegalitarian scenario outlined in Figure 1. Sometimes the answer to that question will be yes; sometimes it will be no. At other times, the answer will be mixed: the scenario may apply in one aspect—either the intranational or international—but not in the other. Social democratic law reformers who are blind to the fact that this is a question which needs to be asked will never discover when their "egalitarian" policies to control corporate crime are likely to have inegalitarian effects.

One can only speculate on the general conditions that are likely to produce the paradox. On the intranational level, to the extent that corporate interests affected by a particular law are more concentrated, and to the extent that the interests of victims are more diffuse, one would expect enforcement of the law to be relatively ineffectual. In contrast, when victims can effectively mount class actions, the structural advantages of their corporate adversaries are attenuated.[47] Perhaps a team of sailors overboard has a better chance against a shark than a single sailor.

Analogous arguments might be built around Galanter's distinction between persons who have only occasional recourse to the courts ("one-shotters") and persons ("repeat players") who engage in many similar legal contests over time.[48] Galanter outlines a number of advantages that repeat players enjoy over one-shotters. Of particular

46. At least this is the view expressed to me by practitioners of food and drug law whom I interviewed.

47. *See* note 26 *supra* for works discussing class actions. In addition, there are principles which do not add to the complexity of law, but rather put a focus on the existing body of law which places more power in the hands of those with more diffuse interests. For example, there is the notion in contract law, that standard form contracts (*i.e.*, adhesion contracts) should be interpreted most favorably to the weaker party; any ambiguities are resolved against the drafter of the document. *See generally* Slawson, *Standard Form Contracts and Democratic Control of Lawmaking Power*, 84 HARV. L. REV. 529 (1971).

48. Galanter, *supra* note 36.

relevance to the present discussion is the interest of repeat players in "playing for rules" as well as for immediate gains.[49] The one-shotter, because he or she is unconcerned about the outcome of similar litigation in the future, has little interest in that element of the outcome that might influence the disposition of the decisionmaker next time around. The repeat player, however, has considerable interest in the effect of a decision on future litigation. In time, therefore, the law tends to become more accommodating to the interests of repeat players. Hence, to the extent that in a given area of law corporations are repeat players and their adversaries are one-shotters, corporations may be better able to turn the web of law to their advantage. It is not always the case, however, that it is the corporate offender which has the advantage of being a repeat player. In the course of my research on the pharmaceutical industry, executives from large corporations complained of the fact that the Food and Drug Administration had established case law suitable to its interests as a prosecutor by picking off small companies (one-shotters) in strategic early cases.[50]

Further, the capacity of large corporations to turn the complexity of law to their advantage would seem to be greater when complexity of law is combined with complexity of the books, or is overlaid with organizational complexity. Certain organizational forms are inherently more complex than others—large organizations more so than small, transnational more so than national. In addition, some aspects of organizational life do not permit ready definition of lines of accountability. With a tax offense, the production manager, the taxation advisor, the finance director, the president, and the auditors may all in part be responsible for a violation for which no one of them fully accepts responsibility. On the other hand, it may be relatively easy to prosecute a quality assurance manager for a good manufacturing practices violation which falls neatly within his or her responsibilities.

Corporate offenders are more likely to be able to use legal complexity to their advantage when investigations, pretrial hearings, and other preliminaries are drawn out. As Sir Richard Eggleston has observed, pretrial hearings in such cases are frequently unproductive because corporate defendants are interested in confusing issues rather than clarifying them.

---

49. *Id.* at 100.

50. If this is true, it should give pause to consumerists who criticize the FDA for overly concentrating on small-time violators. Geis summarizes the Nader investigation of the food industry as concluding that "rather than launch campaigns against major firms that routinely break the law, the FDA pursues small and inconsequential violators, so as to give the appearance of activity with a record of successful prosecution, while allowing major depredators to proceed unmolested." Geis, *Upperworld Crime*, in CURRENT PRESPECTIVES ON CRIMINAL BEHAVIOR: ESSAYS ON CRIMINOLOGY 129 (A. S. Blumberg ed. 1974).

> I did not explain my reasons for thinking that pre-trial con-
> ferences would not be of much assistance if their success
> depended upon the defence making admissions; in fact, my
> reason for expressing this view was that I do not think
> counsel for the accused can be expected to make admissions
> in this class of case when his best chance of success is to
> make the whole so complicated that the jury is unable to say
> that it is satisfied beyond reasonable doubt.[51]

More simply, with the passing of time, witnesses' memories fail and
aging defendants retire. The latter was well illustrated in 1975 when
Gulf Oil was charged in connection with a Bahamian slush fund
through which some $12.3 million in largely illegal foreign political
contributions had been channeled. Of the eleven executives with direct
knowledge of the fund, only two remained with the company. Three
had died and six had retired.[52] Because the government has the
burden of proof, these effects of delayed and protracted proceedings
work to the corporate defendant's advantage.

It might be that areas of the law characterized by a long history
of running repairs, such as taxation, are those which corporations can
most readily exploit. On the other hand, Food and Drug Administration lawyers with whom I have spoken contend that one reason they
have been able to maintain a relatively strong bargaining position with
their corporate adversaries is that, whenever a new set of regulations
is issued under the Food, Drug and Cosmetic Act, all case law applicable to the old regulations is superseded. It may be that the
complexity of case law is more critical than the complexity of legislation. As Townsend has remarked of United States antitrust law:
"While the operative sections of the Sherman Act can be expressed in
a few lines, its precedents can fill entire libraries." [53] It has been
argued that corporate defendants enjoy reduced structural advantages
in civil law countries in part because the disinclination in those jurisdictions to grant formal legal authority to judicial precedent reduces
the number of mines in the legal minefield.[54]

---

51. *White Collar Crime: Can the Courts Handle It?* 23 Proc. Inst. Criminology, U. Sydney 13 (1977).

52. L. Sobel, Corruption in Business 126 (1977).

53. J. Townsend, *The Sherman Act and the Overseas Market Entry Strategy
of Selected Multinational Manufacturing Corporations* (D.B.A. Dissertation, George
Washington University, 1976).

54. This point was made at the Meeting of Experts on Topic III of the Agenda
for the Sixth United Nations Congress on the Prevention of Crime and Treatment
of Offenders: "Crime and the Abuse of Power: Offences and Offenders Beyond the
Reach of the Law?", New York, July, 1979. It does not mean that complexity of
case law is intrinsically more critical than the complexity of codes, but simply that
eliminating cases as one of the parameters in decisions should, other things being
equal, make for less complexity. Certainly it is not difficult to find examples of
common law judges complaining about the weight of the large number of cases
they must consider in reaching judgments concerning companies: "There is no

It is perhaps easier to specify the conditions under which the international side of the scenario depicted in Figure 1 is likely to hold up. Transnationals are less able to transfer their operations around the world to evade legal controls in industries where capital investment in fixed assets is high, where start-up costs are high, or where an experienced workforce is vital. In addition, there are other, more intangible constraints on a transnational's capacity to follow a law evasion strategy. Consider transfer pricing. Internal company politics frequently do not permit a corporation to set the optimal transfer prices suggested by its computer simulations. The general manager of a powerful subsidiary might be unwilling to see his or her paper profits diminished to bolster the profits of a corporate competitor who runs another subsidiary. Some companies entirely ignore the impact of taxes on transfer prices, arguing that simple and consistent pricing practices tend to minimize tax investigation problems.[55]

All of this is good news for those who wish to control transnational corporate crime. It means that transnational corporations have a less than perfect capacity to shift their activities around the world in order to evade legal constraints. The governments of the world therefore do not have to perfectly harmonize their laws in order to curtail the transnational from playing off one set of laws against another.[56] Indeed the practical economic constraints on law evasion are sometimes such that one country that sets higher regulatory standards can effectively impose its higher standards on all other countries in its region. To illustrate, a Central American Regional Director for one transnational pharmaceutical company has told me

---

dearth of cases in this province of the tax law. So large is their number and disparate their facts, that for every parallel found, a qualification hides in the thicket. At most they offer tentative clues to what is debt and what is equity for tax purposes . . . ." *American Processing & Sales Co. v. United States*, 371 F.2d 842, 848 (Ct. Cl. 1967).

55. Shulman, *Transfer Pricing in the Multinational Firm*, EUROPEAN BUSINESS (Jan. 1969).

56. If the problem is that the transnational shifts operations to nations with little regulation, then the perfect solution lies with setting international minimum standards (for pollution, industrial safety, etc.) below which no nation is allowed to fall. But so long as the disparities in regulatory stringency are kept within certain limits the costs to the transnational of playing the law evasion game will be made to exceed the benefits. In fostering a modicum of international harmonization of controls, an internationalization of the consumer and trade union movements, acting as a countervailing force against the internationalization of capital, can play an important role. Gaedeke & Udo Udo-Aka, *Toward the Internationalization of Consumerism*, 17 CALIF. MANAGEMENT REV. 86-92 (1974). Blake, *Corporate Structure and International Unionism*, COLUM. J. WORLD BUS. 20-26 (March 1972). The launching of Ralph Nader's *Multinational Monitor* is a start. Clearly, the United Nations can also play an important role. The activities of the United Nations Center on Transnational Corporations in conducting workshops for officials from Third World countries on negotiation with transnationals is also a valuable beginning. My forthcoming book on the pharmaceutical industry will give detailed consideration to strategies for harmonizing internationally the regulation of drugs.

that when Costa Rica banned a suspected carcinogenic additive in one of its products, the company took the additive out of the product being distributed in all Central American countries, since the cost of special production runs for the Costa Rican market was prohibitive.

Conclusion

In conclusion it must be admitted that no profound generalizations have been adduced as to when laws to control corporate crime will have inegalitarian effects and when they will not. Partly this is because of our nebulous understanding of corporate crime. One wonders, however, whether a search for such generalizations would ever bear fruit. Economists, after all, have tended to abandon the attempt to generalize about when investments will have certain national and international economic effects. Rather, they tend to look at particular investment proposals and consider the likely national and international effects of those specific investments given the structure of the economy at that point in time. Lawyers can surely not aspire to do more. Hopefully, the foregoing paragraphs have sensitized the reader to some of the issues that should be raised when an evaluation is made of whether a particular legal reform to control corporate crime might have unintended inegalitarian effects.

The analogy with economies is worth pursuing. Economists are now beyond arguing that because a country needs ball bearings it must be a good idea to build a ball bearing factory. They realize that before making such a decision the consequences for the structure of the economy, both nationally and internationally, must first be considered. How many legislators, though, are beyond arguing that because a particular form of conduct is severely damaging to the public interest, it must be desirable to enact laws to control that conduct?

[4]
Poverty, Power, White-Collar Crime and the Paradoxes of Criminological Theory

Sutherland's aspiration for a general theory of both white-collar and common crime can be pursued by focusing on inequality as an explanatory variable. Powerlessness and poverty increase the chances that needs are so little satisfied that crime is an irresistible temptation to actors alienated from the social order and that punishment is non-credible to actors who have nothing to lose. It may be theoretically fruitful to move away from a positivist conception of need to needs socially constructed as wants that can be satisfied (contrasted with greed — socially constructed as insatiable wants). When needs are satisfied, further power and wealth enables crime motivated by greed. New types of criminal opportunities and new paths to immunity from accountability are constituted by concentrations of wealth and power. Inequality thus worsens both crimes of poverty motivated by need for goods for use and crimes of wealth motivated by greed enabled by goods for exchange. Furthermore, much crime, particularly violent crime, is motivated by the humiliation of the offender and the offender's perceived right to humiliate the victim. Inegalitarian societies, it is argued, are more structurally humiliating. Dimensions of inequality relevant to the explanation of both white-collar and common crime are economic inequality, inequality in political power (slavery, totalitarianism), racism, ageism and patriarchy. Neither of these lines of explanation is advanced as the whole story on crimes of the powerless or crimes of the powerful; but they may be a theoretically interesting and politically important part of the whole story.

Unlike many contemporary criminologists, I continue to be motivated by the goal that Edwin Sutherland set for us of developing criminological theory of maximum possible generality. Like most contemporary criminologists, I accept that Sutherland's revelation of the nature and extent of white-collar crime creates some acute problems for traditional criminological theories. And as Sutherland so convincingly argued, the dominant tradition of criminological theory that excises white-collar crime from its explanatory scope lays the foundations for a class-biased criminology and criminal justice policy.

Having accepted all this, in this article I want to reject Sutherland's view that the widespread reality of white-collar crime means that poverty and inequality cannot be important variables in a general theory of crime. Sutherland is provocative on this point: 'If it can be shown that white collar crimes are frequent, a general theory that crime is due to poverty and its related pathologies is shown to be invalid' (Sutherland, 1983:7). Sutherland did show that white-collar crime is frequent, when white-collar crime is defined as 'a crime committed by a person of respectability and high social status in the course of his occupation' (Sutherland, 1983: 7). Indeed, work since Sutherland leaves little doubt that more of the most serious crimes that cause the greatest property loss and the greatest physical injury are perpetrated by the rich than by the poor (eg, Cullen, Maakestaad and Cavender, 1987; Clinard and Yeager, 1980; Pepinsky and Jesilow, 1984; Geis, 1973; Pearce, 1976).

My contention is that inequality is relevant to the explanation of both crime in the streets and crime in the suites. I will seek to argue that this is true of various forms of inequality — based on class, race, age and gender. Yet how do issues of inequality of wealth and power connect with my explanatory theory of crime in *Crime, Shame and Reintegration*? In a sense, what I do in this article is couple the work in that book to my 1979 book, *Inequality, Crime and Public Policy.* This first attempt to make sense of the connection between the analysis of inequality and crime and the analysis of shaming and crime has only become possible thanks to a number of recent and exciting contributions to the criminological literature. These are Jack Katz's (1988) *Seductions of Crime,* the work of Scheff and Benson on humiliation and rage, and Cohen and Machalek's (1988) 'General Theory of Expropriative Crime'.

In this article I will not summarise the evidence for the inequality-crime association compiled in *Inequality, Crime and Public Policy,* nor the evidence accumulated since. The purpose of the article is simply to advance a theoretical solution to a problem left with us by Sutherland. It is to show that the claim that poverty is causally implicated in crime can in fact be reconciled with the widespread reality of white-collar crime documented by Sutherland. While the reconciliation is theoretically interesting, whether it is empirically right is something which I simply leave on criminology's research agenda. Even if it is right, inequality is advanced only as a partial explanation of crime of modest explanatory power. More impressive explanatory capacity is only likely when inequality is integrated with other explanatory variables, perhaps in the way I suggested in *Crime, Shame and Reintegration,* perhaps in some other way.

I regard the theoretical work in this article as relevant to explaining crime conceived in either of two ways. First, as in *Crime, Shame and Reintegration,* it can be read as an attempt at explaining what Glaser (1978: 31-2) conceived as predatory crime (crime where an offender preys on others). What is advanced does not seem to me a very good theory of nonpredatory crimes such as drug use.

Alternatively, it can be read as theory concerning that domain of crimes which republicans ought to regard as crimes. Republican normative theory contends that acts ought only to criminalised when they threaten the dominion of citizens, and when there is no less intrusive way of protecting that dominion than criminalisation (Braithwaite and Pettit, 1990). Dominion includes the sphere of control citizens properly enjoy over their persons, their property and their province. To enjoy dominion, a citizen must live in a social world where other citizens respect their liberty and where this mutual respect is socially assured and generally recognised. An attraction of the republican definition for our present purposes is that it connects with a key empirical claim I will advance: when inequality of wealth and power is structurally humiliating, this undermines respect for the dominion of others. And a society where respect for dominion is lost will be a society riddled with crime.

Republican normative commitments direct us to take both political and economic inequality (Montesquieu, 1977: Chs 3-4; Pettit, 1990) and community disapproval (Pocock, 1977; Braithwaite and Pettit, 1990) seriously as issues. Sunstein (1988) advances 4 commitments as basic to republicanism: (1) deliberation in government which shapes as well as balances interests (as opposed to simply doing deals between pre-political interests); (2) political equality; (3) universality, or debate to reconcile competing views, as a regulative ideal; and (4) citizenship, community participation in public life.

Opportunity Theory

In this section, I argue:
  (1) that crime is motivated in part by needs;
  (2) that needs are more likely to be satisfied as we move up the class structure; and

42

(1991) 24 ANZJ Crim

(3) that redistributive policies will do more to increase the need satisfaction of the poor than to decrease the need satisfaction of the rich.

Notwithstanding these 3 hypotheses, greed motivates crime even after need is satisfied. More importantly, wealthly actors who have their needs satisfied will want to accumulate goods for exchange rather than use. Accumulations of goods for exchange enable the constitution of illegitimate opportunities for the rich that cannot be constituted for the poor. Hence, I will argue that inequality causes crime by:

    (i) decreasing the goods available for *use* by the poor to satisfy needs; and

    (ii) increasing the goods available to rich people (and organisations) who have needs satisfied, but whose accumulation of goods for *exchange* constitute criminal opportunities to indulge greed.

Inequality therefore at the same time causes:

crimes of *poverty*	Crimes of *wealth*
motivated by *need*	motivated by *greed*
for goods for *use*	enabled by goods for *exchange* (that are surplus to those required for use).

Inequality, Crime and Public Policy began to explore the theory and empirical evidence in support of the proposition that societies with more unequal distributions of wealth and power will have deeper crime problems. An account was advanced as to why inequality will often worsen both crime in the streets and crime in the suites. Through building on Cohen and Machalek (1988), I believe we can more clearly theorise the dynamics of this proposition than I was able to manage in *Inequality, Crime and Public Policy*.

The traditional account of opportunity theory as an explanation for crimes of the powerless continues to hold great attraction. This starts with Merton's (1957) observation that in any society there are a number of widely shared goals which provide an aspirational frame of reference. The most important of these in capitalist societies is material success. In addition to cultural goals held up as worth striving for, there are defined legitimate institutionalised means for achieving the cultural goals. When these are blocked, crime is more likely. Elaborating on Merton, Cloward and Ohlin (1960) maintained that if delinquency is to result from blockage of legitimate means to achieving a cultural goal, then there is a second requirement: illegitimate means for achieving the goal must be open.

The problem is reconciling white-collar crime within this framework. White-collar crime highlights the fact that illegitimate opportunities are grasped not only to satisfy need but also to gratify greed. In a sense, what I will set up here is explication of a transition as we move up the class structure from crime motivated by beliefs about the importance of satisfying needs to crime motivated by greed — even by the belief, in the immortal words of Michael Douglas from the movie 'Wall Street', that 'greed is good'.

But first things first — crime motivated by beliefs about needs. I am not interested in a positivist definition of need. I am interested in the phenomenon of need being socially constructed in culturally contingent ways that motivate crime. So we have criminals who act on a subsistence model of need, as in the classic case of English slum dwellers transported to Australia for stealing a loaf of bread to feed their family. There are criminals who act on models of need represented at every point of Maslow's (1954) hierarchy of needs. There are criminals motivated by the need for a decent standard of living, where 'decent' can mean what they perceive most people in their community to enjoy, what whites but not blacks enjoy, what they used to enjoy before they lost their job, what they were led to expect to enjoy by the advertising and dramatisation of bourgeois lifestyles on television. In short, the social construction of needs which motivate crime is culturally relative.

However relative they are, I advance one claim about them of general import. This claim is that as we become wealthier, it becomes more likely that any and all conceptions of need will be satisfied. If my income doubles, irrespective of whether my needs are framed in terms of subsistence, the average standard of living, or unrealistic expectations or aspirations, it is likely that I will view those needs as better met than they were before. The general claim is that as we move up the class structure, people are more likely to view their needs as satisfied. This, of course, is an empirically rebuttable claim.

Substituting the term needs in Cloward and Ohlin's (1960) formulation, the theory becomes that when legitimate means for satisfying needs are blocked and illegitimate means are open, crime is more likely. Controlling for aggregate national wealth, let us then compare a society with an equal distribution of wealth and one with an unequal distribution. It follows that because the poor will be poorer in the unequal case, those toward the bottom of the class structure will be less likely to perceive their needs as met (whether those needs are of a subsistence, absolute or relative sort). Because they view so few of their needs as met, the poor are also more likely to take the view that they have little to lose through a criminal conviction. More polemically, the more unequal the class structure, the more of scarce national wealth is devoted to gratifying greed among people whose needs are satisfied, the less is devoted to satisfying unmet need.

Consider a socially defined need for housing. The more unequal the class structure, the greater the proportion of housing expenditure that will be devoted to building bigger and bigger mansions for the rich, the greater the number of homeless, and the more the poor will turn to crime in preference to being put on the street. A more equal class structure may reduce the incidence of crimes of the poor connected to the need for housing.

Because wealthier people are more likely in a position where most of their needs are met, they are less likely to steal for this reason. As in standard welfare economics, let us assume that as we get richer we progressively work down our needs, starting with those that are most important to us. The wealthier we are, the lower the marginal returns to need satisfaction from acquiring a dollar of extra wealth through crime. Our first dollar is worth more to us than our ten millionth dollar. Hence, the crime-preventive effects of redistributing wealth from rich to poor to satisfy the needs of the poor will not be fully counterbalanced by crime-instigating effects on wealthy people who suffer reduced satisfaction of their needs.

Yet we know that even when wealthy people have all of their self-defined personal needs fully met, the extra dollar is not valueless to them. Even though a dollar has less value to a person whose needs are mostly satisfied than to one whose needs are not, the dollar will mostly continue to have some value to people with satisfied needs. Such people can continue to be motivated to pursue wealth for many other reasons — to signify their worth by conspicuous consumption, to prove success to themselves, to build an empire, to leave an inheritance.

For this reason, it is sensible to also apply a Mertonian framework to the economic aspirations of the upper class. We can readily conceive of the blocked aspirations of the already wealthy man to become a millionaire. We might understand his behaviour in paying a bribe in these terms: legitimate means for securing a contract are blocked at the time and an illegitimate opportunity to do so corruptly is open. Vaughan (1983: 59) suggests that a cultural emphasis on economic success motivates the setting of a new goal whenever the old one is attained. While needs are socially constructed as wants that can be satisfied, greed is distinguished as a want that can never be satisfied: success is ever-receding; having more leads to wanting more again.

> While it is meaningless to accumulate certain sensual use-values indefinitely, since their worth is limited by their usefulness, the accretion of exchange-value, being merely quantitative, suffers no such constraints. (Haug, 1986: 18)

Wheeler's (1991) paper directs us to the motivational importance of fear of falling as well as greed for- gain in white-collar crime. There is no problem in accommodating this within the theoretical framework of the present analysis. Crime can be motivated by: (a) a desire for goods for use; (b) a fear of losing goods for use; (c) a desire for goods for exchange; or (d) a fear of losing goods for exchange. My proposition is that (a) and (b) are more relevant to motivating the crimes of poor people; (c) and (d) are more relevant to motivating the crimes of wealthy people and organisations. These distributional tendencies can hold even though (a) to (d) might all be involved in the mixed motives driving say a single corporate crime. Some individuals who play a part in the crime may be motivated by (a), others by (b), others (c) and others (d). Indeed, within some individuals there may be mixed motives that range across the four categories. This does not change the distributional hypothesis that use-motivations will more often be involved in the criminal choices of the poor, exchange-motivations more often involved in the criminal choices of the rich.

I will now argue that just as the poverty of the poor in unequal societies contributes to crime, so does the wealth of the wealthy. We have established that the latter cannot be true because of a purely Mertonian analysis of legitimate opportunities to satisfy needs because the rich have more of their needs satisfied by ready access to legitimate means of need satisfaction.

One line of argument here is that conspicuous concentrations of wealth increase the illegitimate opportunities available to the poor (and indeed the non-poor). Being a car thief is more remunerative when there are many $50,000 cars available to be stolen than when $20,000 cars are the best one can find. Evidence that wealthy neighbourhoods located near slums are especially likely to be victimised by property offenders supports this line of analysis (Boggs, 1965). But it is not a theoretical path I wish to pursue here.

The theoretically important criminogenic effect of increasing concentrations of wealth is in enabling the constitution of new forms of illegitimate opportunity that are not available to the poor or the average income earner, opportunities that can be extremely lucrative. It is important to understand here that increasing wealth for the poor or the average income earner does not constitute new illegitimate opportunities in the way I will discuss.

Marx's distinction of value for use and value for exchange is helpful here. In his 'Economic and Philosophical Manuscripts', use is associated with need: 'every real and possible need is a weakness which will tempt the fly to the gluepot' (Marx, 1973: 148). Also every product that can be used 'is a bait with which to seduce away the other's very being, his money'. Up to the point where legitimate work generates for the worker only value for use (in meeting needs), she has no surplus. Up to this point, extra income is used instead of invested in the constitution of illegitimate opportunities. But when surplus is acquired (value for exchange rather than for use), it can be invested in the constitution of illegitimate opportunities.

A limitation of Cloward and Ohlin's (1960) analysis is that it tends to view illegitimate opportunities as a fact of society independent of the agency of the criminal actor — ready and waiting for the criminal actor to seize. This conception forgets the point that, if they are powerful enough, criminals can actively constitute illegitimate opportunities. This power is not totally explained by control of surplus value — the working class juvenile can constitute a gang as a vehicle for collective criminal enterprises that would be beyond her grasp as an individual. But surplus value can be used to constitute criminal opportunities of an order that is not available to the poor. As Weisburd et al (1989: 79) found in their systematic study of white-collar criminals in New York: 'The most consequential white-collar crimes — in terms of their scope, impact and cost in dollars — appear to require for their commission, that their perpetrators operate in an environment that provides access to both money and the organisation through which money moves.'

Persons with some spare capital can start up a company; the company can be used as a vehicle to defraud consumers or investors; the principal can siphon off funds into a personal account, bankrupting the company and leaving creditors stranded. They can set up a Swiss bank account and a shell company in a tax haven. But to launder dirty money, to employ the lawyers and accountants to evade taxes, they must have some surplus to start with. And the more they have, the more grand the illegitimate opportunities they can constitute. When they become big enough, shares in their company can be' traded publicly. They can then indulge in some very lucrative forms of insider trading and share ramping. If they become billionaires like Nelson Bunker Hunt and W Herbert Hunt, they can even try to manipulate the entire market for a commodity like silver (Abolafia, 1985). If they become an oligopolist in a market, they can work with the other oligopolists to fix prices and breach other trade practice laws. If they become a monopolist, a further array of illegal predatory practices become available. The proposition is that capital can be used to constitute illegitimate opportunities, and the more capital the bigger the opportunities. And obversely to our analysis of need, an egalitarian redistribution of wealth away from surplus for the rich in favour of increased wealth for the poor will not correspondingly expand illegitimate opportunities for the poor. This is because in the hands of the poor, income is for use; it is not available as surplus for constituting illegitimate opportunities.

Other things being equal, the rich will prefer to stay out of trouble by investing in legitimate rather than illegitimate opportunities. But when goals are set with the expectation that they will be secured legitimately, environmental contingencies frequently intervene to block legitimate goal attainment. Powerful actors regularly have the opportunity in these circumstances to achieve the goal illegitimately. The production target cannot be achieved because the effluent treatment plant has broken down. So it is achieved by allowing untreated effluent to flow into the river late at night. Most capital investment simultaneously constitutes a range of both legitimate and illegitimate means of further increasing the wealth of the capitalist. The wealth that creates legal opportunities at the same time brings illegal opportunities for achieving the same result into existence. In this additional sense, investment creates criminal opportunities in a way that use does not. It is just that there is a difference in the way we evaluate illegitimate opportunities that are inherent in any legitimate investment compared with illegitimate opportunities that are created intentionally. The former are unfortunate side-effects of mostly desirable processes of creating wealth. The latter are the main and intended effects of a mostly undesirable process of criminal exploitation. Whatever the mix of desirable and undesirable effects of shifting wealth from the poor to the rich, the

(1991) 24 ANZJ Crim

only effect we are theoretically interested in here is the creation of more illegitimate opportunities for the rich. My main point is that surplus can be used intentionally to constitute illegitimate opportunities — whether by setting up an illegal traffic in arms or drugs or by setting up a tax evasion scheme — in a way that income for use cannot.

Here it is useful to think of the implications of Cohen and Machalek's (1988) evolutionary ecological approach to expropriative crime. The first point in this analysis is that the returns to an expropriative strategy vary inversely with the number of others who are engaging in the same strategy. In nature, a behavioral strategy of predation is more likely to persist if it is different from that used by other predators. There is no 'best' strategy that will be adopted by every predator because it is the best; for a predator to opt for a strategy, it must be one that is not crowded out by others using a similar strategy. Minority strategies can flourish.

Extreme wealth fosters extraordinarily lucrative minority strategies. The wealthy can pursue illegitimate strategies that are novel and that excel because they cannot be contemplated by those who are not wealthy. Where there is no limit on what can be spent on an expropriative strategy, it can be designed to beat all alternative less adequately funded strategies against which it must compete. This is why the most damaging and most lucrative expropriative strategies are white-collar crimes. Those who have no inhibitions against duck-shooting out of season, who need spare no expense on their artillery, for whom no strategy is too novel (even shooting other hunters), are likely to get the best haul of ducks.

Anyone can stage a bank robbery. But bank robbery is not a particularly cost-effective form of illegitimate work. Very few people can buy a bank. Yet as Pontell and Calavita (1990) quote in their paper on Savings and Loans fraud, 'The best way to rob a bank is to own one'.

Cohen and Machalek (1988) suggest that the 'resource holding potential' (RHP) of the poor means they will commit crimes that amount to 'making the best of a bad job'. The RHP of the rich, in contrast, allows them to 'take advantage of a good job'. The rich will rarely resort to the illegitimate means which are criminal staples among the poor because they can secure much higher returns by pursuing either legitimate or illegitimate means to which the poor have no access. There will be little direct competition between the powerful and the powerless criminal. Instead, they will develop different minority strategies that reflect their different RHPs. Where there is direct competition, it is fragile. The small drug dealer can be crushed by the powerful organised criminal unless she finds a way of complementing him, picking up his crumbs or operating outside his area instead of competing with him.

The other peculiar advantage that powerful criminals have is in the domain that the evolutionary ecologists call counter-strategy dynamics. Fast predators activate a selective force favouring faster prey and vice versa (Cohen and Machalek, 1988). The expropriative strategy of conning consumers into buying dangerous or ineffective patent medicines was countered by the strategy of regulatory agencies seizing drugs which had not been through a pre-Marketing clearance process. The most ruthless participants in the industry used their considerable resources to short-circuit such counter-strategies, however. They bribed those responsible for pre-marketing clearance decisions; they paid unethical researchers to produce fraudulent evidence that their products were safe and efficacious (Braithwaite, 1984). To indulge this kind of thwarting of the counter-strategy process requires abundant resources of a sort unavailable to indigent criminals. Box (1983: 59) has written at length on how the greatest comparative advantage of corporate criminals 'lies in their ability to prevent their actions from becoming subject to criminal sanctions in the first place'. Again Pontell and Calavita's (1990) case study of the Savings and Loans crisis illustrates: the counter-strategy relevant there was the deregulatory reforms that the financial sector extracted from the Congress and the Executive in the early 80s, thus rendering their power less accountable.

In *Inequality, Crime and Public Policy*, I developed in some detail the proposition that it is the unaccountable power that accrues to the most wealthy that explains why they can get away with crimes of extreme seriousness. It was argued there that power corrupts and unaccountable power corrupts with impunity.[1] The upper class use their resources to ensure that their power is unaccountable; they benefit from a hegemony that renders their power corrupting. At its most basic level, only people in positions of power have the opportunity to commit crimes that involve the abuse of power, and the more power they have, the more abusive those crimes can be. As Taylor, Walton and Young (1973: 30) put it:

> ... radical deviancy theory has the task of demonstrating analytically that such rule-breaking is institutionalized, regular and widespread among the powerful, that it is a given result of the structural position enjoyed by powerful men — whether they be Cabinet ministers, judges, captains of industry or policemen.

In this analysis, power as well as money is conceived as something that can be exchanged, invested to generate more power. Hence, the crimes of a J Edgar Hoover (Geis and Goff, 1990) can be interpreted as motivated by an insatiable desire to accumulate more power for exchange. The extreme manifestation of this problem is seen in a Marcos or Ceausescu, whose power is inestimable, whose immunity from accountability is total, whose capacity for crime knows no bounds. In contrast to the insatiable demands of a totalitarian ruler to control more totally more and more people, the criminogenic powerlessness of the poor is bounded. It is bounded by the need to assert control over the life of just one person — their own person.

Inequality, Crime and Public Policy argued that if crime in the suites arises from the fact that certain people have great wealth and power, and if crime in the streets arises from the fact that certain other people have very little wealth or power, then policies to redistribute wealth and power may simultaneously relieve both types of crime problems.

I have been led to the same conclusion by the considerations in this article. If it is wealth and power that enable a range of extremely harmful expropriative strategies that are distinctive to those at the top of the class structure, then redistribution of wealth and power in favour of the upper class will increase that which enables their crimes. Redistribution of wealth and power away from the poor will worsen the 'bad lot' of which the best they can make is crime. It will further exacerbate the blockage of legitimate means, thereby increasing the attraction of illegitimate means for satisfying needs. And it will increase the alienation, the hopelessness, the live-for-the-moment desperation of those who feel that they do not have power over their own future.

Moreover, it may be that extremes of wealth and power mean that the rich justify their exploitative class position with exploitative and criminogenic ideologies not so unlike the caricature, 'greed is good'. It may be that just as the criminality of the rich is accounted for in terms of the fact that they exploit, the criminality of the poor is accounted for by the fact that they are exploited. While the forms of crime that predominate at the two ends of the class spectrum are sharply distinguishable minority strategies, they may be different sides of the same coin, both products of the same inequality, of the exploitation perceived by those who are exploited and of the exploiting legitimated for those who exploit.

48 (1991) 24 ANZJ Crim

At both ends, criminal subcultures develop to communicate symbolic reassurance to those who decide to prey on others, to sustain techniques for neutralising the evil of crime (Sykes and Matza, 1957) and to communicate knowledge about how to do it. Black criminal subcultures in America collect, dramatise and transmit the injustices of a society dominated by whites and ruled by an oppressive Anglo-Saxon criminal justice system. The subcultures of Wall Street rationalise exploitative behaviour as that which made America great. Business subcultures of tax evasion are memory files that collect the injustices of the Internal Revenue Service (cf Matza, 1964:102) and communicate resentment over the disproportionate tax burden shouldered by the rich. An oligopolistic price fixing subculture under the auspices of an industry association communicates the social benefits of 'orderly marketing'; it constitutes and reproduces an illegitimate opportunity structure.

The focus of the discussion so far has been excessively on property crime. But it need not have been. A business subculture of resistance to an occupational health and safety agency can foster methods of legal defiance, circumvention and counter-attack that kill. The unaccountable power of a Marcos or a Ceausescu can be used to kill. A wealthy person can use their capital to establish a toxic waste disposal company that directs the violence of cancer against an unsuspecting community by illegal dumping of toxins. The resentment of a black person who feels powerless and exploited because of his race can be manifested by violent as well as acquisitive crime. There are, however, some arguments about inequality that may have some special force in the domain of violent crime. To these I now turn.

The Social Structure of Humiliation

A stunning recent contribution to criminology is Jack Katz's (1988) *The Seductions of Crime*. On the central issue of this paper, Katz stands with Sutherland: 'Because of its insistence on attributing causation to material conditions in personal and social backgrounds, modern social thought has been unable either to acknowledge the embrace of evil by common or street criminals, or, and for the same reason, develop empirical bite and intellectual depth in the study of criminality by the wealthy and powerful' (Katz, 1988:10).

The importance of Katz's work resides in his analysis of violence or rage as 'livid with the awareness of humiliation' (Katz, 1988: 23). Rage both recalls and transforms the experience of humiliation. The experience of a sense of righteousness is the stepping stone from humiliation to rage; the embrace of righteous violence resolves humiliation 'through the overwhelming sensuality of rage' (Katz, 1988: 24; see also Marongiu and Newman, 1987). For Katz it is not coincidental that spouse assault is so often associated with taunting about sexual performance or innuendo of sexual infidelity. Domestic homicide transforms such sexual degradation 'in a last violent stand in defence of his basic worth' (p 26). Rage transcends the offender's humiliation by taking him to dominance over the situation.

Katz's analysis of righteous slaughter is a useful complement to the rather instrumental analysis of opportunity and strategy in the first part of this paper precisely because it is such a non-instrumental analysis. Katz notes the frequency with which murderers cease an attack long before death and indeed in the midst of evidence of persistent life such as screams and pleas for mercy (p 32). The inference that rage is not instrumentally concerned with causing death is also warranted in cases where death is not a *sufficient* concern:

> In a 'stomping', the attacker may announce to his victim the objective of 'kicking your eyes out of your head'. The specific practical objective — to remove precisely the condition of

the attacker's humiliation, the victim's offending gaze — is more imaginatively related to the project of transcending humiliation than would be the victim's death. (p 33)

Violence transcends humiliation by casting the person who degraded the offender into an ontologically lower status. Mounted in a flurry of curses, the attack 'will be against some morally lower, polluted, corrupted, profanized form of life, and hence in honor of a morally higher, more sacred, and — this bears special emphasis — an eternally respectable realm of being' (p 36). The claim that rage is about asserting respect, I will argue, is fundamental to distinguishing forms of shaming that provoke crime and forms that prevent it. Shame and respect are the key concepts for understanding crime. Far from being a self-interested instrumental evildoer, the attacker is immersed in a frenzy of upholding the decent and respectable. Just as humiliation of the *offender* is implicated in the onset of his rage, so the need to humiliate the *victim* enables her victimisation.

Katz reached these conclusions from an analysis of several hundred criminal acts quite independently of similar conclusions reached by psychiatric scholars. Kohut (1972), a psychoanalyst, identified 'narcissistic rage' as a compound of shame and rage. Lewis's (1971) cases led her to conclude that unacknowledged shame and anger causes a feeling trap, alternation between shame and anger that can produce explosive violence she calls humiliated fury. The work of Lansky (1984, 1987) and Scheff et al (1989) similarly emphasises the importance of humiliation that is unacknowledged. Innuendo, underhanded disrespect more than overt insult, opens up a cycle of humiliation, revenge, counter-revenge, ultimately to violence. Scheff (1987) identified two ways of reacting to scorn — shame or anger. But sometimes humiliated actors alternate between the two in what Scheff calls a shame-rage spiral.

Katz denies that material circumstances have anything to do with his conclusions about humiliation and rage. Here I believe he is wrong. Some societies and institutions are structurally more humiliating than others. For a black, living in South Africa is structurally more humiliating than living in Tanzania. Living in a prison is structurally more humiliating than living in a nursing home and the latter is more humiliating than dwelling in a luxury apartment. Slavery is structurally more humiliating than freedom.

School systems such as I experienced as a child, where children are linearly ordered in their classroom according to their rank, 'dunces' sitting at the front, are structurally humiliating for those who fail. These are school systems where dunces are regularly afflicted with degradation ceremonies. And there are alternative structures which are less humiliating, less the mouse race that caricatures the rat race for which children are prepared. An example is Knight's (1985: 266) conception of redemptive schooling:

> A redemptive schooling practice would aim to integrate students into all aspects of school learning and not build fences around students through bureaucratic rituals or prior assumptions concerning student ability. A clear expectation from teachers must be that all students can be taught, and in turn an expectation on the part of students that they can learn. A school succeeds democratically when everyone's competence is valued and is put to use in a variety of socially desirable projects. Indeed, the same may be said to hold for a good society.

More generally, *inegalitarian societies are structurally humiliating.* When parents cannot supply the most basic needs of their children, while at the same time they are assailed by the ostentatious consumption of the affluent, this is structurally humiliating for the poor. Where inequality is great, the rich humiliate the poor through conspicuous consumption and the poor are humiliated as failures for being poor. Both sides of this equation are important. The propensity to feel powerless and exploited among the poor and the propensity of the rich to see exploiting as legitimate both, as we have seen, enable crime.

Racist societies are structurally humiliating: These are societies where the despised racial group is viewed as unworthy of respect, where the superordinate group humiliates the subordinate group, where the subordinate group feels daily humiliation. Such racist oppression can be criminogenic.

Patriarchy is structurally humiliating: Patriarchy is a condition where women enjoy limited dominion, where men do not respect the dominion of women, where women are humiliated by men. However, it is common in patriarchal societies for women not to feel humiliated. Similarly, it is not uncommon for oppressed racial minorities and for the poor *not* to feel humiliated in racist and inegalitarian societies. Here the Gramscian (1971) concept of hegemony is useful. It often happens that part of the success of the domination by the superordinate group is in persuading the subordinate group that they should accept the ideology of superordination; they identify their own interests with those of their rulers.[2] Their subordination is regarded as something natural rather than something to resent (see also Scheff, 1990).

But hegemony never works perfectly. A substantial fraction of the oppressed group is always humiliated by their oppression. It is just that historically, hegemony has tended to work better with the oppression of women than it has with the oppression of racial minorities. In the US or Australia, for example, even though there are many more women than blacks, there are more cases of blacks than of women who feel humiliated to the point of daily seething rage which explodes into violence.

To understand why women commit less crime than men, in spite of their oppression, we need to understand why it is that women, instead of feeling humiliation and rage, feel shame and guilt. I have begun to address this in *Crime, Shame and Reintegration,* and will return to the issue later in this article. For the moment, I note only how I would propose to deal with the critical issue of the operationalisation problem with the infamously vague concept of hegemony. It is through measuring the things to which the theory proposes hegemony leads — shame and guilt when it is present, humiliation and anger when it is not (see further Scheff, 1990).

The fact that patriarchy does not engender feelings of humiliation and rage among most women does not absolve patriarchy of criminogenesis. Remember, there are two sides to our story. The hypothesis is that humiliation both motivates violence among those humiliated and enables violence among those who humiliate. Hence, the degradation of women countenanced by men who do not grant women dominion enables rape and violence against women on a massive scale in patriarchal societies, not to mention commercial exploitation of the bodies of women by actors who might ambiguously be labelled white-collar criminals. Empirical work on homicides by men against women confirms that homicide can be viewed as an attempt by the male to assert '. . . their power and control over their wifes' (Wallace, 1986: 126; Polk and Ranson, 1991). In passing, it is important to note that the willingness to humiliate women should, according to the theory, be more profound among men who see themselves as having been humiliated — as a black humiliated by whites, as an American soldier in Vietnam humiliated by protesters back home, by 'Gooks' who defeat him militarily, and by an authoritarian military.

Ageist societies are structurally humiliating: Where the very young or the very old are not worthy of respect, where they do not enjoy the dominion accorded human beings at the peak of their powers, the young and the old will be abused, including physically abused — both in the home and in institutions specialising in their care (schools and nursing homes). While the very old rarely have the physical power to transcend their humiliation with violent rage, the young do, especially as they become older, stronger young males. The physical powerlessness of the very old makes their abuse the most invisible and insidious in complex societies. As Joel Handler (1989: 5) points out, even prisoners can riot, but the frail aged have neither muscle nor voice. The very young, and particularly the very old (Fattah and Sacco, 1989:174-7), are also vulnerable and attractive targets for consumer fraud.

Ageist and gendered exploitation interact in important ways. Contemporarily we see this in many studies of elder abuse which report over 70%, and sometimes over 80%, of victims of elderly abuse to be female (Hudson, 1986; Wolf and Pillemer 1989:33).[3] Historically, we see it in the victimisation of older women labelled as witches in the 16th and 17th centuries in many parts of the western world (Stearns, 1986: 7).

Totalitarian societies are structurally humiliating: Totalitarian societies are, by definition, disrespectful of the dominion of ordinary citizens. They are societies that trample on the dominion of individual citizens to serve the interests of the ruling party. Atrocities by the state are enabled by disrespect for its citizens. The disrespect that degraded citizens in turn accord to the laws of the totalitarian state is also criminogenic.

Retributive societies are structurally humiliating[4]: These are societies where evildoers are viewed as unworthy of respect, as enjoying no right to have their dominion protected, as worthy of humiliation. The degraded status of prisoners in retributive societies frees those responsible for their daily degradation from restraints to respect the dominion of prisoners. The result can be the systematic violence directed against prisoners that we saw documented in the Royal Commission into New South Wales Prisons (Jewson, 1978) and which was a central cultural fact of the first 100 years of our colonial history. We can see this in Stotland's interpretation of the slaughter of prisoners at Attica: 'For both troopers and guards, sense of competence, violence and self-esteem . . . are linked' (Stotland, 1976: 88). 'A person's self-esteem can be threatened by failure [and] insults' (p 86) (see also, Scheff, 1989: 187; McKay Commission 1972). In another study of the 1970 killings by National Guardsmen at Kent State University, Stotland and Martinez (1976: 12) reached the same conclusion:

> The events . . . leading up to the killings were a series of inept, ineffectual, almost humiliating moves by the Guardsmen against the 'enemy' . . . The answer to these threats to their self-esteem, to their sense of competence, was violence . . . Another aspect . . . which added to the threat to the self-esteem of the Guardsmen [was that] during their presence on . . . campus . . . the students insulted Guardsmen. . . [and the Guardsmen] were not in a position to answer back. Their relative silence was another humiliation for them.

Scheff et al (1989) have discussed both of these cases of collective violence. They focused on the 'brutality and humiliation of the inmates' (such as forcing prisoners to crawl through mud) documented in the McKay Commission (1972) report. But the prison officers were also humiliated by the assertion of inmate power, the mistreatment of hostages and the recognition their superiors in the prison administration gave to prisoner demands (treating them 'as if they were equals'), and their denunciation by the prisoners on television. Scheff et al (1989: 193) interpreted this as a triple shame/rage spiral:

The guards were shamed by the behaviour of the administration and the inmates, were powerless to confront the administration, and became hostile toward the inmates, who in turn were shamed by the guards' lack of respect and reacted with an angry lack of respect towards the guards.

When two parties are each stigmatising the other, on both sides stigmatisation enables one's own violence and provokes the violence of the other.

In *Crime, Shame and Reintegration,* I have developed in more detail the criminogenic consequences of stigmatisation. Because I mainly talk of stigmatisation there rather than humiliation, it is important to clarify the difference between the two terms. Humiliation means disrespectful disapproval. Stigmatisation is humiliation that is sustained over an indefinitely long period. In *Crime, Shame and Reintegration* I partitioned shaming into reintegrative shaming (which prevents crime) and stigmatisation (which encourages it).[5] Reintegrative shaming is disapproval extended while a relationship of respect is sustained with the offender. Stigmatisation is disrespectful, humiliating shaming where degradation ceremonies are never terminated by gestures of reacceptance of the offender. The offender is branded an evil person and cast out in a permanent, open-ended way. Reintegrative shaming, in contrast, might vigorously shame an evil deed, but the offender is cast as a respected person rather than an evil person. Even the shaming of the deed is finite in duration, terminated by ceremonies of forgiveness-apology-repentance. The preventive effect of reintegratively shaming criminals occurs when the offender recognises the wrongdoing and shames himself. This distinction also appears in the work of Katz (1988: 26-7): 'Thus I may "become ashamed of myself" but I do not become humiliated of myself'.

The case is made in *Crime, Shame and Reintegration* that stigmatisation fosters crime by increasing the attraction of criminal subcultures to the stigmatised; we have also in this article seen that humiliation directly provokes violence. Here we have sought to suggest that stigmatisation not only encourages crime *by* those stigmatised; it also enables crime to be targeted *against* those stigmatised. For example, carers for the aged who have stigmatised images of the elderly are more likely to be found among those who abuse their old folk (Phillips, 1983).

The empirical claims derived from the theory in this chapter can be simply summarised. Nations will have more crime the more they are unequal in wealth and power, racist, patriarchal, ageist, totalitarian and retributive. To the extent that hegemony works to convince the subordinate fractions of the population that their oppression is natural rather than humiliating, these effects will be attenuated — we will see evidence of feeling ashamed rather than feeling humiliated, perhaps of more inwardly-directed rather than other-directed violence. The prediction of the theory, nevertheless, is that even where hegemony is strong, inequality will still have some effect on the crime rate because: (a) hegemony will never be total, and (b) because hegemony undermines feelings of being exploited without undermining the ideology of exploitation that enables the victimisation of the exploited. These hypotheses are not banal; they cut against the grain of some popular alternative accounts of crime — for example, the account of Sutherland, Katz and others that materialist explanation does not work, the account that a high crime rate is a price we pay for freedom, the account that retributive crime control policies will have crime-reducing deterrent effects. In the years ahead, I will be doing my best to apply some international comparative data to crude preliminary tests of these propositions.

It may be that when humiliation is deeply structured into a social system, it is not only the subordinate who suffer frequent humiliation. In a class system where the motivation to conspicuously flaunt superior wealth is profound, in a school system motivated by ranking in the class, dropping from number one to number two can be humiliating. Merton saw this point, quoting a well-to-do Hollywood resident of the 30s: 'In this town, I'm snubbed socially because I only get a thousand a week. That hurts.' (Merton, 1968: 190). We also saw this in the case of the Attica riot: in a social system where the prisoners were totally subordinated, the very willingness of the administration to negotiate with the prisoners was humiliating to the prison officers.

This two-way street is perhaps most vivid in the domain of gender and sexuality. Patriarchy is often manifested as measuring the worth of women against a yardstick of youthful physical beauty, while machismo is about male domination of women by sexual virility — the revered male is he who conquers the largest number of beautiful women. Needless to say, societies where success is so measured are structurally humiliating for women who inevitably lose their youth and who resent being used as a score. But when resentment and humiliation is structured into sexuality, the male is also at risk. Katz's (1988) work shows how women taunt men for their poor sexual performance and how violence can be unleashed when they do so.

The key to a feminist criminology of some explanatory power, I submit, is to understand the relationship between gender and my two types of shaming. The sexually stratified structure of shame is why women kill less than men (Braithwaite, 1989). The sexually stratified structure of humiliation is why when women do kill, it is rarely other women (Zahn, 1980: 125; Katz, 1988; Polk and Ranson, 1991).

Just as in the first half of this article the disproportionate emphasis was on property offences, in the second half we have been developing an approach which seems most powerful in the domain of traditional violent offences. However, the analysis is by no means without relevance to the explanation of property and white-collar offences as well.

Katz (1988) makes much of the 'badass' who takes pride in a defiant reputation as bad:

> The badass, with searing purposiveness, tries to scare humiliation off; as one ex-punk explained to me, after years of adolescent anxiety about the ugliness of his complexion and the stupidness of his every word, he found a wonderful calm in making 'them' anxious about *his* perceptions and understandings. (Katz, 1988: 312-3)

The point here is that pride in a badness that transcends humiliation might just as well be the badness of vandalism or theft as the badness of violence. This has been a repeated theme in street-corner criminological research. It is most strongly expressed in Albert Cohen's (1955) notion of reaction formation. Humiliation at school brings about a status problem for the children who fail in a competitive school system. This status problem is solved collectively with other students who have been similarly humiliated by the school. The outcasts set up their own status system with values which are the exact inverse of those of the school — contempt for property and authority instead of respect for property and authority, immediate impulse gratification instead of impulse control, toughness instead of control of aggression. This inverted status system is one in which the delinquent is guaranteed some success. It is clear that many non-violent forms of delinquency will do for dealing with humiliation by rejecting one's rejectors.

Benson (1990) has shown the importance of humiliation and rage among 30 convicted white-collar property offenders. Adjudication of their cases engendered anger and rage as well as shame and embarrassment. The way humiliation unfolded meant that anger usually won out over shame as a way of dealing with the situation. The likely result of feeling unfairly stigmatised, according to Benson, is reduced commitment to the legitimacy of the law. In this sense, Benson argues, a criminal justice system based on reintegrative shaming is less likely to be counter-productive than one based on stigmatisation.

It would be perverse indeed to interpret the second half of this article as only a story about the explanation of common violence in the streets. In the same year that Edwin Sutherland introduced white-collar crime into our lexicon, the greatest white-collar criminal of our century set the world alight. His name was Adolf Hitler. Thomas Scheff points out that 'Every page of Hitler's Mein Kamp bristles with shame and rage' (Scheff, 1987: 147). Indeed Hitler's appeal was the appeal of humiliated fury, an appeal which struck a responsive chord with many German people who felt they had been tricked and humiliated at Versailles[6], defeated by 'traitors, Communists and Jews'. War crimes are partly about blocked legitimate opportunities to achieve national economic objectives. But they are also about being humiliated, wanting to humiliate, and fear of being humiliated on both sides of a conflict.

> There is fear of defeat and fear of humiliation. There is the great fear of being seen to be a loser. It could be argued that the reason the British war fleet was sent to the Falklands was really the fear of humiliation. The preservation of a self-image on a personal or national level is extremely important and fear of losing that image is a strong motivator. Indeed, Enoch Powell goaded Mrs Thatcher in the House of Commons with exactly this approach: how could she, of all people stand for this Argentine insult. (de Bono, 1985:145).

When Saddam Hussein broadcast his appeal of 10 August 1990 to all Arabs, humiliation was a key repetitive element of his text: 'Rise up, so that the voice of right can be heard in the Arab nation. Rebel against all attempts to humiliate Mecca. Make it clear to your rulers, the emirs of oil, as they serve the foreigner; tell them the traitors there is no place for them on Arab soil after they have humiliated Arab honour and dignity.' (*The Times,* 11 August 1990, p1)

Criminology as a Model of how to do Social Theory?

In all of these recent developments in criminological theory, it seems to me that we can do more than satisfy Sutherland's ideal of criminological theory which brings in white-collar crime, which is maximally general in its scope. We can bring class back in (in a way that Sutherland would not approve) and gender, race, age and politics as well. We can call on normative theory which is articulated to explanatory theory to define objects of explanation that are not trivial to the human condition. Philip Pettit and my republican theory (Braithwaite and Pettit, 1990) is, we hope, the most comprehensively developed such normative theory of criminal justice. But there are Marxist, socialist realist, liberal and retributivist models available which are also specified with increasing coherence.

Nevertheless, the most important accomplishment which might be within our grasp is at a more meta-theoretical level. This is to integrate theoretically four ideas:

(1) the reasoning individual (the strategist) and the reasoning collectivity (the corporate strategist);
(2) the somatic, the body, emotions (humiliation, rage, shame, forgiveness, love, respect);
(3) the micro interaction (the degradation ceremony, the assault, the proffering of forgiveness, apology, the ceremony to decertify deviance);
(4) the macro, the structural (relations of production, patriarchy, communitarianism, age structure, urbanisation).

Each of these four levels can be shown to be actively shaping, enabling and constraining each of the others. In *Crime, Shame and Reintegration,* I made much of the reasoning individual acting in ways enabled and constrained by structural factors, but exercising agency in micro encounters that both reproduce and transform those very structures.

Where I did not go far enough was in playing up a similar recursiveness among the somatic, the micro and the macro. Yet we should be emboldened by the work of Scheff and Katz to take this extra step. As Barbalet and Lyon (1989) have pointed out, we have Foucault more than anyone to thank for bringing the body back in to social theory. But for Foucault the body is little more than a text on which is inscribed disciplinary practices, relations of power. Agency is rarely conceded to the somatic. Yet the non-trivial role of Hitler's humiliation and sustained rage in events which transformed the world shows that social theory which writes out somatic agency will have truncated explanatory power.

Katz failed to go beyond the interface between the compelling force of emotions and individual reasoning in the micro encounter. It is the failure for which an earlier generation of micro-sociologists was so eloquently condemned by Taylor, Walton and Young (1973). Why can we not put all of these newer elements together with the legacy of Sutherland to make criminology one of the best exemplars we have in the social sciences of how to do social theory and praxis? It is within our grasp to constructively bring together normative and explanatory theory. And explanatory theory is possible which illuminates the mutual shaping that occurs among reason, emotion, micro-process and macro-structure.

NOTES

1 Sorokin and Lunden (1959: 37) make essentially the same point: 'The greater, more absolute, and coercive the power of rulers, political leaders, and big executives of business, labor and other organisations, and the less freely this power is approved by the ruled population, the more corrupt and criminal such ruling groups and executives tend to be ... With a progressive limitation of their power, criminality of rulers and executives tends to decrease qualitatively (by becoming less grave and murderous) and quantitatively (by decreasing the rate of criminal actions)'.

2 Merton was not unaware of this issue. He conceded that where the poor do not aspire to the same material success goals held out as important for the upper classes, where there are 'differential class symbols of success', they will not suffer the same frustration from blocked legitimate opportunities (Merton, 1968: 201).

3 The exception to this finding is the victim survey of Pillemer and Finkelhor (1988). In this study elderly males were significantly more likely to be abused than elderly females, though the female victims suffered more severe victimisations than the males.

4 Retributiveness may not seem to be a dimension of inequality. But I have argued elsewhere (Braithwaite, 1982; Braithwaite and Pettit, 1990) that under retributive policies 'just deserts' tends to be imposed successfully on the poor and unsuccessfully on the rich. Retributivism exacerbates important inqualities under any feasible programe of implementation.

5 Stigmatisation at least encourages crime among those who are stigmatised, though it will discourage crime among others who witness the stigmatisation (see Braithwaite, 1989:Ch 5).

6 Certainly the emotions attributed to the Germans at the time were in the vocabulary of humiliation. The Australian press observer at Versailles described the arrival of the German foreign minister thus: 'Count von Brockdorff-Rantzau appeared to feel the humiliation of his position, and stood bareheaded ...' (*Sydney Morning Herald*, 3 May, 1919).

REFERENCES

Abolafia, Mitchel Y (1985) 'Self-Regulation as Market Maintenance: An Organization Perspective; in R G Noll (ed) *Regulatory Policy and the Social Sciences.* Berkeley: University of California Press.

Barbalet, Jack and Margot Lyon (1989) unpublished paper presented to Sociology Department Seminar, Australian National University.

Benson, Michael (1990) 'Emotions and Adjudication: A Study of Status Degradation Among White-Collar Criminals' unpublished Paper. Department of Sociology, University of Tennessee.

Boggs, S L (1965) 'Urban Crime patterns' *American Sociological Review* 30: 899-908.

Box, Steven (1983) *Power, Crime and Mystification.* London: Tavistock.

Braithwaite, John (1979) *Inequality, Crime and Public Policy.* London: Routledge and Kegan Paul.

— (1982) 'Challenging Just Deserts: Punishing White-Collar Criminals' *Journal of Criminal Law and Criminology* 73: 723-60.

— (1984) *Corporate Crime in the Pharmaceutical Industry.* London: Routledge and Kegan Paul.

— (1989) *Crime, Shame and Reintegration.* Melbourne: Cambridge University Press.

Braithwaite, John and Philip Pettit (1990) *Not Just Deserts: A Republican Theory of Criminal Justice.* Oxford: Oxford University Press.

Clinard, Marshall and Peter C Yeager (1980) *Corporate Crime.* New York: Free Press.

Cloward, Richard A and Lloyd E Ohlin (1960) *Delinquency and Opportunity: A Theory of Delinquent Gangs.* Glencoe, Ill: Free Press.

Cohen Albert K (1955) *Delinquent Boys: The Culture of the Gang.* Glencoe, Ill: Free Press.

Cohen, Lawrence E and Richard Machalek (1988) 'A General Theory of Expropriative Crime: An Evolutionary Ecological Approach' *American Journal of Sociology* 94: 465-501.

Cullen, Francis T, William J Maakestaad, and Gray Cavender (1987) *Corporate Crime Under Attack: The Ford Pinto Case and Beyond.* Cincinnati: Anderson.

de Bono, Edward (1985) *Conflicts: A Better way to Resolve them.* London: Harrap.

Fattah, E A and V F Sacco (1989) *Crime and Victimization of the Elderly.* New York: Springer-Verlag.

Geis, Gilbert (1973) 'Victimization Patterns in White-Collar Crime' in I Drapkin and E Viano (eds) *Victimology: A New Focus,* vol V. Lexington, Mass: Lexington Books.

Geis, Gilbert and Colin Goff (1990) 'Edwin Sutherland and the FBI: The Evil of Banality' paper to Edwin Sutherland Conference on: White-Collar Crime, Indiana University.

Glaser, Daniel (1978) *Crime in Our Changing Society.* New York: Holt, Rinehart and Winston.

Gramsci, Antoniono (1971) *Selections from the Prison Notebooks of A. Gramsci,* ed and Trans, Q Hoare and G Nowell-Smith. London: Lawrence and Wishart.

Handler, Joel F (1989) 'Community Care for the Frail Elderly: A Theory of Empowerment' unpublished Paper.

Haug, W F (1986) *Critique of Commodity Aesthetics: Appearance, Sexuality and Advertising in Capitalist Society,* Trans Robert Bock. Cambridge: Polity Press.

Hudson, Margaret (1986) 'Elder Mistreatment: Current Research' in Karl A Pillemer and Rosalie S Wolf (eds) *Elder Abuse: Conflict in the Family.* Dover, Mass: Auburn House.

Jewson, Bob (1978) 'The Prisoners' Action Group's Summary of the Royal Commission into NSW Prisons Following the Hearing of Evidence" in P R Wilson and J Braithwaite (eds) *Two Faces'of Deviance: Crimes of the Powerless and Powerful.* Brisbane: University of Queensland Press.

Katz, Jack (1988) *Seductions of Crime: Moral and Sensual Attractions of Doing Evil.* New York: Basic Books.

Knight, Tony (1985) 'Schools and Delinquency' in A Borowski and J M Murray (eds) *Juvenile Delinquency in Australia.* Melbourne: Methuen.

Kohut, H (1972)'Thoughts on Narcissism and Narcissistic Rage' *The Psychoanalytic Study of the Child* 27: 360-400.

Lansky, M (1984) 'Violence, Shame and the Family' *International Journal of Family Psychiatry* 5:21-40.
— (1987) 'Shame and Domestic Violence' in D Nathanson (ed), *The Many Faces of Shame.* New York: Guilford.
Lewis, Helen (1971) *Shame and Guilt in Neurosis.* New York: International Universities Press.
McKay Commission (New York State Special Commission on Attica) (1972) Attica: A Report. New York: Praeger.
Marangiu, Pietro and Graeme Newman (1987) *Vengeance: The Fight Against Injustice.* Totowa, New Jersey: Rowan & Littlefield.
Marx, Karl (1973) *Ecomonic and Philosophic Manuscripts of 1844.* Trans M Milligan. London: Lawrence and Wishart.
Maslow, Abraham H (1954) *Motivation and Personality.* New York: Harper and Row.
Matza, David (1964) *Delinquency and Drift.* New York: Wiley.
Merton, Robert K (1968) *Social Theory and Social Structure.* Glencoe, Ill: Free press.
Montesquieu, Barron De (1977) *The Spirit of Laws,* Abr and ed by D W Carrithers, Berkeley, California: University of California Press.
Pearce, Frank (1976) *Crimes of the Powerful: Marxism, Crime and Deviance.* London: Pluto Press.
Pepinsky, Harold E and Paul Jesilow (1984) *Myths That Cause Crime.* Washington DC: Seven Locks Press.
Pettit, Philip (1989) 'Liberty in the Republic' *John Curtin Memorial Lecture,* Research School of Social Sciences, Australian National University.
Phillips, L R (1983) 'Abuse and Neglect of the Frail Elderly at Home: An Exploration of Theoretical Relationships' *Journal of Advanced Nursing* 8: 379-92.
Pillemer, Karl and David Finkelhor (1988) 'The Prevalence of Elder Abuse: A Random Sample Survey' *The Gerontologist* 28: 51-7.
Pocock, J G A (ed) (1977) *The Political Works of James Harrington.* New York: Cambridge University Press.
Polk, Ken and Ranson, D L (1991) 'Homicide in Victoria' in D Chappell, P Grabosky and H Strang (eds) *Australian Violence: Contemporary Perspectives.* Canberra: Australian Institute of Criminology.
Pontell, Henry and Kitty Calavita (1990) 'Bilking Bankers and Bad Debts: White-Collar Crime and the Savings and Loan Crisis' paper to Edwin Sutherland Conference on White-Collar Crime, Indiana University.
Scheff, Thomas J (1990) *Microsociology.* Chicago: University of Chicago Press.
— (1988) 'Shame and Conformity: The Deference-Emotion System'. *American Sociological Review* 53: 395-406.
— (1987) 'The Shame-Rage Spiral: A Case Study of an Interminable Quarrel' in H B Lewis (ed) *The Role of Shame in Symptom Formation.* Hillsdale, NJ: LEA.
Scheff, Thomas J, Suzanne M Retzinger and Michael T Ryan (1989) 'Crime, Violence and Self-Esteem: Review and Proposals' in A Mecca, N Smelser and J Vasconcellos (eds) *The Social Importance of Self-Esteem.* Berkeley: University of California Press.
Sorokin, P A and W A Lunden (1959) *Power and Morality.* Boston: Porter Sargent.
Stearns, Peter N (1986) 'Old Age Family Conflict: The Perspective of the past' in Karl A Pillemer and Rosalie S Wolf (eds) *Elder Abuse: Conflict in the Family.* Dover, Mass: Auburn House.
Stotland, Ezra (1976) 'Self-Esteem and Violence by Guards and Troopers at Attica' *Criminal Justice and Behavior* 3: 85-96.
Stotland, Ezra and J Martinez (1976) 'Self-Esteem and Mass Violence at Kent State' *International Journal of Group Tensions* 6: 85-96.
Sundstein, Cass (1988) 'Beyond the Republican Revival' *Yale Law Journal,* 97: 1539-90.
Sutherland, Edwin H (1983) *White Collar Crime: The Uncut Version.* New Haven: Yale University Press.
Sykes, Gresham and David Matza (1957) 'Techniques of Neutralization: A Theory of Delinquency' *American Sociological Review* 22: 664-70.

Taylor, Ian, Paul Walton and Jock Young (1973) *The New Criminology: For a Social Theory of Deviance.* London: Routledge and Kegan Paul.

Vaughan, Diane (1983) *Controlling Unlawful Organizational Behaviour: Social Structure and Corporate Misconduct.* Chicago: University of Chicago Press.

Wallace, A (1986) *Homicide: The Social Reality.* Sydney: New South Wales Bureau of Crime Statistics and Research.

Weisburd, David, Stanton Wheeler, Elin Warning and Nancy Bode (1989) *Crimes of the Middle Classes,* unpublished manuscript.

Wheeler, Stanton (1990) 'White-Collar Crime: Some Reflections on a Socio-Legal Research Program' paper to Edwin Sutherland Conference on White-Collar Crime, Indiana University.

Wolf, Rosalie S and Karl A Pillemer (1989) *Helping Elderly Victims: The Reality of Elder Abuse.* New York: Columbia University Press.

Zahn, Margaret A (1980) 'Homicide in the Twentieth Century United States' in James A Inciardi and Charles E Faupel (eds) *History and Crime.* Beverley Hills: Sage.

[5]
Inequality and Republican Criminology

In this chapter I show that the struggle for equality and checking of power is central to republican political theory. Although a republican normative theory of criminal justice does not prescribe maximum equality in criminal sentencing, it prescribes a principle of parsimony in sentencing that would have the effect of producing more egalitarian punishment practices than competing models, such as just deserts. Just as with republican normative theory, republican explanatory theory is strongly focused on inequality (as a cause of crime). Theories are most valuable when they help us to see a problem differently and to see changed and effective ways of responding to it. Republican criminology achieves this because it replaces pessimism that nothing works in reducing crime with an optimistic vision. Republican theory enables us to see that: (a) the most serious crime problems in contemporary societies are precisely the crime problems we are in the best position to reduce; and (b) the changes needed to effect these reductions have gathered considerable momentum in Western societies such as Australia since the mid-1970s. These changes are not so much in criminal justice policies as they are in the support for an effectiveness of social movements with egalitarian criminal justice agendas. Republican criminological praxis involves active support for social movements such as feminism, the environmental movement, the consumer movement, and the social movement against drunk driving and drug-promoting industries such as the alcohol, tobacco, and pharmaceutical industries.

This chapter explains that republicans have moral commitments to both political and economic equality and community involvement in disapproving of criminality. The objective is to show how it follows from these commitments that political support for certain progressive social move-

Reprinted with kind permission of the original publisher.

ments is the best way for republicans to respond to the crime problem. After setting out the basics of a republican normative framework, empirical foundations for the efficacy of this kind of response are hypothesized— that reintegrative shaming prevents crime and that stigmatization causes crime. Next we address the worry that even if these empirical foundations are right, they are foundations for a repressive response that is a threat to freedom. It is concluded that *republican* shaming constitutes freedom rather than threatens it. I show that shaming of our most serious crimes has been historically muted because these types of criminality have been sheltered from shame by concentrations of power. Then I show how progressive social movements are finally mobilizing community disapproval against our protected criminal species. Having made a case for the greater efficacy of community mobilization over criminal justice system mobilization, I then return to why republican normative commitments argue for political support for social movements such as feminism. Finally, I advance a model of the synergy republicans ought to seek between community mobilization against crime and state enforcement.

In my book with Philip Pettit, *Not Just Deserts*, we began a detailed fleshing out of why and how our criminology is republican (Braithwaite and Pettit 1990). Whereas this book advances a normative theory of criminal justice, *Crime, Shame and Reintegration* advances an explanatory theory of crime (Braithwaite 1989a). These theories may be found to be wrong in some important respects. My purpose here is not to defend them, but to go beyond the two books to show how the republican criminologist will view the state and the nature of the struggle against crime in a different way. *Not Just Deserts* is a normative analysis of how to design criminal justice policies. Yet in a way this emphasis is misplaced because the republican criminologist must see the best strategies for dealing with crime as outside the criminal justice system. In this chapter I seek to remedy the preoccupation with criminal justice institutions and to set forth what should be at the center of the political agenda of republican criminology.

For the benefit of readers who are unfamiliar with *Not Just Deserts*, I first explain the basic idea of that book—that the pursuit of dominion is a useful normative framework for criminologists. Then I explain the basic idea of *Crime, Shame and Reintegration*—that reintegrative shaming is the key to crime control.

What is Republicanism?

Republican normative commitments direct us to take both political and economic inequality (Montesquieu 1977, chaps. 3–4; Pettit 1989) and community disapproval (Braithwaite and Pettit 1990; Pocock 1977) seriously. Sunstein (1988) advances four commitments as basic to republicanism: (1) deliberation in governance in order to shape as well as balance interests (as opposed to deal making between prepolitical interests); (2) political equality; (3) universality, or debate to reconcile competing views, as a regulative ideal; and (4) citizenship, community participation in public life.

Consistent with these commitments, in *Not Just Deserts* Pettit and I seek to define in a more foundational way the political objective republicans pursue. We develop a consequentialist theory that posits the maximization of dominion as the yardstick against which to measure the adequacy of policy. What is this dominion that we wish to maximize?

Dominion is a republican conception of liberty. Whereas the liberal conception of freedom is the freedom of an isolated atomistic individual, the republican conception of liberty is the freedom of a social world. Liberal freedom is objective and individualistic. Negative freedom for the liberal means the objective fact of individuals' being left alone by others. For the republican, however, freedom is defined socially and relationally. You only enjoy republican freedom—dominion—when you live in a social world that provides you with an intersubjective set of assurances of liberty. You must subjectively believe that you enjoy these assurances, and so must others believe. As a social, relational conception of liberty, by definition it also has a comparative dimension. To fully enjoy liberty, you must have equality-of-liberty prospects with other persons. If this is difficult to grasp, think of dominion as a conception of freedom that, by definition, incorporates the notions of *liberté*, *égalité*, and *fraternité*; then you have the basic idea.[1]

This conception of dominion as a target for the criminal justice system has two attractive political features for progressive criminologists. First, we show that it motivates a minimalism in state criminal justice interventions. This is the principle of parsimony: If in doubt, do less by way of criminal justice intervention.

Second, at the same time, dominion requires a highly interventionist state policy to secure equality-of-liberty prospects. This is the relational element built into the definition. When women or Aborigines enjoy lesser liberty prospects, affirmative action and redistributive tax and economic policies are commended by the theory. So we have a theory that can require minimalism in criminal justice policy alongside interventionism in economic policy.

The principle of parsimony does important theoretical work. Pettit and I show that it motivates a theoretically driven incrementalism in criminal justice policy—actually a decrementalism. Republicans, we argue, are required to struggle politically alongside the budget-cutting economic rationalists for progressive reductions in criminal justice interventions. The right level of punishment is not determined by the just deserts of offenders. The right level of punishment, according to the theory, is as low as we can take it without clear evidence emerging that crime has increased as a result of cuts to the system.

Not Just Deserts argues that a consequence of implementing this approach will be more equitable punishment practices than we have seen, or could ever see, by following competing philosophies—notably just deserts. We argue that even though the policy of just deserts is based on equal punishment for equal wrongs and republicanism is not, it is republicanism that in practice can deliver more egalitarian punishment practices. Because just deserts tend to be successfully imposed on the poor and unsuccessfully on the rich, a parsimonious policy will be more equitable than a policy of pursuing just deserts. Minimalist policies will tend to be more equitable because of the structural theorem that says where desert is greatest, punishment will be least.

The Explanatory Idea

The notion that shaming controls crime is an old one. But so is the seemingly contradictory notion that stigmatization makes crime problems worse. The only originality of *Crime, Shame and Reintegration* is in positing a theoretical resolution of this contradiction. Reintegrative shaming is posited as a shaming mechanism that prevents crime, stigmatization as a mechanism that increases the risks of crime by the shamed actor. Moreover, the partitioning of shaming mechanisms into two types with these opposite effects is advanced as a missing link in criminological theory. It enables us to integrate previously irreconcilable theories—control, subcultural, labeling, opportunity, and learning theories.

Reintegrative shaming is disapproval extended while a relationship of respect is sustained with the offender. Stigmatization is disrespectful, humiliating shaming where degradation ceremonies are never terminated by gestures of reacceptance of the offender. The offender is branded an evil person and cast out in a permanent, open-ended way. Reintegrative shaming, in contrast, might shame an evil deed, but the offender is cast as a respected person rather than an evil one. Even the shaming of the deed is finite in duration, terminated by ceremonies of forgiveness-apology-repentance.

A crucial preventive effect of reintegratively shaming criminals occurs when the offender recognizes the wrongdoing and shames him- or herself. Hence, a particular type of crime will be less common in a community when that type of crime is subjected to extensive and intensive reintegrative shaming. Extensive stigmatization, in contrast, will have equivocal effects on crime. On the one hand, it will reduce crime through the general deterrent effects of social disapproval. On the other hand, specific deterrence will be worse than a failure because stigmatization will foster the rejection of one's rejectors and the formation of subcultures of resistance to the law.

A Repressive Idea?

Seeking to bring crime under control by community shaming seems more benign than relying on the punitive state. Shaming is not as oppressive as imprisonment. Nevertheless, shame can be a tool of extraordinarily powerful oppression. The most common and profound concerns that come to mind are not about shaming crime, but about shaming forms of deviance that are not criminal—unconventional political and religious views or unconventional sexuality, for example. And the types of shaming of criminals that are most often raised as unconscionable are examples of stigmatization rather than reintegrative shaming. Reintegrative shaming, as a communicative, dialogic form of shaming that seeks to persuade offenders to disapprove of their own criminal conduct is not equivalent to ridiculing wrongdoers as persons by putting them in the stocks.

Even though reintegrative shaming is more respecting of persons than stigmatization, it can be oppressive. Just because it avoids the worst repressive excesses of the punitive state and the stigmatizing community, that is not to deny that reintegrative shaming is a dangerous game. Victims of violence, after all, are often ashamed of their victimization (Stanko 1990: 55, 67). Republicans cannot support reintegrative shaming as the dominant crime control strategy unless they have a clear moral position on what should and should not be shamed. Saying that all that is being advocated is the shaming of criminal conduct is not good enough, because this warrants the shaming of a soldier who refuses to fight in an evil war against Iraq. Pettit and I argue that conduct should never be criminalized unless we can be confident that its criminalization will increase dominion (the republican conception of liberty) in the community (Braithwaite and Pettit 1990). Our contention is that republicans must reserve the reprobation of criminal conduct for conduct that passes this test. Republicans are

therefore required to actively support the reintegrative shaming of conduct whose criminalization uncontroversially protects dominion (such as criminal acts of violence). They are also required to actively oppose the shaming of deviant conduct that poses no threat to dominion.

Republicanism is a consequentialist theory that motivates a strong concern about rights (Braithwaite and Pettit 1990). Yet rights have meaning only as claims that rich individuals and corporations can occasionally assert in courts of law unless community disapproval can be mobilized against those who trample on the rights of others. Liberals and republicans can agree that gay men and lesbian women have a right to be deviant outside the constraints of the criminal law. Yet because liberals are squeamish about mobilizing community disapproval against those who trample on the rights of others, liberalism lacks a practical political program for protecting gays from harassment by the police and other citizens. The liberal idea of a practical political program is that gays should be able to take the police to court when they harass them. Although the republican supports this, it must be viewed as a rather empty gesture. For the republican, rights to diversity acquire genuine power only when socializing institutions and community campaigns foster in citizens a concern to be rights-respecting. Liberal rights can be sterile legalist gestures; republican rights are active cultural accomplishments. Strong gay and lesbian rights movements are the medium for securing these accomplishments.

Another way to think about the dangers of shaming is in terms of Scheff and Retzinger's (1991) framework about the bipolar evils of isolation and engulfment. Engulfment, they claim, was responsible for the violence of Nazi Germany. According to Scheff and Retzinger, societies in which the group is everything (the individual is engulfed) as well as societies of rampant individualism (the individual is isolated) risk endemic violence. Engulfment entails individuals' giving up parts of self in order to be accepted by others; it means fusion of individual needs with the needs of the group, as opposed to differentiation of individual needs from the needs of the group.

We all know what a family that isolates its children is like and what one that engulfs its children is like. Interdependency, mutual respect, love, community are needed to avoid isolation in families. But paradoxically, interdependency and mutual respect are needed to avoid engulfment as well. An engulfing family, the members of which have traditionally gone into the professions, might ridicule or label as a drop-out a member who decides to be an artist. The individuating family, in contrast, while communicating honest disappointment and disagreement with a choice of art over medicine, also communicates satisfaction that the child is capable of thinking for him- or herself, capable of breaking the mold set by parents and siblings. The individuating family uses interdependency and mutual respect as resources to ensure individuality; social bonds enable the constitution of a secure individual self that cannot be engulfed by a fascist or totalitarian state.

At the level of normative theory, individuating social bonds are one reason for rejecting a liberal conception of freedom (the freedom that isolated individuals perfectly enjoy) in favor of a republican conception of freedom (the freedom citizens enjoy in a social world where other citizens grant them social assurances of liberty) (Braithwaite and Pettit 1990: 55–59). A social world where individuals are what Scheff and Retzinger call "in attunement" with other human beings is not just a happy medium between isolation and engulfment. It is a world of social assurances and rights that secure individuation. Families in such an attuned social world will mobilize strong disapproval to protect one member from an act of violence by another; they will mobilize disapproval against a member who undermines another member's right to be deviant in ways that do not threaten dominion. What then is the crucial mechanism that guarantees individuation in families? Reintegrative shaming is that mechanism. Shaming is as essential to guaranteeing freedom as it is to preventing crime.

The republican does not struggle politically for a world in which shaming is used in a way that trades a reduction in freedom for a reduction in crime. Such a trade-off manifests a liberal way of thinking about crime. The republican struggles for a world where shame is used both to increase freedom and to reduce crime. The widespread liberal belief that a high crime rate is a price we pay for free society, that freedom and crime are locked into some hydraulic relationship, is wrong. Republican theory opens our eyes to this theoretical error.

A Useful or a Utopian Idea?

The explanatory theory of *Crime, Shame and Reintegration* is not alone in concluding that tinkering with criminal justice policies will not make a great difference to the crime rate (see, e.g., Gottfredson and Hirschi 1990: 272–73). Like Gottfredson and Hirschi's, my theory concludes that what families do is much more important to the causation and prevention of crime than what police forces do. Does this mean that the republican criminologist shares with theorists of this ilk a structurally impotent psychologism? Does this mean accepting the patriarchal family as our salvation? After all, *Crime, Shame and Reintegration* hypothesizes that it is women much more than men who are susceptible to being both effective subjects and objects of reintegrative shaming (see Hagan et al. 1979). Does it follow, then, that we should struggle to keep women locked into the moral guardianship role within families, which they have demonstrably performed more effectively than men?

A proper republican answer to all three questions, I will argue, is no. For the republican, the family is not a man's castle, but part of a community of citizens. The family is not and should not be immune from outside disapproval resulting from the deliberative processes of an active democracy. The concern for equality of prospects for dominion that republicanism requires means that the republican must struggle against patriarchy (Pettit 1989). Patriarchy is an institutional order that secures systematically lesser prospects of dominion for women than for men. Thus patriarchy must be resisted by the republican. Furthermore, I argue later that patriarchy is a cause of crime.

Patriarchy surely means a gendered patterning of reintegrative shaming. But it is hardly an effective strategy of resistance for women to jettison the obligations they feel to disapprove the wrongdoing of family members as they continue to nurture those family members in bonds of love. For one thing, if my analysis is correct on what is required to secure rights, reintegrative shaming is needed to assure women of their right to equal prospects of dominion. The republican solution is to struggle for equality of obligation to engage in reintegrative shaming. The republican priority is to change men in this respect, not women.

On how to do this, the republican political theorist is anything but individualistic, even though the objective is to change individuals and families. As Sunstein (1988) has argued, active citizenship, community participation in public life, is fundamental to republican ideology. The republican must take seriously social movements of citizens, organized influence from below, as vehicles for progressive change. Such social movements are precisely the vehicles that can and do deliver the changes that will bring a lower crime rate. There is little prospect of top-down solutions to the problem of families that raise violent boys because they fail to disapprove of violent episodes when they first occur. If the state mandated parent effectiveness training, these families probably would not attend. Even if they did attend and understand, they still might not confront members who perpetrate violence (Wilson and Herrnstein 1985: 386–87).

Social Movement Activism

Deeper cultural changes are needed. For these, we must look to social movements like feminism. To the extent the state can make a contribution, it can do so by cutting the budgets of police and prison services somewhat and handing these resources over to feminist women's refuges. The women's movement may be the most important social movement engaged in the struggle for a society more free of crime, but it is not the only one.[2] Before briefly discussing some of these other social movements, I will make some general points about where our greatest crime problems lie and why social movements are especially well placed to have an impact on these crimes.

In Australia, the types of crimes that cause the greatest harm to persons are domestic violence (Hopkins and McGregor 1991; Scutt 1983), occupational health and safety and other corporate crimes of violence such as those of the pharmaceutical industry (Braithwaite 1984; Braithwaite and Grabosky 1985: 1–41), and drunk driving (Homel 1988). The property offenders who cause the majority of criminal losses are white-collar criminals (Braithwaite 1979; Grabosky and Sutton 1989; Wilson and Braithwaite 1978).

There is a common structural reason why these particular offense types are Australia's greatest crime problems. All have enjoyed a historical immunity from public disapproval because of certain structural realities of power. The worst of Australia's white-collar criminals have been not only unusually respectable men, but also men who have been hailed as great entrepreneurial heroes. Violent men have enjoyed historical immunity even from the disapproval of the police when they engaged in acts of domestic assault (Hatty and Sutton 1986; Scutt 1983: chap. 9; Wearing 1990). This has been because of shared values between the offenders and the police about the prerogatives of men to engage in violence in the personal kingdoms of their homes. Since police who answer calls about domestic violence are the main window through which public disapproval might enter the domestic domain, this patriarchal collusion has been effective until very recently in preventing domestic violence from becoming a public issue.

Australian patriarchy takes the culturally specific form of a male mateship culture in which gender-segregated drinking is important (Sergeant 1973).[3] Women were not to be found in public bars in Australia until the 1970s. Pub and club drinking followed by driving is something that most Australian males have done many times, something which they regard as important to sustaining patterns of mateship, and something which they find difficult to regard as shameful. As a consequence of the strong support drunk driving has enjoyed in such a patriarchal context, informal disapproval by friends and formal disapproval by the courts has been historically muted.

These then are the bases for my claim that the particular crime problems that do most harm in Australia have been allowed to continue because of the muted or ambivalent disapproval they elicit, where this limited disapproval arose because of patterns of power. However, since the mid-1970s all of these forms of crime have been targeted by social movements concerned to engender community disapproval about them. The most important of these was the women's movement. Domestic violence was an important issue for the Australian women's movement in the late nineteenth century (Allen 1986). At first the resurgent women's movement of the early 1970s did not give any significant priority to domestic violence (Hopkins and McGregor 1991). By the mid-1970s, this was changing. Major conferences, including rather important conferences organized by feminists at the Australian Institute of Criminology, drew attention to the issue, as did subsequent criminological research (Hatty 1985; O'Donnell and Craney 1982; Scutt 1983; Stubbs and Powell 1989). The most important momentum, however, came from the feminist refuge movement, strategically supported by "femocrats" working within the state (Hopkins and McGregor 1991).

This social movement has had a considerable impact. Media current affairs programs now carry a regular fare of stories exposing the evils of domestic violence. Police education curricula, responding to feminist critiques (Hatty and Sutton 1986; Scutt 1982), have begun to push the line that domestic violence is a crime and a priority concern for Australian police services (McDonald et al. 1990; see also Stubbs and Powell 1989). Domestic violence is now much more out in the open in Australia. While private condoning of domestic violence continues, the public voices heard today are the voices of condemnation. And this is progress.

The social movement against white-collar crime in Australia has not been as vigorous as that in the United States (Ayres and Braithwaite 1992: chap. 1; Cullen et al. 1987; Katz 1980). However, in the 1970s and 1980s, the Australian consumer movement took up the issue with a vigor that had not been seen in previous decades. The specific issues that provoked high-profile public campaigns ranged from nursing home malpractice to used car fraud, tax scams, unsafe consumer products, and finance company rip-offs and misrepresentations. The Australian criminological research community has also given the issue a priority higher than it has been given in any other country.

In the area that has been of greatest interest to me, corporate crime in the pharmaceutical industry (Braithwaite 1984), social movement activism took some big strides in the 1980s. The Australian Consumers' Association and the Australian Federation of Consumer Organizations took much more interest in the issue. A national peak council, The Consumers' Health Forum, was established in 1985, which also gave considerable priority to malpractice in the pharmaceutical industry. These groups linked up with Health Action International and the International Organization of Consumers' Unions to deal with the transnational character of the problems they were confronting. Consumer Interpol began in the 1980s to send out alerts from Penang in Malaysia about dangerous pharmaceuticals that had been dumped in other parts of the world so that national consumer groups could draw attention to the problem if the product was being distributed in their own country. A particularly important development in the 1980s was the establishment in Adelaide of the Medical Lobby for Appropriate Marketing. This group organized letter-writing campaigns and adverse publicity among doctors when pharmaceutical companies were found to be making promotional claims about drugs that were untrue or that covered up side effects, particularly when it was third world consumers who were being victimized. The international reach of the social movement against pharmaceutical industry malpractice indicates a strength that social movement activism enjoys as an approach to transnational crime, a strength not shared by state law enforcement. Intriguingly, the pharmaceutical industry's counterstrategy today is to recruit the social movement against AIDS to resist "unreasonable regulation of the industry" in the forlorn hope that this will speed the desperate search for a cure of AIDS.

The late 1970s and early 1980s saw a social movement against occupational health and safety offenses organized by the trade union movement. Today this movement has almost run out of steam because its vision was limited in most states to achieving legislative reforms. When these were achieved in the mid-1980s, the movement lost focus and direction. Even so, in the state of Victoria over 14,000 workplace health and safety representatives have been appointed and trained by the trade union movement, giving an ongoing, if rather quiescent, grass-roots basis for a continuing movement (Carson et al. 1990).

The environmental movement has cultivated a strong surge in community support since the mid-1970s (McAllister 1991). In terms of organization, resources, and ideological coherence, it is certainly the most politically impressive social movement in Australia. It has, however, been less focused on violations of environmental laws by business than environmental movements in other countries. Instead, it has been more concerned

288

with Australia's biggest environmental problem—soil erosion caused by agricultural practices—and with struggles to declare national parks beyond the reach of the logging and mining industries. Nevertheless, the organization of community disapproval against environmental degradation has changed to the point where powerful business leaders can no longer afford to be shameless about acts of environmental despoliation (McAllister 1991). Moreover, substantial internalization of genuine respect for the environment is evident among many in the business elite.

Both the consumer movement and conservative women's groups such as the Country Women's Association were among several community organizations that made small contributions to the social movement against alcohol abuse in Australia during the 1970s and 1980s. Australia lacked the focused, organized anti-drunk-driving movement that emerged in the late 1970s in the United States—Remove Intoxicated Drivers (RID), Mothers Against Drunk Driving (MADD), and Students Against Drunk Driving (SADD) (Jacobs 1989: xv)—though there is a MADD chapter in Australia. Although the Australian movement against drunk driving was more diffuse than the American movement, this diffuseness may not have been a weakness since changes in Australian attitudes in this area have been dramatic. This movement has less of a grass-roots quality than the others we have discussed; many of the key players were employees of the state or activists from the professions. The medical profession, the road safety research community, and the alcohol and drug education and research community played the leadership roles in this social movement which, for all its diffuseness, attracted widespread public support. Random breath testing to detect drunk driving was supported by only 37 percent of the people of New South Wales in 1973 but by 91 percent in 1983, the year of its introduction (Homel 1988: 114). The punishment of drunk driving is less severe in Australia than in many, perhaps most, other countries, with resort to imprisonment being extremely rare, but the intensity of detection efforts through the use of random breath testing in the states of New South Wales and Tasmania exceeds that to be found anywhere else in the world (Homel 1988). Perhaps because of this, the evidence of the effect of random breath testing (and the associated public campaigning against drunk driving in these states) is of a substantial impact in reducing alcohol-related road fatalities (Homel 1988), in contrast to the equivocal results of evaluation studies on the effect of more halfhearted American experiments (Ross 1982; 1984). Surprisingly, in the late 1980s we had survey evidence suggesting that drunk driving is somewhat more shameful in Australia than the

United States, though considerably less so than in Norway (Berger et al. 1990: 461).

In spite of some spirited opposition from the pub and club industry in New South Wales (Homel 1988: 117), which suffered from reduced alcohol sales, nervous politicians held firm with the reforms. In the end, the alcohol industry was in a sense co-opted by the movement against drunk driving via the introduction and aggressive marketing for the first time in Australia of low-alcohol beers. The marketing campaigns for the new products were notable for their reference to the risks of drunk driving, as in Toohey's "breathe easy" advertising campaign for low-alcohol beer.

Beyond Statist Criminology

All of the social movements I have described became strong only from the mid-1970s onward. What an irony this is for criminology when the mid-1970s was precisely the historical moment for the disillusionment of the "nothing works" era to set in. In the late 1970s, criminologists deserted utilitarianism in droves to join the "just deserts" movement that ultimately became a "get tough" movement (S. Cohen 1985; Cullen and Gilbert 1982). Perhaps nothing does work particularly well if our vision is limited to statist responses to the crime problem.[4] Republican criminology opens our eyes to the limited relevance of statist criminology—the sort the state gives money to—to practical ongoing struggles to reduce the crime rate.

If I am right, it is the most severe crime problems Australians confront that social movements have been making the greatest progress against over the past fifteen years. I do not suggest that the progress has been decisive or overwhelming: patriarchy is not about to breathe its last gasp; the environment continues to collapse; even if some pharmaceutical companies have adopted a markedly more responsible attitude today, most corporate cowboys do not yet seem overwhelmed by remorse; drunk driving is not a problem of the past.

If some progress is being made in the places that count most, statist criminology is tied to statist statistical methodologies that leave it blind to such changes. The methodologies of statist criminology churn out data that are artifacts of the very patterns of power at the heart of my argument. Crimes of domestic violence were not counted very seriously by patriarchal police forces before the social movement against domestic violence, which gained momentum in the mid-1970s. Similarly, victim surveys conducted by the Australian government provided a doubtful baseline because interviews were conducted in the households where domestic violence occurred, presumably in many cases within sight or sound of the persons who committed the violent acts. In fact, statist methodologies show that the problem is getting worse because the social movement against domestic violence has made police more sensitive to domestic violence and has provided support to women who wish to lodge complaints against violent spouses (Hopkins and McGregor 1991).

This is also true of white-collar crime and of crime generally; when a form of crime becomes more shameful, the community discovers more instances of that form of crime. So if bank robbery is shameful and insider trading is not, the community will have the impression that bank robbery is the more common and more serious of these two problems. This when we know the fact of the matter to be that "the best way to rob a bank is to own it."

Taking state statistics on white-collar crime seriously is a similarly foolish enterprise. Criminologists such as Hirschi and Gottfredson (1987) have done just this and reached startling conclusions, such as that white-collar criminals in the United States are disproportionately black! Statist criminology is an edifice built on methodological foundations that render it incapable of knowing the things most worth knowing about crime.[5]

One response to directing shame against specific forms of crime is that this is a utopian enterprise, because shaming is not an effective mechanism of social control in modern, urbanized, heterogeneous societies. Elsewhere I have argued that there is no unidirectional historical trend either toward or away from the effectiveness of shame-based social control (Braithwaite 1991a). Like Elias (1982) and Goffman (1956), I contend that there are some features of interdependency in modern urban societies that actually increase our vulnerability to shame, and others that reduce it.

It is more important to address the specific forms of crime that are the locus of my argument here. I have already said that criminological research gives us no way of knowing whether there is more or less domestic violence today than in the past. What we can say with some confidence, however, is that domestic violence has become more shameful in the nineteenth and twentieth centuries. The following description of the shamelessness of male violence in fifteenth-century England could not be regarded as an accurate description of the situation in that country today.

Wife-beating was a recognized right of man and was practiced without shame by high as well as low. Similarly, the daughter who refused to marry the gentleman of her parents' choice was liable to be locked up, beaten, and flung about the room, without any shock being inflicted upon public opinion. (Trevelyan 1985: 196)

This fact is not only recorded in the history books, but in the courts as well. Even after World War II, there is evidence of English lower courts finding domestic assault to be legitimate as a punishment for a wife who had disobeyed her husband (Stratmann 1982: 121), and indeed it was a matter of right rather than shame in English law until 1891 that a husband could beat his wife. At least in public forums, the beating of wives and daughters today surely does invoke more shame. Public outcry would surely ensue if a ducking stool for the disciplining of nagging wives were installed in any English town today.

More generally, the American evidence shows that concern about white-collar crime and mistrust of business has increased substantially since the mid-1970s (see the studies cited by Cullen et al. 1987: 43). When Edwin Sutherland (1983) wrote in 1949 that white-collar crime flourished because of a lack of organized community resentment against respectable criminals, he may have been right. But contemporary American and Australian data, as well as data from many other countries, suggests that this is no longer true (Grabosky et al. 1987).

Community attitudes toward white-collar crime today should be a worry for the republican, but not for lack of shame; rather my concern is that attitudes can be so stigmatic and punitive. In a study of eight countries (the United States, the United Kingdom, Finland, Sweden, Norway, Denmark, the Netherlands, and Kuwait), Scott and Al-Thakeb (1977) found that in every country the recommended sentence for the manufacture and sale of potentially harmful pharmaceuticals was more severe than for auto theft, larceny (felony), burglary, aggravated assault, and robbery. When this study was replicated some years later in Australia, respondents were even more punitive on this item ("The offender is an executive of a drug company who allows his company to manufacture and sell a drug knowing that it may produce harmful side effects for most individuals"), recommending an average of nine years' imprisonment for the offense (Broadhurst and Indemaur 1982). Some respondents in an Australian Institute of Criminology survey even recommended capital punishment for serious environmental and industrial safety offenses (Grabosky et al. 1987). When I visited Ralph Nader's office in 1990, they had recently lost the services of a person who supported the death penalty for business executives who sold consumer products that caused loss of life. He believed that such convicted corporate criminals should not be executed in the normal way, but in a defective electric chair. I am pleased to report that Ralph Nader was not persuaded by this idea.

Similarly, as I reported above, in Australia at least, community atti-

tudes have become more intolerant of drunk driving. So it seems that the
types of crime that are our most serious problems in Australia have become
more shameful during the last fifteen years. Levi's (1988) study and recent
annual reports of the Australian Commissioner for Taxation even suggest
that for tax evasion, an offense low in moral opprobrium the world over,
but seemingly even less shameful in Australia than in a number of other
countries (Grabosky et al. 1987: 37), the extraordinary moral crusade of
the 1970s and 1980s against tax dishonesty has improved tax compliance
among the wealthy and brought to an end the era when wealthy Australians openly bragged about tax evasion.[6]

While we need much more systematic data on these questions, we have
enough to suggest that social movements can affect attitudes in a way that
increases social disapproval and causes pangs of conscience in those con-
templating breaking the law. The empirical point applies equally to types
of offenses that republicans should not regard as a high priority. Take drug
use, an offense that Pettit and I contend republicans should not regard as a
crime at all (Braithwaite and Pettit 1990: 97–99). The conventional wisdom
of criminology might lead one to believe that drug use is an unsolvable
problem. This view seems unduly pessimistic in light of what I would hypothesize to be the contribution the temperance movement made to the
dramatic reduction in English-speaking countries of drunkenness and excessive drinking during the nineteenth century right up until its Pyrrhic
victory in securing prohibition in the United States. In Australia, the long
period of falling alcohol consumption from the mid-nineteenth century
corresponds with the rise of the temperance movement, and the long rise
in alcohol consumption from the 1930s to the 1970s corresponds with the
decline and virtual demise of the old temperance movement (Powell 1988).[7]
The decline of alcohol consumption since the mid-eighties (McAllister
et al. 1991) may be associated with the rise of a new social movement
against the alcohol industry grounded in the consumer and health education movements. In the late nineteenth and early twentieth centuries,
the temperance movement was a movement of both Christians and feminists who were involved in the women's franchise campaign and who were
deeply concerned about prostitution in public houses and domestic violence (Beresford 1984; Gusfield 1963; Tyrell 1984). Just as contemporary
Alcoholics Anonymous meetings rely heavily on self-shaming in a nurtu-
rant collectivity (Trice and Roman 1970), so the nineteenth-century American temperance movement gave pride of place to the reintegrative power
of the reformed (Powell 1988: 46). Similarly, the Australian temperance
movement of the first half of the nineteenth century was oriented to per-

suading the wayward to "sign the pledge," rejecting at that time the idea of reform through government intervention (Beresford 1984: 3).

Within the narrow ahistoricism of contemporary social science, researchers wax pessimistic at the results of drug education programs of very short duration because of the rather small or insignificant preventive effects they secure (Ogborne 1988; Wragg 1987; 1990). Yet any plausible model of how social movements might transform community attitudes to drugs (and consumption patterns of drugs) would surely involve gradual cumulative change over a historical period of many years such as we have observed with male consumption of tobacco since World War II. A change strategist operating with a model of gradual change over a long historical haul would take comfort from American data on small but significant annual reductions in consumption of drugs such as marijuana and cocaine in recent years (Bachman et al. 1988; 1990a). This research shows that during the years when the social disapproval and perceived health risk of marijuana and cocaine use were declining, usage increased; during the years when social disapproval and perceived risk increased, usage decreased for both drugs (Bachman et al. 1990a: 176). The change strategist would not become pessimistic because the changes are small; her project only makes sense with a reform timetable measured in decades rather than years.[8] But this may be of limited interest to statist criminology, which is loath to fund projects grounded in historical vision. Parliamentary terms and periods of incumbency at the head of government research units do not readily accommodate historical farsightedness.

Confronting the Paralysis of Pessimism

A further basis for pessimism about the capacity of social movements to reduce crime arises from devotion to what Hindess (1982) calls a "capacity-outcome" approach to understanding struggles. According to such an understanding, it is naive to believe that disorganized social movements can secure any more than symbolic victories against powerful organized interests. The capacity-outcome approach assumes that in order to determine the likely outcome of a struggle all one need do is identify what resources or capacities are available to the contending parties; the outcome can then be read off in *a priori* fashion. Hence, if the alcohol industry is a powerful and affluent industry with many political friends and the temperance movement is an economically disorganized collection of women, you can read off the outcome—the alcohol industry will win. Yet the mechanics of history are not so simple. The environmental and consumer movements perhaps do lose more battles than they win, but often enough they win against industries with superior resources. Hopkins and McGregor's (1991) analysis of the Australian movement against domestic violence addresses the structure-agency issue, the extent to which the agency of social movements can prevail against structures of domination:

An American study found that the existence of local feminist groups was a more important predictor of community programmes for battered women throughout the USA than per capita income, political liberalism or the existence of state domestic violence legislation (see Tierney 1982: 211). The movement against domestic violence does seem to be a case of, in this instance, women making their own history. (Hopkins and McGregor 1991: 138)

It seems that social movements can make progress in moral crusades that appeal to the sense of justice of people. Progressive change is possible by asking citizens to challenge a hegemony that unjustly acquiesces in a certain type of crime's being less serious because it is perpetrated by men in a position of some national or familial power. The appeal of such crusades can be broad because what is demanded is really so little and so consistent with the rhetoric of Western justice systems. It is a demand simply that we should not afford criminals an advantage in our perceptions of the evil of their deeds simply because they are powerful. It is a plea for the uncontroversial notion of treating equal crimes with equal seriousness. This is certainly part of what makes progress against the odds more possible for social movements when they demand that the criminal law be taken seriously.

Progress may be easier here than in so many of the other domains where social movements struggle. The truly difficult part of the republican criminologist's political agenda is to find or build social movements to mobilize against the excesses of the criminal justice system. Just as the symbolic power of the criminal law makes mobilization against criminal justice neglect comparatively easy, this symbolic power makes mobilization against criminal justice excess difficult.

One of the more sophisticated versions of the capacity-outcome approach to struggles is Edelman's (1964) account that diffuse, disorganized publics win symbolic victories, while organized interests receive tangible rewards. So, for example, the social movement against white-collar crime gets the symbolic victory of enacting new laws to regulate business, but the powerful players of the industry win the tangible victory of ensuring that the new laws are enforced only against marginal operators whom the powerful corporations are quite pleased to have harassed (Carson 1975; Hopkins and Parnell 1984; O'Malley 1980). Although this model has explanatory power in some criminal justice domains, it would be more of a concern to the republican if her job were primarily to secure tougher state enforcement. But in fact, when confronted with a domain where the criminal law is not being taken seriously enough, the republican is more concerned with symbolic victories than with tangible changes to state policies. The republican analysis is that crime rates are more responsive to patterns of community disapproval of crime than to state enforcement patterns. So it is the symbolic victory for the hearts and minds of citizens that is more important than securing tangible changes to state criminal justice practices. This is not to say that republicans are unconcerned about reforming criminal justice practices (the nature of such concerns is developed at length in Braithwaite and Pettit 1990), it is just to say that the republican pursues the objective of reducing crime with more of an eye to community organization than to criminal enforcement.

Although all of these social movements seem to have succeeded in turning community attitudes against the conduct of concern to them, the crime control dividends may have been less than expected because a significant proportion of the campaigning has been stigmatic. These social movements have failed to grasp the crucial difference between reintegrative shaming and stigmatization. Hence, stigmatic features of the social movement against alcohol have motivated a culturally specific form of resistance within Australian male mateship culture—the denunciation of antialcohol activists as "wowsers" (Dunstan 1974). Recent community disapproval of illicit drug use has been stigmatic in a way that has enabled drug subcultures to assure drug users that their rejectors are worthy of rejection. In contrast, the Australian antitobacco movement has been at pains not to stigmatize users while disapproving of their practices. Even here, though, a stigmatizing fringe to the movement has fueled subcultures of resistance in the form of smokers' rights movements, which are supported by the tobacco industry.

Similarly, while the social movement against white-collar crime in the United States has dramatically changed community attitudes to disapproval, many white-collar criminals have acquired an immunity to this disapproval. They also reject their rejectors. An important study by Benson (1990) found that convicted white-collar criminals were more likely to feel mad than bad about their offending. The reason, I have argued, is that the stigmatic features of the social movement against white-collar crime in the United States have fueled business subcultures of resistance to regulatory laws (Braithwaite 1989b). Consequently, the social movement regularly fails to bring offenders to a position of shame about their crime.

296

Instead, offenders feel angry about being unfairly picked on by antibusiness prosecutors.

Similarly, many violent men in Australia reject their rejectors as manhaters. One reason they may be able to do this is that there is a fringe of the Australian women's movement who are in fact man-haters. While the Australian women's movement in general eschews the stigmatization of men, managing to communicate disapproval within a continuum of respect for men, occasional stigmatic excess has provided symbolic ammunition for chauvinist cultures of resistance that sustain the moral ambiguity of domestic violence.

The Egalitarian Thrust of Republican Support for Social Movements

In this section I briefly sketch five additional reasons why republican political theory counsels the consideration of support for the social movements I have mentioned. These are (1) the republican commitment to economic and political equality; (2) the commitment to active participation of citizens in community life; (3) the effect of inequality on crime, not only through the historical muting of disapproval toward crimes of the powerful but also, for example, through the effect of patriarchy on the structuring of humiliation; (4) the way social movements can inculcate pride in being law-abiding and rights-respecting as well as shame at violating these norms; and (5) the way social movements can encourage the evolution of cooperation in regulatory regimes while preventing the evolution of capture and corruption.

The republican supports social movements that represent the egalitarian aspirations of less powerful groups because a concern with political and economic equality is basic to republicanism (Pettit 1989; Sunstein 1988). For Philip Pettit and me, this concern defines republicanism—the republican wants to maximize the dominion of citizens, defined in a social or relational way as equality-of-liberty prospects (Braithwaite and Pettit 1990: 64–65). Women living under the thumb of a patriarch or men living in abject poverty cannot enjoy equality-of-liberty prospects with the wealthy. Because republicans also support the active participation of citizens in community life, they have two reasons for supporting the women's or consumer movements besides their concern about crime prevention—an equality-based reason and a participation-based reason.

A third consideration is the belief that inequality is a direct cause of crime. Inequality of power has allowed our most serious crime problems to fester because the powerful have been able to sustain immunity from community disapproval. Elsewhere I have argued that for more direct theoretical reasons, economic inequality, inequality in political power (slavery, totalitarianism), racism, ageism, and patriarchy are causes of crime (Braithwaite 1991b). There is both a noninstrumental and an instrumental side to this argument. First, much crime, particularly violent crime, is motivated by the humiliation of the offender and the offender's perceived right to humiliate the victim. Inegalitarian societies, it is argued, are structurally more humiliating than egalitarian societies. For example, it is structurally more humiliating to be a black in South Africa than in Tanzania. The more instrumental analysis of the motivation of crime also rejects Sutherland's (1983) interpretation that poverty cannot be a cause of crime because it is the rich and not the poor that commit greater numbers of more serious crimes. According to my more instrumental analysis, inequality worsens crimes of *poverty* motivated by *need* for goods for *use* and crimes of *wealth* motivated by *greed* enabled by goods for *exchange* (Braithwaite 1979, 1991b). Inequality worsens both crimes of the exploited and crimes of exploitation.

Social movements affect crime not only by mobilizing shame against criminal behavior, but also by mobilizing pride in prosocial patterns of behavior that provide alternatives to crime. For example, the state contributed to the campaign against drunk driving in Australia with television advertisements showing role models for responsible male drinking. One member of the drinking group would in a nonthreatening way "be a mate" by insisting that he drive home a drinking companion who had consumed too much. Tom Scheff has rightly criticized *Crime, Shame and Reintegration* for not giving enough importance to pride as a complement to shame (Scheff and Retzinger 1991: 175). It may be that pride in being law-abiding, caring, responsible, and rights-respecting has more marked effects than shame does on the thought of being criminal or trampling on the rights of others. I give more prominence to shaming in *Crime, Shame and Reintegration* only because the partitioning of shaming resolves the central theoretical contradictions of criminology. At the same time, pride does seem to be an even more important emotion for the women's movement to cultivate than shame—pride in being a woman, pride in resisting patriarchal domination, pride in persuading men to respect the rights of women, and pride among the men who are so persuaded.

Finally, Ian Ayres and I have argued that business regulation schemes can be more effective if they are transformed from bipartite games between the state and a regulated industry to tripartite games in which the third

298

player is a community group with an active interest in the particular regulatory domain (Ayres and Braithwaite 1992). Republican empowerment of community groups in regulatory deliberation can improve the cost effectiveness and decency of regulatory institutions. Tripartite regulation, it is argued, can secure the advantages of the evolution of cooperative regulation (Scholz 1984) while preventing the evolution of capture and corruption. This analysis is of more general criminal justice import than one might think. This is because the republican believes that many social problems that are currently dealt with by criminal law would be better dealt with by regulatory law (Braithwaite and Pettit 1990). Hence, for example, the republican is interested in abandoning bipartite state criminal control of prostitution in favor of multiparty dialogic regulation that gives both the women's movement and sex workers' unions seats at the negotiating table when regulatory arrangements are put in place (Ayres and Braithwaite 1992).

I have sketched only summary references to these other works that give further reasons why the political program of republican criminology is support for empowering social movements of the powerless. I do this only to give some sense of the theoretical interconnections within the wider corpus of my work and why they converge on the political program of support for the social movements I have discussed.[9]

Synergy Between State and Social Movement Activism

Thus far I have overplayed the juxtaposition between preventing crime through state enforcement and preventing crime by mobilizing social movements. I have done this to make as effective a break as possible with the entrenched *étatisme* of conventional criminological thinking. But in fact, my view is that social movements are more effective when they eschew both a total preoccupation with changing state policies and a total preoccupation with grass-roots consciousness raising (see also Grabosky 1990). Social movements are effective when their strategies recognize the synergy between these two thrusts.

The purpose of my book with Ian Ayres is to show how a creative synergy can be sustained between state regulation of business and public interest group activism. First, we argue for state empowerment and resourcing of weak and disorganized public interest groups so that they can become credible participants in tripartite regulation. From the public interest group point of view, they must lobby for their empowerment by the state. The synergy between femocrats and the refuge movement in Aus-

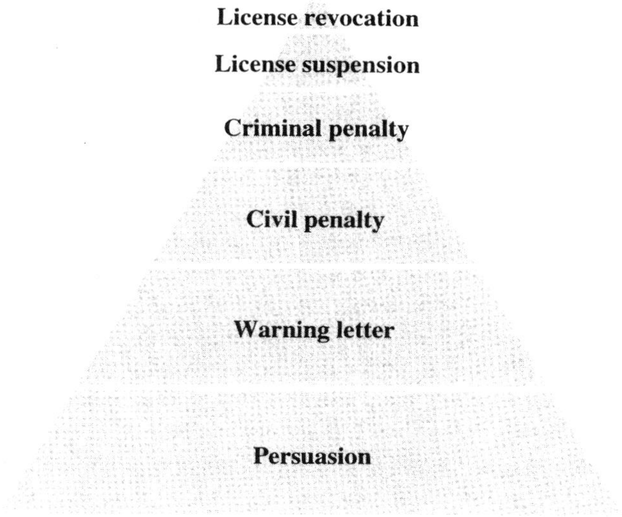

License revocation

License suspension

Criminal penalty

Civil penalty

Warning letter

Persuasion

Fig. 12.1. Example of an enforcement pyramid. The proportion of space at each layer represents the proportion of enforcement activity at that level.

tralia is a strategic model of how this can be done (Hopkins and McGregor 1991; Yeatman 1990).

It is also important that progressive social movements lobby for credible state sanctioning capacities against crimes of the powerful. This is not because social movements should seek to achieve results by relying on the state to deter crime. Unfortunately, this is precisely the miscalculation social movements often make. A credible capacity for sanctioning the powerful is necessary for enabling dialogic regulation, regulation based on reasoning about what sort of conduct should cause us to be proud or ashamed.

In *Responsive Regulation*, Ayres and I make this point with the idea of the enforcement pyramid (Ayres and Braithwaite 1992; see also Braithwaite 1985). An example of a pyramid is given in Figure 12.1. In this model, the state signals that it has a range of sanctioning possibilities through which it can escalate if the firm does not cooperate with dialogic regulation. The agency has the capacity to escalate right up to corporate capital punishment (license revocation). The paradox of the model is that by carrying a big stick, the state is able to speak softly. More crucially for the present argument, by carrying a big stick, the state is also able to require the firm to hear the voices of its critics from public interest groups. Tripartite dialogic regulation at the base of the enforcement pyramid is enabled by the capacity of the state to escalate in punitiveness. Paradoxically, if we lop the top off such an enforcement pyramid, the state may have less capacity to do this. By weakening the criminal enforcement capability of the state, we end up with a more litigious, less cooperative regulatory regime in which public interest movements can have effects only by going to court.

We can translate the same basic model to the arena of domestic violence. My theoretical position is that violence within families is least likely when those families themselves succeed in persuading their members to internalize an abhorrence of violence, to take pride in respecting the rights of women and caring for others. But sometimes families will fail in accomplishing this. Then they must be able to look for support outside. A battered woman might seek help from a refuge. With a refuge worker, she might then seek help from the civil law (an order restraining a man from entering his own house) and ultimately the criminal law (imprisonment of the man). Just as with the business regulation pyramid, the capacity of the victim of domestic violence to show the offender how continued violence will lead inevitably to more and more dire outside intervention is empowering for the victim. If the victim is afraid to signal this power that the state enables her to have, another member of the family may have the courage to do so. Family members or domestic violence workers are likely to get the attention of violent men only when they can signal to the offender with genuine credibility that he is on a slippery slope leading to more and more forceful state intervention until the violence stops. Equally important to mobilizing outside legal support is outside support that gives women and their children the economic power to leave a violent household and to credibly threaten to leave should future violence occur. Obviously, state policies are essential here, and the women's movement is the crucial political force for securing those state policies.

The hope is not that state enforcement will be so powerful and so regularly used that it will deter rational offenders. The hope is that state enforcement will be sufficiently credible to empower informal processes of social control, to enable dialogic regulation of violence. State criminal enforcement capabilities are a resource that women, children, and domestic violence workers can use to demand that violent offenders take seriously their disapproval of acts of violence. Of course, state criminal enforcement capability is also important for securing the incapacitation of some men who are beyond reform or civil restraint and for signifying the shamefulness of crime. Neither of these latter reasons for criminal enforcement

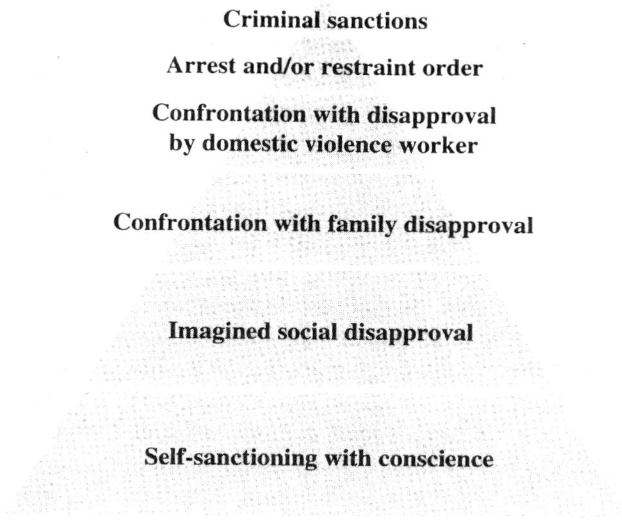

Inequality and Republican Criminology 301

Criminal sanctions

Arrest and/or restraint order

**Confrontation with disapproval
by domestic violence worker**

Confrontation with family disapproval

Imagined social disapproval

Self-sanctioning with conscience

Fig. 12.2. Example of a domestic violence enforcement pyramid.

justifies, however, widespread or automatic resort to imprisonment. They justify only the capability for and the occasional use of imprisonment.

Philip Pettit and I have derived from the republican objective of maximizing dominion a presumption in favor of being parsimonious in the use of the criminal law (Braithwaite and Pettit 1990: 87). What the enforcement pyramid shows, however, is a paradox about the way the world works. The very capacity to escalate state intervention enables social control to work better at less coercive levels. While republicans should be faithful to the simple principle of parsimony by supporting reductions in the maximum prison sentence that can be imposed for assault, it would not serve the objective of parsimonious punishment to abolish imprisonment altogether as a sentence for assault. One reason for this is that a consequence of throwing away the big stick is that middle-sized sticks would be used more often. This at least follows if I am right that the tough sanctions at the peak of the enforcement pyramid channel social control down to the dialogic base of the pyramid.

For the republican, then, credible criminal enforcement capability strengthens the hand of communitarian crime control; it does not supplant it. We can conceptualize an enforcement pyramid for domestic violence as in Figure 12.2.[10] The republican envisages that a long historical process of

302

community and state involvement in shaming acts of domestic violence will result in most citizens' internalizing the shamefulness of violence. Consequently, most social control will work at the base of the enforcement pyramid by self-sanctioning with pangs of conscience. If this fails, the history of community shaming of violence will persuade the perpetrators that others will disapprove of them after they have committed an act of violence. Note that no one has to confront the offender directly with shame at this level; an offender who understands the culture will know that those who find out about the violence will be gossiping disapprovingly. As I was at pains to argue in *Crime, Shame and Reintegration*, on most of the occasions when gossip hits its target, it will do so without being heard by the target; it will be effective in the imagination of a culturally knowledgeable subject. If the offender is incapable of imagining the disapproval others feel about the violence, then someone must make clear that disapproval. If family members are too intimidated to do it, then a domestic violence worker must do it. If disapproval, dialogue, and counseling do not work, then the formal law must be invoked: first a court order restraining the freedom of movement of the offender (perhaps associated with arrest after a specific outburst [see Hopkins and McGregor 1991; Sherman and Berk 1984]) and if that fails, criminal enforcement. The republican, therefore, does not call simply for informalism rather than formalism; she calls for a formalism that empowers informalism. The effect of successful implementation of an enforcement pyramid is, however, that most social control is communitarian control rather than state control and that most of the day-to-day successes are achieved by dialogic regulation, with state regulation stepping in to mop up the failures. This is also the story of Homel's (1988) work on the reduction of drunk driving in Australia—the formalism of random breath testing empowered the informalism of dialogic regulation within drinking groups or by bar attendants.

The real power of reintegrative shaming is at the level of prevention: conscience building. With the very worst cases of deep-seated violence, reintegrative shaming is quite likely to fail, but then so is everything else. When things come to this pass, we must do our best with clumsy protective measures for victims. But the heart of a political program that I suspect is shared by feminism and republicanism is to struggle for cultural and economic changes that prevent violence long before it becomes unpreventable.

Summary

1. The partitioning of shaming into reintegrative and stigmatizing modalities is the key theoretical move for criminology to take.

2. Social movements like the women's movement can affect the level of crime not only by shaming crimes of violence but also by inculcating pride in solving problems nonviolently, pride in caring for others and pride in respecting the rights of women.

3. Australia's most serious crime problems are domestic violence, white-collar crime, and drunk driving. These have been allowed to become our major crime problems because of historical failures of the community and the state to mobilize shame against these offenses. This historical failure is explained by the structural position of men and the structural position of those in command positions in the economy.

4. Since the mid-1970s, social movements have worked with the state and the mass media in a progressively more effective way to raise voices against the muted and ambiguous disapproval these offense types have attracted. Social movements such as the women's, environmental, and consumer movements can be more effective in campaigns to get the state and the community to take seriously the crimes of powerful people than in many of the other domains in which they struggle.

5. The republican way of thinking about crime therefore encourages the view that since the mid-1970s in Australia we may have been making slow but significant progress with the crime problem. This is not being achieved without setback and reversal. The excesses of financial deregulation caused a surge in certain types of corporate crime in the mid-1980s. The stigmatizing of men by some sections of the women's movement has fostered resistance and backlash to feminist thought in some quarters, most tragically among Aboriginal women (Ridgeway 1986). The stigmatization of business executives by some sections of the consumer and environmental movements has at times engendered business subcultures of resistance to regulatory law. But on balance, there has been progress.

6. There is no inexorable march with modernization and urbanization toward a society where reintegrative shaming cannot work. It is likely that in many Western countries, like Australia, domestic violence, drunk driving, environmental crime, corporate crimes of violence, and other types of white-collar crime have become more shameful in recent times.

7. This empirical view of historical shifts in patterns of community disapproval can be detached from republican normative commitments. My theory would be that illicit drug use can never be successfully controlled

by a state deterrence policy; it can be better controlled by a social movement against drug use, as long as that movement does not stigmatize drug users. The nineteenth- and early twentieth-century temperance movement is not in every way a model of the social movement I have in mind. However, it may be that its dialogism and its disapproval of drug abuse contributed to the dramatic decline in alcohol consumption that occurred during its heyday. The contemporary antismoking movement is another in which my analysis would place confidence as a strategy for change. Social movements do not have to be ideologically coherent, and they certainly do not have to accept republicanism, to be effective in changing patterns of disapproval for crime.

8. Progress with crime does not depend on cultural changes that are especially dramatic. It does not require our transformation into a society of busybodies, constantly prying into the affairs of other individuals. Such an individualistic vision would be politically impotent and an authoritarian threat to dominion. Progress requires us to support progressive social movements whose agendas include the disapproval of our most serious crimes. These social movements have effects at the microlevel. Consequently, shaming will work most of the time in the consciences and imaginations of potential wrongdoers who dislike the thought of people gossiping about them. We are not required to confront others daily with our disapproval (except our children, who are still learning how to imagine what others will disapprove of). This is not to deny that every now and then during a lifetime, most of us will encounter violent people who lack conscience, who fail to imagine the depth of disapproval others feel toward their violence. These people we certainly must confront. For most of us, this is not a month-to-month demand on our republican obligations. The month-to-month demand is to be active in one progressive social movement or another. Republicans do not have to be busybodies of daily private life so much as activists of public life, participants in a collective struggle for a republican culture.

9. Social movements can reduce crime not only by mobilizing disapproval of crime but also by attacking the structural roots of crime. Patriarchy is a structural cause of domestic violence, feminism a social movement that addresses this cause. Corruption in business-government relations is one reason why regulatory agencies cover up corporate crimes; consumerism (in the Nader public-citizen mold) is a social movement concerned with addressing this structural basis of crime.

10. Reintegrative shaming directed at the kinds of crime that republicans struggle to have recognized as crime is not repressive. Reintegrative

shaming is as necessary to increasing freedom as it is to reducing crime. Liberals are wrong to conclude that a high crime rate is a price we pay for freedom. A high crime rate is one of the consequences of the limited conception of freedom in liberalism.

11. Republicans believe in individuation, because dominion is something individuals enjoy as individuals. For republicans, both individual isolation and engulfment by the group are evils. Individuation in a social world is secured by a system of social assurances, including rights. Republican rights are best secured by reintegrative shaming of those who are not rights-respecting. Liberal rights, in contrast, are empty legal gestures of limited practical use to securing individuation in a social world infused with relations of power.

12. The republican is interested in exploring synergies between social movement action and state action that will increase dominion for citizens. In the domain of crime control, the task is not so much to get the state to do the job but for the state to empower citizens and movements of citizens who are ultimately our best hope for a reduction in crime.

326

Notes

This chapter is in part stimulated by discussions of my earlier work with Ngaire Naffine, the late June Fielding, and Betsy Stanko. Unfortunately, I have taken only pathetically small steps down the three paths suggested by these scholars. My thanks to Ross Homel, Andrew Hopkins, Toni Makkai, David Nelkin, and Philip Pettit for extremely helpful comments on an earlier draft of this work.

· 1. For the philosophers who are shocked by such a casual definitional gestalt, here is a formal definition. A person enjoys full dominion, we say, if and only if:

    a. She enjoys no less a prospect of liberty than is available to other citizens.

    b. It is common knowledge among citizens that this condition obtains, so that she and nearly everyone else knows that she enjoys the prospect mentioned; she and nearly everyone else knows that the others generally know this too, and so on.

    c. She enjoys no less a prospect of liberty than the best that is compatible with the same prospect for all citizens (Braithwaite and Pettit 1990, 64–65).

2. Needless to say, I am not impressed by the theoretical or empirical bite of Adler's (1975) arguments on the effect of the women's movement in causing the rise of a new female criminal (see Adler 1975; Box and Hale 1983; Scutt 1980; Smart 1979; Steffensmeier and Steffensmeier 1980).

3. It should also be noted that this social formation accounts for Australia's other major violence problem, beyond domestic violence. This is male-on-male violence,

macho responses to insult or humiliation, mostly by young working-class males, in the context of drinking at pubs, clubs, and other entertainment venues (Tomsen et al. 1991).

4. Purists who claim that statism does not exist in the English language can read it as a translation from the French (*étatisme*), a language more accommodating to republican writing.

5. According to republican criminology, among the many things that are critical to know, two of the distinctively republican things are: (1) Is it true that when we come to view a certain type of crime as shameful, we are less likely to engage in it? (2) Is it true that an effect of the campaigning of social movements has been to make some of the most serious types of crime more shameful?

6. The high point of this moral crusade was the extraordinary event of a National Tax Summit. Business, union, and community leaders were invited to the chamber of parliament to address the prime minister on what needed to be done to return to a fair tax system that citizens would respect.

7. As Gusfield says of the nineteenth-century heyday of the American temperance movement, "Sobriety was virtuous and in a community dominated by middle-class Protestants, necessary to social acceptance and to self-esteem." In contrast, by the mid-twentieth century or earlier, "Abstinence has lost much of its ability to confer prestige and esteem" (Gusfield 1963: 4).

8. A fully fleshed out theory of this sort would have to give an account of how entrepreneurs can create new waves of drug use until an effective community reaction takes hold—marijuana in the 1960s, heroin in the 1960s, cocaine in the 1980s, amphetamines and LSD in the 1960s with a resurgence in the 1990s. Does community reaction occur wave by wave, drug by drug? Is there a hopeful new ideological turn in community reaction today, where *all* drugs, tobacco and alcohol included, are being bundled together as harmful things to put into your body? Are parents today who fail to educate their children about the generic undesirability of drugs at risk of being cast as negligent parents? Are smoking parents now vulnerable to community expectations that they have an obligation to confess their own stupidity to their children?

9. The republican commitment also implies support for the crime victims' movement more generally (Braithwaite and Pettit 1990: 91–92). But this is a more difficult question I must leave for another paper.

10. I am grateful to the late June Fielding for suggesting in a seminar that the enforcement pyramid idea might be extended to the domain of crimes against women.

REFERENCES

Adler, Freda (1975) *Sisters in Crime: The Rise of the New Female Criminal*. McGraw-Hill: New York.

Allen, Judith (1986) 'Desperately Seeking Solutions: Changing Battered Women's Options Since 1880', in Suzanne E. Hatty (ed.), *National Conference on Domestic Violence, Volume 1*, Australian Institute of Criminology Seminar Proceeding No. 12: Canberra.

Ayres, Ian and John Braithwaite (1992) *Responsive Regulation: Transcending the Deregulation Debate*. Oxford University Press: New York.

Bachman, Jerald G., Lloyd D. Johnston and Patrick M. O'Malley (1990a) 'Explaining the Recent Decline in Cocaine Use Among Adults: Further Evidence that Perceived Risks and Disapproval Lead to Reduced Drug Use', *Journal of Health and Social Behaviour* 31: 173–84.

Bachman, Jerald G., Lloyd D. Johnston, Patrick M. O'Malley and Ronald H. Humphrey (1988) 'Explaining the Recent Decline in Marijuana Use: Differentiating the Effects of Perceived Risks, Disapproval, and General Lifestyle Factors', *Journal of Health and Social Behaviour* 29: 92–112.

Benson, Michael (1990) 'Emotions and Adjudication: A Study of Status Degradation Among White-Collar Criminals', Unpublished Paper. Department of Sociology, University of Tennessee.

Beresford, Q. (1984) 'Drinkers and the Anti-Drink Movement in Sydney, 1870–1930', Unpublished Ph.D. Thesis, Australian National University.

Berger, Dale E., John R. Snortum, Ross J. Homel, Ragnar Hauge and Wendy Loxley (1990) 'Deterrence and Prevention of Alcohol-Impaired Driving in Australia, the United States and Norway', *Justice Quarterly* 7: 453–65.

Box, Steven and Chris Hale (1983) 'Liberation and Female Criminality in England and Wales', *British Journal of Criminology* 23: 35–49.

Braithwaite, John (1979) Inequality, *Crime and Public Policy*. Routledge and Kegan Paul: London.

Braithwaite, John (1984) *Corporate Crime in the Pharmaceutical Industry*. Routledge and Kegan Paul: London.

Braithwaite, John (1985) *To Punish or Persuade: Enforcement of Coal Mine Safety*. State University of New York Press: Albany.

Braithwaite, John, (1989a) *Crime, Shame and Reintegration*. Cambridge University Press: Melbourne.

Braithwaite, John (1989b) 'Criminological Theory and Organizational Crime', *Justice Quarterly* 6: 333–59.

Braithwaite, John (1991a) 'Shame and Modernity', *British Journal of Criminology* 33: 1–18.

Braithwaite, John (1991b) 'Power, Poverty, White-Collar Crime and the Paradoxes of Criminological Theory', *Australian and New Zealand Journal of Criminology* 24: 40–58.

Braithwaite, John and Peter Grabosky (1985) *Occupational Health and Safety Enforcement in Australia*. Australian Institute of Criminology: Canberra.

Braithwaite, John and Philip Pettit (1990) *Not Just Deserts: A Republican Theory of Criminal Justice*. Oxford University Press: Oxford.

Broadhurst, R. and D. Indemaur (1982) 'Crime Seriousness Ratings: The Relationship of Information Accuracy and General Attitudes in Western Australia', *Australian and New Zealand Journal of Criminology* 15: 219.

Carson, W.G. (1975) 'Symbolic and Instrumental Dimensions of Early Factory Legislation: A Case Study in the Social Origins of Criminal Law' in R. Hood (ed.), *Crime, Criminology, and Public Policy*. Free: Glencoe.

Carson, Kit, W.G. Creighton, C. Henenberg and R. Johnstone (1990) *Victorian Occupational Health and Safety: An Assessment of Law in Transition*. La Trobe University: Melbourne.

Cohen, Stanley (1985) *Visions of Social Control*. Polity Press: London.

Cullen, Frank and Karen E. Gilbert (1982) *Reaffirming Rehabilitation*. Andersen Publishing Co.: Cincinnati.

Cullen, Frank T., William J. Maakestaad, and Gray Cevender (1987) *Corporate Crime Under Attack: The Ford Pinto Case and Beyond*. Anderson: Cincinnati.

Dunstan, Keith (1974) *Wowsers*. Cassell: Melbourne.

Edelman, J.M. (1964) *The symbolic Uses of Politics*. University of Illinois Press: Urbana.

Elias, Norbert (1982) *State Formation and Civilization: The Civilizing Process*. Basil Blackwell: Oxford.

Goffman, Erving (1956) 'Embarrassment and Social Organization', *American Journal of Sociology* 62: 264–71.

Gottfredson, Michael R. and Travis Hirschi (1990) *A General Theory of Crime*. Stanford University Press: Stanford.

Grabosky, Peter (1990) ' Crime Control and the Citizen: Non-Governmental Participants in the Criminal Justice System', Paper to East Meets West Conference: International Trends in Crime, Bali, Indonesia.

Grabosky, Peter, John Braithwaite and Paul R. Wilson (1987) 'The Myth of Community Tolerance Toward White-Collar Crime', *Australian and New Zealand Journal of Criminology* 20: 33–44.

Grabosky, Peter and Adam Sutton (eds) (1989) *Stains on a White Collar*. Federation Press: Sydney.

Gusfield, J. (1963) *Symbolic Crusade*. University of Illinois Press: Urbana.

Hagan, John, J.H. Simpson and A.R. Gillis (1979) 'The Sexual Stratification of Social Control', *British Journal of Sociology* 30: 25–38.

Hatty, Suzanne (ed.) (1985) *National Conference on Domestic Violence*. Australian Institute of Criminology: Canberra.

Hatty, Suzanne and Jeanna Sutton (1986) 'Policing Violence Against Women', in Suzanne E. Hatty (ed.), *National Conference on Domestic Violence, Volume 2*, Australian Institute of Criminology Seminar Proceeding No. 12: Canberra.

Hindess, Barry (1982) 'Power, Interests and the Outcomes of Struggles', *Sociology* 16: 498–511.

Hirschi, Travis and Michael Gottfredson (1987) ' Causes of White Collar Crime', *Criminology* 25: 949–74.

Homel, Ross (1988) *Policing and Punishing the Drinking Driver: A Study of General and Specific Deterrence.* Springer-Verlag: New York.

Hopkins, Andrew and Heather McGregor (1991) *Working for Change: The Movement Against Domestic Violence.* Allen and Unwin: Sydney.

Hopkins, Andrew and N. Parnell (1984) 'Why Coal Mine Safety Regulations in Australia Are Not Enforced', *International Journal of Sociology and Law* 12: 179–84.

Jacobs, James B. (1989) *Drunk Driving: An American Dilemma.* Chicago: University of Chicago Press.

Katz, J. (1980) 'The Social Movement Against White-collar Crime' in E. Bittner and S.L. Bessinger (eds), *Criminology Review Yearbook, Vol. 2.* Sage: Beverly Hills.

Levi, Margaret (1988) *Of Rule and Revenue.* University of California Press: Berkeley.

McAllister, Ian (1991) 'Community Attitudes to the Environment, Forests and Forest Management in Australia', Resources Assessment Commission: Canberra.

McAllister, Ian, Rhonda Moore and Toni Makkai (1991) *Drugs in Australian Society: Patterns, Attitudes and Policy,* Longman Cheshire: Melbourne.

Montesquieu, Baron de (1977) *The Spirit of Laws,* abr. and ed. D.W. Carrithers. University of California Press: Berkeley.

O'Donnell, J. and J. Craney (eds) (1982) *Family Violence in Australia.* Longman Cheshire: Melbourne.

Ogborne, Allan C. (1988) 'School-based Educational Programs to Prevent the Personal Use of Psychoactive Drugs for Non-medical Purposes', *Australian Drug and Alcohol Review* 7: 305–14.

O'Malley, P. (1980) 'Theories of Structural Versus Causal Determination: Accounting for Legislative Change in Capitalist Societies' in R. Tomasic (ed.), *Legislation and Society in Australia.* Allen & Unwin: Sydney.

Pettit, Philip (1989) 'Liberty in the Republic', John Curtin Memorial Lecture, Research School of Social Sciences, Australian National University.

Pocock, J.G.A. (ed.) (1977) *The Political Works of Hames Harrington.* Cambridge University Press: New York.

Powell, Keith C. (1988) *Drinking and Alcohol in Colonial Australia 1788–1901 for the Eastern Colonies.* National Campaign Against Drug Abuse, Monograph Series No. 3, Australian Government Publishing Service: Canberra.

Ridgeway, Beverly (1986) 'Domestic Violence: Aboriginal Women's Viewpoint', in Suzanne E. Hatty (ed.), *National Conference on Domestic Violence, Volume 1,* Australian Institute of Criminology Seminar Proceeding No. 12: Canberra.

Ross, H. Lawrence (1982) *Deterring the Drinking Driver: Legal Policy and Social Control.* Lexington Books: Lexington.

Ross, H. Lawrence (1984) 'Social Control Through Deterrence: Drinking and Driving Laws', *Annual Review of Sociology* 10: 21–35.

Scheff, Thomas and Suzanne Retzinger (1991) *Emotions and Violence: Shame and Rage in Destructive Conflicts*. Lexington Books: Lexington, MA.

Scholz, John T. (1984) 'Deterrence, Cooperation and the Ecology of Regulatory Enforcement', *Law and Society Review* 18: 179–224.

Scott, J.C. and F. Al-Thakeb (1977) 'The Public's Perceptions of Crime: A Comparative Analysis of Scandinavia, Western Europe, the Middle East and the United States', in C. Huff (ed.) *Contemporary Corrections*, Sage: Beverly Hills.

Scutt, Jocelynne (1980) 'Crime and Sexual Politics', in E. Windschuttle (ed.), *Women, Class and History*. Fontana: Melbourne.

Scutt, Jocelynne (1982) 'Domestic Violence: the police response', in C. O'Donnell and J. Craney (eds), *Family Violence in Australia*. Longman Cheshire: Melbourne.

Sergeant, Margaret (1973) *Alcoholism as a Social Problem*, University of Queensland Press: Brisbane.

Sherman, L. and R. Berk (1984) 'The specific Deterrent Effects of Arrest for Domestic Assault', *American Sociological Review* 49: 261–72.

Smart, Carol (1979) 'The New Female Offender: Reality or Myth? *British Journal of Criminology* 19: 50–59.

Stanko, Elizabeth (1990) *Everyday Violence*. Pandora: London.

Steffensmeier, D. and R.H. Steffensmeier (1980) 'Trends in Female Delinquency', *Criminology* 18: 62–85.

Stratmann, P. (1982) 'Domestic Violence: The Legal Responses', in C. O'Donnell and J.Craney (eds), *Family Violence in Australia*. Longman Cheshire: Melbourne.

Stubbs, Julie and Diana Powell (1989) *Domestic Violence: Impact of Legal Reform in N.S.W.* Sydney: New South Wales Bureau of Crime Statistics and Research.

Sunstein, Cass (1988) 'Beyond the Republican Revival', *Yale Law Journal* 97: 1539–1590.

Sutherland, Edwin H. (1983) *White Collar Crime: The Uncut Version*. Yale University Press: New Haven.

Tierney, K. (1982) 'The Battered Women Movement and the Creation of the Wife-beating Problem', *Social Problems* 29: 208–20.

Tomsen, Stephen, Ross Homel and Jenny Thommeny (1991) 'The Causes of Public Violence: Situational 'versus' Other Factors in Drinking Related Assaults', in D. Chappell, R. Grabosky and H. Strang (eds) *Australian Violence: Contemporary Perspectives*. Canberra: Australian Institute of Criminology.

Trevelyan, G. M. (1985) *A Shortened History of England*. Penguin: Harmondsworth.

Trice, H. M. and P. M. Roman (1970) 'Delabeling, Relabeling and Alcoholics Anonymous', *Social Problems* 17: 538–46.

Tyrell, I (1984) 'International Aspects of the Women's Temperance Movement in Australia: The Influence of the American W.C.T.U., 1882–1914', *Journal of Religious History* 12: 184–304.

Wearing, Rosemary (1990) 'A Longitudinal Analysis of the 1987 Crimes (Family Violence) Act in Victoria'. Report to Criminology Research Council, Canberra.

Wilson, James Q. and Richard Herrnstein (1985) *Crime and Human Nature*. Simon and Schuster: New York.

Wilson, Paul R. and John Braithwaite (eds) (1978) *Two Faces of Deviance: Crimes of the Powerless and Powerful*, University of Queensland Press: Brisbane.

Wragg, Jeffrey (1987) 'The Development of a Model for Drug Education: Programme Implications Derived from Past Education Studies and Known Causative Factors', *Drug Education Journal of Australia* 1: 1–5.

Wragg, Jeffrey (1990) 'The Longitudinal Evaluation of a Primary School Drug Education Program: Did It Work?' *Drug Education Journal of Australia* 4: 33–44.

Yeatman, A. (1990) *Bureaucrats, Technocrats and Femocrats*. George Allen and Unwin: Melbourne.

PART II

Responsive
Regulation

[6]
Preventive Law and Managerial Auditing

Introduction

The corporate sector has learnt some expensive lessons in recent decades on the costs of inadequate auditing systems to ensure compliance with the law — the Lockheed bribery scandal, thalidomide, Bhopal, Allied Chemical and Kepone, A.H. Robins and the Dalkon Shield, asbestos; and these are just the high-profile cases which generate newspaper headlines. In more mundane ways, large corporations are confronted every year with instances of employees breaking the law on behalf of the corporation in their enthusiasm to achieve the goals they have been set by the organisation.

Of course, it is sometimes in the corporation's interest to break the law, but most large corporations rightly take the view that to allow a culture of lawlessness to develop within the organisation will be to the long-term disadvantage of the corporation. The corporations which allow employees to play fast and loose with the law are the ones that end up with billion dollar legal disasters. Moreover, the American foreign bribery scandals of the 1970s taught us that corporations that turn a blind eye to slush funds find that while that eye is closed their own executives are helping themselves to the monies poured into off-books accounts. In short, corporations which have a climate of tolerance towards illegal means of corporate goal attainment in a variety of ways tend themselves to become victims of corporate crime.

The Corporate Response

The upshot of this realisation has been that many companies are now responding constructively with preventive law programmes which draw on the experience of managerial auditing. These have been devised in a variety of areas, notably the following:

- product liability;
- occupational health and safety;
- companies and securities law requirements;
- restrictive trade practices;
- revenue law;
- consumer protection;
- environmental protection, and
- data protection.

Why the importance attached to compliance controls? The main reason is clear; prevention is often more cost-effective than cure. The costs to be avoided are well known but bear repeating:

- heavy civil damages (e.g. for products liability);
- product recalls or other corrective action;
- trading losses resulting from unauthorised acts of employees;
- disqualification of licence or authority to transact business;
- disruption and loss of morale as a result of involvement in litigation or a publicity crisis;
- fines, or, in some instances, even jail;

- legal costs in defending claims or prosecutions;
- increases in insurance premiums, and
- spectre of increased regulation.

Beyond these obvious motivations for having effective internal controls, there is a trend towards enforced self-regulation, with the state delegating its enforcement role to private enterprise and coercing private enterprise to discharge that role on its behalf.

How, then, can large organisations respond to the challenge of making their self-regulatory systems work better to ensure compliance with the law?

The Essential Requirements of an Effective Self-regulatory System

One of the authors examined, largely on the basis of interviews with executives, the characteristics of the internal compliance systems of the five American coal mining companies with the lowest accident rates for the industry in the early 1980s, and also reviewed other empirical work on the organisational characteristics associated with safety in mines[1]. A characteristic which consistently emerged was that companies with good safety records had detailed plans of attack to deal with identifiable hazards. This may be a characteristic which is not so relevant to determining the effectiveness of other kinds of internal compliance functions as it is for occupational health and safety. However, the other features which emerged from this empirical work seem to us of likely general relevance. Effectively, self-regulating companies:

(1) give a lot of informal clout and top management backing to their compliance personnel (safety inspectors in the case of mine safety);

(2) make sure that clearly defined accountability for compliance performance is placed on line managers;

(3) monitor that performance carefully and let managers know when it is not up to standard;

(4) leave effective communication of compliance problems to those capable of acting on them, and

(5) do not neglect training and supervision (especially by front-line supervisors) for compliance.

These characteristics of successfully self-regulated corporations will be considered in turn.

Clout for Internal Compliance Groups

At a recent seminar on laws to control animal experimentation, one of the authors asked the animal welfare officer from a very large Australian research institution how she dealt with researchers who refused to comply with Australia's voluntary code on the use of animals in experiments. "Easy," she said. "If they don't do what I ask, I don't give them any more animals." Her role encompassed the ordering and delivery of animals to experimenters. This gave her organisational clout in dealing with researchers. Most fundamentally, then, clout for internal compliance groups comes from their control of resources which are important to those who must be made to comply.

Clout is central in the same way to the success of government regulators. Health departments find it easier to control drug companies than food outlets, and find it much less necessary to resort to law enforcement to do so, because health departments hold sway over so many decisions which affect the success of pharmaceutical companies. They decide whether new drugs will be allowed on the market and, if so, with what promotional claims, at what price and with what quality control requirements during manufacture. Organisational actors are more compliant with requests from actors who control vital resources (such as approvals and licences) for the organisation.

Often, it is organisationally difficult to give compliance staff control over contingencies which matter to those regulated. In these circumstances, it is important for top management clearly to communicate the message to the organisation that, in any dispute, it is likely to stand behind its compliance staff. Regrettably, in most organisations, the opposite message is part of the folklore of the corporate culture — that, when the crunch comes, management will stand behind its production people and allow them to push aside that which impedes output. In contrast, with the coal mining safety leaders visited, when a company inspector recommended that a section of a mine be closed down because it was unsafe, in all five companies it was considered inadvisable for line managers to ignore the recommendation because of the substantial risk that top management would back the safety staff rather than themselves.

Quality control directors in many pharmaceutical companies are given clout by quite formal requirements that their decisions can only be overruled by a written directive from the corporation's chief executive. This gives quality control unusual authority, because not many chief executives want to risk their careers by overruling their technical people for the sake of a single batch of drugs when the danger, however remote, is that this batch could kill someone.

Clearly Defined Accountability

A senior pharmaceutical company executive once explained: "There's a Murphy's Law of a kind: If someone else can be blamed, he will be." Active policies to resist this tendency are needed for companies to be effectively self-regulating. At all five coal mines, leading in safety, the line manager, not the safety staff, was held responsible for different types of safety breakdowns. They were all companies which avoided the problem of diffused accountability: people knew where the buck stopped for different kinds of failures.

In contrast, companies with little will to comply sometimes draw lines of accountability with a view to creating a picture of diffused responsibility so that no one can be called to account should a court enquire into the affairs of the company. Everyone is given a credible organisational alibi for blaming someone else. Perhaps worse, other non-self-regulating companies calculatedly set out to pass blame on to others. Thus, some pharmaceutical and pesticide companies have their most dicey toxicological testing done by contract laboratories which survive by telling large companies what they want to hear. They get results which indicate the safety of their products without risking the consequences of a conviction for the presentation of fraudulent data. The use of sales agents to pay bribes is perhaps the best documented device of this sort in the corporate crime literature.

At three of the large American pharmaceutical companies visited by one of the authors, it was revealed that there was a "vice-president responsible for going to jail", and two of these were interviewed[2]. Lines of accountability had been drawn in these organisations such that, if there were a problem and someone's head had to go on the chopping block, it would be that of the "vice-president responsible for going to jail". These executives probably would not have been promoted to vice-president had they not been willing to act as scapegoats. If they performed well, presumably they would be shifted sideways to a safer vice-presidency. Corporations can pay someone to be their fall-guy in many ways. Exceptionally generous severance pay is the simplest method.

Admiral Poindexter's role in the Iran-Contra operation was that of a classic "vice-president responsible for going to jail". On 16 July 1987 he told the US Congressional investigators that the "buck stopped" with him, not with the President, that he had decided not to tell the President even though he knew that the President approved of what he was doing "so I could insulate him and provide some future deniability should it leak out"[3]. In the Nixon White House, in contrast, staff did not show Nixon the solicitude of shielding him from the taint of the knowledge of Watergate, so the buck did stop with the President — where it belonged.

In summary, most companies make little effort clearly to define lines of responsibility for compliance; the result is that when something does go wrong the complexity of the organisation is usually sufficient to make it difficult to convict any individual. Calculatedly non-compliant companies sometimes create lines of accountability which will point the finger of responsibility away from their top managers. And effectively self-regulating companies have principles of responsibility which make it clear in advance which line managers will be held responsible should certain types of non-compliance occur. However, a number of the pharmaceutical companies visited had an each way bet; they had clearly defined lines of accountability for their internal disciplinary purposes, while contriving to portray a picture of confused accountability to the outside world. The fact that the latter does occur is one reason why "private police" can be more effective than "public police", and why self-regulation has the potential more effectively to punish individuals than Government regulation.

Monitoring Compliance Performance

Two of the surprising findings from the survey of the organisational characteristics of coal mining safety leaders were that the size of the safety staffs of these companies varied enormously, as did the punitiveness of their approach to disciplining individuals who breached safety rules. It was expected that among the defining characteristics of companies which were leaders in safety would be that they would spend a lot of money on safety staff and would be very tough on safety offenders. While a large safety staff is not necessarily a characteristic of safety leaders, putting enormous accountability pressures for safety on line managers is. While a policy of sacking or fining safety offenders on the spot is not typical, communication of the message that higher management is deeply concerned when individuals break the rules is universal for safety leaders.

Ultimately, there is, of course, no standard recipe to be followed; as the director of safety at Bethlehem Steel put it: "You can't cookbook safety." However, there is a framework for legal risk management and companies are well advised to heed the basic elements of that framework when building up their own preventive programmes.

The annals of corporate disasters contain numerous examples of companies which have failed to take even the elementary step of identifying areas of prime risk. One case in point is the explosion at the Flixborough plant of Hypro Ltd in the mid-1970s. The explosion, which killed 28 people, occurred in an environment where the awareness of such a risk seemed to be minimal if present at all:

> . . . the plant operated by this organisation held over 360,000 gallons of cyclohexane, naphtha, toluene and gasolene on a site which was licensed to store only 8,500 gallons; . . . there were associated "shortcomings" in its safety procedures and uncertainties about responsibilities for safety; . . . a major repair to a plant processing very large quantities of cyclohexane at high temperatures and pressures was carried out with limited design, inspection and test procedures. . . Hazards on the scale which emerged were not being "responded to" by Hypro, simply because they were not imagined or considered. . . The Flixborough case presents in perhaps an extreme form the characteristics of intelligence failure or of the failure of foresight which is charted in most retrospective inquiries into accidents[4].

Risk identification can be conducted at an ethereal mathematical level, but legal risk management typically requires the use of check-lists, systematic reviews of corporate operations, "what if" projections and other down-to-earth techniques of managerial control. Indeed, a notable development in the literature on preventive law is the use of risk management theory to generate highly practical guides for decision making.

Warning Systems

Another infamous area of neglect is the need for warning systems to help ensure that management is alerted to compliance problems which threaten the company. There are numerous examples of compliance problems being concealed at lower or middle levels of management and of companies being taken by surprise when the bad news leaks to the public (e.g. Exxon in relation to allegations of the payment of bribes by its Italian subsidiary). The solution adopted by many companies (e.g. General Electric, Exxon, and United Airlines) has been to supplement one-over-one reporting relationships with extra reporting channels to top management.

The best advice for avoiding communication blockages can be summed up in these terms:

- Make sure that routine formal reporting relationships are designed well and appropriately enough to the unique environment of the company, to ensure that most recurrent problems of non-compliance are reported to those with the power to correct them.

- Make sure there is a free route to the top, by-passing line reporting relationships, to reduce the likely success of conspiratorial blocking of bad news.

- Create a corporate culture with a climate of concern for compliance problems which are not an employee's own responsibility — an organisation "full of antennae" in which there is a commitment to being alert to noticing and reporting how others, as well as oneself, can solve compliance problems.

Training and Supervision for Compliance

It is not enough for top management to know when non-compliance is occurring and then to tell those with clearly defined responsibility for the problem to bring the company into compliance. Often, the problems are complex, so formal and systematic training is needed to ensure that all employees know *how* to comply in their area of responsibility, and supervision is needed to ensure that the lessons of the training have been learnt.

Thus, all legal and marketing personnel require training in restrictive trade practices, and industrial relations staff training in labour relations law. All production people need occupational health and safety training. The mistake which many non-compliant companies make is in communicating the relevant knowledge to middle management and then glibly assuming that they will pass it down.

The five coal mine safety leaders were all characterised by extraordinary measures to ensure that first-line supervisors were training and supervising their workers. At US Steel, for example, department heads are responsible for developing training plans which ensure that foremen provide all workers with training in a set of safe job procedures which are written by the foreman

19

for the job of each employee in his care. Each foreman must make at least one individual contact each week with each employee under his supervision to consolidate this training. With inexperienced workers, these contacts are usually "tell-show" checks, whereby the worker is asked to explain what should and should not be done and why the approved procedure is the safest one. Foremen are required to make at least two planned safety observations of each employee each month. The safety observations are planned so that they cover systematically all job operations for which the employee has received instruction. In addition to the safety observations, which are planned and scheduled at the beginning of each week, foremen are expected to perform additional "impromptu observations" following chance recognition of unsafe practices. Whenever a foreman observes an unsafe condition or work method, whether in a planned or impromptu safety observation, he must correct it immediately and report the occurrence to higher management on a "supervisor's safety report". The foreman can tell whether a worker who deviates from a procedure or rule has been trained in it by looking at the employee's record. For all employees, a record is maintained by their foreman, noting their safety history — basic training, safety contacts, planned safety observations, unsafe acts, violations, discipline and injuries. When workers move from foreman to foreman, their records move with them, so a new foreman can discover at a glance what safety training a worker lacks for his new job.

In short, effectively self-regulating companies do not tell middle managers how to comply and assume they will tell the troops; they have training policies and programmes to guarantee that training is happening and working down to the lowest reaches of the organisation. They audit compliance with compliance training programmes as assiduously as they audit compliance itself.

Watching Pressures for Non-compliance

Having covered the five basic principles for creating an effectively self-regulating company, consideration might be given to another even more basic principle. This is that companies must be concerned not to put employees under so much pressure to achieve the economic goals of the organisation that they cut corners with the law. The role of excessive performance pressures on middle managers in creating corporate crime has been frequently pointed to in the literature[5]. *Corporate Crime in the Pharmaceutical Industry*[2] illustrated the problem thus:

> Take the situation of Riker, a pharmaceutical subsidiary of the 3M corporation. In order to foster innovation, 3M imposes on Riker a goal that each year 25 per cent of gross sales should be of products introduced in the last five years. Now if Riker's research division were to have a long dry spell through no fault of its own, but because all of its compounds had turned out to have toxic effects, the organisation would be under pressure to churn something out to meet the goal imposed by headquarters. Riker would not have to yield to this pressure. It could presumably go to 3M and explain the reasons for its run of bad luck. The fact that such goal requirements do put research directors under pressure was well illustrated by one American executive who explained that research directors often forestall criticism of long dry spells by spreading out discoveries — scheduling the programme so that something new is always on the horizon.
>
> Sometimes the goal performance criterion which creates pressure for fraud/bias is not for the production of a certain number of winners but simply for completing a predetermined

number of evaluations in a given year. One medical director told me that one of his staff had run ten trials which showed a drug to be clear on a certain test, then fabricated data on the remaining 90 trials to show the same result. The fraud had been perpetrated by a scientist who was falling behind in his work-load and who had an obligation to complete a certain number of evaluations-for the year (p. 94).

One might say that this is an inevitable problem for any company that is serious about setting its people performance goals. But there are differences in the degrees of seriousness of the problem. At one extreme are companies which calculatedly set their managers goals that they know can only be achieved by breaking the law. Thus, the pharmaceutical chief executive may tell her regional medical director to do whatever he has to do to get a product approved for marketing in a Latin American country, when she knows this will mean paying a bribe. Likewise, the coal mining executive may tell his mine manager to cut costs when he knows this will mean cutting corners on safety.

The mentality of "do what you have to do but don't tell me how you do it" is widespread in business. Eliminating it is easy for executives who are prepared to set targets which are achievable in a responsible way. It is a quesiton of top management's attitudes. IBM is one example of a company which we found to have the approach to target setting which we have in mind. IBM representatives have a sales quota to meet. There is what is called a "100 Per Cent Club" of representatives who have achieved 100 per cent or more of their quota. A majority of representatives make the 100 Per Cent Club, so the quotas are achievable by ethical sales practices. IBM, in fact, has a policy of ensuring that targets are attainable by legal means. Accordingly, quotas are adjusted downwards when times are bad.

As Clinard found, unreasonable pressure on middle managers comes from the top, and most top managers have a fairly clear idea of how hard they can squeeze without creating a criminogenic organisation[5 pp. 91-102, 140-4]. In the words of C.F. Luce, Chairman of Consolidated Edison: "The top manager has a duty not to push so hard that middle managers are pushed to unethical compromises"[5 p. 142].

This "duty", however, takes us back to the fundamental problem of self-regulation. Companies must have a desire to comply with the law sufficiently strongly to let this override other corporate goals. This sixth "principle" therefore really reduces to companies being motivated to be effectively self-regulating. We believe companies can be so motivated from their internal deliberations as moral agents, from their self-interested concerns to minimise risks, but, more importantly, from external pressures calculated to make effective self-regulation an attractive policy. The design of these external pressures is a topic for another day. ∎

References

1. Braithwaite, J., *To Punish or Persuade: Enforcement of Coal Mine Safety*, State University of New York Press, Albany, 1985.
2. Braithwaite, J., *Corporate Crime in the Pharmaceutical Industry*, Routledge and Kegan Paul, London, 1984.
3. *Australian Financial Review*, 17 July 1987, p. 10.
4. Turner, "Organizational Responses to Hazard", in Kunreuther, H. (Ed.), *Risk: A Seminar Series*, 1981.
5. Clinard, M., *Corporate Ethics and Crime: The Role of Middle Management*, Sage, Beverly Hills, 1983.

[7]
Convergence in Models of Regulatory Strategy[1]

INTRODUCTION

There is an emerging convergence between rational actor and normative accounts of what works in securing compliance with regulatory laws. This convergence is about the efficacy of tit-for-tat enforcement - regulation that is contingently tough and forgiving. Building on this convergence, the possibility is considered that regulatory agencies will be best able to secure compliance when they are Benign Big Guns. That is, regulators will be more able to speak softly when they carry big sticks (and crucially, a hierarchy of lesser sanctions). Paradoxically, the bigger and the more various are the sticks, the more regulators will achieve success by speaking softly.

CONVERGENCE IN MODELS OF REGULATORY STRATEGY

A deal of contemporary social science is a stalemate between theories assuming economic rationality on the part of actors and theories counterposing action as variously motivated by the desire to comply with norms, to maintain a sense of identity, or to do good. The contention of this paper is that theory is most likely to be robust where there is convergence between the implications of rational actor and moral actor accounts. So in the culture of our social science, we might well search for arenas of convergence between materialist and idealist analysis instead of continuing to seek battlegrounds for new clashes between these traditions.

Much barren scholarly disputation has raged between a majority view that corporations will only comply with the law when faced with rational incentives and a minority view that corporate actors internalise the values in the law in a way that leaves them open to persuasion and self-regulation. Empirically, among regulators themselves, the latter has been found to be the majority account.[2]

---

1   Paper delivered at a Public Seminar entitled "Occupational Health and Safety and Environmental Protection: Current Policies and Practices in the Social Control of Corporate Crime", convened by the Institute of Criminology, 25 October 1989

2   See the studies cited by Hawkins, K., **Environment and Enforcement: Regulation and the Social Definition of Pollution** (1984) p 3

Attempts have recently been made to model the intuition that regulatory agencies do best at securing compliance with their statutes by striking some sort of sophisticated balance between punishment and persuasion. At the same time that I was struggling with such an attempt in Australia,[3] Scholz was doing so in a very different way in the United States.[4] Although Scholz and Braithwaite posit contrary premises about human motivation and different intervening processes, their theories converge at a key point, namely the efficacy of regulation that is contingently tough and forgiving.

Scholz models regulation as a prisoner's dilemma game wherein the motivation of the firm is to minimise regulatory costs and the motivation of the regulator is to maximize compliance outcomes.[5] A tit-for-tat enforcement strategy is shown to be that most likely to establish mutually beneficial cooperation. Tit-for-tat (TFT) means that the regulator refrains from a deterrent response so long as the firm is cooperating. But when the firm yields to the temptation to exploit the cooperative posture of the regulator and cheats on compliance, then the regulator shifts from a cooperative to a deterrent response. Confronted with the matrix of payoffs typical in the enforcement dilemma, the optimal strategy is for both the firm and the regulator to cooperate until the other defects from cooperation. Then the rational player should retaliate (to deterrence regulation on the part of the state; to a law evasion strategy by the firm). If the retaliation secures a return to cooperation by the other player, then one should be forgiving, restoring the benefits of mutual cooperation in place of the lower payoffs of mutual defection. Drawing on the work of Axelrod,[6] Scholz contends that in prisoner's dilemma games TFT has been demonstrated mathematically, experimentally and through the use of computer simulation tournaments against other sophisticated strategies to maximize the payoffs of players in many circumstances.

Scholz's theory of the evolution of cooperation is a positive theory of why cooperation should evolve by virtue of the rationality of players seeking optimum payoffs. Second, it is a positive theory of what is the best strategy for securing compliance with the law. Third, it can be the basis of a normative theory of how regulators ought to act. In this comment, discussion will be limited to the potential for the second kind of theoretical contribution. Scholz has a limited theory of the first type - of the political realities of how regulators and corporations in fact act - particularly because of its implied assumption of equality of power between regulatory players. But my own work is even more fallible in this regard since it includes no theory at all of how regulatory strategies evolve. While my work is

---

3   Braithwaite, J., "Enforced Self-Regulation: A New Strategy for Corporate Crime Control" (1982) 80 **Michigan Law Review** pp 1466-1507; and Braithwaite, J., **To Punish or Persuade: Enforcement of Coal Mine Safety** (1985)

4   Scholz, J.T., "Deterrence, Cooperation and the Ecology of Regulatory Enforcement" (1984) 80 **Law and Society Review** pp 179-224 and Scholz, J.T., "Voluntary Compliance and Regulatory Enforcement" (1984) 6 **Law and Policy** pp 385-404

5   **ibid.**

6   Axelrod, R., **The Evolution of Cooperation** (1984)

embedded in a normative account of how business regulation ought to be done, here we will consider it simply as a positive theory of what regulatory strategy will be most effective in securing compliance with a pre-given law.

Thus reconstructed, Braithwaite's theory[7] is based on six postulates:

- Some corporate actors will only comply with the law if it is economically rational for them to do so. Most corporate actors will comply with the law most of the time simply because it is the law. All corporate actors are bundles of contradictory commitments to values about economic rationality, law abidingness and business responsibility. Business executives have profit-maximising selves and law-abiding selves; at different moments, in different contexts, the different selves prevail.
- A strategy based totally on persuasion and self-regulation will be exploited when actors are motivated by economic rationality.
- A strategy based mostly on punishment will undermine the good will of actors when they are motivated by a sense of responsibility.
- Punishment is expensive; persuasion is cheap. A strategy based mostly on punishment wastes resources on litigation that would be better spent on monitoring and persuasion. (A highly punitive mining inspectorate will spend more time in court than in mines.)
- A strategy based mostly on punishment fosters an organized business subculture of resistance to regulation wherein methods of legal resistance and counterattack are incorporated into industry socialisation.[8] Punitive enforcement engenders a game of regulatory cat-and-mouse whereby firms defy the spirit of the law by exploiting loopholes, and the state writes more and more specific rules to cover the loopholes. The result can be:
  - rulemaking by accretion that gives no coherence to the rules as a package, and
  - a barren legalism concentrating on specific, simple, visible violations to the neglect of underlying systemic problems.
- Heavy reliance must be placed on persuasion rather than on punishment in industries where technological and environmental realities change so quickly that the regulations which give detailed content to the law cannot keep up to date.

If these premises are correct, a strategy for mixing punishment and persuasion is needed. At one level, TFT is the mix that resolves these contradictions. By cooperating with firms until they cheat, the counterproductivity of undermining the good faith of socially responsible actors is averted. By nurturing expectations of responsibility and cooperation within the regulatory culture,[9] the regulator can coax and caress fidelity to the spirit of the law even in contexts where the law is riddled with gaps or loopholes. By getting tough with cheaters, actors are made to suffer

---

7   Braithwaite (1985) **op.cit. supra** n. 3
8   Bardach, E. and Kagan, R., **Going by the Book: The Problem of Regulating Unreasonableness** (1982)
9   Meidinger, E., "Regulatory Culture: A Theoretical Outline", (1986) 9 **Law and Policy** pp 355-86

when motivated by their rational economic selves, and are given reason to favour their socially responsible, law-abiding selves. In short, they are given reason to reform, more so because when they do reform they find the regulator forgiving.

   To Punish or Persuade argued, however, for a more elaborate strategy for mixing punishment and persuasion than just TFT. The contention was that compliance was most likely when the regulatory agency displayed an explicit enforcement pyramid. An example of an enforcement pyramid appears in Figure 1.

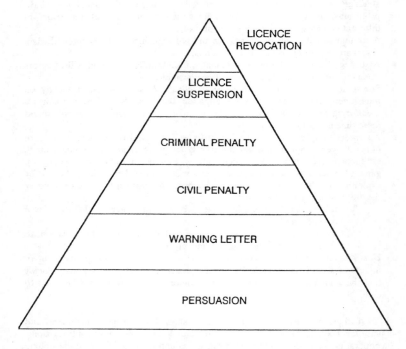

Figure 1   **Example of an enforcement pyramid. The proportion of space at each layer represents the proportion of enforcement activity at that level.**

Most regulatory action occurs at the base of the pyramid where initially attempts are made to coax compliance by persuasion. The next phase of enforcement escalation is a warning letter; if this fails to secure compliance, civil monetary penalties are imposed; if this fails, criminal prosecution ensues; if this fails, the plant is shut down or a license to operate is suspended; and if this fails, the license to do business is revoked. This particular enforcement pyramid would be appropriate to some regulatory arenas but not others. The form of the enforcement pyramid is the subject of the theory, not the content of this particular pyramid.

The idea of the enforcement pyramid has advantages over the bipolar TFT notion of switching between cooperation and deterrence. Defection from cooperation is a less attractive option for a firm when confronted with a regulator armed with an enforcement pyramid than when confronted with a regulator having only one deterrence option. This is true even where the deterrence option is maximally potent. Actually, it is especially true where the single deterrence option is cataclysmic. It is not uncommon for regulatory agencies to have the power to withdraw or suspend licenses as the only effective power at their disposal. The problem is that the sanction is such a drastic one (for example, putting a TV station off the air), that it is politically impossible and morally unacceptable to use it with any but the most extraordinary offenses. Hence, such agencies often find themselves in the situation where their implied plea to "cooperate or else" has little credibility. Regulators have maximum capacity to lever cooperation when they can escalate deterrence in a way that is responsive to the degree of uncooperativeness of the firm, and the moral and political acceptability of the response.

It follows from the postulate of the theory about an organized business subculture of resistance, that we should transcend the view of regulation as a game played with single firms. In some respects industry associations can be more important players. For example, individual firms will often follow the advice of an industry association to cooperate on a particular regulatory requirement because if the industry does not make this requirement work, it will confront a political backlash which may lead to more intervention. Hence, the importance of a pyramid of regulatory strategies pitched at the entire industry (see Figure 2), as well as a pyramid of sanctions directed at individual firms (see Figure 1).

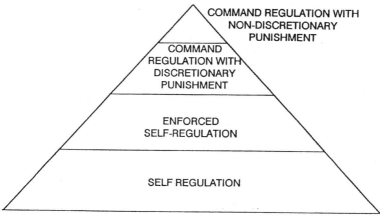

Figure 2   **Example of a pyramid of enforcement strategy**

To Punish or Persuade argued that the state is most likely to achieve regulatory goals at least cost to taxpayers and industry by communicating to industry that in any regulatory arena the preferred strategy is industry self-regulation. However, given that industry will often exploit the privilege of self-regulation, the state must also communicate its willingness to escalate regulatory strategy up the further pyramid of interventionism exemplified in Figure 2. Again the content of the pyramid (defended in To Punish or Persuade) is not the issue. One could conceive of another regulatory pyramid that might escalate from self-regulation to negative licensing,[10] to positive licensing, to taxes on harm.[11]

Any appropriate pyramid of interventionism enables the state to communicate its preparedness to escalate up the pyramid, thereby giving both the industry and regulatory agents incentives to make regulation work at lower levels of intervention. The key contention is that the gradients and peaks of the two enforcement pyramids create downward pressure which causes most of the action to occur at the base of the pyramid - in the realms of persuasion and self-regulation. The irony is that the existence and signalling of the capacity to get as tough as is needed can usher in a regulatory culture more voluntaristic and less litigious than is possible when the state rules out adversariness and punitiveness as an option. Lop the tops off the enforcement pyramids and there is less prospect of self-regulation and less prospect of persuasion as an alternative to punishment.

I now want to suggest that we can build further on the convergent theoretical foundations of Scholtz's work and my own. This elaboration was stimulated by the emergence of a "Benign Big Gun" cluster of agencies from the application of a variety of multivariate techniques to taxonomize 96 Australian regulatory agencies according to patterns of enforcement behavior.[12] The Benign Big Guns were agencies that walked softly while carrying very big sticks. The agencies in the cluster were distinguished by having enormous powers: the power of the Reserve Bank to take over banks, seize gold, increase reserve deposit ratios; the power of the Australian Broadcasting Tribunal to completely shut down business by revoking licenses; or the power of oil and gas regulators to stop production on rigs at stupendous cost. The core agencies in this cluster had such enormous powers but never, or hardly ever, used them. They also never or hardly ever used the lesser power of criminal prosecution. The Broadcasting Tribunal's strategy was once characterized by counsel for the Australian Consumers' Association as "regulation by raised eyebrows" and the Reserve Bank strategy has been described as "regulation by vice-regal suasion".

The data from this study are not adequate for measuring the relative effectiveness of these 96 agencies in achieving their regulatory goals. Nevertheless, the empirical association between speaking softly and carrying big sticks is an

---

10   See Grabosky, P. and Braithwaite, J., **Of Manners Gentle: Enforcement Stratefies of Australian Business Regulatory Agencies** (1986)

11   Anderson, F.R., et al., Environmental Improvement Through Economic Incentives (1977)

12   Graboksy and Braithwaite, op.cit. supra n. 10; and Braithwaite, J., et al., "An Enforcement Taxonomy of Regulatory Agencies" (1987) 9 **Law and Policy** pp 325-350

interesting basis for theoretical speculation. Might it be that the greater the heights of punitiveness to which an agency can escalate, the greater its capacity to push regulation down to the base of the enforcement pyramid? A flat pyramid (with a truncated range of escalations) will exert less downward pressure to keep regulation at its base than a tall pyramid. A tall enforcement pyramid can be used to apply enormous pressure from the heights of its peak to motivate 'voluntary' compliance. Thus, the key propositions of a Benign Big Gun theory of regulation would be that successful pursuit of cooperative regulation and maximum compliance with the law is predicted by:

- use of a tit-for-tat strategy;
- access to a hierarchical range of sanctions and a hierarchy of interventionism in regulatory style (the enforcement pyramids); and
- how extreme in punitiveness is the upper limit of the range of sanctions.

In presenting this conceptual note, I wish to be clear and provocative about these three interconnected ideas. But I also mean to be tentative. The first need is for fieldwork, in the tradition exemplified by Hawkins,[13] to ground if and how regulators come to be granted the credibility of being Benign Big Guns. Hawkins' work raises questions about how direct is the link between the image of invincibility regulators can sustain and the calibre of their firepower. What are the limits, if any, on the capacity of regulators to bluff their way to an image of invincibility?

The important point concerns the possibilities for convergence between theories derived from rational and normative accounts of human motivation. Analyses of what makes compliance rational and what builds business cultures of social responsibility can converge on the conclusion that compliance is optimized by regulation that is contingently tough and forgiving. For Scholz, forgiveness for firms planning to cooperate in future is part of maximizing the difference between the cooperation and confrontation payoffs. In *To Punish or Persuade*, forgiveness is advocated more for its importance in building commitment to comply in future. In Scholz's formulation, punishment is all about deterrence. I place greater importance on the moral educative effects of punishment, and on the role of punishment in constituting an image of invincibility within a regulatory culture.

Both accounts, from their different premises, move away from the notion of an optimum level of stringency in the law, an optimum level of enforcement, and an optimum static strategy, and instead converge toward an optimum way of playing a dynamic enforcement game. Of course it remains to be seen whether the product of this convergence is empirically robust, and whether we can build upon it a Benign Big Gun theory of regulatory power.

---

13   Hawkins, op.cit. supra n. 2

[8]
Beyond Positivism: Learning from Contextual Integrated Strategies

Good criminologists are interpretively flexible, searching to read situations from the different angles illuminated by multiple theories. Plural understandings of a crime problem stimulate a disparate range of action possibilities that can be integrated into a hedged, mutually reinforcing package of preventive policies. Positivist criminology has its uses in informing the kind of research-policy interface advanced. Its limitation is that it focuses on short-term, decontextualized policies that are intentionally disentangled from integrated policy packages. This when it is long-term, dynamically responsive, and contextualized, integrated assaults that are more likely to bear fruit. Some suggestions are made on how to reform criminology so that its creative and evaluative focus is more directed at what Bateson in 1972 called "systemic wisdom." The alternative is to settle for a positivism that almost inevitably leads to a policy analysis of despair about the intractability of the crime problem. That "nothing works" is not an empirically established fact, but an artifact of the epistemology of a science with a particular structure. This structure can be reformed.

Imagine for a moment that another applied scholarly discipline—international relations—were run like criminology.[1] The core activity of the field would then involve regressions where variables like the size of nations' armies and arsenals were used to predict which nations were more likely to end up in wars; regressions in which aspects of the personality and structural location (gender, class, etc.) of national leaders were used to predict propensity to lead their nations into violence; tests of strain theories of violence (Will the Russians become less prone to violence if they have bread in their stomachs?); experiments in which the effects of functional equivalents to street lighting, such as satellite monitoring to make missile movements visible, were monitored. Of course, the discipline of international relations is nothing like this.[2] If it were, then my prediction is that the predominant view in the discipline would be that "nothing works." Most studies would

Thanks to Don Weatherburn for comments on an earlier draft of this article. This article was prepared for presentation at the American Society of Criminology Meeting, Phoenix.

384   JOURNAL OF RESEARCH IN CRIME AND DELINQUENCY

find no significant effects in preventing war of deterrence by large armies, personality and structural characteristics of national leaders, strain variables, or deployment of new prevention technologies. Because of the discipline's nihilism, political leaders would take little notice of it.

Why do I predict a nothing works nihilism, scientific surrender before the dreadful challenge of preventing war, were international relations to go the way of criminology? Well, for the same reason that we have produced a nihilistic scientific culture from the dogged positivism of criminology, a nihilism reinforced by the critical legal studies, Marxist, and postmodern critics of the mainstream tradition (Handler 1992). Positivism produces an avalanche of nonsignificant findings, even in a system of scientific production that is biased in favor of highlighting significant effects, because specificity of context is overwhelmingly important in deciding whether a crime will occur or a war will break out. Even positivist theories that are empirically robust in terms of certain kinds of static tests will generally fail to predict effective intervention because they will not be sufficiently dynamic to cope with the way context unfolds in specific instances.

If this kind of positivist science is not the mainstream of international relations, then what is its "classical approach" (Bull 1966)? It is, I would suggest, to analyze integrated policy packages as they operate in the context of a particular period of history—to analyze, for example, the successes and failures of the Reagan administration's foreign policy with the Soviet Union and to learn from that history. Four departures from criminology's positivist model are involved here: (a) focus on integrated policy packages; (b) contextual analysis; (c) eschewing static models in favor of dynamic "thinking in time" (Neustadt and May 1986); and (d) intertwining rather than separating normative theories (about what ought to be) and explanatory theories (about what is).

I do not want to suggest that international relations has got it right and we got it wrong. Clearly, the kind of science we need for understanding crime is rather different from what is required to understand international relations. I have used the other discipline simply as a device to open our eyes to the fact that there are radically different ways of organizing our science. Now I will develop a brief case for a different scientific model for criminology. First, I will suggest what might be the role of theory in informing context-specific integrated policy packages. Second, I will advocate what I see as a more marginal, but still important, role for the type of positivist criminology that is currently the mainstream of the discipline. Third, I will find virtue in a more internationalized culture of evaluation that nurtures thinking in time and thinking across cultures about the contextual successes and failures of integrated policy packages.

THEORY AND INTEGRATED STRATEGIES

Theory matters. But I don't think it matters in the way that positivist criminology would have it. The positivist vision about which I am doubtful is of theory constructed from a set of eternally true propositional building blocks, each supported by a substantial body of empirical evidence. This vision is limited because truth changes over time and truth about humans is changed by the fact of humans discovering it to be true.[3] At the end of several decades of hard work confirming all the building blocks of a theory, some of the building blocks that were verified early on will have become no longer true. Because positivist science progresses slowly, it never delivers anything better than theoretical structures that are half true, half crumbling, as more and more older blocks fall out of place. This is the lesson we should have learned from the history of positivist economics.

The important way I think we should use theory is metaphorically. Competing theories supply us with competing ways of imagining how to construct integrated policy packages. Let me give you a practical example of the constructive, commonsense use of theory in developing integrated strategies for dealing with a contextually conceived problem. Sydney in the 1980s had a motor vehicle theft rate that was very high by any world standard. The New South Wales Police responded by calling together the key players for a roundtable discussion that came to be known during the early 1990s as the "Motor Vehicle Theft Forum." It included senior police, motor vehicle manufacturers, insurers, media organizations and the Motor Traders' Association (representing vehicle sellers). The police also sent some staff out to the streets and correctional institutions to talk to young people who stole cars. The latter feedback was viewed using an opportunity theory metaphor. These young offenders were often unemployed, facing long-term unemployment, from impoverished neighborhoods (blocked legitimate opportunities). Their illegitimate opportunities to steal cars were constituted in part by white-collar criminals in the used-car trade, who used computerized lists of parts (or whole cars) that had been ordered by customers to supply juveniles with written lists of car models for which they would pay. Opportunity theory provided a way of understanding the social context of these unusually high car-theft rates, and it supplied policy implications. It motivated a search for ways of reforming juvenile justice that might give young people more hope for the future (see Juvenile Justice Advisory Council of NSW 1993). It led to the comprehension that some of the enforcement effort should be directed to the white-collar criminals who constitute the illegitimate opportunity structure for car theft.

The theory of moral hazard was also an important metaphor, though the participants hardly spoke of it in such high-flown terms. Insurance companies had been happy to take (higher) insurance premiums that valued cars well beyond their worth. The New South Wales practice was to insure on "agreed value" rather than "market value." This did engender a temptation to leave cars so that it was easy for them to be stolen (or to actively arrange for them to be stolen) when owners wanted to deal with a financial problem by cashing out their overinsured asset. The preventive remedy here was the insurance companies' undertaking to move the industry away from agreed value toward market value.

Finally, some simple crime prevention theory (Clarke 1993) was instructive. The marking of car engines with compliance plates and engine numbers was supposed to prevent theft by aiding traceability. But the context of the Sydney car-theft market was one where cars were being stolen substantially for parts that were not marked. So the vehicle manufacturers agreed at the roundtable discussion to move to individual marking of separate salable parts. In addition to the opportunity, crime prevention, and moral-hazard theories that illuminate the policy choices in this context, the whole process of the roundtable problem solving was explicitly motivated by the theoretical metaphor of "community policing," to which the New South Wales police hierarchy had been converted several years earlier. The total policy package may have worked. By mid-1992, the number of motor vehicle thefts in New South Wales had dropped by one third, compared with the level prevailing during 1990 (Police Board of New South Wales 1992, p. 25).

The metaphors of criminological theory do get translated into the commonsense thinking of police practitioners. I am regularly surprised at how often I even discover my own (not-so-straightforward) metaphor of reintegrative shaming being imaginatively applied by Australian police. This makes me increasingly suspicious that I got the idea from them more than they got it from me. Criminology is like that: theory plagiarizes and reconceptualizes the common sense of practitioners. The implication of this is that accomplishing the level of theoretical literacy required to make the strategy advanced in this article work is not as difficult as it might seem.

The positivist priority of discovering which of a number of competing theories explains more variance does not seem centrally important to me. What is important is that criminology develop a range of theories that are sometimes useful. Practitioners can then scan through the list of useful theories to see which supplies a revealing metaphor in the particular problem context. Naturally, this will often be different theories from the ones the positivists say explain most variance across sets of decontextualized cases. In the world of problem solving that matters, it is contextualized usefulness that counts, not decontextualized statistical power.

Usually, as in the Sydney car-theft problem solving, there will be multiple competing theories that supply useful interpretive metaphors. The crime is, at the same time, a seizing of an illegitimate opportunity, a response to blocked legitimate opportunity, taking advantage of a moral hazard, an assertion of macho independence, and so on. The art (rather than the science) of applied criminology is the gift of being able to perceive multiple theoretical significances in a practical problem, thus bringing the practitioner to a nuanced understanding of the problem. This nuanced understanding, seeing the problem in many ways at once, seeing it through different theoretical prisms, enables an integrated strategy of problem solving.

REENTER POSITIVIST CRIMINOLOGY

Traditional positivist criminology has an extremely important prior role in this process. This is, first, the role of demonstrating which theories are nonsense. Many theories tend to consistent irrelevance or to revealing more falsity than truth. In other words, we should want the discipline to help limit the number of theories scanned by practitioners to theories that explain significant amounts of variance a fair proportion of the time. Positivist criminology can help by locating which theories have some partial explanatory power some of the time and which theories are best not to clutter our thinking because they rarely explain anything. Of course, even prior to this empirical sifting, there is a need to weed out theories that are logically incoherent, based on concepts that cannot be identified in the world, or infertile (making no new predictions that other, better theories have not already made).

Second, for an applied discipline like criminology, positivist methods have the crucial role of testing key policy claims of the theory. But in light of what I said earlier about the limits of positivist testing of a policy across a large number of decontextualized cases, I want to reformulate the role for positivist science so it serves those concerned to find integrated, contextualized policy packages. Consider demand-reduction theories of drug control as alternatives to supply reduction through criminal enforcement.[4] Within the narrow ahistoricism of positivist social science, researchers wax pessimistic about the impact of drug education programs of very short duration because of the rather small or insignificant preventive effects they secure (Ogborne 1988; Wragg 1987, 1990). But surely any credible demand-side strategy must be integrated and long term? It stretches credibility to hope that an education program run for young people over days or weeks could overwhelm influences mediated by peers with whom they interact for many hours every day, by adult role models they see daily, and by a continuous barrage of media influences. The credible integrated strategy here involves political and social movement leadership to transform the culture, in the long haul, away from a drug use culture, away from a hard-drinking culture in which smoking is a symbol of adulthood, a culture wherein a little pill can be found for every ill. This means an integrated long-term strategy to move toward a society whose citizens just don't want to solve their problems through drugs. Some societies, of course, are already somewhat like this; not all societies have drug problems like those of the United States. The historical record shows that such transformation need not be pie in the sky. In Australia, a long period of sharply falling alcohol consumption from the mid-19th century corresponds with the rise of the temperance movement, and the long rise in consumption from the 1930s to the 1970s corresponds with the decline and virtual demise of the old temperance movement (cf. Powell 1988). This decline of the temperance movement occurred after its international leadership in the United States made the tactical mistake of supporting prohibition, a supply-side addition to their demand-reduction strategy, which disintegrated and discredited their total policy package.

In the context of aspiring to change via long historical struggles in which social movements and states seek to transform cultural attitudes toward drugs, what is the relevance of piecemeal, necessarily short-term, positive evaluation of drug education programs? There is a relevance, I think. The long-term reformer should not be discouraged by nihilistic positivists who summarize short-term evaluation literatures with the conclusion that most of these things make no difference most of the time. But one should definitely be discouraged in one's support for a particular element of an integrated long-term strategy if all the evaluation studies show that in the short term, this element never makes any significant difference. One would be wise to be in the business of only supporting elements of a policy package that have some empirical basis of support from the positivist evaluation literature. But one should not become a nothing works nihilist in the face of some short-term interventions being found to have no significant effect whereas others do. One will take heart from the fact that a short-term intervention can sometimes effect change when the theory is that only long and deep cultural change will turn the problem around. One will delve into the positivist studies to grasp what clues they can offer about the contexts for success versus failure for which we might watch in the process of contextual implementation.

In summary, positivist criminology can do two things for us. First, it can rule out certain theories as making consistently unsupportable claims. Second, it can tell us which interventions sometimes show evidence of working, even if they do not always work. It will never deliver us a unified explanatory edifice that is any more than a very partial, crude, and flawed explanation of the world.

INTEGRATED, CONTEXTUAL, DYNAMIC IMPLEMENTATION

Let me now illustrate the scientific process I have in mind with deterrence theory. Empirical tests of deterrence theories lead most criminologists to the conclusion that deterrence theories have relatively weak explanatory power (see, for example, the reviews in Zimring and Hawkins 1973; Gibbs 1975; Blumstein, Cohen, and Nagin 1978; Tittle 1980; Roth, Scholz, and Witte 1989). Moreover, specific interventions in policy to increase deterrence mostly, though not invariably, fail to reduce crime. Consistent with the analysis I have outlined above, we should not react to this literature as nothing works nihilists about deterrent interventions. I take the (mostly negative) literature to show that deterrence can have an effect, but that the positivist literature has not revealed a lot about the contexts in which this is true and the contexts in which it is not. The literature does give a few limited clues, for example, about the greater contextual significance of informal as opposed to formal controls (Burkett and Jensen 1975; Kraut 1975; Anderson, Chiricos, and Waldo 1977; Meier and Johnson 1977; Jensen and Erickson 1978; Akers, Krohn, Lanza-Kaduce, and Radosevich 1979; Tittle 1980; Meier 1982; Paternoster, Saltzman, Waldo, & Chiricos 1983a, 1983b; Bishop 1984; Williams 1985; Paternoster and Iovanni 1986; Paternoster 1989; Nagin and Paternoster 1991; Grasmick, Bursik, and Kinsey 1991; Grasmick, Bursik, and Arneklev 1993; but see Piliavin, Gartner, Thornton, and Matsueda 1986; Williams and Hawkins 1989; Simpson 1992) and about contexts in which deterrent threats can foster defiance (Sherman 1992) or stigmatization (Makkai and Braithwaite 1993) that actually increase crime.

What I am concluding is that, weak as it is, there is enough positivist support for deterrence to take it seriously as a theoretical option to scan during the design of an integrated strategy for dealing with a particular crime problem. More provocatively, I want to reject nihilist positivism even more strongly by saying that even if a positivist test of deterrence theory fails to support it with regard to that particular crime problem, deterrence is still a theory the policy analyst should be scanning in designing an integrated policy strategy. Toni Makkai, Valerie Braithwaite, Diane Gibson, Anne Jenkins, David Ermann, and I have been involved with just such a problem in our research on compliance with quality of care standards by Australian nursing homes. Our positivist research shows that perceptual deterrence models do not explain compliance (Braithwaite and Makkai 1991; Makkai and Braithwaite 1993). Yet the careful in-context fieldwork we have done observing regulatory encounters shows that the across-context regressions obscure many dynamic contexts where deterrent threats have moments of considerable force and others where deterrent threats get managers' backs up, hardening determination to resist.

The regression findings imply that it surely would be folly to seek to improve compliance with nursing home laws based on a purely deterrent strategy. Equally, the qualitative research suggests designing an integrated strategy for improving compliance that includes discretion to swing in with deterrent threats when this is contextually appropriate and to deliver on the threats when this is needed. As consultants, what we have done for the Australian government is design such an integrated strategy (Braithwaite, Makkai, Braithwaite, and Gibson 1993). It is a dynamic approach that seeks to avert most of the counterproductive contexts for deterrent threats by always trying persuasion, appeals to professionalism, and caring for the patients as first strategies. If this continues to fail, nursing homes are banned from admitting new residents until they can show that they are capable of acceptable care for them and so that they can concentrate all their energies on putting things right for the residents they already have. Although this is presented as a protective, preventive measure, it also has clear deterrent implications, which can be communicated without the kind of threat that incurs resistance. When this fails, escalation of deterrent threats right up to the ultimate incapacitative measure of corporate capital punishment (closing the home) is mobilized when social control fails at each lower level of an enforcement pyramid. The theory of such a dynamic enforcement pyramid has been outlined in more detail elsewhere (Ayres and Braithwaite 1992). Therein deterrence is integrated into a strategy that tries persuasion first, then deterrence when that fails, then incapacitation when deterrence fails.

One problem with deterrence theory in criminology has been that it has tended to be limited to what the international relations theorists call passive deterrence, neglecting the possibility that when passive deterrence initially fails, more active kinds of deterrence based on graduated escalation might yet succeed (Schelling 1966, p. 78). Whether deterrence is working in a particular context is not something one assumes on the basis of prior positivist research; it is something one discovers by observing specific reactions during regulatory encounters.

The key ideas here are therefore to move on from (a) accepting deterrence as a theory that can be relevant in some contexts but not others to (b) designing an integrated strategy in which deterrence finds a place that is contingent on its contextual relevance, where (c) that strategy is dynamic and responsive to how the players of an unfolding crime control game react to events as they occur.

TOWARD A MORE PRODUCTIVE
CULTURE OF EVALUATION

It follows that the most useful kind of evaluation research focuses on entire integrated strategies evaluated in a stream of time. Quantitative skills in interrupted time series analysis can be relevant to this kind of evaluation, assessing changes in levels of crime that occur as different elements of a package swing into action in different ways during a history of interventions. At least equally relevant, however, are the skills of the historian and of the qualitative fieldworker. The historian, unlike the positivist, sees the future as requiring a different explanatory frame from the past, always flowing in a stream of time from the past, where the past has predictive value of sorts, but where that predictive value is compromised by the way time always changes context.

This historical attitude has it that the situation evaluated in a previous positivist study may be analogous, but that analogies are dangerous in learning the lessons of any history, including the history of criminological research. So the evaluator with an historical attitude always asks both how is this situation different and how is it similar to the one studied in the positivist research. It will always be different in time and place and almost always in nation if one is a non-U.S. criminologist. Concomitantly, there will be major cultural differences in the people involved.

Criminologists interested in making policy prescriptions in a particular sociohistorical context must get their hands dirty—go out and talk to the people involved, observe them doing their job, so that they can appreciate the way differences in time, place, and culture matter. The evaluator of an integrated solution should do the same. Then the evaluator can write a rich report on what was special about this context, particularly if it is one where a dramatic success or an unexpected failure occurs. This, in turn, enables other criminologists to discern how such a dramatic success or failure is different and similar to the implementation context they confront.

My advocacy is of rich, detailed descriptions of integrated strategies, especially where the integrated strategies would seem to have been successful. This is crucial to my remedy for nothing works nihilism. We should be looking for criminological equivalents to international relations classics like Allison's 1971 book on the Cuban missile crisis.[5]

I am amazed at some of the obvious success stories of integrated social control strategies that have been completely ignored by researchers. Millions of dollars are spent on researching drug control, but no one in Australia has fully studied the integrated strategy used to deal with what was, apart from alcohol and tobacco, the biggest drug problem of my parents' generation, a

392   JOURNAL OF RESEARCH IN CRIME AND DELINQUENCY

drug to which both my parents at one time were addicted and which killed my aunt. This drug was a combination of phenacetin, aspirin, and a megadose of caffeine (over-the-counter brandnames Bex and Vincents). It was marketed particularly aggressively on radio and television during the 1950s to mothers as a pick-me-up to deal with the stresses of family life.[6] Why is this integrated strategy worth studying? Because it was completely successful. You cannot buy this drug in Australia today and, as far as I know, there are no addicts left, though many ended their addiction through death. The police were not key actors in this integrated drug control strategy. The key actors were a social movement against the drug led by the Australian Kidney Foundation, certain specialist colleges of the medical profession, certain journalists who campaigned against the drug, and health regulators who eventually banned advertising and negotiated agreements with the manufacturers to withdraw the product from the market in a way that gave them time to diversify into safer drugs. You can actually still buy Bex and Vincents in Australia, but the addictive and destructive phenacetin-aspirin-caffeine combination has long been removed from their formulations.

Progress in learning how to better control the problems we call crime will come through studies of such integrated strategies, which combine analyses of quantitative outcomes, historical methods, and interview-based fieldwork. In every country, I suspect such success stories are to be found. But like the Bex and Vincents campaign, like the Sydney car-theft campaign, like cleaning up the Australian nursing home industry (Braithwaite et al. 1993), like the current campaign against insurance industry fraud in Australia (Fisse and Braithwaite forthcoming; Braithwaite 1993), criminal enforcement is often not one of the most important ingredients in an integrated strategy that reduces crime. In other integrated strategies, like the successful efforts against drunk driving in Australia during the past decade (Homel 1988), criminal enforcement has been central within an integrated strategy. Homel's book on drunk driving is close to the kind of evaluation I am advocating here, though I would have liked more historical and qualitative work on the social movement and informal drinking-group contributions to the success story.

Maximum benefit will flow from this kind of transformation of criminology if the process of learning becomes more internationalized. There is no more barren view than that you only need attend to research findings from your own country because results from other lands will not translate at home. My story is that results from your own country don't translate either: they are best viewed as analogies that demand systematic listing of differences and similarities to the sociohistorical context in which you propose to use the findings. There is virtue, not fault, in opening our horizons to integrated strategies that work in contexts that are massively different. This is precisely how leaps of inductive insight relevant to here-and-now contexts occur. Horizon-broadening difference opens up our policy imaginations to new ways of fashioning interventions, ways rather different from anything that has ever been done anywhere else before.

AN INTEGRATED STRATEGY
FOR REFORMING CRIMINOLOGY

A summary of where we have gotten so far is that the best chance of fashioning an intervention to deal with a crime problem arises when:

1. The policymaker has a commonsense grasp of how to use good criminological theories as metaphors, usually applying multiple theoretical metaphors, arriving at a nuanced understanding of the crime problem by seeing it as many things at once.
2. The policymaker reads literature reviews on the results of the best positivist research. This reading enables the policymaker to drop some theories off the list of those scanned under point 1. It gives one clues on what kinds of interventions can work some of the time, even if not most of the time.
3. The policymaker engages with the people living and working in the context in which one wishes to intervene. The qualitative understanding one gets from talking with these people enables a listing of the ways this context is different from and similar to the contexts in which successful interventions (point 2) have been previously applied, based on the common theoretical relevance (point 1) one apprehends in the context.
4. One designs (with stakeholders) an integrated strategy that is redundantly responsive to the theoretical relevances one sees in point 1, the positivist findings one understands in point 2, and the contextual differences one discerns in point 3. One has acquired wisdom in the design of integrated strategies by reading the histories and evaluations of integrated strategies in point 5.
5. Where it seems there might be lessons from the implementation of the integrated strategy, the policymaker writes down the history of the strategy's discovery and unfolding, the outcome data at different points of this unfolding, and the perceptions of key players at different points during the implementation dynamic. This enables professional researchers to come in and do different kinds of evaluations of the entire integrated strategy process.

Perhaps this seems a demanding set of expectations of policymakers. This is only true if we view policymakers as individuals in the abstracted way I have found it convenient to present them. For civic republicans like me, policy-making is a communal process of dialogue, wherein different mem-

394   JOURNAL OF RESEARCH IN CRIME AND DELINQUENCY

bers of a policy-making community can be relied on for different kinds of knowledge, insight, and creativity.

So what is the integrated reform agenda for criminology that follows from opting for this approach to fashioning integrated strategies to crime problems? It is:

1. Take criminological theory more seriously. Don't have the view that theory is a waste of time because it does not deliver master explanations that account for massive proportions of variance. Theories that are wrong most of the time can be extremely useful. Don't be shy about theory of very general sweep. The more general the theory, the more likely it is to be worth keeping on the list of theories that merit scanning by policy practitioners.
2. Put positivist criminology in its place. Reject the prescriptions of the critical theorists and postmodernists who want to write off positivist criminology.[7] Nurture in particular the most rigorous positivist criminology, such as random-allocation policy experiments and big cohort studies. But reject the view that the ultimate value in science is discovering that single unified set of law-like statements that offers the best explanation of the phenomenon.
3. Nurture the contextual art of identifying similarities and differences from other contexts where important research discoveries have occurred. Nurture historical criminology. Nurture a cross-cultural criminology of discovery and diagnosis of past and present successful integrated crime control strategies from around the world.
4. Shift research resources to policymaker-researcher teams who design long-term integrated strategies and who then undertake a combination of historical, qualitative fieldwork and quantitative evaluations across the (long) time span of these multifaceted assaults on the problem.
5. Give the design of integrated dynamic strategies a greater status in criminology than the design of static explanatory theories.

What I am describing here is a very different set of scientific practices from contemporary criminology. The latter I see as consisting of three main groups of practitioners who essentially spin the field in circles. One group is a small class of explanatory theorists of crime; the second is a large class of positivist researchers who test the static explanatory models generated by the first group or who just do atheoretical description; the third group is a rabble of critical theorists peddling a plethora of mutually incompatible critiques, but unified in their desire to tear down the more conservative contributions coming from the first two groups. Of course, there are anthropologists, historians, and a good number of other misfits who don't squeeze into any of these groups. But in the broad, the discipline does not go anywhere worth going because the first group develops static theories that the second group endlessly, repetitively discovers to be mostly not true. The third group (without offering much in the way of an alternative) endlessly and repetitively critiques the first two for bothering with their whole enterprise. From the ashes of this cycle of theory, refutation, and derision, every now and then a new theorist manages to dress up in new clothes an old theory that was demolished in some previous cycle of destruction. And the wheel turns again. My critique is that the first two groups are entrapped in a scientific culture that persists with a pretense (that most of the participants know to be a delusion) of the pursuit of a single unified set of law-like statements that offers the best explanation of the phenomenon. My enterprise has been to give these two groups a more useful role (see points 1 and 2 above) in a criminology that moves forward to making a contribution to reducing crime instead of moving in circles.

I have said very little about the third group. They have an absolutely important role that begins with note 1 to the first sentence of this article. Critical theorists keep us all on our toes with regard to our presuppositions. What is this crime that is worth preventing? When is defiance of the state something to be nurtured rather than crushed? Whose interests are being served by this reform process we are being offered? Why even talk of this social problem as crime? The latter is often the most important question to ask. My theoretical bias is that the most important crime control accomplishments of integrated strategies flow from those parts of the strategies that react to crime rather in the way that abolitionists would have it—as troubles, problems of living, mistakes, conflicts—as matters for dialogue. Those of us who are republicans and intellectual pluralists truly do believe that it is good for us to be regularly smitten by these kinds of critiques. Hence I want a criminology wherein the scholarship and praxis of those who work on each of my five agenda items are continually under attack from critical theorists. Indeed, sometimes I would want to join in on these attacks. The blood sport of critique is both socially productive and a good recreational activity for those of us who normally toil at the more frustrating and compromising work of reform. But I would also like to tempt some critical theorists to have a go at developing contextual, integrated strategies of dynamic intervention. If nothing else, the experience would make them better critics.

CONCLUSION

In other publications with various colleagues, I have begun to set down in more detail what dynamic integrated strategies might look like to deal with occupational health and safety violations in Australia (Braithwaite and Grabosky 1985; Braithwaite, Grabosky, and Fisse 1986), Australian nursing home regulation (Braithwaite et al. 1993), Australian antitrust and consumer

396 JOURNAL OF RESEARCH IN CRIME AND DELINQUENCY

protection (Fisse and Braithwaite 1993; Braithwaite 1993), domestic violence and rape (Braithwaite and Daly forthcoming), and Australian juvenile justice (Braithwaite and Mugford forthcoming). In this article, I have made all too brief reference to integrated strategies for dealing with drug abuse, drunk driving, and motor vehicle theft. Doubtless the descriptions have been tantalizing rather than convincing.

The meta-theory of dynamic and contextual response in this work is that there is no right or best policy for responding to a particular type of crime that can be revealed by positivist science. What is the best strategy depends on the history of other strategies that have succeeded or failed. I illustrated with the enforcement pyramid for Australian nursing home regulation: persuasion is a better strategy than deterrence until persuasion fails; deterrence is better than persuasion when the trust implied by persuasion has been abused; incapacitation is a better strategy than deterrence when deterrence has failed.

The idea of combining competing theories into integrated strategies is not just a matter of hedging bets—try one after the other until you find one that works. There should be a theory of integration that justifies an ordering of the strategies. For example, there are three grounds for trying persuasion before deterrence in the contexts I have mentioned:

1. Persuasion is cheaper.
2. Persuasion is more respecting of persons and of their freedom, being based on dialogue rather than coercion.
3. "Defiance" reactions that exacerbate crime (Sherman 1992) are more likely when deterrent threats are the port of first call.

Hence the idea of integrated strategies is a temporal sequencing that minimizes the weaknesses of each theory by covering them with the strengths of another. It follows that criminologists need to become theoretically eclectic rather than theoretically committed. The appreciative understanding that Bateson (1972) calls "systemic wisdom" comes from openness to playing with multiple theoretical metaphors. With such systemic wisdom, criminologists can "frame interventions that attempt to influence the pattern of relations defining a system, rather than attempting to manipulate artificial 'causes' and 'effects' " (Morgan 1986, p. 254). Criminological research can be reformed to inform the framing and reframing of such systemic interventions.

NOTES

1. This article proceeds from the belief that most of the time it is a noble enterprise to be a criminologist and to seek to make a contribution to reducing crime, given the way most crimes

are defined in Western democracies. This is not to deny that there are ways of being a criminologist that are ignoble, that there are kinds of crime that one should not struggle to reduce, and that there are ways of doing it that are morally deplorable. My position on when and how it is good to be in the crime control game can be found elsewhere (Braithwaite and Pettit 1990).

2. See, for example, Vasquez (1990). But note that the papers in Section II of the collection, "Debates Over Methods and Theory," show that there is an embattled minority tradition in the field of positivist quantitative scholarship.

3. For example, reporting the truth of an insider trading practice on the stock market will cause other investors to adjust their behavior so that the insider trading is no longer profitable. The most lucrative criminal practices in any economy will be those whose truth has yet to be recognized, a truth that is therefore yet to be incorporated into criminological theory.

4. I am grateful for a conversation with Alfred Blumstein, which helped clarify my thinking on this issue.

5. Allison analyzed the Cuban crisis by, in turn, comprehending the players of this deadly game in terms of a rational actor model, an organizational process model, and a bureaucratic politics model.

6. See the important feminist study of the phenomenon by Hennessy (1993). Unfortunately for present purposes, this book is not primarily about the successful control strategies used to tackle the problem, but rather about the gendered promotion of the drug.

7. In speaking of criminological theories as supplying metaphors and positivist research as analogies, I don't want to be read as a postmodernist who doubts that truth and falsity can be found in the conclusions of theory and research. Even when they are true in the circumstances of their testing, they are still most productively viewed as metaphors and analogies when we attempt to apply them to a different context.

REFERENCES

Akers, R. L., M. D. Krohn, L. Lanza-Kaduce, and M. Radosevich. 1979. "Social Learning and Deviant Behavior: A Specific Test of a General Theory." *American Sociological Review* 83:114-53.

Allison, Graham T. 1971. *The Essence of Decision: Explaining the Cuban Missile Crisis.* Boston: Little, Brown.

Anderson, Linda S., Theodore G. Chiricos, and Gordon P. Waldo. 1977. "Formal and Informal Sanctions: A Comparison of Deterrent Effects." *Social Problems* 25:103-14.

Ayres, Ian and John Braithwaite. 1992. *Responsive Regulation: Transcending the Deregulation Debate.* New York: Oxford.

Bateson, Gregory. 1972. *Steps to and Ecology of Mind.* New York: Ballantine.

Bishop, D. M. 1984. "Legal and Extralegal Barriers to Delinquency: A Panel Analysis." *Criminology* 22:403-19.

Blumstein, Alfred, Jacqueline Cohen, and Daniel Nagin, eds. 1978. *Deterrence and Incapacitation: Estimating the Effects of Criminal Sanctions on Crime Rates.* Washington, DC: National Academy of Sciences.

Braithwaite, John. 1993. "Corporate Crime and Republican Criminological Praxis." Paper to the Queens University Conference on Corporate Crime.

Braithwaite, John and Kathleen Daly. Forthcoming. "Masculinities, Crimes Against Women and Communitarian Control." In *Just Boys Doing Business: Men, Masculinity and Crime,* edited by Tim Newburn and Betsy Stanko. London: Routledge.

398   JOURNAL OF RESEARCH IN CRIME AND DELINQUENCY

Braithwaite, John and Peter Grabosky. 1985. *Occupational Health and Safety Enforcement in Australia.* Canberra: Australian Institute of Criminology.

Braithwaite, John, Peter Grabosky, and Brent Fisse. 1986. "Occupational Health and Safety Enforcement Guidelines." Report to the Victorian Department of Labour, Melbourne.

Braithwaite, John and Toni Makkai. 1991. "Testing an Expected Utility Model of Corporate Deterrence." *Law and Society Review* 25:7-41.

Braithwaite, John, Toni Makkai, Valerie Braithwaite, and Diane Gibson. 1993. *Raising the Standard: Resident Centred Nursing Home Regulation in Australia.* Canberra: Australian Government Publishing Service.

Braithwaite, John and Stephen Mugford. Forthcoming. "Conditions of Successful Reintegration Ceremonies: Dealing With Juvenile Offenders." *British Journal of Criminology.*

Braithwaite, John and Philip Pettit. 1990. *Not Just Deserts: A Republican Theory of Criminal Justice.* Oxford: Oxford University Press.

Bull, Hedley. 1966. "International Theory: The Case for a Classical Approach." *World Politics* 18:361-77.

Burkett, S. R. and E. L. Jensen. 1975. "Conventional Ties, Peer Influence and the Fear of Apprehension: A Study of Adolescent Marijuana Use." *Sociological Quarterly* 16:522-33.

Clarke, Ronald V. 1993. *Situational Crime Prevention: Successful Case Studies.* Albany, NY: Harrow & Heston.

Fisse, Brent and John Braithwaite. Forthcoming. *Corporations, Crime and Accountability.* Sydney: Cambridge University Press.

Gibbs, Jack. 1975. *Crime, Punishment and Deterrence.* New York: Elsevier.

Grasmick, Harold G., Robert J. Bursik, Jr., and Bruce J. Arneklev. 1993. "Reduction in Drunk Driving as a Response to Increased Threats of Shame, Embarrassment, and Legal Sanctions." *Criminology* 31:41-67.

Grasmick, Harold G., Robert J. Bursik, and Karyl A. Kinsey. 1991. "Shame and Embarrassment as Deterrents to Noncompliance With the Law: The Case of an Antilittering Campaign." *Environment and Behavior* 23:233-51.

Handler, Joel F. 1992 "Postmodernism, Protest, and the New Social Movements." *Law and Society Review* 26:697-732.

Hennessy, Eileen. 1993. *A Cup of Tea, a Bex and a Good Lie Down.* Townsville: James Cook University Press.

Homel, Ross. 1988. *Policing and Punishing the Drinking Driver: A Study of General and Specific Deterrence.* New York: Springer-Verlag.

Jensen, Gary F. and Maynard Erickson. 1978. "The Social Meaning of Sanctions." In *Crime Law and Sanctions: Theoretical Perspectives*, edited by M. Krohn and R. Akers. Beverly Hills, CA: Sage.

Juvenile Justice Advisory Council of NSW. 1993. *Green Paper, Future Directions for Juvenile Justice in New South Wales.* Sydney: Juvenile Justice Advisory Council of NSW.

Kraut, Robert E. 1975. "Deterrent and Definitional Influences on Shoplifting." *Social Problems* 23:358-68.

Makkai, Toni and John Braithwaite. 1993. "The Dialectics of Corporate Deterrence." Unpublished paper.

Meier, Robert F. 1982. "Jurisdictional Differences in Deterring Marijuana Use." *Journal of Drug Issues* 12:61-71.

Meier, Robert F. and Weldon T. Johnson 1977. "Deterrence as Social Control: The Legal and Extra-Legal Production of Conformity." *American Sociological Review* 42:292-304.

Morgan, Gareth. 1986. *Images of Organization.* Beverly Hills, CA: Sage.

Nagin, Daniel S. and Raymond Paternoster. 1991. "The Preventive Effects of the Perceived Risk of Arrest: Testing an Expanded Conception of Deterrence." *Criminology* 29:561-87.

Neustadt, Richard E. and Ernest R. May. 1986. *Thinking in Time: The Uses of History for Decision Makers*. New York: Free Press.

Ogborne, Allan C. 1988. "School-Based Educational Programs to Prevent the Personal Use of Psychoactive Drugs for Non-Medical Purposes." *Australian Drug and Alcohol Review* 7:305-14.

Paternoster, Raymond. 1989. "Decisions to Participate in and Desist From Four Types of Common Delinquency: Deterrence and the Rational Choice Perspective." *Law and Society Review* 23:7-40.

Paternoster, Raymond and Leeann Iovanni. 1986. "The Deterrent Threat of Perceived Severity: A Re-examination." *Social Forces* 64:751-77.

Paternoster, Raymond, Linda Saltzman. Gordon Waldo, and Theodore Chiricos. 1983a. "Estimating Perceptual Stability and Deterrent Effects: The Role of Perceived Legal Punishment in the Inhibition of Criminal Involvement." *Journal of Criminal Law and Criminology* 74:270-97.

―――. 1983b. "Perceived Risk and Social Control: Do Sanctions Really Deter?" *Law and Society Review* 17:457-79.

Piliavin, Irving, Rosemary Gartner, Craig Thornton, and Ross C. Matsueda. 1986. "Crime, Deterrence and Rational Choice." *American Sociological Review* 51:101-19.

Police Board of New South Wales. 1992. *Annual Report 1991-92*. Sydney: Police Board.

Powell, Keith C. 1988. *Drinking and Alcohol in Colonial Australia 1788-1901 for the Eastern Colonies. National Campaign Against Drug Abuse*. Monograph Series No. 3. Canberra: Australian Government Publishing Service.

Roth, Jeffrey A., John T. Scholz, and Anne Dryden Witte. 1989. *Tax Compliance: An Agenda for Research*, Vols. 1 and 2. Philadelphia: University of Pennsylvania Press.

Schelling, Thomas C. 1966. *Arms and Influence*. New Haven: Yale University Press.

Sherman, Lawrence W. 1992. *Policing Domestic Violence: Experiments and Dilemmas*. New York: Free Press.

Simpson, Sally. 1992. "Corporate Crime Deterrence and Corporate Control Policies: Views from the Inside." In *Essays in White-Collar Crime*, edited by K. Schlegel and D. Weisburd. Boston: Northeastern University Press.

Tittle, Charles R. 1980. *Sanctions and Social Deviance*. New York: Praeger.

Vasquez, John A. 1990. *Classics of International Relations*. 2nd ed. Englewood Cliffs, NJ: Prentice-Hall.

Williams, F. P., III. 1985. "Deterrence and Social Control: Rethinking the Relationship." *Journal of Criminal Justice* 13:141-54.

Williams, Kirk and Richard Hawkins. 1989. "The Meaning of Arrest for Wife Assault." *Criminology* 27:163-81.

Wragg, Jeffrey. 1987. "The Development of a Model for Drug Education: Programme Implications Derived from Past Education Studies and Known Causative Factors." *Drug Education Journal of Australia* 1:1-5.

―――. 1990. "The Longitudinal Evaluation of a Primary School Drug Education Program: Did It Work?" *Drug Education Journal of Australia* 4:33-44.

Zimring, Franklin E. and Gordon J. Hawkins 1973. *Deterrence: The Legal Threat in Crime Control*. Chicago: University of Chicago Press.

[9]
Transnational Regulation of the Pharmaceutical Industry

ABSTRACT: While the pharmaceutical industry arguably has the worst record of serious corporate crime of any industry, international law evasion rather than outright law violation has been the biggest problem in the industry. To understand how these problems can be and are being brought under control, a legal-pluralist analysis is needed that decenters criminal enforcement by the state. Consumer and professional activism and a variety of levels of self-regulation in combination with state, regional, and international regulation are all important to understanding how progress is possible. Creative work within this web of controls can actually transform lowest-common-denominator regulation into highest-common-factor regulation and self-regulation when actors are capable of thinking strategically in world-system terms.

IN 1984, I published a book on the serious and rather widespread nature of corporate crime in the international pharmaceutical industry.[1] Since that book was published, there has been some improvement in the social control brought to bear against some of the problems I identified. The nature of this progress will be discussed in the present article. The interesting thing is that there has been little progress with criminal enforcement, which remains exceedingly rare in all nations of the world in spite of the fact that serious criminal conduct seems more common in the pharmaceutical industry than in perhaps any industrial sector in the world economy.[2] Implications of this situation for a legal-pluralist approach to the control of international corporate crime will be discussed. First, however, the nature of the problem must be described.

THE PROBLEM

In *Corporate Crime in the Pharmaceutical Industry*, I concluded that bribery is probably a larger problem in the pharmaceutical industry than in almost any other industry.[3] Of the 20 largest American pharmaceutical companies, 19 had been embroiled in bribery problems during the decade before the publication of the book. There was evidence of almost every conceivable type of actor who could strategically affect the interests of pharmaceutical companies receiving bribes from them: health ministers, government price control officials, purchasers for government pharmaceutical benefits systems, tax officials, police, customs officers, hospital administrators, health inspectors, physicians—and so the list went on. Product-safety offenses such as the sale of impure, overstrength, out-of-date, or nonsterile products were also shown to be widespread.[4] Antitrust offenses kept some of the postwar wonder drugs financially out of the reach of most of the world's population for many years, causing countless lives to be lost needlessly.[5] Misrepresentations in printed advertising and by word of mouth by sales representatives were common offenses in the pharmaceutical industry, with particularly serious consequences.[6] The pharmaceutical industry also had its share of tax offenders and fraudsters who duped shareholders and creditors.[7] But the most serious corporate crimes in the pharmaceutical industry were, and still are, in the safety testing of drugs.

Cases were documented of rats and monkeys in drug trials developing terrible symptoms like tumors and blindness and being replaced by healthy animals.[8] Cases of reincarnated rats were documented—rats that died reappeared later in the data as living animals. There were also many cases involving physicians who were paid handsomely to do clinical trials on humans for new drugs.

---

1. John Braithwaite, *Corporate Crime in the Pharmaceutical Industry* (London: Routledge & Kegan Paul, 1984).
2. Ibid., pp. 14-17.
3. Ibid., pp. 11-50.

4. Ibid., pp. 110-58.
5. Ibid., pp. 159-203.
6. Ibid., pp. 204-44.
7. Ibid., pp. 279-89.
8. Ibid., pp. 51-109.

Some had terrible misfortunes on the eve of Food and Drug Administration (FDA) audits of the quality of the data they had collected in support of new drug applications. For example, Dr. James Scheiner of Fairfax, Virginia, who did experiments for Johnson and Johnson, had his office vandalized the night before an FDA audit—the mindless vandals dumping the records relating to the studies to be audited into a whirlpool bath. Dr. Francois Savery, who had earned a fortune testing drugs for Hoffman-La Roche and other leading companies, suffered the catastrophe of accidentally dropping his data overboard while out in a rowboat. Unfortunately, a U.S. court did not believe him; he was sentenced to five years probation for felony fraud. Regrettably, however, safety-testing fraud remains a serious problem, with new allegations involving leading companies and leading researchers continuing to emerge repeatedly.

THE TRANSNATIONAL NATURE OF THE PROBLEM

The internationalized nature of corporate crime in the pharmaceutical industry makes criminal convictions difficult to obtain. The offenses we are discussing are complex to start with, before one adds the problem of international jurisdictional tangles. There is the complexity of the books—paper trails through the finances and the raw scientific data that are difficult to follow. Then there is the scientific complexity of cutting-edge technology. Not many of us are capable of understanding it, certainly not many Federal Bureau of Investigation officers. Then there is

organizational complexity: everyone in the organization has a story as to why the slipups in the system were someone else's responsibility. All of these complexities are to some extent inherent in an international high-technology industry. But pharmaceutical industry informants have explained to me how the complexity is more contrived than inherent. For example, companies generally can get clearly defined internal accountability for things that matter to them. They define accountability clearly for internal purposes on matters like product quality, while setting forth a smokescreen of diffused and confused accountability for projection to the outside world. Three of the U.S. companies I visited a decade ago had "vice presidents responsible for going to jail." Incumbents in these positions explained to me how lines of accountability for purposes of official presentation to the outside world were drawn so that if a head had to go on the chopping block, it would be theirs. After a period of faithful service as the vice president responsible for going to jail, they would be rewarded with promotion sideways to a safe vice presidency.

International complexity is also both inherent and contrived. The bribe from a U.S. company to a Latin American health minister can be arranged so that it is paid in a third country by an intermediary from a fourth country through a Swiss (fifth country) bank account. This is using jurisdictional complexity to make lawbreaking harder to discover and punish. The more fundamental and insidious way that international jurisdictional complexity is used, however, is to evade laws instead of breaking them. International law evasion strategies have reached a high level of sophistication in the pharmaceutical industry.

The paradigmatic law evasion strategy is transfer pricing or profit shifting to avoid tax. A transnational corporation has massive intracorporate sales. Tax liabilities can be avoided by pricing low for intracorporate sales from a subsidiary located in a high-tax country to a subsidiary in a low-tax country and by pricing high when sales are from a low-tax to a high-tax nation. There have been cases where pharmaceutical transnationals have managed to run their worldwide operations at a loss except for a single obscure tax haven, in which massive profits are recorded.[9]

International law evasion in the pharmaceutical industry comes in both cruder and more sophisticated variants than profit shifting. An example of a cruder form of evasion is an impure or understrength product that is forbidden from sale in one country being dumped in another nation with looser laws.[10] With products where there is reason to believe that risks could be high during the experimental stage, initial testing can be done on Third World populations without a practical capacity to sue or to stir up public opinion in the firm's home country.[11] This strategy is often

an element of a much more sophisticated international law evasion strategy whereby the firm develops an integrated plan of where it will do the early testing and where it will do its final testing; where it will seek marketing approval first, second, third, penultimately, and ultimately; and where it will locate manufacturing of the new product. While a remote jungle clinic may be ideal for initial testing, sophisticated final testing will have to be done by internationally reputable clinicians in the First World if the U.S. FDA is to be impressed. As far as marketing is concerned, after the initial testing in a Third World market, an Organization for Economic Cooperation and Development country with permissive standards for approval might be the next choice; Belgium was such a country at the time of my research a decade ago. Belgian approval might then be used to justify entry to a number of large Third World markets such as Brazil. The first manufacturing plant could be located in Belgium, so that Belgium could issue the certificate of free sale required by most Third World nations these days—a certificate indicating that the product is approved for marketing in the country of manufacture.[12] Then the firm might work its way up through First World markets with progressively more demanding registration requirements, using evidence from the safe and efficacious use of the products in the less sophisticated

9. Ibid., p. 285.

10. See David A. Bryan, "Consumer Safety Abroad: Dumping of Dangerous American Products Overseas," *Texas Tech Law Review*, 12:435-58 (1981).

11. Braithwaite, *Corporate Crime in the Pharmaceutical Industry*, p. 266.

12. Rosemary Pierce Wall, "International Trends in New Drug Approval Regulation: The Impact of Pharmaceutical Innovation," *Rutgers Computer and Technology Law Journal*, 10:129 (1984).

markets to gain entry to more sophisticated markets.

Hence using people in the Third World as guinea pigs is part of a rather complex totality. It is a complexity that manifests the rationality of the transnational corporation in finding the line of least resistance to early marketing through the complex jungle of the international regulatory nonsystem. Transnationals use system against nonsystem. While the transnational's worldwide goals are coherent, the goals of the regulatory agencies of the world are conflicting. So the transnational plays one off against the others. Corporations exploit the fact that regulatory goals have coherence only at a national level while corporate coherence is transnational. Transnational corporations also sometimes use—or turn a blind eye to—intermediaries who smuggle a product into countries where marketing approval has not been obtained. But such blatant lawbreaking is not the main game. In fact, it is a rather unimportant one for the transnational pharmaceutical corporation. The main game is the more subtle business of computer-assisted strategizing to find the path of least legal resistance through the international regulatory thicket. Instead of one nation's laws being viewed as an obstacle to be broken through by law violation, compliance with these laws becomes a resource for getting around the spirit of another nation's laws. In other domains of regulatory failure, we see the same paradigm of an international evasion strategy. The Bank of Credit and Commerce International (BCCI) used the laws of each country in which it operated to set itself up in such a way that it was effectively offshore in every country where it operated.[13] Compliance with the letter of some national laws can be used to avoid the spirit of all national laws.

SOME SOLUTIONS

When criminologists discover the great subtlety, sophistication, and power that enable transnational corporations to achieve their objectives with international law evasion strategies, the tendency is to evince a policy analysis of despair. National governments will be outmaneuvered every time by an adversary with a coherent international strategy in a game that is played in an international market. The alternative of an international regulatory agency is pie in the sky, so effective regulation in the public interest is hopeless.

This despair is warranted only if one's vision is restricted to national states as the sole regulators who matter. I will attempt to move to a legal-pluralist model of regulation that helps us to understand why prospects for protecting the public interest from exploitation by pharmaceutical transnationals are actually improving. My contention will be that we must view intervention to protect the public interest in safe and efficacious drugs as possible at a number of levels: national regulatory enforcement, regional regulatory cooperation, international regulatory

13. Albert Reiss, Jr., "Detecting, Investigating and Regulating Business Law-Breaking," in *The Future of Regulatory Enforcement in Australia*, ed. P. Grabosky and J. Braithwaite (Canberra: Australian Institute of Criminology, 1993).

coordination, intrafirm regulation through both individual executive consciences (for example, professional values) and organizational consciences (internal compliance groups), interfirm self-regulation through national and international industry associations as well as through the work of reforming individual firms, and private regulation by product liability suits and consumer activism.

National regulatory enforcement

Criminal law enforcement to deal with the problems of corporate crime in the pharmaceutical industry has been practically nonexistent in every country in the world. This is a result of the technological, jurisdictional, legal, and organizational complexities discussed earlier. Given these realities, consistent criminal enforcement against known corporate lawbreaking is an impossible aspiration. An attraction of a legal-pluralist policy analysis is that the belief that there are constructive ways of solving problems of lawbreaking and evasion without recourse to the criminal law means that we can harbor our criminal enforcement resources for the rather small number of cases where criminal prosecution is the best way to have an impact on the problem. Policymakers who believe that the 100 criminal cases they know about should be investigated and prosecuted with an eye to criminal sanctions set themselves an impossible goal in the domain of complex corporate crime. Policymakers who believe that there are better ways of dealing with 99 out of 100 corporate crimes than taking them to court leave themselves with a superior capacity to concentrate their enforcement resources on the 1 case in 100 that they think is best handled by a criminal prosecution. Then when they score a major enforcement success by concentrating their scarce litigation resources on that 1 case in 100, this success strengthens their hand with the more negotiated approach they adopt toward the other 99 cases.[14]

Within the sphere of national criminal enforcement, there is a capacity for sanctioning that contains a rather more international reach than existing practice has. Brent Fisse and I develop this approach in a book we have almost completed on reforming corporate criminal law.[15] The book offers an approach to the problem of the limits of national law for dealing with conduct in international markets. The approach would force corporate offenders to use their private justice systems to take remedial action. Our accountability model proposes that, having proved the *actus reus* of the offense—for example, that the corporation distributed nonsterile products—the court would invite the corporation to prepare, perhaps with outside consultants, a report indicating the reasons for the offense, those responsible for its execution,

14. The enforcement-pyramid philosophy I am alluding to here is outlined and defended in much more detail in Ian Ayres and John Braithwaite, *Responsive Regulation: Transcending the Deregulation Debate* (New York: Oxford University Press, 1992), chap. 2.

15. This book is tentatively titled *Passing the Buck: Accountability and the Control of Corporate Crime.*

the organizational reforms to be taken to prevent recurrence, and the disciplinary measures to be taken against those responsible. If the package of measures proposed by the corporation in its self-investigation report is unsatisfactory to the court, the judge can allow the ax he or she has been holding over the corporate head to fall. If the package of measures is satisfactory to the needs of justice and community protection, then corporate sanctioning is withheld.

I will not attempt a detailed treatment of all the problems with the proposal and how these can be addressed. Instead, I want to emphasize one advantage of this approach that is relevant to the concern of this article—the limits of national enforcement for dealing with internationalized lawbreaking or law evasion. While the court or a regulatory agency cannot act directly against misconduct beyond its jurisdictional authority, our proposal allows it to hold a national threat over the head of an international corporation, which can use its private justice system to exert some international control. For example, if one reason for an offense occurring in the United States is certain actions of French executives at a French manufacturing plant, the self-investigation report to the U.S. court could recommend disciplinary action by the corporation against the French executives. While our accountability model does not enable an American court to put the French executives behind bars, it can lever private justice measures that cost them their jobs or their annual bonuses or can

interrupt their career paths. These are not inconsequential levers, and national courts could use them against offenses that involve multiple offshore offenders within the employ of a transnational corporation.

There are many other measures that can be taken to improve national regulatory enforcement, but since I have discussed a number of these at length in the earlier book,[16] I shall not dwell upon them here. Rather, the purpose of this article is to show how this is only one of many control options from the perspective of a legal pluralist.

Regional regulatory cooperation

National governments do not have to harmonize their laws perfectly to prevent transnational corporations from playing one country's set of laws off against another's. Indeed, the practical economic constraints of law evasion are often such that a country that sets higher regulatory standards can effectively impose its higher standards on all other countries in a region. This is particularly so when the country is a large and powerful one such as the United States. But strategic government intervention even by small countries can change lowest-common-denominator regulation into highest-common-factor regulation. For example, a Central American regional director for a transnational pharmaceutical company explained to me that when Costa Rica banned a suspected carcinogenic additive in one of its prod-

16. Braithwaite, *Corporate Crime in the Pharmaceutical Industry*, pp. 290-383.

ucts, the company took the additive from all products being distributed in all Central American countries, since the cost of special production runs for the Costa Rican market was prohibitive. Similarly, Costa Rica has long ruled that all disclosures and warnings made on the drug packages and inserts in the country of origin should be identically made in Costa Rica. The same executive explained, "From our point of view, that means they all have to say what we say in [our home country] because the cost of having different packaging for the different Central American countries is too great."

Again, though, because of the capacity of the transnational to shift its activities around the world, there are limits to how high Costa Rica can push up all Central American standards. The same executive noted:

Let me put it this way. It would not be in our interests to locate more of our manufacturing in the United States. For [one of the company's main products], our literature in Europe, Africa, Australia, South America, and so on claims some 10 indications for the product. In the U.S., the FDA approves only 3. We don't want to be forced by Costa Rica and others to suggest only three indications worldwide when we believe in 10.

Even though Costa Rica did not push this European company's standards up to those of the United States, the interesting thing is that they can push them up to some degree across the whole of Central America. Where international conventions fail, little Costa Rica can succeed in harmonizing minimum standards upward.

The Costa Rican situation illustrates the fact that within a region of

the world, harmonization is possible. There are costs for transnationals in playing the international law evasion game—shuffling operations, product, and money around the world is never frictionless. A progressive nation does not always have to bring the whole world with it to defeat international law evasion in its region. The European Community and the European Free Trade Association provide various examples of this, though they also provide examples of nations with higher regulatory standards being pegged back to a regional norm.[17] The Benelux countries (Belgium, the Netherlands, Luxembourg) and the Andean Pact (Peru, Ecuador, Bolivia, Colombia, and Venezuela) both have made progress toward establishing some uniformity in drug regulation within their regions. The United States, like many other nations, has signed a number of bilateral memoranda of understanding. These memoranda bind the FDA and the foreign regulator to common standards for good laboratory practices and preclinical testing.[18]

Overall, the regional harmonization game can be a win-win game for the industry and its consumers. While harmonization cuts down possibilities for international law evasion by industry, having a single uniform set of regulatory requirements also reduces the costs of compliance. Even if consumers in some countries some of the time get products meeting lower standards under harmonized rules, they also get improved protection against products designed

17. Wall, "International Trends in New Drug Approval Regulation," p. 334.

18. Ibid., p. 335.

to meet much lower standards creeping into their market. And as we have seen, consumers in a lot of countries a lot of the time will get products that meet higher standards. This is because in regional regulatory forums, a captured or corrupt bureaucrat who wants to set standards well below the international average tends to be less persuasive than a crusading bureaucrat from a country that, because of a history of special problems with the product in his or her homeland, wants to set standards well above the international average.

International regulatory cooperation

The United Nations, preeminently the World Health Organization (WHO), provides a forum where more ambitious harmonization of laws is facilitated to thwart international law evasion strategies.[19] WHO's international drug adverse-reaction-reporting scheme does not work wonderfully well, but it effects some opening up of regulatory exposure in sophisticated markets for companies who test and dump in unsophisticated markets. The exposure is limited, however, because the unsophisticated markets are precisely those where problems are not reported into the scheme. Advocacy groups, as we will see later, have targeted their windows of exposure more effectively on these unsophisticated markets. The Certification Scheme on the Quality of Pharmaceutical Products

Moving in International Commerce is a successful harmonization project of the WHO. The large number of participating countries certify on request from another participant country that specified pharmaceutical exports meet the Good Manufacturing Practices Standards set down under the scheme, that the plants are subject to periodic inspection, and that the product is authorized for sale in the exporting country. Good Laboratory Practices are now becoming increasingly internationalized, thereby increasing the auditability of data from other countries and bringing the problem of fraud in the international safety testing of drugs under somewhat improved control. International regulatory cooperation on such matters under the auspices of the WHO and other international agencies has no panaceas to offer in a complex world, but it can effect limited improvements in international regulatory capability.

Professionalism and self-regulation

One of the analytical mistakes that scholars of white-collar crime repeatedly make is to assume that when an executive works for a criminogenic corporation, the executive's corporate identity is the only identity that matters to him or her. The 131 interviews I conducted with executives in the international pharmaceutical industry demonstrated clearly how executives have plural identities and multiple loyalties to multiple organizations. The Lilly research executive may have a loyalty to her research team that is more

19. Ellen N. Cohn, "International Regulation of Pharmaceuticals: The Role of the World Health Organization," *Virginia Journal of Transnational Law*, 23:331-61 (1983).

profound than the more remote loyalty to Lilly as a corporation. She may have a loyalty to her profession, to her patients if she is a doctor, and so on. The identity "Lilly executive" is just one of many identities.

An important conclusion from my earlier study was that the consumers of the world receive more protection from the higher standards that these competing identities bring into the firm than from enforcement of the law. This is particularly true with regard to the Third World. As many have demonstrated, drug companies have double and triple standards when it comes to marketing drugs in the Third World.[20] It is also true, however, that most, if not all, transnational pharmaceutical companies set much higher standards in the least regulated Third World markets than they are required to meet by the laws of those countries. They set higher standards because it would simply be intolerable to the professional standards of the people who work for them to stoop to the levels allowed by lax laws. There are other reasons that we will get to later. But in my fieldwork, and in my work as a consumer advocate, I have encountered many instances of responsible professionals within transnational corporations exposing the unethical conduct of certain of their own executives to the professional disapproval of their peers within the firm, and this in the firms that are among the worst law-

breakers in an industry with an unusually bad record for lawbreaking.[21]

Those in the best position to know about corporate wrongdoing are within the corporation. Those in the best position to understand whether organizationally and technologically complex corporate conduct actually amounts to wrongdoing are those imbued with an understanding of the organization, its technology, and the potential effects of that technology. The actors in the best position to mobilize informal sanctioning and disapproval that wrongdoers will care about are peers with whom they share a daily professional life. These are reasons why intracorporate self-regulation by employees with consciences is the form of regulation that almost certainly saves the greatest number of lives. If transnational pharmaceutical companies really did meet the minimum standards in the law of all the countries in which they operated, and never performed above those legal standards, the death toll from prescription drugs would be horrific. This observation points to the fundamental limitation of state law enforcement as a control strategy.

In all firms, there are constituencies that are supportive of the intent of regulatory laws. In pharmaceutical companies, the office of the medical director and the quality assurance group are often such constituencies, and in some cases the general counsel's office is a constituency that also pushes for compliance with the law. Effective self-regulation depends to a considerable extent on

20. See, for example, Charles Medawar, *Insult or Injury?* (London: Social Audit, 1979); M.N.G. Dukes and B. Swartz, *Responsibility for Drug-Induced Injury* (Amsterdam: Elsevier, 1988); Milton Silverman, Philip R. Lee, and Mia Lydecker, *Prescriptions for Death* (Berkeley: University of California Press, 1982).

21. Marshall Clinard and Peter Yeager, *Corporate Crime* (New York: Free Press, 1980), pp. 119-22.

strengthening the hand of such offices. An example is the strategy, now widespread throughout the industry, of allowing decisions of quality control on batches of drugs to be overruled only by the signature of the chief executive. This eliminates much of the day-to-day nullifying of quality control by production managers who insist on meeting production targets when they deem attainment of specifications to be good enough. Such a management policy strengthens the hand of a pro-regulation internal constituency enormously.

Interfirm self-regulation

Interfirm regulation is one of the things that can constitute the intrafirm self-regulation that I concluded was so important in the last section—but so can it be constituted by state regulation, such as law requiring the signature of the chief executive when quality control is overruled, or by consumer activism. Interfirm regulation can occur at a number of levels. National industry associations can write and enforce self-regulatory codes, as can international industry associations. Then there is the work of single firms seeking to upgrade the standards of their corporate peers. Each of these levels of interindustry regulation will now be illustrated.

An example of national industry association self-regulation is the Australian Pharmaceutical Manufacturers' Association Code of Conduct.[22] The code relates primarily to the

promotion of prescription drugs. Throughout the 1980s, I was a highly public advocate, along with leaders of the Australian consumer movement, of the view that self-regulation was not the way to go for the control of pharmaceutical advertising, that tougher government regulation was needed. I still believe that in principle this is an area in which government regulation ought to be more effective and efficient than self-regulation. In the aftermath of the total failure of such regulation during the 1970s and 1980s, however, the government decided to give a rejuvenated self-regulation scheme a three-year trial beginning in 1988. It turned out that self-regulation during this period was more effective in improving the integrity of pharmaceuticals promotion than the limp government regulation of the previous decade had been.[23] While Australian consumer activists such as myself who have been involved in a hands-on way with this issue do not doubt the finding that self-regulation worked better than the feeble government regulation that it replaced, we still believe that inappropriate marketing practices are widespread and unremedied. Nevertheless, improvement is improvement, and it warrants the concession that historical circumstances arise that result in self-regulation's working better than government regulation even in an area where in principle the reverse should be true. The reasons for the

22. Australian Pharmaceutical Manufacturers' Association, *Code of Conduct of the Australian Pharmaceutical Manufacturers' Association Inc.* (North Sydney: APMA, 1990).

23. See Trade Practices Commission, *Report by the Trade Practices Commission on the Self-Regulation of Promotion and Advertising of Therapeutic Goods* (Canberra: Trade Practices Commission, 1992).

success of this scheme were contingent; they included a substantial industry investment in prepublication monitoring of advertisements for compliance with the code, repeated postpublication surveys of the percentage of ads that complied that were conducted independently by the Australian Society of Clinical and Experimental Pharmacologists,[24] and knowledge that the self-regulation scheme would be evaluated by the Trade Practices Commission to determine if it should be replaced by government regulation.

This case illustrates that consumer advocates and regulatory strategists must avoid myopic rejection of strategies on the basis of theoretical dogma. Where self-regulation does outperform government regulation, pragmatism is needed to give credit where credit is due, rewarding improved protection for consumers in a plural regulatory order, so that improved protection may be achieved.

The International Federation of Pharmaceutical Manufacturers' Association (IFPMA) has also been in the business of self-regulation. Indeed, the Australian Pharmaceutical Manufacturers' Association code, discussed in the last two paragraphs, received part of its impetus from pressure for increased self-regulation from the IFPMA.[25] In turn, the fear of de facto international and national regulation by the WHO in conjunction with Third World governments in order to implement the WHO list of essential drugs—that is, to eliminate nonessential drugs from the market so that scarce health budgets could be concentrated on lifesaving products—prompted the IFPMA in 1982 to start supplying essential drugs to a few pilot countries.[26] In countries such as Gambia and Sierra Leone, the initiative seems to have been responsible for some improvement in primary health care and in the availability of lifesaving drugs.[27] By and large, however, one would have to say that the IFPMA efforts at self-regulation have been tokenistic and that it is only in a few countries such as Australia that they have been taken seriously because of extra pressure from professional and consumer constituencies.

An interesting more recent development in interfirm regulation has been at the level of a single firm—the Swiss giant Ciba-Geigy—that has sought to persuade its corporate peers to upgrade self-regulatory standards voluntarily. Ciba-Geigy was a pariah firm until the late 1980s as far as the international consumer movement was concerned.[28] It had done terrible things in product testing, such as spraying Third World agricultural workers with experimental chemicals from the air without their consent and aggressively

24. R.F.W. Moulds and L.M.H. Wing, "Drug Advertising," *Medical Journal of Australia,* 150:410-11 (1989).

25. The IFPMA introduced a code of pharmaceutical marketing in 1981. IFPMA, *IFPMA Code of Pharmaceutical Marketing Practices* (Geneva: IFPMA, 1987).

26. Cohn, "International Regulation of Pharmaceuticals," p. 352.

27. Andrew Chetley, *A Healthy Business? World Health and the Pharmaceutical Industry* (London: Zed Books, 1990), pp. 133-34.

28. See Olle Hansson, *Inside Ciba-Geigy* (Penang: International Organization of Consumers' Unions, 1989).

marketing products such as cli-oquinol that had disastrous side effects, which were covered up. Ciba-Geigy also persisted in the marketing of products in the Third World after they had been demonstrated to be unsafe and had been withdrawn from First World markets. Cynics will say that it was the public relations setbacks associated with the consumer movement perception of Ciba-Geigy as a killer corporation, combined with the threat of an international consumer boycott, that caused the corporation to change its spots. Greater cynics will say that Ciba-Geigy has not altered its spots at all. My view is that Ciba-Geigy has changed, if not completely changed. At the end of 1986, the company initiated a program called the Risk Assessment of Drugs—Analysis and Response (RAD-AR). RAD-AR's goal is to get leading companies to be more open about the risk factors associated with their products and to foment a more constructive dialogue about the risks and benefits of particular pharmaceuticals, a dialogue in which industry critics take part.[29] RAD-AR's success has been patchy, varying from one part of the world to another. Representatives of many companies have attended RAD-AR seminars, but not many have acted to make their safety and efficacy data more genuinely open to their competitors and their critics. The U.S. company G. D. Searle, formerly a prominent practitioner of reincarnated rat research, is one organization that has moved significantly in the direction of greater openness about its prod-

ucts.[30] It is both interesting and theoretically significant that the companies that have taken the most determined steps toward greater openness and dialogue about the risks of an industry that markets tamed poisons have been those such as Ciba-Geigy and Searle that have been subjected, with good reason, to some of the strongest consumerist vilification.

Consumer activism

The interplay between interfirm regulation and consumer activism became clear in the last section. National and international industry associations have stepped up their self-regulatory activities when they have been put under pressure from consumer groups. The individual firms that have been preeminent in leading the industry in the direction of a more responsible regulatory culture[31] in recent decades have been firms that have been effectively targeted by the consumer movement. This self-regulatory improvement is in considerable part an attempt to fend off strengthened state and international regulation. And the threatened state and international regulation is itself a threat largely, or at least partly, because of the lobbying of national and international consumer groups. Another threat the industry fears is strengthened consumer product liability laws and class action legislation. Where this strengthening has

30. Chetley, *Healthy Business?* p. 139.

31. Regulatory culture includes firms, regulators, and public interest groups. I see regulatory culture as a very useful concept; see Errol Meidinger, "Regulatory Culture: A Theoretical Outline," *Law and Policy,* 9:355-86 (1986).

29. An important forum for this discussion is the periodical *RAD-AR Report.*

occurred, it largely has been through consumer movement activism. This in turn brings in another level of analysis to a legal-pluralist examination of the social control of drug risks, that concerned with private consumers punishing corporations in the courts for taking unjustified risks with their bodies. All these levels are interconnected, and very often interconnected in a way that suggests that an initial impetus from consumer movement activism was crucial. The industry itself recognizes this. Consequently, a new tactic in its appeals for partial deregulation of drug safety testing has been to work with gay and lesbian groups concerned about red tape holding up new drugs to combat acquired immune deficiency syndrome (AIDS).

In the United States, Ralph Nader's organization, Sidney Wolfe and the Health Research Group, and the Consumers' Union all have been important players in the drug regulation game, working hand in hand with sympathetic journalists such as Morton Mintz of the *Washington Post* and sympathetic legislators such as Edward Kennedy and Howard Metzenbaum. Internationally, the preeminently important group has been Health Action International, an arm of the International Organization of Consumers' Unions. These two groups now have a regional office structure that puts them on the battlefront of the worst abuses of the industry in the Third World.

In Australia, professional groups with strong links to the consumer movement have been particularly important in effecting change in industry practices. Dr. Ken Harvey has been a leading activist from the medical profession in promoting peer guidelines for the appropriate use of different drugs. Use of the guidelines within Australian hospitals has both reduced irrational prescribing and cut drug costs. The most interesting group in Australia has been the Medical Lobby for Appropriate Marketing (MLAM). The MLAM strategy has been relatively simple. Dr. Peter Mansfield, the inspiration behind MLAM, writes to a large number of doctors who are MLAM members around the world with information about a product that is being marketed inappropriately by a particular company in a particular country. These medical professionals then write to the company—generally at its world headquarters or in the country where the offense occurred or in their own country—demanding an explanation for the alleged inappropriate marketing practice. A naive strategy, hard-bitten advocates of state deterrence might say. Not really. It is a strategy that works enough of the time to make it an extremely cost-efficient method of social control for activists with scarce resources. Writing letters is cheap. Moreover, it is a decent method of social control based on a reasoned appeal to corporate and medical responsibility.[32] Sometimes MLAM decides that it wrongly assessed a situation and writes back to the company with an apology. Pharmaceutical executives, even some of the very worst of them, do have a better side, a re-

32. See Clifford Shearing, "A Constitutive Conception of Regulation," in *Future of Regulatory Enforcement in Australia*, ed. Grabosky and Braithwaite.

26   THE ANNALS OF THE AMERICAN ACADEMY

sponsible side, to which appeals to professional and corporate responsibility can be made. They have multiple selves that make it worth considering a strategy that encourages them to put their best self forward. When that does not work, there are other strategies available to advocacy groups—muckraking in the media and calls for state enforcement, for example, and in extreme cases threats of consumer or professional boycotts.

In addition to corporate executives having a socially responsible self that can, surprisingly, often be brought to the fore, pharmaceutical companies have self-interested reasons to listen and respond seriously to rising ground swells of professional concern about their marketing practices. Pharmaceutical companies survive in the marketplace by persuading physicians to prescribe their products. In other words, they depend for success on convincing health care professionals that they are trustworthy. Sometimes they make the judgment that the best way to promote their long-term success is to actually be trustworthy, to admit a mistake and put it right. Five of 17 MLAM letters between January 1988 and June 1989 resulted in an agreement by the targeted company to alter claims or withdraw the product in question.[33] This strike rate increased to 5 of 9 for the period from July 1989 to June 1990.[34]

CONCLUSION

State regulation is very important for controlling corporate crime in the pharmaceutical industry. But inappropriate state regulation can deter innovation and push up the costs of drugs that are desperately needed in many parts of the world.[35] In this article, I have said very little about these crucial issues because they always are the focus in debates on the regulation of the pharmaceutical industry. Here I have sought to decenter the state. My argument has been that while the state is very important, its importance to market ordering and regulation of abuse is overrated. Underrated sources of regulation of abuse are market ordering by international organizations, mobilization of community disapproval by consumer and professional groups, intrafirm self-regulation at the level of individual executive professionalism, and interfirm self-regulation mobilized by national and international industry associations and individual firms, such as Ciba-Geigy.

All of these forms of social control may seem weak, but their weakness can be overstated if we fail to realize that their strength comes from the way they are interrelated. Pharmaceutical companies are not exactly enmeshed in a Foucauldian carceral archipelago,[36] but they are sur-

33. V. A. Wade, P. R. Mansfield, and P. J. McDonald, "Drug Company Evidence to Justify Advertising," _Lancet_, Nov. 1989, pp. 1261-64.

34. Peter R. Mansfield, "Classifying Improvements to Drug Marketing and Justifications for Claims of Efficacy," _International Journal of Risk and Safety in Medicine_, 2:171-

84 (1991). Of course, with such data one can never be sure that the company would not have changed its marketing practices without the pressure from MLAM.

35. See, for example, Robert I. Chien, _Issues in Pharmaceutical Economics_ (Lexington, MA: Lexington Books, 1979).

36. Michel Foucault, _Discipline and Punish: The Birth of the Prison_, trans. A. Sheridan (London: Allen Lane, 1977).

rounded by a web of controls that must be taken more seriously than any single strand of that web. Consumer groups might seem disorganized and weak. But when they can mobilize media assaults, sow seeds of professional distrust of the industry, foment consumer cynicism about the products the industry sells, heighten the threat of government regulation, nurture industry self-regulation to fend off the latter threat, and initiate mass tort litigation, the entire web of influences can change industry conduct. Most crucially, advocates engaging in a critical public dialogue with the industry flush out sympathizers within the industry. The pharmaceutical industry has within it thousands of public citizens who believe in corporate responsibility, who care about human health, and who have standards of professional integrity. In a pinch, some of these executives with a conscience will blow the whistle; at the drop of a hat, a good number of them will discreetly provide useful information to industry critics. Because the industry cannot exile its huge fifth column of responsible professionals, to a certain extent it actually listens to them and responds to their internal critiques. This is why intracorporate self-regulation is the main game. But it is a main game that gets a lot of its power from outside forces—consumerist critics, scientific journals, the popular media, professional societies, the professional socialization practices of universities, and, yes, criminal law. Criminal law must be seen, therefore, in proper perspective as one of the critical outside forces that empowers a web of market-ordering

mechanisms. Criminal law is too clumsy and costly a device to be the frontline assault weapon that routinely strikes the blows that are decisive for winning the battle. Rather, criminal law has enormous importance as heavy artillery that provides the backing to push the frontline troops forward into hand-to-hand combat with the mercenaries.[37]

The United States is the country that is the heaviest user of criminal law as a control mechanism for regulatory problems in the pharmaceutical industry. Even so, criminal law is used in U.S. pharmaceuticals regulation with extreme rarity.[38] All nations should be using criminal law much more against the worst corporate crimes of the pharmaceutical industry. Although all nations have in common the fact that criminal law is rarely or never used against pharmaceutical transnationals, countries vary enormously in the levels of unwarranted risk that drug companies take with consumers' lives. A quick visit to a pharmacy in Guatemala and one in Sweden, neither country being one that uses criminal law against pharmaceutical companies, immediately communicates the enormous difference in the risk that consumers confront in these two societies. What accounts for the differences in drug morbidity and mortality is the total fabric of the web of controls I have outlined previously. Criminologists who eschew a legal-

37. See the enforcement-pyramid philosophy in Ayres and Braithwaite, *Responsive Regulation: Transcending the Deregulation Debate*, chap. 2.

38. Braithwaite, *Corporate Crime in the Pharmaceutical Industry*.

pluralist analysis will never get to the bottom of what really protects the lives of consumers from corporate crime.

A policy analysis of despair is no longer warranted in the face of the reality of international law evasion strategies, as deep and deadly as the problem remains. International harmonization efforts are slowly moving forward, particularly in a European Community that is increasingly setting the international agenda. Guarded support for these harmonization moves is coming from the industry and many national regulators and consumer and professional groups who see some prospect for win-win change. More striking, there is a new view gaining momentum in the industry that the international law evasion game is not the way to go. This view is succinctly summarized in the advice of Harvard Business School guru Michael Porter in his paradigm-shattering book, *The Competitive Advantage of Nations.*

Establish norms exceeding the toughest regulatory hurdles or product standards. Some localities (or user industries) will lead in terms of the stringency of product standards, pollution limits, noise guidelines, and the like. Tough regulatory standards are not a hindrance but an opportunity to move early to upgrade products and processes.[39]

Find the localities whose regulations foreshadow those elsewhere. Some regions and cities will typically lead others in terms of their concern with social problems such as safety, environmental quality, and the like. Instead of avoiding such areas, as some companies do, they should be sought out. A firm should define its internal goals as meeting, or exceeding, their standards. An advantage will result as other regions, and ultimately other nations, modify regulations to follow suit.[40]

Firms, like governments, are often prone to see the short-term cost of dealing with tough standards and not their longer-term benefits in terms of innovation. Firms point to foreign rivals without such standards as having a cost advantage. Such thinking is based on an incomplete view of how competitive advantage is created and sustained. Selling poorly performing, unsafe, or environmentally damaging products is not a route to real competitive advantage in sophisticated industry and industry segments, especially in a world where environmental sensitivity and concern for social welfare are rising in all advanced nations. Sophisticated buyers will usually appreciate safer, cleaner, quieter products before governments do. Firms with the skills to produce such products will have an important lever to enter foreign markets, and can often accelerate the process by which foreign regulations are toughened.[41]

Here we have an intriguing emerging international dynamic. Firms that have upgraded their safety standards early because of their location in states that are early movers to higher standards have an interest in getting other states to follow the lead. There is thus a connected strategy for those of us who are active in the international consumer movement. It is to persuade targeted national governments to be first movers to up-

---

39. Michael Porter, *The Competitive Advantage of Nations* (London: Macmillan, 1990), p. 585.

40. Ibid., p. 588.
41. Ibid., pp. 648-49.

grade regulatory standards through the argument that they can actually benefit their national economy by doing so. Porter supplies many examples of nations that constructed important competitive advantages by being first to establish tougher health and safety standards.[42] Then home-base transnationals from those first nations can be recruited to support upgrading standards in other nations, thus setting back their competitors from laggard nations.

42. Empirically, it is simply not the case that it is the countries with weak business regulations that are flourishing in the world economy. The toughest environmental or consumer protection legislation in the world on any given hazard will usually be found in the United States, Japan, or Germany. Porter provides an account of some of the reasons why this is the case. Australia's BHP spent a 9-figure sum during the 1980s on new doors to reduce the hazardous emissions from its coke ovens. The doors were bought from Japan. Why? Japan was the leader in tightening regulatory controls over coke oven emissions, and as a consequence it was Japanese steelmakers that developed the control technology and sold it to the rest of the world. The Japanese Energy Conservation Law of 1979 set demanding standards for energy saving in air conditioners, refrigerators, and cars, resulting in a variety of product improvements that have benefited Japan's international position. America more than Japan has historically led the world in the export of pollution-control equipment and services as a result of its tough environmental regulation. However, when certain deregulatory tendencies in the United States allowed Germany, Sweden, and Denmark to move ahead of the United States on some environmental standards, these countries increasingly came to supply world markets for the relevant technologies. Sweden led the world in regulations requiring special access and aids for handicapped persons. Consequently, Swedish companies dominate world markets in technology to aid the disabled.

Porter's way of thinking about the constitution of competitive advantage is gaining wider acceptance in business and regulatory communities. Pharmaceutical companies can see that it is actually a competitive disadvantage to have as a home base an Eastern European country that might have cheap labor costs and minimal regulatory standards. The absence of demanding regulators and demanding consumer groups gives companies from these countries totally inadequate preparation for competing in sophisticated markets.

What is it that is generating this shift among some industry strategists from an interest in seeking the lowest possible standards to finding the highest standards? It is "sophisticated buyers . . . [who] . . . appreciate safer . . . products before governments do." To the sophisticated buyers we might add sophisticated health care professionals, sophisticated corporate insiders, and sophisticated industry association leaders. Shifts toward a search for the highest standards are caused by the web of influences that has been the subject of this article. Increasingly one does meet pharmaceutical industry executives who are actively committed to shooting for the highest regulatory standards in the way Porter commends. Shifts away from lowest-common-denominator regulation in the world system toward highest-common-factor regulation can be a result of the web of interconnections among regulatory, self-regulatory, and consumerist actors in a plural international ordering of markets. Comparatively poorly resourced players of the regulatory game, such as consumer groups, need not be powerless actors if they are smart. To be smart, they must have an internationalist strategy that recognizes and works with the plural sources of market ordering.[43]

43. For a sophisticated discussion of the theoretical foundations for a pluralist analysis of market ordering see Shearing, "Constitutive Conception of Regulation."

PART III

Republican Legal Institutions

[10]
The Politics of Legalism: Rules Versus Standards in Nursing Home Regulation

PRECISE RULES give more explicit guidance than vague standards. It would seem to follow that regulators will enforce precise rules more reliably than vague standards. This article demonstrates empirically that this is not necessarily so. It also induces from data on nursing home regulation the beginnings of a theory of a reliability paradox. We show how pursuit of reliability for a part of the law can increase the unreliability of a whole body of law. Reliability is used here with the standard scientific meaning of the extent to which measures give consistent results, as contrasted with validity, which means the extent to which measures assess the 'true' position. A 12-inch ruler that in truth is 13 inches long gives reliable (consistent) but invalid (untrue) measurement.

Our aim is to contribute to the rules-versus-standards debate in law, to regulatory policy analysis and to debates about reliability in science. A rule is taken to be a legal norm of the form, in circumstance X, do Y or not-Y. A standard, in contrast, enjoins the pursuit or achievement of a value, a goal or outcome, without specifying the action(s) required to do so. The divide is not a neat one, the world being full of rules about standards and standards about rules. Nevertheless, some bodies of law are more dominated by standards and others more by rules.

Reprinted by permission of Sage Publications Ltd.

308

The Reliability Paradox of Regulatory Inspection

The sociolegal literature on rules versus standards is itself paradoxical. On the one hand, there is a literature claiming to show that American law is more standards-oriented, British law more oriented to rules. The most important contribution to this literature, Atiyah and Summers' (1987) *Form and Substance in Anglo-American Law*, makes the more general claim that American law is more substantive, British law more formal (see also Krotoszynski, 1990). On the other hand, the comparative literature on regulatory enforcement concludes that enforcement in other nations is less formal than in the United States (see generally, Bardach and Kagan, 1982; Braithwaite, 1987), including Britain (Day and Klein, 1987; Hawkins, 1984; Vogel, 1986), Sweden (Kelman, 1981), Australia (Grabosky and Braithwaite, 1986) and Japan (Badaracco, 1985; Haley, 1988; Upham, 1987; Vogel, 1979). Data collected for the present study of nursing-home regulation fit both stories in terms of the British–American comparison, in that British nursing-home regulation operates with more precise and formal rules than the more substantive, standard-like American nursing-home regulations, while British regulatory practice is more discretionary, more oriented to securing improvement in the quality of care and less interested than in the USA with collecting evidence for litigation concerning non-compliance with rules. While American law is more substantive and less formal than British law, British nursing-home regulatory practice is less formal than is American practice.

It may be that these opposite tendencies are indeed both true and have their origins in the same historical variable: the greater distrust of the state in America, compared to Europe and Asia (see Kagan, 1991; Vogel, 1986). Distrust of the legislature by the courts and by litigants energized by the more vigorous American separation of powers (an institutionalization of distrust) is one factor that may have resulted in the creation of a more substantive jurisprudence by American courts. Distrust of the executive by interest groups (litigants) and the courts has led them to pursue the limitation of administrative discretion, driving regulators to more formal regulatory enforcement. In other words, courts and interest groups in America operationalize institutionalized distrust of the state by going substantive with statutory interpretation and by driving the executive to go formal with application of the law. Courts and interest groups play the separation of powers to seize power from the legislature by judicial discretion in the interpretation of statutes, just as they seize power from the executive by limiting its discretion.

While this is a way of reconciling two literatures on the greater formality of British jurisprudence and the greater formality of American regulatory enforcement, in this article we deal with a different comparison. We find that both Australian nursing-home law and Australian nursing-home regulatory practice are less formal than in the USA, which may express a higher degree of trust among the legislature, the executive, the industry and advocacy groups – tripartite consensus building. This has meant in this arena (since 1987 reforms) that private interests rarely used courts or lobbied parliamentarians for more formal laws to achieve their objectives (Braithwaite, 1994).

The cross-national comparison illuminates themes from the American Critical Legal Studies (CLS) literature on rules versus standards, particularly the work of Duncan Kennedy (1976) and Mark Kelman (1987). Kennedy and Kelman see a reliance on standards as premised 'on the hope of moral dialogue and ultimate consensus, since the standards will remain contentless unless such moral dialogue succeeds in overcoming the skeptical sense that one person's conception of what is just is nothing more than either a whimsical taste or a rhetorical cover for a self-serving program' (Kelman, 1987:62; see also Michelman, 1986). Our case study shows this hope being more or less realized in Australia at least for one little domain of regulation for a very short period of history.[1] The point that Kelman and Kennedy make is that rules do not depend on communities seeking consensus; standards do.[2] Kelman and Kennedy contend that the rule mentality is therefore a liberal individualist one, a contention disputed by Pierre Schlag (1985; see also Radin, 1989:806 and n. 88; Rose, 1987:606–10; Sullivan, 1992).

From another ideological perspective, we would put it that a rule-orientation in law conduces to liberal individualism, whereas a standard-orientation can both conduce to and depend on a degree of republican community. Rather, if it does not depend on a degree of republican community among those concerned with a particular issue, like nursing-home regulation, a standards-orientation will conduce to unchecked domination. Meidinger (1987) reports the existence of 'regulatory communities' even in the USA.

In the rules-versus-standards debate, CLS scholars pick up themes from American Legal Realists, who were fond of showing how the presumed precision of rules enabled imprecision. One reason they pointed to was that courts usually confront a choice of which of a number of precise yet contradictory rules they choose to invoke in a particular situation: 'each rule was in fact radically undercut by its fratricidal twin' (Kelman, 1987:48; see Schlag, 1985:409). Moreover, both realists and critical scholars indicate that often when the nominal rule is formally clear and consistent, the real operative rule for invoking it is opaque and inconsistent. The speed limit is 60, but the operating rules are that anything up to 65 or so will be ignored or let off with a warning (unless contempt is shown to the police officer or the officer wants to detain a person to check out compliance with some other rule). Hence the law and society injunction: study the law in action rather than the law in books. If your concern is consistency, you are bound to be misled unless you study consistency of the law in action. Our present study seeks some clarification of the rules-versus-standards debate by examining law in action. It shows empirically what CLS scholars assert when they say 'the text cannot define its context' (Schlag, 1985:410):

> If we concede that the sector of the social world cordoned off by directive can be affected by the external world, then the only way in which a directive can be certain is if it is sufficiently flexible to accommodate the effects of the external world.

This refutes the view that 'the choice between formulating or interpreting a legal directive as a rule or as a standard is a choice between . . . certainty or flexibility, uniformity or individualization' (Schlag, 1985:399). Rather, there are contexts

310

where standards are both more certain and more flexible, more uniform and more individualized than rules. Nursing home regulation we find here to be one such context. It will be shown to be a context where plural dialogue framed by few standards (rather than many rules) is better.

Consistency of compliance assessments has come to assume pre-eminent importance in policy-making within regulatory bureaucracies. This is especially true of political debates about nursing-home reform and regulation in Western democracies. It is our contention that this central regulatory preoccupation with consistency is misplaced and that reliability is not the most important desideratum of a set of standards for inspecting nursing homes or any other industry. We propose a paradox in which reliability is more likely to be achieved when reliability is not the central objective of public policy. When we make other objectives our central concern – such as designing standards which best foster a regulatory dialogue about how a nursing home can improve quality of life outcomes – an indirect effect may be that better reliability of ratings is achieved. We advance this paradox by considering recent reforms in Australia and then comparing them to the state of American nursing-home inspection.

NURSING-HOME REFORM IN AUSTRALIA

Following a series of nursing-home scandals, consumer activism and two parliamentary enquiries (McLeay Report, 1982; Giles Report, 1985), the Australian government launched a package of nursing-home reforms in 1987. The first element of the package was a new set of 31 outcome-oriented standards negotiated through the active collaboration of federal and state governments, industry and professional, union and consumer groups. The consensus standards that attracted the assent of all these groups were so broad that they were attacked as 'motherhood statements' by many who were not immediately engaged in their negotiation. We agreed with these critics at the time. Moreover, while the standards were marketed as 'Outcome Standards for Australian Nursing Homes', many of them (listed in Table 1) did not look like outcomes to us. Since then, we learned that degree of outcome-orientation is primarily a matter of regulatory process design rather than standard-wording (Braithwaite et al., 1990: 135–41), a point to which we return.

Another fundamental concern we had about the new Australian standards was that they just could not be reliable. They were broad, subjective, lacking in detailed protocols,[3] and the process by which they were to be rated was absolutely unattentive to sampling issues. Moreover, the process was resident-centred when we knew that a high proportion of residents would be confused and unreliable informants. Compounding these problems was a shift toward the inclusion of many 'soft' social and resident rights standards, in contrast to the previous exclusive focus on 'harder' structural or health-care inputs, that could be checked with a ruler, a thermometer or by confirming a doctor's signature. It was inconceivable to us that standards concerned with the resident's right to 'privacy and dignity' or a 'homelike environment' could be rated reliably. We certainly thought these standards were a 'good thing' because they would stimulate a dialogue that was sorely needed. But we harboured the deepest of doubts that they could be legally enforceable, doubts shared at the time also by the government's lawyers, industry's legal advisers, and the consumer movement.

In 1987, when we started an international comparative study of nursing-home regulation in Australia, the USA, Britain and Japan, we were rather embarrassed by the Australian standards. We would say to American regulators: 'We know they are only a start and we have a lot of work to do to flesh out the kinds of guidelines and protocols that you have built up over the years.' They in turn would look aghast at how broad, vague, undefined and unenforceable these quaint Antipodean standards were. Since that time, our research findings provided quite strong grounds for believing that the broad, unrefined Australian standards are not just more reliable than US standards but more reliable by a wide margin. Furthermore, observations of 59 nursing-home inspections in Australia and 44 in the USA between 1988 and 1993 suggest that the reason Australian ratings are more reliable is precisely because they are more (a) broad, (b) subjective, (c) undefined with regard to protocols, (d) resident-centred and (e) devoid of random sampling.

THE AUSTRALIAN RELIABILITY STUDY

Inter-rater reliability studies are extremely rare in the literature on regulatory inspectorates. In fact, the nursing-home inspection data from the USA and Australia that we discuss in this article are almost the only reliability data of which we are aware on any type of regulatory inspectorate in any country.[4] There are two reasons for the rarity of such research. First, government agencies are normally fearful of studies which might show that their judgements about compliance with the law are arbitrary and capricious. Such data might be used by defence lawyers to destroy the legal foundations of the regulatory regime. Second, such studies are difficult to do – expensive, logistically a nightmare, and intrusive for the organizations being inspected. Funding agencies, governments and regulated organizations are all therefore resistant to regulatory reliability research.

Elsewhere (Braithwaite et al., 1991:12) we discuss how these sources of resistance were overcome in this study. An essential step toward overcoming industry resistance was the need to avoid compounding the disruption of a government inspection with a reliability inspection immediately before or after. We did this by placing a single reliability rater in the nursing home at the same time as the government inspection team. The government inspection team of two or three inspectors spends an average of 6.5 hours inspecting the facility. Australian facilities tend to be much smaller than US facilities, the median number of beds being 38. Because the reliability raters had to do the job alone, they generally arrived before the team and left after them, occasionally having to come back for a second day.[5] The single reliability raters could compensate for the need to do the work of two and sometimes three others in five additional ways, beyond spending more time in the facility: (1) they did not need to stop to

312

explain problems to facility staff and management; (2) they did not need to take extensive notes for use in an official report; (3) they did not need to collect the evidence to document a finding in the event of enforcement action; (4) they did not need to stop to compare notes with other team members; and (5) they also had the advantage of being more senior, experienced nurses. We were able, therefore, to sell the study to nursing homes on the grounds that the only extra disruption they would confront was having one additional inspector in their home for the duration of the normal standards monitoring visit, and perhaps a little longer.

Methodologically, there are both advantages and disadvantages to this approach. A disadvantage is that guidelines had to be enforced to prevent the team and the independent rater from communicating with each other in any way about standards during the visit. This we believe was successfully negotiated (Braithwaite et al., 1991). An advantage is avoiding the problem of sequential visits whereby the nursing home has the opportunity of rectifying problems identified by the visit of the first team before the second team arrives.

SAMPLE

Details on the selection of the two independent raters, the 30 inspection teams from New South Wales and Victoria, and the sampling frame for the nursing homes are provided elsewhere (Braithwaite et al., 1991: 13–15). Only one nursing home refused to cooperate in a quota sample of 50 nursing homes with quotas for (a) number of beds in the home, (b) non-profit-for-profit status, (c) state and (d) composition of the inspection team. The sampling for the reliability study had to be quota sampling because the inspectors at the time were in the midst of working through the stratified random sample of homes that we had selected for our wider evaluation (Braithwaite et al., 1990). Within the discretion allowed by their quotas, independent raters were instructed to be especially on guard against a bias toward 'easy' nursing homes. They were told: 'If you have to err, err on the side of homes which are more likely to be problem homes, because these will be the homes which give you more opportunities to disagree with the team.' As it turned out, independent raters did err quite significantly on the side of homes with more problems. While the average number of 'met' ratings for all homes was 23, the average number of 'met' ratings for homes in the reliability study was 18.

RESULTS

Agreement between the independent rater and the government inspection team was measured at three points in time. After the team completed its visit, the team met (usually the next day) to discuss as a team the positives and negatives observed on each standard and to agree on initial ratings. Soon after, they would meet with the independent rater to compare their (blind) initial ratings. The percent of agreement between these initial (totally independent) ratings are provided in the first column of Table 1. The standards are rated into three categories – 'met', 'action required' and 'urgent action required'.[6] On Standard 1.1, 84 percent agreement means that for 84 percent of the nursing homes, the team and the independent rater gave the home exactly the same rating on this 3-point scale. Once both sides had been apprised of each other's ratings, they were asked to discuss why they had reached different conclusions on certain standards. During this discussion, one side would sometimes persuade the other that they were wrong. On occasion, the combining of their information caused both sides to conclude that they had been wrong. This generated the 'after conferring' ratings, the measure of agreement in the second column of Table 1. After the team had been back to the nursing home for a further visit to advise the nursing home of their ratings (giving the nursing home an opportunity to provide further information that might rebut them), the team passed this information on to the independent rater. Both sides then had the opportunity to change their ratings again in light of the feedback from the nursing home. These final ratings were the basis for calculating agreement in the third column of Table 1. At each stage, the reasons for disagreement and changes of heart were recorded. Data on the reasons for disagreement on different standards are elaborated elsewhere (Braithwaite et al., 1991: 18–30). Broadly, disagreements based on the collection of different information were equal in number to disagreements based on different interpretations of the standards.

A high level of overall agreement was recorded for all standards. Not surprisingly, this level of agreement increased slightly after conferring. Receipt of negotiation feedback from the nursing home made only a minor difference – on some standards increasing agreement slightly, on others reducing it slightly. There are some surprising results in Table 1. For example, the 'homelike environment' standard (4.1), which no one we know would have predicted to be reliable, was rated quite consistently – with 88 percent blind agreement rising to 94 percent after conferring. Similarly, it was assumed that reliability was implausible on the 'soft' social and residents' rights standards. Yet soft standards such as 5.1, 'The dignity of residents is respected by nursing home staff,' were rated with impressive reliability.

The first suspicion one should harbour about the exceptionally high agreement in Table 1 stems from an assumption that in a majority of cases both teams and independent raters give nursing homes met ratings. As a statistical artifact, it follows therefore that met-met agreement will be very common. For example, if the probability of getting 'a met' is 0.9, the likelihood of getting two mets on purely statistical grounds from two independent assessors is going to be 0.9×0.9, that is, 0.81. Conversely, if the probability were lower for a met, that is 0.5, the likelihood of two mets is much lower (0.25). Two considerations render this explanation for high reliabilities implausible. First, with the Australian standards, 12 of the 31 had proportions of mets under 50 percent. In the US system, the distribution tends to be more extreme (met ratings often over 90 percent). Second, with the Australian data, independent raters are not more likely to agree with teams on 'met' ratings than they are on 'action required' and 'urgent action required' ratings. It is simply not true that our high reliabilities

314

TABLE I
Overall Agreement between the Team and the Independent Rater[a] and the Kappa Coefficient[b] (n = 50)

Standard	Initially (%)		After Conferring (%)		After Negotiation (%)	
1.1 Residents are enabled to receive appropriate medical care by a medical practitioner of their choice when needed.	84	(0.76)	90	(0.85)	92	(0.88)
1.2 Residents are enabled and encouraged to make informed choices about their individual care plans.	90	(0.81)	92	(0.85)	90	(0.81)
1.3 All residents are as free from pain as possible.	90	(0.61)	94	(0.75)	94	(0.70)
1.4 All residents are adequately nourished and adequately hydrated.	90	(0.86)	92	(0.87)	94	(0.90)
1.5 Residents are enabled to maintain continence.	78	(0.56)	86	(0.73)	86	(0.73)
1.6 Residents are enabled to maintain and, if possible, improve their mobility and dexterity.	90	(0.81)	96	(0.92)	96	(0.92)
1.7 Residents have clean healthy skin consistent with their age and general health.	98	(0.91)	98	(0.91)	98	(0.90)
1.8 Residents are enabled to maintain oral and dental health.	96	(0.91)	96	(0.91)	96	(0.91)
1.9 Sensory losses are identified and corrected so that residents are able to communicate effectively.	84	(0.66)	86	(0.71)	88	(0.74)
2.1 Residents are enabled and encouraged to have visitors of their choice and to maintain personal contacts.	90	(0.77)	94	(0.86)	96	(0.90)
2.2 Residents are enabled and encouraged to maintain control of their financial affairs.	94	(0.86)	94	(0.86)	96	(0.90)
2.3 Residents have maximum freedom of movement within and from the nursing home, restricted only for safety reasons.	94	(0.85)	98	(0.95)	94	(0.75)
2.4 Provision is made for residents with different religious, personal and cultural customs.	94	(0.84)	98	(0.94)	96	(0.88)
2.5 Residents are enabled and encouraged to maintain their responsibilities and obligations as citizens.	90	(0.62)	94	(0.77)	98	(0.90)
3.1 The nursing home has policies which have been developed in consultation with residents and which, regarding their daily activities, – provide an appropriate balance between residents' rights and effective management of the nursing home, – and are interpreted flexibly taking into account individual resident needs.	88	(0.75)	92	(0.84)	92	(0.83)
3.2 Residents and their representatives are enabled to comment or complain about conditions in the nursing home.	84	(0.71)	94	(0.89)	90	(0.81)
4.1 Management of the nursing home is attempting to create and maintain a homelike environment.	88	(0.77)	94	(0.89)	94	(0.89)
4.2 The nursing home has policies which enable residents to feel secure in their accommodation.	86	(0.73)	90	(0.81)	92	(0.84)
5.1 The dignity of residents is respected by nursing home staff.	92	(0.88)	98	(0.97)	98	(0.97)
5.2 Private property is not taken, lent or given to other people without the owner's permission.	96	(0.94)	98	(0.94)	98	(0.97)
5.3 Residents are enabled to undertake personal activities, including bathing, toileting and dressing in private.	88	(0.82)	94	(0.91)	94	(0.91)

Standard	Initially (%)		After Conferring (%)		After Negotiation (%)	
5.4 The nursing home is free from undue noise.	94	(0.87)	96	(0.91)	92	(0.82)
5.5 Information about residents is treated confidentially.	90	(0.80)	96	(0.92)	96	(0.92)
5.6 Nursing-home practices support the residents' right to die with dignity.	96	(0.86)	98	(0.94)	98	(0.93)
6.1 Residents are enabled to participate in a wide range of activities appropriate to their interests and capacities.	92	(0.84)	94	(0.88)	94	(0.88)
7.1 The resident's right to participate in activities which may involve a degree of risk is respected.	94	(0.85)	96	(0.90)	94	(0.82)
7.2 Nursing-home design, equipment and practices contribute to a safe environment for residents, staff and visitors.	82	(0.71)	92	(0.87)	90	(0.84)
7.3 Residents, visitors and staff are protected from infection and infestation.	92	(0.87)	98	(0.97)	96	(0.94)
7.4 Residents and staff are protected from the hazards of fire and natural disasters.	94	(0.91)	94	(0.91)	96	(0.94)
7.5 The security of buildings, contents and people within the nursing home is safeguarded.	98	(0.96)	98	(0.96)	98	(0.96)
7.6 Physical and other forms of restraint are used correctly and appropriately.	92	(0.87)	92	(0.87)	90	(0.83)

[a] Overall agreement means the team and the independent rater gave exactly the same rating. These were for ratings made using the new format of met, action required and urgent action required. The percent agreement was identical under the old format (met, met in part, not met) with the exceptions of Standard 5.6: 94 96 96; and Standard 7.2: 84 90 88.
[b] The kappa coefficients are in parentheses next to the percent figures of overall agreements.

reflect ease of agreement when the standard is met compared with difficulty in reaching agreement when it is not met (agreement for all standards by rating categories is presented in Braithwaite et al., 1991: 19–22).

Based on factor analytic work, we elsewhere argue that it is psychometrically defensible to add scores on the 31 standards to obtain a total compliance score (Braithwaite et al., 1990, 1992), something that would probably not be defensible on American Medicaid survey results. Overall, the inter-rater reliability coefficient for the blind ratings of the total compliance score is 0.93, increasing to 0.96 after conferring and remaining at 0.96 after negotiation with the nursing home. These reliability coefficients show no major variation by raters, state, size of home, level of disability of residents or ownership status. While these data show impressive intrastate reliability within the two largest Australian states, they do not demonstrate interstate reliability. That is, while two inspectors trained in the same state give the same ratings, they may both give different ratings from an inspection in a different state. Indeed, our qualitative fieldwork inclines us to agree with critics who say there are serious problems of interstate reliability.

The weakness of this reliability study is that the reliability rater is an individual rather than another team. Our expectation, however, was that reliance on an individual as the reliability rater would reduce rather than increase reliability. We expected that the reliability rater would fail to pick up information that the team picked up by virtue of having at least one extra set of eyes and ears. We tried to

316

compensate for this by allowing the reliability rater to stay in the nursing home longer than the team did and by using reliability raters who, in our opinion, were more experienced and acute observers than the average team member, but we never expected that this would fully allow the reliability rater to overcome the information-gathering deficit. This interpretation of why reliance on a single rater would reduce rather than increase reliability was borne out by the results of the study. At the conferring and negotiation stages, there were more cases of the reliability rater agreeing that she had made an erroneous rating by missing vital information than there were cases of teams agreeing that they had made erroneous ratings by failing to pick up some vital piece of information.

In addition to this reliability work, we also report some encouraging validation studies on the standards (Braithwaite et al., 1991; Braithwaite et al., 1992). Of particular interest here is that we asked 410 directors of nursing[7] to give their own nursing homes ratings on the 31 standards soon after an inspection team had visited their nursing home. The average agreement of directors of nursing with team ratings across the 31 standards was 92 percent, the lowest being 84 percent on homelike environment ratings (4.1). Directors of nursing naturally gave themselves higher ratings than did the teams, but the correlation between their total compliance scores and scores given by teams was 0.88. The consensus of industry understanding on the meaning of these standards that permits such a result is based on 93 percent of directors of nursing in Australia having attended a course on the standards. This process also led to an extraordinarily high level of belief in the 'clarity', 'desirability' and 'practicality' of the standards by directors of nursing and proprietors (Braithwaite et al., 1990, 1991, 1992). The worst result for any of the standards on these three criteria was on Standard 2.2, 'Residents are enabled and encouraged to maintain control of their financial affairs,' for which 24 percent of directors of nursing had doubts about the standard's practicality.

AMERICAN RELIABILITY STUDIES

How then do these Australian reliability results compare with the results of American reliability work? The first major empirical study of nursing home inspection was the Wisconsin Quality Assurance Project. That project piloted its own quality of care measure which was independent of the state regulatory process (Gustafson et al., 1980). Based on just 11 criteria, it was a much simpler measure than that used by Wisconsin state inspectors. Five two-person teams of nursing-home professionals visited nine nursing homes, giving 45 data points for the calculation of reliabilities. An average reliability coefficient on this simple measure of quality of care of 0.78 was obtained. This measure was also validated against a global 0–100 assessment of the quality of care of each home (r = 0.76), the global assessment itself having been found to be reliable (Gustafson, 1977). This pilot therefore demonstrated that two-person teams could rate the quality of care in nursing homes with reasonable reliability. Unfortunately, when the two measures of quality of care were correlated with the number of deficiencies cited by the last government inspectors to visit the nursing home, the correlations were not statistically significant at the 0.05 level. This early study thus gives us the first clear clue to the direction in which we are led by our results: Reliable ratings of the quality of care in nursing homes are possible when professional raters use a limited number of criteria; *but* when raters use the large number of specific American regulations as their criteria, reliability is lost. This was the pilot study on the Wisconsin quality of care instrument.

In the final study, 12 homes were visited by 3 teams (36 data points). The reliability and validation of the simple quality of care instrument improved slightly compared to the pilot, but a very low association of this simple instrument with the number of citations issued by government inspectors of 0.12 was found on another sample of 65 homes (Gustafson et al., 1982). So we get the same general picture as in the pilot – reliable rating of a simple quality of care measure combined with a poor relationship of this reliable measure with compliance ratings from government inspections.

Another particularly discouraging finding of the Wisconsin project is summarized in the final report:

> The final important result in problem identification came from a comparison of problems identified by federal validation teams versus the QAP and traditional processes. There were no differences in methods in terms of the number of conditions found out of compliance. However, there were substantial differences between state and federal teams at the standard and element level. (Gustafson et al., 1982:5)

This sounds discouraging but it was actually something of an understatement. It is true that 'There were no differences . . . in the number of conditions found out of compliance.' Neither the state inspectors nor the federal validation inspectors found any 'conditions' out of compliance, so there was perfect agreement! Condition-level was the most serious level of non-compliance rating and was rarely given. A freedom of information request to the funding agency, the United States Department of Health and Human Services, by Dr John Gardiner revealed that at the next level of seriousness of citation – the standard level – the state inspectors had cited three standards as out of compliance for the 20 homes in the study, while the federal validation team cited 28. Total deficiencies cited at the standard and element levels (the latter being the lowest level of seriousness) for the 20 nursing homes were 437. There was agreement on only 8 percent of these between the state and federal validation teams. For 92 percent of these deficiencies, one team was citing something that the other team had not cited.

One reason for these disturbing differences could be that the federal validation surveys (inspections) were done on average 30.5 days after the state survey. However, the internal memorandum secured by Dr Gardiner's freedom-of-information request pointed out: 'While changes at the facility between surveys do cause differences in findings, most facility changes are corrective actions which would reduce the deficiencies between the first (State) and second (Federal) surveys.' In fact, deficiencies rose sharply between the first set of

318

inspections and the second. Moreover, the memorandum pointed out: 'The majority of deficiencies found on the second (Federal) survey existed, and should have been identified during the first (State) survey.'

Another major University of Wisconsin study was published in 1985 on data from New York, Massachusetts and Wisconsin (Zimmerman et al., 1985). While the number of data points for the reliability coefficients was only 13 (two teams visiting 13 homes in New York and Massachusetts), the results were much better. This time, with the teams in the nursing homes at the same time and in different states, 58 percent of deficiencies cited were cited by both teams. An impressive 84 percent of deficiencies detected by state teams were also detected by independent teams, though there was a much larger number of deficiencies detected by independent teams which were not detected by state teams.

Both teams returned to these nursing homes four months later to assess whether the deficiencies on which the two teams agreed had been corrected. The state teams judged 96 percent to be corrected and the independent teams 71 percent. In this study multiple regressions using the Wisconsin quality of care indicator found only weak validation of the number of deficiencies detected by inspectors ($p < 0.1$), but much stronger validation of the total severity of deficiencies detected ($p < 0.05$).

The third American reliability study of the ratings of compliance with nursing-home regulations was based on double inspections of 21 Tennessee homes (Spector et al., 1987). There was a one-day interval between visits to the nursing home. Both teams were inspectors from the Tennessee Department of Health and Environment. Both teams were large (averaging 8.7 for the (official) first team and 5.5 for the second validation team); and both had unusual breadth of disciplinary coverage – always including nurses, a generalist, a social worker, physiotherapist and pharmacist. The official team also included a dietician, sanitarian and fire inspector.

Only 25 percent of the regulations cited by the official team were also cited by the validation team (Spector et al., 1987: 119–23). Again, one might have expected that the second team would have found less because the nursing home would have acted to correct the deficiencies detected by the first team. The second team, however, found twice as many deficiencies as the first.[8] These studies highlight the reliability paradox. How can the US system which involves many more inspector-hours in the nursing home, larger multidisciplinary teams and more sophisticated protocols on more precisely specified standards produce such low reliability, while the Australian system produces such high reliability?

While all the studies we are comparing from both sides of the Pacific have considerable deficiencies, the tenor of the findings are so diametrically opposed that it is hard to make sense of them in terms of method error.[9] This is especially so since we believe that the very extensive fieldwork we have undertaken since 1987 (see Braithwaite et al., 1993: Appendix A, 'Data and Methods'), including observing nursing-home inspectors doing their work during 103 inspections in the two countries, makes sense of our counterintuitive findings. To this interpretive work we now turn.

WHY ARE AUSTRALIAN STANDARDS MORE RELIABLE?

We advance five answers to the question of why Australian nursing-home standards are more reliable than US standards: It is because they are (1) broad; (2) undefined with regard to protocols; (3) subjective; (4) resident-centred; and (5) devoid of random sampling. Put even more provocatively, we will show why the very desiderata revered within the received scientific wisdom of American gerontology are responsible for the unreliability of nursing-home inspection. The tendency of the gerontological consultants who advise US governments on nursing-home inspection policies is to cast blame at the competence of nursing-home inspectors. Our experience is that American nursing-home inspectors seem of better-than-average competence compared to business regulatory inspectors from many fields that we have observed in Australia and other parts of the world. What our investigation calls into question is the competence of the scientific analysis that has been offered of the American process.

1. THE EFFECT OF BROADNESS OF STANDARDS ON RELIABILITY

The Australian standards in the words of one consumer advocate are 'wishy-washy and blunt'. Their breadth and vagueness certainly makes them appear an implausible regulatory instrument. Consequently, there is pressure under the surface in Australia for standards that look more scientifically and legally respectable. Before we succumb to such pressures, it is well to contemplate how those pressures have been played out in the USA during the past 25 years.

Historically, what has happened in the United States is that key political players in the nursing-home regulatory game came to be critical of broad, vaguely defined standards. The industry has been at the forefront of this criticism; when nursing home X gets a not met rating on a broad standard on which nursing home Y in similar circumstances gets a met rating, home X screams about inconsistency. It complains to its industry association about the vagueness of the standard leading to 'subjective' and 'unfair' judgements by inspectors. The industry association representing these member grievances pleads for the standard to be 'tightened up'. Consumer groups also agree that the standards should be made more specific, but for different reasons. They are concerned that vague standards are unenforceable. Legislators have been responsive to these pleas because they feel frustrated that inspectors are not cleaning up the industry the way they had hoped; their analysis fits nicely with that of the industry and consumer groups. These standards, the legislators conclude, are so vague that they give the inspectors too much discretion to subvert the legislative mandate. This indeed is also the analysis of many top regulatory bureaucrats in the federal government. They are frustrated at the failure of the states to deliver federal hopes. Part of the blame they lay at the door of standards so vague as to allow wide discretion for inaction. Finally, the technocrats – the behavioural and medical scientists and the lawyers – despair at

320

vague standards. The scientists believe in tight protocols to ensure that the same things are being assessed in exactly the same way using precisely defined criteria. The lawyers believe, like the consumer advocates, that vague standards are difficult to enforce in the courts and, like the industry associations, they believe that vague standards result in abuse of discretion.

Hence, if there is one thing that all of the influential players of the American regulatory game have agreed upon it is that broad standards which are not tightly specified must be narrowed. The consequence has been an historical process of all these constituencies succeeding in having one broad standard broken down into two narrower standards; then later each of those two standards being subdivided into three standards.

By 1986 the logical conclusion to this process was reached to the point where there were over 500 federal standards ('Tag numbers'). Outcome-oriented reforms in 1986 reduced these to 357, but this was short-lived respite with the 1987 Omnibus Budget Reconciliation Act (OBRA) reforms[10] adding a large number of new and tighter standards. Moreover, in some states, the number of state standards exceeds the federal standards by a factor of two or three. In most states, federal and state standards are surveyed simultaneously. The upshot is that most of the people who inspect US nursing homes are checking compliance with over a thousand regulations – a stark contrast with the 31 Australian standards. How do they cope with such a daunting task? The answer is that they do not. Some of the standards are completely forgotten, not suppressed by any malevolent or captured political motive, just plain forgotten. Such standards are never cited in the states where they are forgotten. Then there are those that become familiar by some accident of enforcement history that gave prominence to a particular standard in a particular state. Referring to state regulations, one midwestern inspector said: 'We use 10 percent of them repeatedly. You get into the habit of citing the same ones. Even though possibly you could use others [for the same offence]. Most are never used.'

The professional background of the inspection-team members is one important criterion that selects which standards will be attended to. Administrator: 'If you've got a nurse, it will be nursing deficiencies in the survey report; if a pharmacist, you'll get pharmacy deficiencies; a sanitarian, sanitary deficiencies; a lawyer, patient rights, etc.' We observed a Medicaid survey team to rate all dietary standards in a facility 'met' for the reason that the dietary problems looked so serious. How can that make sense? The team felt that the dietary problems were so bad that they could not check them all out properly and get all the other standards checked in the time-frame required by the Health Care Financing Administration (HCFA) to complete the survey; so they 'deferred' the dietary problem for two weeks until a dietician could be booked for a specialist survey. When we went out with the dietician two weeks later on this survey, sure enough, a great number of the dietary standards rated met in the survey report submitted to the federal government were rated 'not met'.

The point of these examples is that when surveyors have an impossible number of standards to check, arbitrary factors will cause particular standards to be checked in some homes but neglected in others, causing endemic unreliability. At its best, the American process works in the following way. The inspectors meet together at the conclusion to their information-gathering, as they do at certain intermediate points during the inspection, to share the problems they have found. When a number of negative findings are judged to constitute a pattern of non-compliance of a particular type, a search begins for a 'Tag number' which can be written up as not met. Once all the problems have been agreed and Tag numbers found to write not mets for them, the team leader ticks met for all the remaining standards. As she does so, she does not read them or think about them and she certainly does not check with her colleagues that someone has collected the information necessary to reach that met rating. Usually she will not discuss with her colleagues the possibility that the same pattern of conduct that caused one standard to be rated not met should also cause several other standards to be out of compliance (for example, an inappropriate use of restraint may cause standards concerned with restraint, following physician's orders, resident choice, mobility and freedom of movement to all be out of compliance).[11] In other words she makes one valid not met rating and several invalid met ratings as a result of this strategy. This we said was the American process at its best. At its worst, the team partitions responsibility for the standards, each writing up their own standards with little input from the other team members.

What is the relevant contrast with the Australian process in this regard? It is not easy for Australian teams to keep 31 standards in their heads even though none of them has mandated protocols. Yet they can make a fist of it. More critically, after their visit the team can (and generally does) sit down to discuss, standard by standard, the evidence collected by all team members relevant to each one. This dialogue is formalized by the team agreeing on a list of positives and negatives to be written beside each standard. Sometimes they will find that they have not collected the data necessary to reach a reliable rating on the standard. They must then take steps to collect the extra information. There is no escape from this because the team is required to sit down with the management of the nursing home, to summarize the positives and negatives on each standard and to give reasons for their final ratings. Again the American 'exit conference' is different in that it reports only exceptions. Nothing is said about standards that have been ticked met. It would be difficult to do so since the team has neither debated compliance with them nor assured themselves that they have collected the data relevant to them. The crucial difference is that Australian teams actually do deliberate on all their standards and collect the evidence that they judge sufficient to support that deliberation.

It is not the fault of American inspectors that they do not do this – the number of standards and protocols with which they must live makes this quite impossible. The end result of demands for more specific standards with more clearly defined protocols that cover all the things judged to be important for nursing homes is an inspection package that is structurally unreliable. The pursuit of the reliability of parts causes the unreliability of the whole.

If American inspectors give up on keeping all these standards in their heads, what is their cognitive coping strategy? It seems to us that they have a gestalt of the prohibitions codified in the regulations – for example, that good infection

322

control is required; that privacy must be protected; that good nursing practice should be followed. It is likely that professional training informs these gestalts more than the law does. They then decide whether a citation ought to be written by deciding whether it offends against one of these gestalts. Then they search for the appropriate regulation under which to cite it. 'What will we call it? How about 1220 A? What about 1220 B? Why don't we use both of them?'

After explaining to a number of surveyors this interpretation, based on our observation of how they coped, they agreed that this was basically how they did it. When we pointed out that the most troubling implication of this process from the point of view of reliability was that depending on how hard they searched through the standards, they might find one or two or three deficiencies to write out, one of them said, tellingly: 'Or they might find none at all and have to mush it in.' Decisions about how hard to search for multiple citations for essentially the same problem are driven by a 'professional judgment' of 'how serious overall their problems have been' or 'how hard they've been trying.' 'You can write it out under [X] and create a repeat violation because they got a deficiency on [X] last time. Or you can write it out under [Y] so its just an element, which has no real consequences. Or you can put it out under both [X] and [Y], putting out a whole standard.'[12]

Hence, hand-in-hand with a paradox of reliability is a paradox of discretion. More and more specific standards are written by lawmakers in the misplaced belief that this narrows the discretion of inspectors. The opposite is the truth: the larger the smorgasbord of standards, the greater the discretion of regulators to pick and choose an enforcement cocktail tailored to meet their own objective. A proliferation of more specific laws is a resource to expand discretion, not a limitation upon it (Baldwin and Hawkins, 1984).

The beauty of a small number of broad standards is therefore that one can design a regulatory process to ensure that the ticking of a met rating means that a proper process of information-gathering and team deliberation has occurred on that standard. One accountability check in Australia is that whenever enforcement action is appealed, the team's worksheets listing all of the positives and negatives they found under each of the 31 standards must be tabled before the Standards Review Panel. Until 1990, teams were required to write a report for the nursing home with a statement in support of the rating for each of the 31 standards. This proved an impossible burden with reports often running over 50 typed pages. As a result, from 1990, the report gives a statement in support of the compliance ratings of standards grouped under seven objectives. This makes for 10-page reports which are more consumer-friendly.

In summary, the smaller the number of standards, the better the prospects of ensuring that (a) the most vital information for assessing the total quality of life and quality of care of residents is pursued; (b) lying behind each rating is a collective deliberative process on what that particular rating should be; (c) there is effective public accountability to audit that (a) and (b) actually occur; and (d) inspectors have the capacity to stand back to document the wider patterns in the problems they have identified, to see the wood for the trees. These indeed are just some of the ways that 'loose laws' can make for better public policy (Goodin, 1982: 59–72).

2. THE EFFECT OF PROTOCOLS ON RELIABILITY

The same argument against the proliferation of standards can be extended to the proliferation of protocols for rating standards. The misplaced faith of the legislator for narrowing broad discretion results in the enactment of more specific laws. The misplaced faith of the consultants from the scientific establishment of gerontology results in protocols to narrow discretion. When there are the number of protocols that are supposedly followed in the American process, all the inspector can do is fill out the forms mandated for certain protocols and essentially fudge the other protocols that cannot be checked. Realizing that this is the way the game is played, advocates of protocols for certain standards that they regard as especially important lobby the federal government to mandate auditable protocol forms that the state inspectors must fill out. While this improves the attention given to the lobbyist's cherished regulation, it further worsens the structural malaise of the process.

The commendable shift to resident interviews in the OBRA reforms to the survey process introduced in October 1990 has already fallen prey to the disease of the proliferation of protocols. Our observations during the early months of the new process illustrated the unintended consequences. Interviewers started at the beginning of the schedule for the resident interviews only to find that either they ran out of time or the resident became exhausted before they had got very far through the schedule. Thus, items placed early in the schedule were done according to protocol, and later items were fudged or ignored. For this and other reasons we will come to soon, we therefore agree with the exasperated surveyor who said to us: 'Our own questions are better than the nonsense on the OBRA forms.' When we raised this and other examples of OBRA protocols being selectively and partially followed, one state survey manager replied: 'We'll streamline it. In time we'll do it our way rather than follow the HCFA protocol.' The trouble is of course that every state has no choice but to streamline, and each state streamlines in its own way. Streamlining error is the inevitable consequence of overly ambitious pursuit of reliability through the proliferation of protocols.

Protocols can work well in the context of a social science evaluation, but fail in practice because in the evaluation study the protocol does not have to compete for limited time with 30 other protocols. There are, however, other reasons why a protocol that succeeds in the evaluation study fails in inspection practice. An evaluation might show that a protocol of putting a tick in a box for the name of every resident that participates in each activity can be done reliably. Moreover, scores from following the protocol are validated against more sophisticated detailed assessments of the effectiveness of activities programmes. Unfortunately, however, what was valid at the evaluation stage quickly becomes invalid at the implementation stage.

Administrators are quick learners in the business of getting good survey results. If ticks in activities boxes are what count, droves of sleeping residents will be wheeled into activities programmes to get the numbers up. Never mind that the quality of the activities programme will be compromised by the clutter of sleeping residents; it's beating the protocol that counts. This is why nursing-home administrators love protocols: 'Give us the rules and we'll play the game.' Imprecision, undefined evidence-gathering procedures, make it harder for the efficient administrator to beat the system. In Australia, because there are no defined protocols for inspectors, nursing-home management has no choice but to focus on the outcomes for which the inspectors are searching. This makes their life more painful and uncertain. When protocols are defined, the administrators showed us how they create a documentation system, a paper trail that matches the protocols the inspectors follow: 'You can achieve paper compliance without real compliance. You can fool most inspectors on most standards with paper compliance.'

The source of unreliability then becomes the rare inspector who looks behind the paper trail to the quality of care that is actually being given. Validity then becomes the major source of unreliability!

American evaluators have been systematically blind to these possibilities. When they fail to find reliability after innovations to 'tighten up' the standards and protocols, they call for more of the same. They conclude that the tightening and refinement did not go far enough. Consider, for example, the evaluation of the state of New York's methodologically sophisticated and pace-setting Sentinel Health Events (Office of Health Systems Management, 1985). The Sentinel Health Events were not legal standards but outcome measures designed to be at the heart of the innovative New York regulatory system. When this study obtained poor reliabilities for nursing-home ratings using the Sentinel Health Events, the evaluators concluded:

> It is important to note that although the Stage I and Stage II reliabilities were disappointing, it is expected that the old system in New York State of PaCS (the system to be implemented nationally in April 1986) would have even less reliability. This is because the new system in New York has far more structure than either the old system or PaCS. (Office of Health Systems Management, 1985: 105)

The assumption that more structure is better was particularly obstinate in light of the reasons for unreliability that were diagnosed in the New York study. The first and 'extremely prevalent' reason found was that 'some surveyors (incorrectly) extended protocol requirements by noting a quality issue when no such quality issue is defined in the Protocol' (Office of Health Systems Management, 1985: 39). An illustration of an 'incorrect' deviation from protocol arose when one surveyor who was supposed to assess improvement of a decubitus ulcer on the basis of 'chart review' found inadequate care and deterioration by *observing* care being given:

> The protocol states that only a chart review is necessary for this protocol, so the first cause for difference of opinion was a result of one surveyor doing more than he/she was instructed to do. (Office of Health Systems Management, 1985: 36)

This clearly illustrates the pathology of punishing surveyors for looking beyond the trees specified in their protocols to the wood. The orthodoxy of science is to disapprove of the nurse who used her/his initiative to follow her/his suspicion by digging deeper and to approve the nurse who reached the wrong conclusion because she/he followed the protocol. The orthodoxy of science is naïve here. It is naïve to believe that nurses, who are socialized to care about the patients they encounter, who are trained to use their initiative as professionals to get to the bottom of problems, can be turned into uncaring, mindless automatons who simply stick to the protocols.

Given that many nurses will be caring enough and have the initiative to follow the evidentiary trail toward conclusions of poor quality care, we think it best to design inspection systems which both assume and encourage this, rather than systems that attempt to control it. We think that when a resident is being seriously neglected, two different nurses, with free rein to follow whatever evidentiary trail they pick up, are both more likely to detect the neglect than are two nurses who we ask to be automatons by following a standard protocol. This is particularly so with the many idiosyncratic types of neglect that the designers of the protocol never foresaw. As one Australian inspector pointed out: 'There are a hundred different reasons for residents to be incontinent.' The advantage of wide procedural discretion over tight definition of protocols in generating valid ratings seem to us especially profound when we are considering team inspections. This is because when one team member fails to latch on to an evidentiary trail that will lead to a not met rating the other team member may succeed in latching on to it, or one may discover the missing link in an evidentiary chain pieced together by the other. With our own reliability data, after all, the main source of disagreement was the single independent rater failing to pick up information that the team had detected (and vice versa to a lesser extent).

Inspectors boxed in by a proliferation of protocols cope in another way that makes it difficult for them to see the wood for the trees: *task-specialization*. One surveyor takes responsibility for filling out the forms required from record interviews and another completes the reviews of resident records. We observed very little reading by one surveyor of the protocols filled out by another. In the busy work of getting the huge number of survey forms completed, the process of following up problems identified in a resident interview by tracking down residents' records (and vice versa) is profoundly compromised. This is not to say such follow-through does not occur in the USA; it is just to say that it occurs more freely in the more free-wheeling Australian process. Protocols kill initiative under a pile of paper. With nursing-home staff and nursing-home inspectors alike, excessive demands for task-orientation distract attention from the outcomes that matter. The result is the creation of nursing-home bureaucracies and regulatory bureaucracies that miss the big picture.

This pathology of protocols is just a specific illustration of the more general problem of formalized regulation forgetting that 'policy problems can be solved only by taking account of numerous interdependent and highly variable factors which oblige decision-makers to manage a kind of cybernetic process involving tentative probe, feedback, adjustment, and reconciliation' (Schuck, 1979: 29). The pursuit of precision, either by protocols or by the proliferation of ever-narrower rules, causes an unreliability that is a symptom of a deeper and many-sided malaise of regulatory failure. This is especially depressing since the

326

pursuit of precision usually fails in its own terms – it fails to deliver precision. There might be 30 or 40 US regulations for every one in Australia, but the American standards still seem vague. In the language game of regulation, the problem of one vague concept is solved by splitting into three vague concepts or by defining protocols with other vague concepts. An alternative we suggest to the perpetual struggle to get the words right is to concentrate more on getting the processes of dialogue right. Certainly there is merit in keeping the words simple. This is a necessary precondition to accomplishing processes of dialogue that will deliver reliable judgements on those simple words.

3. THE EFFECT OF SUBJECTIVITY OF STANDARDS ON RELIABILITY

When we spoke to senior regulatory bureaucrats in the United States and to social scientists who had been involved in the development and evaluation of nursing home surveys, a common type of comment was: 'There are some things that the process cannot do reliably. So you don't do them. Examples are: "Are the staff pleasant? Is the room tastefully decorated?"' The thought occurred to us that if the Hyatt Hotel group adopted the view that decor and staff pleasantness were matters for which it could not set reliable standards (and therefore should not bother with), it would soon be bankrupt. In business, a head office effectively enforces all manner of 'soft' standards on franchisees by adopting a qualitative approach to evaluation of performance. In these cases, dialogue informs an evaluation that is made against the yardstick of 'What is it, subjectively, that consumers want?' Admittedly, some of these subjective assessments are easy and some are hard. You don't have to talk to many consumers to realize that they don't like vermin running around their hotel room or their nursing home. But to judge reactions as to how warm and non-institutional is the decor or what they think of their continental breakfast, you really need to work hard at talking to consumers. Surely one reason that American nursing homes are so cold, institutional, and unattentive to decor compared for example to English nursing homes is precisely the attitude that such things are so subjective as to be beyond control.

The reliability of the 'homelike environment' standard (4.1 in Table 1) in Australia shows that this American posture is in error. A properly subjective approach on a standard such as this involves talking to residents about whether they feel free to put up personal mementos in an area they define as their private space, whether there are spaces in the facility that they feel are inviting and homelike for chatting with friends, whether they feel there are inviting garden areas they can use. This subjectivity often comes under attack in Australia. For example, managers of nursing-home chains complain to us that they have provided exactly the same food to two nursing homes; the team in one home gives them a 'met' rating for the food and in the other home they get an 'action required' rating. There is absolutely no inconsistency here if the residents at the two homes have different subjective views about the food. Two teams will never agree on what is nice food, but we have found that they can agree, with high reliability, on whether the residents in a nursing home generally like the food they are getting. Reliability is accomplished by rejecting objectivity in favour of subjectivity.

The impetus to reform subjectivity in standards through objective criteria and protocols is dangerous because quality of life, which is what nursing-home care should be about, is ultimately an irreducibly subjective matter. The paradox of objectivity is that its pursuit undercuts a desideratum on which the industry, politicians, consumer groups and gerontologists (if not the lawyers) generally agree. This is that the regulatory process should be more outcome-oriented. The trouble is that inputs (the temperature of the food as it leaves the serving line; the size of the room) are generally more 'objective' than outcomes (satisfaction of residents with the food and the comfort of the room). Objectivity disempowers residents and empowers nursing-home managements who know how to get objective inputs in a row for inspection day – reams of documentation of the temperatures on food lines. Subjectivity, in contrast, means that residents are empowered because it is no longer the documents under the control of management that matter; it is what they as residents think and want that counts.

Even the vision of outcomes which enjoys most support within the American gerontological establishment is an 'objective' conception – counting the number of residents with decubitus ulcers or the number of restrained residents (Institute of Medicine, 1986; Office of Health Systems Management, 1985; Phillips, 1987). Collecting such objective outcome information is something we applaud. However, it must be pointed out that it is a process that does little to shift power over the definition of regulatory problems out of the hands of management into the hands of consumers. Administrators can handle a regulatory process that counts decubitus ulcers or restraints. They can keep control of their own evaluation because they know what the score is objectively before the inspector walks through the door. Consequently, they are ready with a defensive documentary record to prove that the residents with the bedsores were all turned two-hourly, that there are physicians' orders, psychiatric assessments to justify the restraints they want to keep and the like (Wiener and Kayser-Jones, 1989). Hence, while the outcome of the number of restrained residents can be measured very reliably and while this is an extremely valuable thing to do, it does not solve the problem of reliably assessing a law that requires proper use of restraints (such as Standard 7.6 in Table 1). Reliable assessment of a legal standard requires investigative common sense, determination and the imagination to uncover leads and follow them. The protocol-following automatons lauded by the objective-outcomes movement will be incapable of doing this job reliably. Their protocols would not allow them reliably to find that over 90 percent of the American nursing homes we have seen fail to meet the Australian restraint Standard 7.6. Instead, they mostly conclude that American homes where half the residents are tied up or chemically restrained meet the US standards, and where they find non-compliance, they find it unreliably.

328

4. THE EFFECT OF BEING RESIDENT-CENTRED ON RELIABILITY

Being resident-centred means two things for us: first, it means relying on residents as a source of information for rating standards and, second, it means participation in a regulatory dialogue where quality of life outcomes for residents are the ultimate criteria of regulatory evaluation. Critics regard this as an orientation that is a prescription for unreliability because most residents are so sick or confused that what is a subjectively good outcome for them is unknowable in most particular cases. Moreover, for the same reason, they are incapable of being meaningfully interviewed. Our research team deals with both these objections elsewhere at greater length (Braithwaite and Makkai, 1993). Briefly, we should at least say here that most resident outcomes that are the focus of debate within any sensible regulatory system will be uncontrovertially bad. We know that getting burnt in a fire, getting pills prescribed for someone else, or getting a decubitus ulcer are outcomes that residents are keen to avoid without having to ask them. Second, we use our fieldwork data to argue elsewhere that skilled inspectors know how to find those residents in a nursing home who will be outstanding informants on those issues that do require subjective feedback from residents and they also know how to get some useful information even from residents who spend most of their life extremely confused (Braithwaite and Makkai, 1993). The critics argue that it is harder, or even impossible, for a nursing home with many extremely high disability or demented residents to comply with standards under the more resident-centred process that we have in Australia. Our data do not show this to be the case (Braithwaite and Makkai, 1993).

In practical terms, the Australian nursing-home regulatory process is more resident-centred than any we know. Yet we have seen that this resident-centred process seems to have high reliability. It is true, as the critics point out, that Australian inspectors are often misled by confused residents. However, we also found it true that these errors are almost invariably corrected long before they affect final ratings. In our reliability study, inspectors being misled by confused residents did not even register as a reason for disagreements, though one side picking up useful information from residents that the other side missed was one of the more important reasons for disagreements (Braithwaite et al., 1991). Moreover, with our study of reasons for 889 disagreements between inspectors and directors of nursing on ratings, in only 3 percent of disagreements was one of the reasons given for disagreement that the director of nursing felt that the team had relied on misinformation from residents (Braithwaite et al., 1990: 73).

These data show that interpretive errors in a subjective, resident-centred process can be and are corrected through a process of dialogue. First, dialogue with residents and their carers is important. Second, with nursing-home staff and within the team, there is dialogue about whether the seven quality of life objectives of the Australian standards are being secured: health care, social independence, freedom of choice, homelike environment, privacy and dignity, variety of experience and safety. Consistency does not easily fall out of such processes of dialogue; it comes painfully and with a lot of backtracking and moving in circles as new inconsistencies are discovered along the way.

Ultimately, however, consistency will be greater to the extent that the *only* debate is about resident outcomes. When the debate is theoretically only about whether an input required in a rule is delivered, in practice the outcomes that motivated the rulemakers' specification of the input will unpredictably intrude into regulatory judgements. This is inevitable because sensible people do not like to enforce the law when its enforcement will defeat the very purposes for which the law was enacted. Because business regulatory laws (such as those that regulate health care) deal with such complex, changing and individually variable problems, mismatch between legally mandated input and desired outcome is exceedingly common.

Let us illustrate with a comparatively simple example. We observed a Chicago sanitarian point out during an exit conference following an inspection that it is against the regulations to have a male and a female in adjoining rooms sharing the same toilet. The sanitarian concedes that in this particular case neither resident is capable of using the toilet and that moving either of them would be upsetting to them. He says that he is going to turn a blind eye to the rule for the sake of the residents, but he warns management that someone else from the department could come along and cite them for this. In other words, he is pointing out that because there is such a mismatch between rule and outcome, he is giving an unreliable ruling. With Australian inspectors confronting such a predicament, there will be no such unreliability. Since what is the best outcome for the residents is clear and since inspectors are instructed only to be concerned about outcomes, dialogue should quickly lead to a reliable result.

Our claim is that dialogue about resident-centred outcomes conduces to more reliability than recourse to authoritative interpretations of the meaning of words in rules. A word like privacy is certainly a very slippery word, as is health or pain as a matter of fact. In a resident-centred process when the question arises 'But is this really an invasion of privacy?', the answer is discovered through a process of dialogue about what are the senses of privacy that are important to this particular resident. Dissension is more likely when the question is to be resolved by pitting one inspector's conception of what privacy means against another's; consensus is more likely when the professional responsibility of both is to focus on the practical sense of privacy that is subjectively important to that resident in that situation. There will always be inconsistency in trans-situational 'objective' judgements of whether privacy has been invaded. Resident-centred contextual dialogue about privacy outcomes, in contrast, can often reach reliable conclusions.

It follows that progress with increasing reliability is less likely to come from handing down more sharply defined authoritative interpretations of what privacy is, more likely to come from improving processes of dialogue. Dialogue occurs at many levels, all of which allow scope for improvement. Inspectors can improve their dialogue with residents by learning how to deal with resident intimidation, how to capture the moments of clarity of thought that normally confused residents experience, how to communicate non-verbally with residents when verbal communication is poor, how to use third parties (roommates, relatives) to draw out uncommunicative residents, how to mobilize translation

330

support with non-English speaking residents. Moreover, group discussions with residents (e.g. with Residents' Councils), something on which American inspectors are much more advanced than those in Australia, can draw out some people who will not be drawn one on one.

Inspectors can improve their dialogue with each other by scheduling interim discussions during the course of an inspection, learning how to be active listeners, learning how to break deadlocks by framing the sticking points on which more subjective information from residents is needed. They can also learn when it is wise to draw on the wider experience of a supervisor or to get the perspective of nursing-home staff on an issue. They can learn how to select crucial conflicts over consistency to be put on the agenda for regular meetings of all inspectors. Training courses can be improved by making them more genuinely dialogic – showing videotapes of real regulatory encounters and asking trainees to debate the appropriate compliance rating, for example. Attempts have been made to improve dialogue at most of these levels in both the USA and Australia, but with highly variable commitment and success.

Focusing reform energy on processes of dialogue rather than on rules recognizes something that the community of scholars who work on regulation and policing have begun to realize. This is that it is simply not true that police officers make decisions mostly by reference to rules (Shearing and Ericson, 1991). They do not, should not and could not do so. Police culture, Shearing and Ericson (1991) point out, is not a book of rules, but a storybook. Police learn how to handle difficult situations by hearing stories about how competent officers handled similar situations or by themselves experiencing and retelling such stories:

> Stories constitute a consciousness, a sensibility, a way of being out of which action will flow without recourse to specific instructions. Unlike rules, stories do not address action directly but rather constitute a sensibility out of which action flows. (Shearing, personal communication, 1993)

Stories instruct the participants in a regulatory culture how to 'read', via a 'poetic apprehension', the layers of meaning in a situation. Shearing and Ericson (1991) show how this poetic apprehension is communicated through analogous reasoning – like advising young officers to avoid provocation in difficult situations by 'acting as if you were on holidays'. Nursing-home inspectors communicate a resident-centred sensibility, for example, with the analogous reason: 'Is this a home that you could be happy for your mother or grandmother to live in?' Reliable ratings will be maximally possible with a regulatory culture that accomplishes a common set of sensibilities through processes of dialogue.

Hence, a hotel chain can get staff pleasantness and decor to a state that appeals to consumers, but it will not accomplish this with a set of decor rules. Rather, it seeks to cultivate the right sort of sensibilities in its management and quality assurance staff with stories, concrete examples and analogies. Staff civility and pleasant decor then follow from these sensibilities.

The importance of legal standards is more in setting the framework and focus for storytelling, less as words that utter explicit guidance. To be good at framework-setting and focusing dialogue, standards must be simple and few in number. Like good poetry, they must engage us by being replete with silences, leaving us to make of them what we can: 'For in leaving to us the talk of making sense of what is before us, this silence forces our continuous and attentive engagement with the poem itself' (White, 1984:27).

5. THE EFFECT OF RANDOM SAMPLING ON RELIABILITY

Yet another way in which the paradox of reliability came about in the past was on the question of the random sampling of residents. The behavioural and medical scientists who were influential in shaping the American process as it emerged in the 1980s believed that randomness was important to valid and reliable ratings. The old-fashioned inspection practice of allowing inspectors to concentrate their evidence-gathering on residents of their choice was viewed as unscientific. Many key players in the industry association were also vigorous advocates of random sampling, but for different and perhaps more sophisticated reasons. Some regulators alleged that these industry players supported random sampling because it would inhibit inspectors from following their noses to the residents who were getting the worst deal out of the nursing home. The lawyers had a hand in this shift as well. Up until October 1990, when the USA abandoned random sampling of residents for nursing-home inspections, standard training practice would confront the American inspector with the scenario of a company lawyer challenging their findings by questioning their competence in the statistical theory which would warrant the judgement that a 'pattern' of non-compliance existed.

Our observations of the random-sampling process revealed endemic cheating by inspectors. They would cheat for both principled and unprincipled reasons. When on the initial tour of the nursing home, the inspector met a resident who complained of mistreatment or who manifested signs of neglectful care, the inspector would sometimes cheat by putting that resident into the random sample even though she/he was not randomly selected. On one occasion, an inspector from another part of the state asked the team to put a friend of hers who was suffering from a decubitus ulcer in the sample. On another occasion, a complainant was fudged into the sample to protect her – so that the problem would appear to have been discovered by the team. In another multistorey nursing home, where care seemed to vary by floor, the team decided to 'improve' on the standard sampling protocol by stratifying the sample by floor. These were all examples of principled cheating.

Examples of unprincipled cheating included the following. The team member met on the tour a resident who was a friend she enjoyed talking to. After a 20-minute chat with her over lunch, she realized that she had already collected half the information she needed from this resident. So she slipped her into the random sample. In another type of fudging repeatedly observed, the inspector would find a resident with multiple problems – restraint, catheter, decubitus ulcer and others. Because the sampling protocol demands a number of residents

332

with each of these types of special problem, this resident became 'a good one to do'. Slipping such a resident into the sample reduced the total number of residents investigated. We say these latter examples are of unprincipled cheating, but the teams did not view it this way. We have already made the point that systematic data collection to rate hundreds of regulations is impossible; the cheating, they contended, made an impossible job a little more possible.

Even when the cheating was clearly principled rather than designed to cut corners, surveyors were under no illusion that it was cheating that required concealment:

Surveyor: 'There are ways of bending these things [the sample]. That doesn't cause us any problem.'
JB: 'How do you mean?'
Surveyor: 'Well you can just number the list of patients where you are selecting every fifth one: 1,2,3,4,6,5.'

It is a sad commentary on the unreflexive empiricism of the behavioural sciences that so many books are written on the statistics of sampling, while no one does empirical studies of random sampling in practice. Our own observations are of a wide gulf between science in the books and science in action, even with surveyors with considerably more education and training in sampling protocols than the average opinion survey interviewer, for example.

The reasons for the gulf in this domain are multiple, but include: (a) laziness; (b) job survival; (c) the view that they have more serious professional obligations than to the numbers games of scientists; and (d) the view that they have a more sophisticated or rounded practitioner's view of randomness than the theoreticians. The last of these is the most interesting: surveyors who stratify by floor or who put into the sample someone they bump into on the tour have a social construction of randomness which they will defend as superior to the protocol they have been given. This then is just a special case of the naïvety of assuming that because protocols exist, they will be followed; because something works in a pilot, it will work in day-to-day practice. Behavioural scientists are empirically neglectful of behaviour in science. One lesson of observing nursing-home inspections is that trained professionals expect and extract working conditions where they exercise professional judgement: they simply refuse to succumb to demands that they follow instructions like machines. Inspection procedures should never be based on the hope that this will not happen; they should be designed on the expectation that it will.

Hence, random sampling in nursing-home inspection in the USA up to 1990 tended to fail in one of two ways. In some cases the team cheated by slipping bad cases into the sample, thereby defeating randomness. In other cases, they refrained from cheating when they saw bad cases; they settled for the randomly selected case and let the bad case slip by that might have been their best chance of getting to the deepest problems in the facility. As argued earlier, our own view is that inspectors are most likely to find problems of non-compliance reliably when their initiative in following evidentiary leads is cultivated instead of controlled.

The final reason why random sampling reduces reliability in regulatory inspections is that it is extraordinarily time-consuming. It distracts a great deal of time from the more important work of gathering evidence on all the standards (or in the US case, at least a larger fraction of the standards). We would observe one team member on the first day of a pre-1990 US inspection do little more than participate in the initial tour and gather all the information on residents and their categories of care in order to select the sample, selecting it with the correct number in each category (variably according to the number of qualified residents in the home), and recording the selected sample to prove that the sampling protocol had been followed. On one occasion, we observed four nurses debate for 37 minutes whether, for sampling purposes, group therapy counted in the 'physical therapy' category. A call to the supervisor was eventually needed to resolve the dispute. All this effort for the dubious statistical virtue of randomly selecting 16 residents from a population of 80! The USA made a sound scientific decision when it abandoned random sampling in October 1990.

DISCUSSION

The first point we should make toward a conclusion is that our hypothesis that the US nursing-home inspection process is much less reliable than the Australian process may simply not be true. None of the quantitative studies has large samples, and all have design flaws. They do, nevertheless, amount to superior information on the reliability of nursing-home inspection than we have on any other area of business regulatory inspection we know. We would be surprised if our hypothesis were wrong, however, not only because of the dramatically different results of the quantitative reliability studies but because of the convergent conclusion from our extensive qualitative fieldwork.

It could be argued that even if our empirical claim about the comparative reliability of nursing-home inspection were right, this is simply a statistical artefact. When an American inspector finds a problem that should be cited, there are 499 different ways he/she can cite it under the wrong standard (if there are 500 standards). When an Australian decides to give a not met rating, there are only 30 ways he/she can get it wrong (with 31 standards). Of course this is an overstatement because clearly there is little risk of fire-safety citations being written under a quality of food standard. Nevertheless, the basic point remains that more standards means more ways classification errors can occur.

To point this out, however, is not to erect a defence of the American standards. It is no comfort to nursing-home operators who feel they have been treated inconsistently to tell them that they unfortunately have been victims of a statistical artefact. If inspectors give the wrong ratings because of the many standards under which they might write non-compliance, then this is a bad feature of the design of a system with too many standards. It is the design features of this system that cause the unreliability. At the outset to this article, we said that reliability is not the only, or even the most important, criterion for evaluating a regulatory process. For one thing, reliability is not validity. A common assertion

334

about nursing homes from industry participants in all the countries we visited for this research is that competent people can assess validity rather easily: 'When I go into a home, I can look around and fairly quickly tell if it is a well-run nursing home or a nursing home with problems. If I can do it, they [surveyors] can because they go to different homes all the time' (Pennsylvanian administrator). This kind of assertion does not sit well with American researchers who find low reliability in the ratings of US inspection teams. It may be, however, that both the genius and the limitation of the Australian process is that it engages with the nursing home only at that rather broad level of the quality of care and life, and it is at this broad level that reliability can be achieved, as in this oft-repeated wisdom of the industry.

Once the team follows protocols that cause it to dig deeper, reliability may become problematic. In failing to dig deep, the process may in some senses be reliable but not valid. Consider Standard 2.2, 'Residents are enabled and encouraged to maintain control of their financial affairs.' This is assessed by a team member asking the person responsible for managing resident accounts (and for liaison with guardians or relatives who manage accounts) to explain the nursing home's system for ensuring that the standard is met. Documentary evidence of these systems will then be sighted. In addition, the team will ask residents and visitors if they are experiencing any problems in maintaining resident control of their financial affairs. What we have found is that different raters who only dig this deep in their investigations of this matter will come up with the same ratings. However, if one of the teams were to dig deeper and conduct a full-scale financial audit of all of the residents' accounts, it might find instances of residents being deceived and defrauded by the nursing home. By one team digging deeper, interteam reliability would have been shattered, but this team would be making a more valid rating. What we may have with Australian standards monitoring is a process that reliably reveals those sorts of problems that can be revealed by shallow digging.

Overall, we doubt that the American process digs deeper than the Australian process does, because Australian facilities that are identified as 'homes of concern' at the initial visit usually get many more follow-up visits than do American homes with comparable problems. However, there is no doubt that at the initial visit stage, there are several important ways in which the American process digs deeper. An example is the US requirement for a systematic survey of errors in the administration of medications. US inspections often uncover quite frightening 'med-pass error rates' of 10 percent and more. Australian standards monitoring visits reliably fail to uncover such problems. American inspectors observe treatments being given to a sample of residents. Mostly these are observations of the treatment of decubitus ulcers. This deeper digging in the American process uncovers many problems that remain reliably submerged in the Australian process – Class III ulcers that are documented and treated as Class II or poor infection-control practice in the treatment of bedsores. The biggest difference is with the deeper digging that American inspectors do in checking the documentation of resident care, though, unlike the other domains of deeper digging we have discussed, we doubt that this is reason for superiority in the US process (Braithwaite, 1994). Moreover, we do not believe that the lower reliability of the US process is caused by its successes in collecting greater amounts of information than the initial Australian visit. On the contrary, the greater unreliability of the American process is caused by the fact that most of its hundreds of ratings are made on the basis of no information or at least no deliberation of any information.

In summary, we think it is fair to describe the initial Australian visit as reliably uncovering problems that can be exposed by shallow digging and reliably failing to uncover problems that can only be exposed by digging deeper. Moreover, it would improve the validity of the Australian process to adopt certain elements of the American process, such as the systematic observation of treatments. This is not to deny our more fundamental assertion that the best way to find the deepest problems is to follow leads rather than follow protocols. A police department that relies exclusively on the most sophisticated regimen of random patrol will not solve murders.

CONCLUSION

The classic work on the optimal precision of regulatory standards has been that of Colin Diver (1980, 1989). Diver identifies three problems with regulatory standards – vagueness, overinclusiveness and complexity. Vague rules leave citizens to guess at their meaning in particular circumstances. Overinclusive rules command actions that are not beneficial (or are harmful). Overinclusive rules accomplish a poor fit between outcomes desired by policymakers and the requirements demanded by literal adherence to the rules. A complex set of rules is long, full of contradictions between one part of the rules and another, and dogged by verbal intricacy.

Diver (1989) advances three qualities of well-drafted legal rules – transparency, congruence and simplicity – to deal respectively with the three problems of vagueness, overinclusiveness and complexity. Clearly, the 31 Australian standards in Table 1 satisfy the criterion of simplicity. Congruence between desired outcomes and legal requirements, we have seen, is accomplished by shifting to a radical outcome-orientation wherein if resident outcomes cannot be shown to be put at risk by an action, then that action involves no violation. The problem of vagueness, however, is not dealt with by making the rules transparent. Different citizens cannot look at the Australian standards as if through a transparent window and see the same image. Transparency is accomplished at the next stage of the process. Vagueness about meaning is clarified by empowering the beneficiaries of the rules to define the meanings of the standard that are important to them in a particular situation. Because there is no way of solving the problem of vagueness at the level of the wording of rules without also rendering the rules overinclusive and complex,[13] the solution is to leave the words vague but to specify the interpretive evidence that is privileged and to require a regulatory dialogue about this evidence. Laws that fail the transparency test as disembodied law can be the starting point for a process that solves the vagueness problem

336

through mandating which subjectivity is privileged (and mandating dialogue focused on that subjectivity). The law fails the vagueness test, but the package of law–outcome–subjectivity–dialogue passes it. That is, two people just applying the law are likely to reach different conclusions about the same evidence; two people who use the law to guide outcome-oriented dialogue are likely to reach the same legal conclusion in a specific context. Dialogic accountability within the process, especially when this includes a requirement for consultation with residents and staff about the ratings given to their nursing home, prevents vague wording from being translated into unbridled discretion for inspectors, and therefore unreliability.

Like any solution, of course, there are limits to it. There will arise interpretations of 'freedom', subjectively defined by residents, that will be disallowed by inspectors as beyond the range of acceptable definitions of freedom or impossible to satisfy in a nursing home context. Freedom to assault other residents is a case in point, but this still allows wide scope for a disparate variety of constructions of freedom that are tolerated in a liberal democracy, even if they are abhorrent to the inspectors. For example, one Australian resident invoked the standards to insist on his freedom to use the services of a prostitute; this conception of freedom was respected.

Whatever its limitations, the Australian policy is an attempt to break radically with the past in an approach to averting overinclusiveness and complexity, while using dialogue and empowerment to render vague wording outcome-accountable. This puts an alternative to an American nursing-home industry that pleads for simplicity in the law at the same time as it drives the law to greater complexity through persistent complaints about inconsistency. It puts an alternative to consumer advocates who call for more outcome-oriented and resident-centred regulation, but who scream unaccountability and unenforcibility as soon as vague wording appears in regulations. It puts an alternative to regulators who want consistency by some means other than back-breaking protocols that actually worsen reliability. It challenges the clarity of thinking in American governmental reports that pretend mutually contradictory critiques such as the following can be reconciled without radical regulatory transformation: 'There are too many regulations'; 'The regulations are too vague'; and 'The regulations are too picky, detailed' (Illinois Legislative Investigating Commission, 1984: 20–1).

The transformations we advocate involve: (a) opting for standards that are simple and few in number (in preference to many specific rules); (b) structuring the regulatory process to be resident-centred and outcome-oriented; and (c) trusting dialogue (not just top-down 'training') among people who have been persuaded to care about those outcomes. These are our conditions for regulatory context that renders text reliable.

These conclusions can be read as part of a more general questioning of the claim that precision and the elimination of discretion though detailed regulatory law is a path to either greater consistency or equity (Hawkins, 1992). Precision tends to 'permit by implication conduct that the rule was intended to forbid' (Posner, 1977: 425). Detailed laws can provide a set of signposts to navigate

THE POLITICS OF LEGALISM 337

around for those with the resources to employ a good legal navigator (Schoer, 1993). While our focus here has been restricted to the effects of precision on consistency, precision-driven inconsistency can be theorized as a strategic resource of the powerful, particularly of repeat players who have an interest in playing for rules as well as for outcomes (thereby opening up a pattern of loopholes that suit the big players). As Max Weber (1954) showed: '[T]he more formal and complex the body of law becomes, the more it will operate in favour of formal rational bureaucratic groups such as corporations' (Sutton and Wild, 1978:195). Marching under the banner of consistency, business can co-opt lawyers, social scientists, legislators and consumer advocates to the delivery of strategically inconsistent regulation of limited potency.

NOTES

This project has enjoyed the funding support of the Australian Department of Health, Housing and Community Services, the Australian Research Council, the American Bar Foundation and the Australian National University. The authors are indebted to the support of their colleagues on the Nursing Home Regulation in Action Project, David Ermann, Diane Gibson, Miriam Landau and Toni Makkai. Valerie Braithwaite benefited from a visiting appointment at the Buehler Center on Aging, Northwestern University, during the US field work. Thanks to Paul Finn and James Morauta for comments on this article.

1. At another point, Kelman (1987:44) puts the hope that has been realized here another way: 'Rules are bad because they inevitably have gaps and conflicts and are thus less mechanically applicable than they might appear. . . . The open invocation of an apparently vague standard, though, may be reasonably predictable in practice because even relatively detailed tacit community norms so converge that application of vague policy sentiments to cases poses little danger of disagreement.' It would be overstating our results to say that we found little disagreement, though one might say these data show 'a surprisingly low level of disagreement'.
2. '[C]onversation and explanation of one's conduct are avoided . . . a rule's a rule, don't complain to me' (Kelman, 1987:63).
3. There is a 20-page set of Standards Monitoring Guidelines (Department of Community Services and Health, 1988). But these instruct inspectors only in 'key issues' and some of the things to 'look for' under each standard.
4. A British study was conducted of the reliability of two standard protocols for the inspection of residential care homes (Gibbs and Sinclair, 1991). Residential care homes are for residents who require less extensive care than those in nursing homes, though in practice the extensiveness of care between the two types of institution overlaps considerably. Gibbs and Sinclair's (1991) results from 48 homes fall between the US and Australian results reported in this article. A global reliability coefficient of 0.38 increased to 0.67 when the instrument was culled to include only high reliability items. This was a test-retest reliability with four weeks between inspections.
5. Part of the study was to check whether unreliability was caused by the reliability rater, in part, being in the facility at different times from the official team. This turned out to be a very minor source of unreliability (Braithwaite et al., 1991).
6. The definitions of these three categories are:
   Met The team considers that residents are experiencing the quality of life and care

338

described in the standard. This does not necessarily mean there is not room for improvement or that the home could not operate more efficiently.

Action Required Either the standard is fully met for the majority of residents and the other residents are not experiencing neglect, abuse, denial of rights or any other significant detriment or substantially met for all residents and the home is taking action to address those minor concerns identified.

Urgent Action Required For one or more residents there is an identified abuse, neglect, denial of rights *and/or* other significant detriment.

7. The Australian director of nursing is the chief executive of the nursing home, combining the functions of administrator and director of nurses in the American system.

8. Another aspect of the same project was to compare the effect of this new survey process (PaCS) with the then existing process on deficiencies cited. Both processes were rating identical standards. However, the new PaCS process, which became the official US process from 1986 to 1990, was slightly more resident-centred than the old process was (though nowhere near as resident-centred as the Australian process). This test was conducted on a larger sample of 51 nursing homes, with the second team entering the home within a day or two of the first departing. PaCS teams cited 50 percent more deficiencies than did the teams surveying the same standards under the less resident-centred process (Spector and Drugovich, 1989).

9. One might hypothesize, for example, that American nursing homes being larger make reliability more difficult. But within our Australian study, the reliabilities are much the same for large and small homes. Large Australian homes are rated much more reliably than those in the Wisconsin study that produced the best US result.

10. This was a major reform to nursing home regulatory law. The new survey process based on the reform came into effect in October 1990. Omnibus Budget Reconciliation Act of 1987, Pub. L. No. 100–203, Paras 4203–4213.

11. A limited amount of such cross-referencing, however, may be done by a 'quality assurance' officer back at head office.

12. This was a 1989 inspection which predated abolition of the distinction among 'elements', 'standards' and 'conditions of participation' in Medicaid.

13. Rorty would say there is no way of solving it at all: 'words take their meaning from other words rather than by virtue of their representative character, and the corollary that vocabularies acquire their privileges from the men who use them rather than from their transparency to the real' (Rorty, 1979:368; see also Wittgenstein, 1972:29–39).

REFERENCES

Atiyah, P. S. and Robert S. Summers (1987) *Form and Substance in Anglo-American Law*. Oxford: Clarendon Press.

Badaracco, Joseph L. (1985) *Loading the Dice: A Five Country Study of Vinyl Chloride Regulation*. Boston, MA: Harvard Business School Press.

Baldwin, Robert and Keith Hawkins (1984) 'Discretionary Justice: Davis Reconsidered', *Public law*: 570–89.

Bardach, Eugene and Robert A. Kagan (1982) *Going by the Book: The Problem of Regulatory Unreasonableness*. Philadelphia, PA: Temple University Press.

Braithwaite, John (1987) 'Negotiation versus Litigation: Industry Regulation in Great Britain and the United States', *American Bar Foundation Research Journal* 2:559–74.

Braithwaite, John (1994) 'The Nursing Home Industry', pp. 11–54 in A. Reiss and M.

THE POLITICS OF LEGALISM 339

Tonry (eds), *Organizational Crime: Crime and Justice: A Review of Research Volume V*. Chicago, IL: University of Chicago Press.

Braithwaite, John, Valerie Braithwaite, Diane Gibson and Toni Makkai (1992) 'Progress in Assessing the Quality of Australian Nursing Home Care', *Australian Journal of Public Health* 16(1): 89–97.

Braithwaite, John, Toni Makkai, Valerie Braithwaite and Diane Gibson (1993) *Raising the Standard: Resident-Centred Nursing Home Regulations in Australia*. Canberra: Australian Government Publishing Service.

Braithwaite, John, Toni Makkai, Valerie Braithwaite, Diane Gibson and David Ermann (1990) *The Contribution of the Standards Monitoring Process to the Quality of Nursing Home Life*. Canberra: Department of Community Services and Health.

Braithwaite, John and Toni Makkai (1993) 'Can Resident-Centred Inspection of Nursing Homes Work with Very Sick Residents?', *Health Policy* 24: 19–33.

Braithwaite, Valerie, John Braithwaite, Diane Gibson, Miriam Landau and Toni Makkai (1991) *The Reliability and Validity of Nursing Home Standards*. Canberra: Department of Health, Housing and Community Services.

Day, Patricia and Rudolf Klein (1987) 'The Regulation of Nursing Homes: A Comparative Perspective', *Milbank Quarterly* 65: 303–47.

Department of Community Services and Health (1988) *Nursing Home Standards Monitoring Guidelines*. Canberra: Department of Community Services and Health.

Diver, Colin S. (1980) 'A Theory of Regulatory Enforcement', *Public Policy* 28: 257–99.

Diver, Colin S. (1989) 'Regulatory Precision', pp. 199–232 in K. Hawkins and J. M. Thomas (eds), *Making Regulatory Policy*. Pittsburgh, PA: University of Pittsburgh Press.

Gibbs, Ian and Ian Sinclair (1991) 'A Checklist Approach to the Inspection of Old People's Homes', Report to the Department of Health. York Department of Social Policy and Social Work, University of York.

Giles Report: Senate Select Committee on Private Hospitals and Nursing Homes (1985) *Private Nursing Homes in Australia: Their Conduct, Administration and Ownership*. Canberra: Australian Government Publishing Service.

Goodin, Robert E. (1982) *Political Theory and Public Policy*. Chicago, IL: University of Chicago Press.

Grabosky, Peter and John Braithwaite (1986) *Of Manners Gentle: Enforcement Strategies of Australian Business Regulatory Agencies*. Melbourne: Oxford University Press.

Gustafson, David H. (Project Manager) (1977) *Monitoring Quality of Nursing Home Care: Final Report*. Madison, WI: Department of Health and Social Services.

Gustafson, David H., Charles J. Fiss, Judy C. Fryback, Peggy A. Smelser and May E. Hiles (1980) 'Measuring the Quality of Care in Nursing Homes: A Pilot Study in Wisconsin', *Public Health Reports* 95(4): 336–43.

Gustafson, David H., Robert Peterson, Sandra Casper, Ann Macco, Richard Van Koningsveld and Edward Kopetsky (1982) *The Impact of the Wisconsin Quality Assurance Project: A Field Evaluation*. Madison, WI: University of Wisconsin.

Haley, John O. (ed.) (1988) *Law and Society in Contemporary Japan: American Perspectives*. Dubuque, IA: Kendall Hunt.

Hawkins, Keith (1984) *Environment and Enforcement: Regulation and the Social Definition of Pollution*. Oxford: Clarendon Press.

Hawkins, Keith (ed.) (1992) *The Uses of Discretion*. Oxford: Clarendon Press.

Illinois Legislative Investigating Commission (1984) *Regulation and Funding of Illinois Nursing Homes*. Springfield, IL: Illinois General Assembly.

Institute of Medicine (1986) *Improving the Quality of Care in Nursing Homes*. Washington, DC: National Academy Press.

Kagan, R. A. (1991) 'Adversarial Legalism and American Government', *Journal of Policy Analysis and Management* 10(3): 369–406.

340

Kelman, Mark (1987) *A Guide to Critical Legal Studies*. Cambridge, MA: Harvard University Press.

Kelman, S. (1981) *Regulating America: Regulating Sweden: A Comparative Study of Occupational Safety and Health Policy*. Cambridge, MA: MIT Press.

Kennedy, Duncan (1976) 'Form and Substance in Private Law Adjudication', *Harvard Law Review* 89: 1685–778.

Krotoszynski, R. J. (1990) 'Autonomy, Community, and Traditions of Liberty – The Contrast of British and American Privacy Law', *Duke Law Journal* 6: 1398–454.

McLeay Report: The House of Representatives Standing Committee on Expenditure (1982) *In a Home or at Home: Accommodation and Home Care for the Aged*. Canberra: Parliament of the Commonwealth of Australia, October.

Meidinger, Errol (1987) 'Regulatory Culture: A Theoretical Outline', *Law and Policy* 9: 355.

Michelman, Frank I. (1986) 'The Supreme Court, 1985 Term – Foreword: Traces of Self-Government', *Harvard Law Review* 100: 4–77.

Office of Health Systems Management (1985) *Evaluation of the New York State Residential Health Care Facility Quality Assurance System*. Standards and Surveillance, Division of Health Care, Office of Health Systems Management. Albany, NY: New York State Department of Health.

Phillips, Colleen (1987) *Developing Outcome Norms to Monitor Quality of Care in Rhode Island Nursing Homes*. Providence, RI: Rhode Island Department of Health.

Posner, Richard (1977) *Economic Analysis of Law*. Boston, MA: Little, Brown.

Radin, Margaret Jane (1989) 'Reconsidering the Rule of Law', *Boston University Law Review* 69: 781.

Rorty, Richard (1979) *Philosophy and the Mirror of Nature*. Princeton, NJ: Princeton University Press.

Rose, Carol M. (1987) 'Crystals and Mud in Property Law', *Stanford Law Review* 40: 577–610.

Schlag, Pierre (1985) 'Rules and Standards', *UCLA Law Review* 33: 379–430.

Schoer, Ray (1993) 'Self-Regulation and the Australian Stock Exchange', in P. Grabosky and J. Braithwaite (eds), *Business Regulation and Australia's Future*. Canberra: Australian Institute of Criminology.

Schuck, Peter H. (1979) 'Litigation, Bargaining and Regulation', *Regulation* 3: 26–34.

Shearing, Clifford D. and Richard V. Ericson (1991) 'Towards a Figurative Conception of Action', *British Journal of Sociology* 42: 481–506.

Spector, William D. and Margaret L. Drugovich (1989) 'Reforming Nursing Home Quality Regulation: Impact on Cited Deficiencies and Nursing Home Outcomes', *Medical Care* 27: 789–801.

Spector, William D., Adrianna H. Takada, Margaret L. Durgovich, Linda L. Laliberte and Richard Tucker (1987) *PaCS Evaluation: Final Report*. Baltimore, MD: Health Care Financing Bureau.

Sutton, Adam and Ron Wild (1978) 'Corporate Crime and Social Structure', in P. Wilson and J. Braithwaite (eds), *Two Faces of Deviance*. Brisbane: University of Queensland Press.

Sullivan, Kathleen, M. (1992) 'The Justices of Rules and Standards – Foreword', *Harvard Law Review* 106(1): 24–123.

Upham, Frank K. (1987) *Law and Social Change in Postwar Japan*. Cambridge, MA: Harvard University Press.

Vogel, David (1986) *National Styles of Regulation: Environment Policy in Great Britain and the United States*. Ithaca, NY: Cornell University Press.

Vogel, Ezra F. (1979) *Japan as No. 1: Lessons for America*. Cambridge, MA: Harvard University Press.

Weber, Max (1954) *On Law in Economics and Society*. New York: Clarion.

White, James Boyd (1984) *When Words Lose Their Meaning: Constitutions and Reconstitutions of Language, Character and Community*. Chicago, IL: University of Chicago Press.

Wiener, Carolyn L. and Jeanie Kayser-Jones (1989) 'Defensive Work in Nursing Homes – Accountability Gone Amok', *Social Science and Medicine* 28(1): 37–44.

Wittgenstein, Ludwig (1972) *Philosophical Investigations*, trans. G. E. M. Anscombe. Oxford: Blackwell.

Zimmerman, David, J. Robert Egan, David Gustafson, Charles Metcalf and Felicity Skidmore (1985) *Evaluation of the Three State Demonstrations in Nursing Home Quality Assurance Procedures*. Baltimore, MD: Health Care Financing Bureau, September.

[11]
Community Values and Australian Jurisprudence*

1. Community Opinion: Superficial and Deep

The then Chief Justice of Australia, delivering the 1987 Fullagar Lecture, contended that, "[it is unrealistic to interpret any instrument, whether it be a constitution, a statute, or a contract, by reference to words alone, without any regard to fundamental values".[1] Earlier, in his Menzies lecture, Anthony Mason contended that when judges take account of values,

> they should be acknowledged and should be accepted community values rather than mere personal values. The ever present danger is that 'strict and complete legalism' will be a cloak for undisclosed and unidentified policy values.... As judges who are unaware of the original underlying values subsequently apply that precedent in accordance with the doctrine of *stare decisis*, those hidden values are reproduced in the new judgment — even though the community values may have changed.[2]

The purpose of this article is to refine the rationale for recent Australian judicial opinion that appellate courts ought to be responsive to "community values" in exercising their responsibility to keep the law in good repair, by which the judges mean relevant to contemporary Australia. A good account of the judicial reasoning I seek to justify is provided by Brennan J:

> The common law has been created by the courts and the genius of the common law system consists in the ability of the courts to mould the law to correspond with the contemporary values of society. Had the courts not kept the common law in serviceable condition throughout the centuries of its development, its rules would now be regarded as remnants of history which had escaped the shipwreck of time.... Legislatures have disappointed the theorists and the courts have been left with a substantial part of the responsibility for keeping the law in a serviceable state, a function which calls for consideration of the contemporary values of the community.... The contemporary

* Professor, Law Program, Research School of Social Sciences, Austrian National University. I wish to thank Clive Bean, Valerie Braithwaite, Frank Brennan, Frank Callaway, Peter Drahos, Paul Finn, Ian Holloway, Susanne Karstedt, Philip Pettit, Cheryl Saunders, Ruth Scott, Michael Smith, Gary Sturgess, Leslie Zines, and participants at a Law and Government Seminar held at ANU in August 1994 for helpful comments on this paper and Nathan Harris and Tonia Vincent for research assistance.
1 Mason, A F, "Future Directions in Australian Law" (1987) 13 *Mon ULR* 149 at 158–9.
2 Mason, A F, "The Role of a Constitutional Court in a Federation: A Comparison of the Australian and United States Experience" (1986) 16 *FLR* 1 at 5.

values which justify judicial development of the law are not the transient notions which emerge in reaction to a particular event or which are inspired by
a publicity campaign conducted by an interest group. They are the relatively
permanent values of the Australian community.... The responsibility for
keeping the common law consonant with contemporary values does not
mean that the courts have a general power to mould society and its institutions according to judicial perceptions of what is conducive to the attainment
of those values. Although the courts have a broad charter, there are limits
imposed by the constitutional distribution of powers among the three
branches of government and there are limits imposed by the authority of
precedent not only on courts bound by the decisions of courts above them in
the hierarchy but also on the superior courts which are bound to maintain the
authority and predictability of the common law.[3]

There are obvious challenges to such a view. In the eighteenth and nineteenth centuries, when courts in England and various American states delivered a plethora of judgments restricting and then abolishing slavery,[4] it is fair
to say that those courts were both right and generally ahead of public opinion.
From 1976,[5] when the United States Supreme Court progressively backed
away from its effective abolition of the death penalty in *Furman v Georgia*,[6] it
engaged in an unprincipled surrender to public opinion. In this article, I introduce a critical distinction between community values and community attitudes
that helps resolve the dilemma such cases pose for the "community values"
doctrine.

According to this distinction, when the courts supported the abolition of
slavery, they correctly applied community values about which there was substantial consensus. The key values at issue were freedom and equal respect for
human beings. From consensually held *values*, they derived judgments which
flew in the face of dissensus in community *attitudes* toward slavery. Similarly,
what courts can do on capital punishment is to reject majoritarian community

---

3 *Dietrich v R* (1992) 109 ALR 385 at 402-3. See also Stephen J in *Onus v Alcoa of Australia Ltd* (1982) CLR 27 at 42: "Courts necessarily reflect community values ..."; Davies, G L,
"The Judiciary: Maintaining the Balance" in Finn, P (ed), *Essays on Law and Government,
vol 1* (forthcoming) at 41: "As part of that function, the judiciary bears responsibility for
articulating and, within legally permissible bounds, developing the body of legal principles which governs the resolution of disputes in the way which will best serve Australian
society; that is, in accordance with community values. It must generally do so in a way
which will maintain the stability, coherence and consistency of the law"; Brown, S,
"Courts and the Community: The Courts, Legal and Community Standards" (1994) *National Conference: Courts in a Representative Democracy*. Thomas J of the High Court of
New Zealand is sympathetic to these views but laments that "the reference to 'community
values' is altogether too imprecise. Is it therefore possible to give these norms or values
any firmer or more specific content?" Thomas J's answer is "both yes and no", given that
we must avoid making "the judges interpreters and ciphers of public opinion and the law
the slave of the public mood": see Thomas, E W, "A Return to Principle in Judicial Reasoning and an Acclamation of Judicial Autonomy" (1993) *Victoria U Wellington LR
Monograph No 5* 1 at 56. The objective of this article is to clarify the "yes" and the "no"
to accomplish both the autonomy and the responsiveness Thomas J seeks.
4 Finkelman, P, *Slavery in the Courtroom* (1985); Finkelman, P, *The Law of Freedom and
Bondage: A Casebook* (1986). In drawing attention to the role of the courts in the demise
of slavery, no implication is intended that their role was as important as the role of legislatures and anti-slavery social movements.
5 Friedman, L M, *Crime and Punishment in American History* (1993) at 316–23.
6 408 US 238 (1972).

attitudes in favour of capital punishment by arguing from consensual community values, such as respect for human life, to the conclusion that capital punishment is an overreaching of state power. The moral reasoning of the judges can be superior to the attitudes of the people, but only if it is reasoning from the foundation of values shared by the people. One reason for this is that most people do not have the time or interest on most issues to argue through the implications of their values for their attitudes on specific subjects like capital punishment. They do not have the expertise to marshal the empirical evidence on whether the introduction of capital punishment would reduce the homicide rate, or whether it would result in many executions of individuals who would subsequently be found to be innocent. As a result, populist attitudes are readily dominated by media stereotypes.

The contention of this article is, therefore, that it is community values and not community attitudes which ought to be the foundation of judicial deliberation about sustaining contemporarily relevant law. While the article begins from the premise that judge-made law is both inevitable and desirable, this is not to devalue the rule of law, particularly since the rule of law is one of the very values which I will show to be subject to an Australian community consensus. Most judicial work does not and should not make law. But we cannot escape the fact that it is the judges who created the common law, and the judges who are therefore responsible for renovating it in contemporary and responsive ways. While the Constitution, statutes and the pre-existing common law should be the main constraints on judicial discretion, when interpretive gaps remain and when changing circumstances require adaptation, judicial law-making becomes inevitable. It is in this judicial work that judges ought to argue from foundations of community values rather than community attitudes.

Section 2, below, explains the distinction between attitudes and values that has come out of the discipline of social psychology since the 1970s. The fact that near-universal consensus exists in Australia over several dozen values will be demonstrated empirically in Section 3. Section 4 then argues that values are a superior foundation for judicial deliberation than attitudes because near-universal values are more likely than attitudes to represent moral truth. Section 5 considers the critique that values which attract near-universal support are so vague and platitudinous as to be of little practical use. Section 6 addresses the concern that grounding of judicial deliberation in consensus values will inhibit the diversity of ideas that might enrich the court's deliberation. Section 7 considers options for incorporating a more principled commitment to considering community values in judicial decision-making, while Section 8 advances the specific notion of a republican Bill of Values and Rights as an alternative to a liberal Bill of Rights.

2. *The Difference Between Attitudes and Values*

The seminal clarifying work on the distinction between attitudes and values was by Milton Rokeach in *Beliefs, Attitudes, and Values*[7] and *The Nature of Human Values*.[8] Rokeach defined an attitude as a set of beliefs about a specific object or situation (such as an attitude toward slavery). A value, in contrast, is a single belief of a specific kind. It is a trans-situational guide to attitudes, actions and judgments. It lifts us above attitudes about specific objects and situations, to more ultimate goals that affect how we should judge a wide sweep of objects and situations. While a value is a standard that transcends objects and situations, an attitude is not a standard. An attitude is simply an organised[9] set of beliefs focused on the specific object or situation that gives the attitude its name. Rokeach contended that:

> a person has as many values as he has learned beliefs concerning desirable modes of conduct and end-states of existence, and as many attitudes as direct or indirect encounters he has had with specific objects and situations. It is thus estimated that values number only in the dozens, whereas attitudes number in the thousands.[10]

Subsequent empirical work, including work done in Australia, seems to have confirmed Rokeach's model that with fewer than a hundred values one can cover exhaustively all of the values that matter for almost all people.[11]

Many values correspond to needs — for example, one could describe freedom from hunger as either a value or a need. But values differ from needs in being an accomplishment of human cognition learned in a community of human beings. "Values are the cognitive representations and transformations of needs, and man is the only animal capable of such representations and transformations."[12] Moreover, sometimes those cognitive transformations are considerably greater than in the case of hunger — for example, the transformation of a need for sex into a value for love or intimacy. Many values, moreover, are not cognitive representations of needs but of societal and institutional demands. Schwartz and Bilsky see values as cognitive representations of three universal requirements: biological needs; interactional requirements for interpersonal coordination; and societal demands for group welfare and survival.[13] Values are finite in number because they tend to be standards grounded in a finite number of trans-situational demands of the human condition. Moreover, their grounding in universal demands is one reason for the near-universal consensus which characterises the most important values. Kluckhohn and Strodtbeck state it this way:

---

7   Rokeach, M, *Beliefs, Attitudes, and Values* (1968).
8   Rokeach, M, *The Nature of Human Values* (1973).
9   "Organized" for psychologists means intercorrelated in ways that enable psychometrically satisfactory scales to be formed.
10 Above n8 at 18.
11 See the data in Section 3 below.
12 Above n8 at 20.
13 Schwartz, S H and Bilsky, W, "Toward a Universal Psychological Structure of Human Values" (1987) 53 *J Personality Soc Psych* 550 at 550.

First, it is assumed that *there is a limited number of common human prob-lems for which all peoples at all times must find some solution.* This is the universal aspect of value orientations because the common human problems to be treated arise inevitably out of the human situation. The second as-sumption is that *while there is variability in solutions of all the problems, it is neither limitless nor random but is definitely variable within a range of possible solutions.*[14]

3. *Values and Consensus*

Public debate over attitudes is characterised by division and dissensus. People irreconcilably hold different attitudes to abortion. During abortion debates, however, they tend not to disagree on the underlying values — respect for hu-man life, health, freedom of choice — on which their attitudes are grounded. The pro-abortionist does not say, "who cares about human life?", but rather argues about the proper context for applying this value and the relative weight to be given to other values.[15] The empirical evidence is that most, though not all, values are characterised by high consensus both internationally and in Australia.

The values paradigm in social psychological research asks citizens to ac-cept or reject certain values "as a guiding principle in my life",[16] or for other people's lives, or public policy. The best studies then ask respondents to think hard about whether there are any other guiding principles not covered by the list they have been given. There are various strategies for prompting the dis-covery of excluded values. Iteratively, this research literature has therefore built up lists of values that fairly exhaustively cover the domain.

---

14 Kluckhohn, R and Strodtbeck, F L, Variations in Value Orientation (1961) at 10 (my em-phasis). See also Brown, D E, *Human Universals* (1991).

15 The Australian sterilisation cases provide interesting examples of how the High Court has grappled with such debates over the proper context for applying and weighting conflicting values. See *Secretary, Department of Health and Community Services v JWB* (1992) 106 ALR 385; *P v P* (1994) 120 ALR 545.

16 This is the wording Schwartz has used in his leading studies in 35 nations, including Aus-tralia and New Zealand. See Schwartz, S H, "Universals in the Content and Structure of Values: Theoretical Advances and Empirical Tests in 20 Countries" (1992) 25 *Advances in Experimental Soc Psych* 1; Schwartz, S H, "Are There Universal Aspects in the Struc-ture and Contents of Human Values?" (1994) unpublished paper presented to International Congress of Applied Psychology, Madrid, 16 July 1994.

The most important Australian contributors to this literature have been Feather,[17] Bill and Ruth Scott,[18] and Valerie Braithwaite.[19] I will illustrate the consensus over values with one of Valerie Braithwaite's data sets, not because it is necessarily superior to the others (in fact, it's rather out of date) but because it is a general population study rather than a study of university students, because it explores the comprehensiveness issue and includes a "values justification study" (interviews in which citizens are asked to give justifications for their values)[20] and because I could get ready access to her raw data!

The study was based on interviews with a stratified random sample of 483 Brisbane adults in 1975. Three types of values were included in the study. Two sets concerned goals in life: personal and social goals. For the personal goals, citizens were asked to say what they felt about the value "as a principle for you to live by". For the social goals, they were asked to accept or reject them as "principles that guide your judgments and actions". Table 1 lists results for these two types of values combined in descending order of community acceptance. Seven response categories were given: "Reject this"; "Inclined to reject this"; "Neither reject nor accept this"; "Inclined to accept this"; "Accept this as important"; "Accept this as very important"; "Accept this as of the greatest importance". In Table 1, the last four response categories

---

17 See the following works by Feather, N T: "Educational Choice and Student Attitudes in Relation to Terminal and Instrumental Values" (1970) 22 *AJ Psych* 127; "Value Systems in State and Church Schools" (1970) 22 *AJ Psych* 299; "Similarity of Value Systems as a Determinant of Educational Choice at University Level" (1971) 23 *AJ Psych* 201; "The Measurement of Values: Effects of Different Assessment Procedures" (1973) 25 *AJ Psych* 221; "Values and Income Level" (1975) 27 *AJ Psych* 23–9; *Values in Education and Society* (1975); "Value Importance, Conservatism and Age" (1977) 7 *European J Soc Psych* 241; "Human Values and the Work Situation: Two Studies" (1979) 14 *A Psychologist* 131; "Value Correlates of Conservatism" (1979) 37 *J Personality Soc Psych* 1617; "Value Systems and Social Interaction: A field study in a Newly Independent Nation" (1980) 10 *J Applied Soc Psych* 1; "Reasons for Entering Medical School in Relation to Value Priorities and Sex of Student" (1982) 55 *J Occupational Psych* 119; "Protestant Ethic, Conservatism, and Values" (1984) 46 *J Personality Soc Psych* 1132; "Masculinity, Femininity, Psychological Androgyny, and the Structure of Values" (1984) 47 *J Personality Soc Psych* 604; "Attitudes, Values, and Attributions: Explanations of Unemployment" (1985) 48 *J Personality Soc Psych* 876; "Cross-Cultural Studies with the Rokeach Value Survey: The Flinders Program of Research on Values" (1986) 38 *AJ Psych* 269; Feather, N T and Cross, D G, "Value Systems and Delinquency: Parental and Generational Discrepancies in Value Systems for Delinquent and Non-Delinquent Boys" (1975) 14 *Brit J Soc Clinical Psych* 117; Feather, N T and Peay, E R, "The Structure of Terminal and Instrumental Values: Dimensions and Clusters" (1975) 27 *AJ Psych* 151.

18 Scott, W A, "International Ideology and Interpersonal Ideology" (1960) 24 *Public Opinion Q* 419; *Values and Organizations: A Study of Fraternities and Sororities* (1965); Braithwaite, V A and Scott, W A, "Values", in Robinson, J P, Shaver P R and Wrightsman L S (eds), *Measures of Personality and Social Psychological Attitudes* (1991) at 661.

19 Braithwaite, V A, "The Structure of Social Values: Validation of Rokeach's Two Value Model" (1982) 21 *Brit J Soc Psych* 203; "Beyond Rokeach's Equality-Freedom Model: Two Dimensional Values in a One Dimensional World" (1994) 50 *J Soc Iss* 67; Braithwaite J and Braithwaite V A, "Delinquency and the Question of Values" (1981) 23 *Int'l J Offender Therapy Comparative Criminology* 129; Braithwaite, V A and Law, H G, "Structure of Human Values: Testing and Adequacy of the Rokeach Value Survey." (1985) 49 *J Personality Soc Psych* 250; Braithwaite, V A, Makkai, T and Pittelkow, Y, "Inglehart's Materialism/Postmaterialism Concept: Clarifying the Dimensionality Debate Through Rokeach's Model of Social Values" (1994) (unpublished).

20 Braithwaite, V A, *Exploring Value Structure* (1979) at 277–90.

are combined into an "Accept" category and the first two into "Reject". Excluded from the table is a another list of 71 ways of behaving, as opposed to goals in life. These have been excluded because most of them are of limited relevance to judicial decision-making. While it is important to know that there is community consensus about the value of "BEING POLITE" or "BEING GENEROUS", such virtues are rarely relevant to the outcomes of judicial decisions.[21] A few of these ways of behaving that enjoy overwhelming consensus in the Australian community are relevant to judges, however, including: "BEING FORGIVING"; "RESPECTING THE PRIVACY OF OTHERS"; and "BEING TOLERANT".

Table 1

Rejection and Acceptance of Guiding Principles in Life by 483 Brisbane Citizens

	Reject	Neither reject nor accept	Accept
	%	%	%
HUMAN DIGNITY Allowing each individual to be treated as someone of worth	0	1	99
THE PROTECTION OF HUMAN LIFE Taking care to preserve your own life and the life of others	0	2	98
WISDOM Having a mature understanding of life	0	2	98
A WORLD OF BEAUTY Having the beauty of nature and of the arts (music, literature, art, et cetera)	0	5	95
SECURITY FOR LOVED ONES Taking care of loved ones	1	1	99
GOOD HEALTH Physical well-being	1	1	99
A WORLD AT PEACE Being free from war and conflict	1	1	98
EQUAL OPPORTUNITY FOR ALL Giving everyone an equal chance in life	1	1	98
SELF-RESPECT Believing in your own worth	1	1	98
HAPPINESS Feeling pleased with the life you are leading	1	2	97
THE RULE OF LAW Punishing the guilty and protecting the innocent	1	2	97
FREEDOM Being able to live as you choose whilst respecting the freedom of others	1	2	97
PRESERVING THE NATURAL ENVIRONMENT Preventing the destruction of nature's beauty and resources	1	2	97
MATURE LOVE Having a relationship of deep and lasting affection	1	2	96

---

21 I am indebted to Leslie Zines for pointing out a recent case where the Full Federal Court invoked the value of "generosity". See *Chaudhary v Minister for Immigration and Ethnic Affairs* (1994) 121 ALR 315 at 318: "True national interest has a concern for Australia's name in the world, and may at times involve a measure of generosity".

	Reject	Neither reject nor accept	Accept
	%	%	%
INNER HARMONY Feeling free of conflict within yourself	1	3	96
TRUE FRIENDSHIP Having genuine and close friends	1	3	96
SELF-IMPROVEMENT Striving to be a better person	1	4	95
SOCIAL PROGRESS AND SOCIAL REFORM Readiness to change our way of life for the better	1	5	93
THE PURSUIT OF KNOWLEDGE Always trying to find out new things about the world we live in	1	6	93
NATIONAL SECURITY Protection of your nation from enemies	2	1	97
A SENSE OF ACCOMPLISHMENT Feeling that you have achieved something worthwhile in your life	2	2	96
COMFORT BUT NOT LUXURY Being satisfied with the simple pleasures of life	2	2	96
A GOOD LIFE FOR OTHERS Improving the welfare of all people in need	2	4	94
SELF-KNOWLEDGE OR SELF-INSIGHT Being more aware of what sort of person you are	2	4	94
NATIONAL ECONOMIC DEVELOPMENT Having greater economic progress and prosperity for the nation	2	5	92
PHYSICAL DEVELOPMENT Being physically fit	2	7	91
RESPECT FROM OTHERS Being thought well of by others	2	10	88
ACCEPTANCE BY OTHERS Feeling that you belong	2	11	88
REWARD FOR INDIVIDUAL EFFORT Letting the individual profit from initiative and hard work	3	3	94
SEXUAL INTIMACY Having a satisfying sexual relationship	3	7	90
PRIVACY FOR YOURSELF Being able to keep your business to yourself	4	8	88
A SENSE OF OWNERSHIP Knowledge that the things you need and use belong to you	5	6	89
SELF-SUFFICIENCY Being able to make the things you need yourself	5	15	79
GREATER ECONOMIC EQUALITY Lessening the gap between the rich and the poor	6	13	80
A SENSE OF TRADITION Having respect for the achievements of our forefathers	6	13	81

	Reject	Neither Reject nor accept	Accept
	%	%	%
RULE BY THE PEOPLE Involvement by all citizens in making decisions that affect their community	7	9	84
ECONOMIC PROSPERITY Being financially well-off	7	18	75
NATIONAL GREATNESS Being a united, strong, independent and powerful nation	8	9	93
AN ACTIVE SOCIAL LIFE Mixing with other people	8	17	75
PERSONAL SUPPORT Knowing that there is someone to take care of you	9	14	77
BEING ALWAYS ON THE GO Keeping busy by having lots of interests	9	14	76
PHYSICAL EXERCISE taking part in energetic activity	9	20	71
AN EXCITING LIFE A life full of new experiences or adventures	9	25	66
STABILITY A life not liable to sudden or unexpected change	12	15	73
UPHOLDING TRADITIONAL SEXUAL MORAL STANDARDS Opposing sexual permissiveness and pornography	13	14	73
SALVATION Being saved from your sins and at peace with God	13	19	68
RELIGIOUS OR MYSTICAL EXPERIENCE Being at one with God or the universe	13	21	66
A LEISURELY LIFE Being free from pressure and stress	14	13	73
CAREFREE ENJOYMENT Being free to indulge in the pleasures of life	14	24	62
RECOGNITION BY THE COMMUNITY Having high standing in the community	15	26	58
AUTHORITY Having power to influence others and control decisions	21	29	49
MAN'S DOMINATION OF NATURE Controlling nature and making use of the forces of nature	22	16	61

The first 45 values listed in Table 1 are all values that can be described as attracting consensus in the Australian community. The final nine on the list — "STABILITY", "UPHOLDING TRADITIONAL SEXUAL MORAL STANDARDS, SALVATION", "RELIGIOUS OR MYSTICAL EXPERIENCE", "A LEISURELY LIFE", "CAREFREE ENJOYMENT", "RECOGNITION BY THE COMMUNITY", "AUTHORITY" and "MAN'S DOMINATION OF NATURE" — are rejected by over 10 per cent of the population and accepted by fewer than three quarters.[22] It might be argued

22 Of course the 10 per cent rejection cut-off is quite arbitrary. Yet the two least supported

that none of them qualifies as the kind of value that courts ought to require themselves to further. A common reason for the lack of consensus with most of these nine values is that they are associated in the minds of good numbers of citizens with past or present state tyrannies on behalf of majorities ("AUTHORITY") — religious tyrannies ("SALVATION, RELIGIOUS OR MYSTICAL EXPERIENCE"), sexual tyrannies ("UPHOLDING TRADITIONAL SEXUAL MORAL STANDARDS"), and tyranny over nature ("MAN'S DOMINATION OF NATURE").

In 1994, Russell Blamey used 18 of these values in the *National Forest Attitudes Survey* of 1680 Australians.[23] Responses were very similar to the 1975 results, the biggest changes being an increase in acceptance of "GREATER ECONOMIC EQUALITY" from 80 per cent to 86 per cent and a drop in acceptance of "NATIONAL SECURITY" from 97 per cent to 90 per cent.

4.   Are Values Moral Truths?

One can accept the claim that community values and not community attitudes ought to ground judicial deliberation without believing that community values are more likely to represent moral truth than community attitudes. Indeed, one can do so even while believing that moral truth does not exist. For example, one can justify values-grounding and reject attitudes-grounding because of the empirical evidence that the people can agree on their values but not on their attitudes (combined perhaps with some view that the people should ultimately be sovereign in a democracy).

No attempt will be made here at any serious argument that moral truth exists and that the near-universal values listed above count among these truths. Better for readers to go to the work of philosophers who argue that there is a fact of the matter about what is right and wrong, such as Michael Smith's recent tour de force, *The Moral Problem*.[24] My objective is the more modest

---

values on the reduced list — "PHYSICAL EXERCISE" and "AN EXCITING LIFE" — may be especially attractive consensus values for Australia, if not for other lands. Some jurists might think of "PHYSICAL EXERCISE" and "AN EXCITING LIFE" as peculiar values for purposes of judicial deliberation, and it must be admitted that cases where these values were at issue would be rare. Yet it may be that the citizens who think of an exciting life as a particularly important value, mainly young citizens, think of High Court judges as "fossils" precisely because of judges' attitudes to their values. And isn't the point of taking community values seriously to correct such judicial myopias? Interestingly, the natural law theorist, Finnis, does include "play" among his list of basic values. His other choices are: knowledge; life; aesthetic experience; sociability (friendship); practical reasonableness; and religion. See Finnis, J M, *Natural Law and Natural Rights* (1980) at 87. Equally, psychologists find a strong biological basis for this value. For example, Schwartz concludes that: "[s]timulation values derive from the presumed organismic need for variety and stimulation in order to maintain an optimal level of activation (Berlyne, 1960; Houston & Mednick, 1963; Maddi, 1961)". See Schwartz, "Universals" above n16 at 7; citing Berlyne, D E, *Conflict, Arousal, and Curiosity* (1960); Houston, J P and Mednick, S A, "Creativity and the Need for Novelty", (1963) 66 *J Abnormal Soc Psych* 137; Maddi, S R, "Exploratory Behavior and Variation-Seeking in Man", in Fiske, D W and Maddi, S R (eds), *Functions of Varied Experience* (1961) 253.

23 Blamey, R, *Citizens, Sumers and Contingent Valuation: An Investigation into Respondents' Behaviour* (1995) Unpublished PhD dissertation, Centre for Research in Environmental Studies, ANU, Canberra.

24 Smith, M, *The Moral Problem* (1994).

one of showing why philosophers who have profoundly incompatible accounts of truth — perhaps cognitivist, perhaps realist, perhaps subjectivist — might agree that moral truth is more likely to reside in the consensus values listed in Table 1 than in community attitudes.

We can and do make moral progress, just as we regress morally at times. The abolition of slavery, the slow lifting of the subjugation of women to men, are examples of moral progress. When such progress comes, it often results from challenging prevailing attitudes with the fundamental truth in underlying values like equal treatment. When moral regress occurs, it is often from failing to do so. The moral progress in the *Mabo* decision[25] was enabled by the near-universal acceptance of the underlying "principle of non-discrimination".[26] Non-discrimination was among the "fundamental values of our common law" that Brennan J found to be trampled upon by the doctrine of *terra nullius*.[27]

One reason why community attitudes are less likely to represent moral truth than values is that attitudes are more dominated by the circumstances of the particular situations which are their objects. Across a range of situations, people acquire an appreciation of the value of equal respect, partly through personal experiences of unequal respect in a number of those situations. However, when it comes to a specific object — say, Aborigines — particular histories of dominating practices in a person's life distort the moral truth of equal respect. One has a racist father. As Leader of the Opposition, one is dominated by the imperative to oppose the government, even on the *Native Title Act* 1993 (Cth). One is dominated by the opportunity to win needed political support from an angry mining lobby. Attitudes to political parties may be dominated by the fact of whether one's parents were Labor or Liberal, and so on. Attitudes are more dominated by churches, husbands, parties, mass media, peers and employers, because they are cognitions focussed on a specific terrain within which one or another agent of domination holds sway. Values, as cognitive standards that transcend all domains, are comparatively more free from specific dominations.

Moreover, it makes sense for agents of domination to invest their scarce resources in shaping attitudes of interest to them rather than in changing values. It makes more sense for husbands to dominate wives into an attitude of subservience to the family than it does to assail the fundamental value of equality because it is the attitude that directly benefits them. Indeed, in other spheres — for example, treatment of their children — the dominating husband may want the wife to respect the principle of equality. In short, as we move from attitudes to values, we move from (a) cognitions more dominated by the forces of domination that prevail in specific situations, to (b) trans-situational cognitions where dominations are dissipated or cross-cutting. The practical upshot is that values are more likely to speak moral truth than attitudes. While attitudes within Australia are racist, patriarchal, homophobic and bigoted in a

---

25 *Mabo v Queensland (No 2)* (1992) 175 CLR 1.
26 Brennan, F, "Securing a Bountiful Place for Aborigines and Torres Strait Islanders in a Modern, Free and Tolerant Australia" (1994) *Constitutional Centenary Foundation Paper* at 22.
27 Above n25 at 41–2.

great variety of ways, the consensus Australian values listed in Table 1 are not. Since domination distorts truth and undominated dialogue is the road to the discovery of truth,[28] and since attitude formation is subject to concerted contextual domination in a way that value formation is not, values are more likely to represent moral truth than attitudes.

This is why we might reject Sadurski's claim that "it is *not* the case that people agree about the fundamental principles while disagreeing about some other, less basic values [read 'attitudes']".[29] Rather, Sadurski argues that the specific attitudes are "the proper test of what one means by the general principle ... it is not that they follow from the principle under certain interpretation, but rather they are constitutive of it".[30] My theory is that attitudes are constituted by dominations and by misunderstandings of the world to a degree that values are not. Therefore, to say that a person's values are constituted by their bundle of attitudes, or worse, by their actual behaviour in circumstances of domination, is to reconstitute values so as to make them as morally flawed as our attitudes and actions. Often, an attitude (X) will be shaped by not one value, but by a set of conflicting values ($V_{1...}V_n$) , a set of empirical beliefs ($E_1...E_n$), a set of conflicting social structures ($S_1...S_n$), and some biological needs ($N_1...N_n$). To read attitude X simply as constituting a value V_X[31] is altogether too simple, as well as collapsing a distinction that has analytic and normative advantages.

5. *Values and Vagueness*

Cynics, of course, reject the propositions that values can be moral truths and are more likely to be morally true than attitudes. It is hard for cynics to lose this debate because, even if they concede that there might be moral truth in values, they switch tack to the contention that they are "motherhood" truths which are so obvious and general as to offer little guidance to practical action. The jurist who believes in the possibility of moral progress, however, sees the challenge as one of progressively expanding the domain of motherhood truth (of sound agreement on a truth that becomes banal because of that agreement). Yesterday's controversy — equal respect for all, including slaves — becomes today's motherhood truth.

For judges who reject both Dixonian "strict and complete legalism" on grounds that it is impossible, and Masonian "community values" on grounds of vagueness, there are alternatives. They can believe that they must sometimes make law, but when they do they should simply rely on their own values because there is no moral fact of the matter to be discovered from others. In this case, moral argument is at bottom no more than a bare exercise of power by judges, an attempt to impose their preferences on the preferences of others.[32] Critics of Murphy J would construe this as the Murphy alternative. Another alternative is for judges to find values that are "immanent" in the law,

---

28 See the references below in nn48–56.
29 Sadurski, W "Conventional Morality and Judicial Standards" (1987) 73 *Virginia LR* 339 at 378.
30 Id at 379.
31 Or attitude X and attitude Y as constituting value (X+Y).
32 See Smith, M, "Realism" in Singer, P (ed), *Companion to Ethics* (1991) at 403–4.

and then apply those values by analogical reasoning to new legal problems. Finally, judges who believe that values-as-motherhood-truth are unhelpful in practical situations, a sham for grounding of judicial deliberation in the will of a sovereign people, can ground their interpretation of the law in community attitudes of a more specific sort.

Judges who take this last path can be led by community attitudes under the sway of a dictator or a sensationalist media to judgments that are oppressive of freedom, or of other values shared by the same community. Paul Finn has raised three objections to the manner in which Australian judges have used "community values" to justify decisions.[33] I will contend that the practices that concern him most are what I would call using community attitudes rather than community values to justify decisions.

First, Finn objects that "there is little in the cases to suggest that the standards or values attributed to the community are grounded in cogent empirical evidence which could sustain the claim made for them".[34] Accountable judicial decision-making does require that judges cite grounds and sources when they allow community opinion to influence their decisions. In general, they dare not do this, for fear of a storm of controversy if they get the empirical facts of community opinion wrong, and for fear that they rely on data extrinsic to the evidence the parties have had an opportunity to rebut. This fear of the judges is well placed when they allow their interpretation of community *attitudes* to influence decisions. They will generally not find the data; when they do, they will find one opinion poll disagreeing with another; and where they do find empirical agreement, it will usually be about the existence of deep divisions in community attitudes, rather than consensus. Community values are a different story, however. There we can find the data rather easily; it tends to greater consistency; and as shown in Section 3 of this article, the evidence is of near-universal community acceptance of the most critical values.

Second, because of the aversion judges prudently have toward citing opinion polls to support their interpretation of community views, they tend to cite authority external to the community — for example, comparative law materials — in their desire to obscure the impression that they are imposing their own value or policy preferences.[35] When an Australian court cites the United States Supreme Court and an international treaty, and then equates the standard therein with community values, these values are actually imposed on the Australian community. Judges marching under the banner of popular sovereignty then actually push sovereignty out the door. Again, however, if judges follow community *values* (according to one of the methodologies described in Sections 7 and 8), they can refer directly to the authority of the Australian people rather than impose upon them beliefs from a foreign forum. From the foundations of Australian law and Australian values, they can still draw on the

---

33 Finn, P, "Of Power and the People: Ends and Methods in Australian Judge-Made Law" (1994) 1 *Judicial Review* 255 at 277–8.

34 Id at 277.

35 Finn cites Gummow J's judgment in *Service Station Association Ltd v Berg Bennett & Associates Pty Ltd* (1993) 117 ALR 393 at 405: "Invocation of 'community standards' may be no more than an invention by the judicial branch of government of new heads of 'public policy'".

wisdom in non-Australian deliberation about how to deliver the objectives of our law and community.

Third, Finn maintains that "to the extent that there is a majoritarian implication in the formula, it is one which in a variety of contexts the courts have every reason to resist and no more so than in the areas of human rights and criminal procedure".[36] Finn is right here when it is majoritarian community attitudes that are at issue. Where the law allows the leeway to choose, judges have a duty to resist majoritarian support for trampling on human rights or cutting corners on just criminal procedures. But which of the consensus Australian values discussed in Section 3 would Finn suggest judges have reason to resist?

Finn is right that much invocation of community values is a contrivance by judges who wish to impose values. Yet in the end he concedes that there may be some "core values" that are so "intrinsic to the social and governmental order we have created in this country" that judges can act upon them in their law-making.[37] Because values tend to be "deeply engrained standards" that "encapsulate the aspirations of individuals and societies",[38] they can indeed be found by culturally knowledgable single judges applying their own cognitions to the institutional order, though they can be found more reliably, less refutably, and more democratically by applying the paradigm of values research to statistically adequate random samples of the people.

My contention is that Finn's arguments should lead us to the conclusion that judicial guidance by community attitudes is a dangerous, if not impossible, path, imposition by judges of their personal values is unacceptable, and total judicial avoidance of law-making cannot be sustained. While judicial guidance by community values (or values immanent in the institutional order) when filling legal silences is the only alternative left standing, the vagueness critique of it has not been answered.

It is true that values give only broad guidance, while attitudes can give quite specific direction to courts. Yet while we should want the courts to get rather specific guidance from the law (as the community value of the rule of law requires), highly specific forms of guidance from community opinion is not desirable. Judicial decision-making, like legislative decision-making, is better to the extent that it is based on rich deliberation where a plurality of community attitudes, interpretive principles and empirical data are available, where relevant, to inform the dialogue.[39] Put another way, the arguments against courts being required to be responsive to community attitudes are similar to the arguments against Citizen Initiated Referenda. Opinion poll democracy is not reflective, deliberative democracy and it risks a tyranny of the majority. Though the virtues of deliberative decision-making are the common reasons why both judicial commitment to reflect community attitudes and Citizen Initiated Referenda are dangerous, there is a key difference. While legislators are ultimately accountable to the people through the ballot box for

---

36 Above n33 at 278.
37 Ibid.
38 Braithwaite and Scott, above n18 at 661.
39 In this respect, I am at one with Sadurski's conclusion, above n29 passim.

how they conduct their deliberation, judges are not (quite properly, given the risk the tyranny of the majority poses to judicial independence). Nevertheless, an accountability problem remains when judges apply moral precepts to resolve the indeterminacies in the law. A way to solve it is for judges to conduct their deliberation in ways that require them to justify decisions in terms of the law, and in terms of community values when the law is indeterminate or when the common law loses touch with societal change.

Community values can provide a sound, comparatively uncontroversial, non-arbitrary foundation in terms of which more controversial reasoning must be justified. Conceived as no more than foundations for the derivation of more controversial moral judgments, a "motherhood" quality is no longer a vice. The cut and thrust of deliberative contestation should focus on the soundness of the derivations rather than on premises which are better for being the people's premises. The judges' arguments: the people's premises.

The logic, interpretations, and empirical assumptions of the judges will ultimately have more effect on decisions than community values. So, of course, will the law. This is as it should be in a democracy that takes both the rule of law and deliberative decision-making seriously. Under the approach to community values advocated here, jurists still must have positions on the big questions of statutory interpretation: what kind of weight should be given to legislative history, to extrapolating the original purposes of the legislators to new situations; how legally mandated rules of statutory interpretation should be applied and so on. How judges come down on these questions will also have more influence on outcomes than community values.

However, one virtue of the community values approach is worth mentioning with regard to the dilemmas of statutory interpretation. The problem with narrow conceptualisations of statutes based on either legislative text, or history, or intention, is myopia.[40] The writers of texts fail to see their indeterminacies. The legislative history and known legislative purposes are silent on unintended consequences and on tacit purposes. Necessarily, these approaches to statutory interpretation therefore blind us to values that are affected by the law. Citizens get a bad deal from the democracy in furthering values they care about to the extent that myopic theories of statutory interpretation rule out of consideration those values that cannot be found in the text, the history, or the known intent. A judicial duty to consider community values when the meaning or relevance of the law is in doubt is the least myopic of all the theories of interpretation. This is because we know it is possible to generate a list of values which comprehensively defines the guiding principles in life that matter to most citizens. To the extent that judges incorporate systematic consideration of community values into their deliberations, they build in a safeguard against the myopias of text, history and intent. To that extent, they are less likely to short-change citizens in terms of the entire range of outcomes that matter to them.[41] Moreover, the empirical claim can be made that such fidelity to the

---

40 See Sunstein, C R, *After the Rights Revolution: Reconceiving the Regulatory State* (1990).
41 Equally, of course, good rules of statutory interpretation protect against these theoretical myopias. But my claim is that one of the grounds for rules of statutory interpretation being sound is that they leave space for the judges to interpolate consensus values into the indeterminacies of the legal text.

value-preferences of citizens is consistent with enhanced fidelity to the considered preferences of legislatures, as Mason commented on this article:

> In the case of statutes which impinge upon fundamental values, it is possible to say that an unambiguous and unmistakable expression of intention is required to justify an interpretation which trenches upon the values. To insist upon the expression of such an intention is to enhance the legislative process by compelling those who introduce legislation to make plain to the legislature what the effect of the legislation will be.[42]

It also should be remembered that for some types of problems the legislature chooses, and rightly chooses, to put less trust in the quality of its own deliberation than in the deliberation of judges or other public officials to whom it delegates discretion. What is the New South Wales Parliament saying when it enacts a *Contracts Review Act* 1980 that provides:

> [Where the Supreme Court] finds a contract or a provision of a contract to have been unjust in the circumstances relating to the contract at the time it was made, the Court may, if it considers it just to do so, and for the purpose of avoiding as far as practicable an unjust consequence or result [make certain orders or refuse to enforce the contract].[43]

My conjecture is that the parliament is saying to the courts: "Please rely on your own deliberation about the community's and the law's conception of justice when deciding what to do about an unjust contract, rather than looking for obscure clues in our text or our intent. All the values that should be considered in these judgments cannot be found there precisely because we do not trust our ability to think them all through".[44]

In such circumstances, a court that persists with strict legalism paradoxically flouts the rule of law, while the court that rigorously considers community values respects the rule of law in the sense of applying the law in the way the parliament implicitly requests. Equally, a judiciary that fails to update the common law in light of changing realities in the community shows scant respect for the rule of law.

6.   *Consensus, Diversity and Deliberation*

One might ask if it is a good thing to search for a foundation of community consensus to ground judicial deliberation. Is there not virtue in diversity, in difference, that we should seek to preserve rather than reduce to a lowest common denominator? Indeed there is.[45] Yet there is a place for both consensus and difference in the way we structure our deliberative institutions. The problem with measuring judicial accountability against sets of contradictory community cognitions, rather than consensus cognitions, is that the former empower judges to select whichever of the contradictory cognitions suits as

---

42   Personal communication.
43   See s7(1).
44   For other examples, and a different interpretation of their significance, see the judgment of Gummow J in *Brennan v Comcare* (1994) 122 ALR 615 at 633–6.
45   See Young, I M, *Justice and the Politics of Difference* (1990); Young, I M, "Justice and Communicative Democracy" (1993) unpublished paper presented at ANU, Canberra, February 1993. See also above n29 passim.

they impose their own attitudes. Where one wants diversity is in the judicial deliberation itself. First, one should aspire to a court which is itself somewhat diverse, perhaps at least in terms of sex, age, region, religion and ethnicity.[46] Second, one should aspire to a court which is exquisitely open to the diversity of ways of thinking in the community — a court which reads widely, which attends educational courses, which talks with ordinary Australians from all walks of life, which is encouraging to interventions of public interest groups and other institutions of civil society as *amicis curiae*, which is hospitable to "Brandeis briefs" on wider social and economic concerns relevant to a case, and perhaps even which commissions social science research to summarise the diverse ways of thinking about the problems before it.[47]

As Bernstein,[48] Handler[49] and Drysek[50] have pointed out, subjectivist philosophers such as Arendt,[51] Gadamer,[52] Habermas,[53] MacIntyre[54] and Barber[55] have very different views on what truth is and how one discovers it. For all their differences, however, they can agree that the way to attack the dilemmas of truth and method is through a plural dialogue, where many voices can be heard, unconstrained by forces of domination. At least they can agree that they are heirs of Aristotle. In addition, objectivists such as Popperian fallibilists can equally agree that robust, pluralist debate is essential for drawing out the refutation of that which is objectively false.[56]

Moreover, MacIntyre[57] may be right that disagreement on basic ethical paradigms is frequently compatible with consensus on the moral status of specific practical questions. Appellate court judges agree a lot of the time, but usually not for identical reasons, and often on the basis of mutually incompatible philosophical positions. This is why deconstructionists can play such havoc with their work. But if we take MacIntyre[58] seriously, nihilism is not justified in the face of such deconstruction. This is because dialogue between incompatible traditions can see one tradition generate solutions for the second in terms that are coherent within the second tradition. After all the wooing and wondering among justices, the High Court decision, woven together from

---

46 One should not expect too much from this reform alone, however. Like so much in this paper, it is relevant only to appellate courts and irrelevant to the bread and butter work of trial courts where only one judge of one gender, age, religion etc presides.

47 On courts facilitating social science research, *amicis curiae* and Brandeis briefs, see Davies, above n3.

48 Bernstein, R J, *Beyond Objectivism and Relativism: Science, Hermeneutics, and Praxis* (1983).

49 Handler, J F, "Dependent People, the State, and the Modern/Postmodern Search for the Dialogic Community" (1988) 35 *UCLA LR* 999.

50 Drysek, J S, *Discursive Democracy: Politics, Policy and Political Science* (1990).

51 Arendt, H, *The Human Condition* (1958).

52 Gadamer, H R, *Truth and Method* (1975).

53 Habermas, J, *The Theory of Communicative Action I: Reason and the Rationalization of Society* (1984).

54 MacIntyre, A, *After Virtue: A Study in Moral Theory* (1984).

55 Barber, B R, *Strong Democracy: Participatory Politics for a New Age* (1984).

56 Mill is another interesting case here. See Mill, J S, *Utilitarianism; Liberty; Representative Government* (1964) at 95–8, 107, 111.

57 MacIntyre, A, "Does Applied Ethics Rest on a Mistake?" (1984) 67 *The Monist* 498 at 500–1.

58 MacIntyre, A, *Whose Justice? Which Rationality?* (1988) at 364–5.

slender and contrary opinion, can knit a fabric of communal conviction that inspires civic purpose and practical problem solving. Consider *Mabo*. The outcome can generally be regarded as sensible, but for several philosophically incompatible reasons. The realistic aspiration therefore is for consensus at the front end and the back end of the judicial process, but not in between. At the front end, there can be consensus on shared community values (pre-eminently, on the rule of law). At the back end, there can be consensus on agreeing to accept a practical solution to the problem, and on at least some shared reasons for that solution. Sandwiched in between the consensual acceptance of the solution and the consensus values that ground the deliberation, we should aspire to being open to the most plural, multicultural, theoretically eclectic deliberation.

Sadly, the dialogue needed between the judges to enable MacIntyre's solving of the problems of one tradition in the terms of another occurs in only a limited way in Australian appellate courts. Conferences to ensure a robust dialogue among the judges are not institutionalised across our highest courts in the way that they are in those of the United States and Canada. An implication of the position articulated in this article is that there is a need to reform the rugged individualism of the deliberative practices of our senior judges.[59] Dialogue can help the judges to help each other to see relevances of community values that they might neglect in their solitary chambers.

The prescription for collective deliberation applies with even greater force when it comes to how one should make judgments about how to balance conflicting community values. This is a topic for another article. Suffice it to say here that there are three basic options: (1) empirical evidence exists on how ordinary citizens balance and trade off existing values and on which values rank higher in a hierarchy of values — these data can be used to inform judicial balancing;[60] (2) the judges can construct or apply a normative theory of how to derive all the shared values from a common yardstick — such as happiness for utilitarians, or dominion (a republican conception of liberty) for republicans such as Philip Pettit and me[61] — then values are traded off according to their contribution to the overarching value; (3) judges can derive from one value conclusions about the contexts where other values ought to apply — for example, the rule of law as a value implies that the value of happiness ought not to be allowed as a reason for convicting an innocent person. Section 7 briefly begins to define a republican approach to trading off the values to be weighed in different fact situations. It would involve a mix of all three of the above strategies. Whichever approach to balancing or contextualising

---

59 Michelman sees O'Connor J's dissenting judgment in *Goldman v Weinberger* 106 S Ct 1324 (1986) as a model of republican collegiality: "The tone of Justice O'Connor J's opinion is as dialogic as its method. Its implicit setting and sense are those of an equal speaking among several, not of solitary, self-contained pronouncement. It directly addresses each of the other four judicial speakers in the case, calling each by name, the only one of the five opinions to do so. It speaks in the voice of colloquy, not authority; of persuasion, not self-justification. Altogether, the opinion seems a model of judicial reconciliatory dialogue". See Michelman, F I, "The Supreme Court 1985 Term — Foreword: Traces of Self-Government" (1986) 100 *Harv LR* 4 at 36.

60 See the studies above in nn16–9.

61 Braithwaite, J and Pettit, P, *Not Just Deserts: A Republican Theory of Criminal Justice* (1990).

values is espoused, it seems likely that collegial dialogue will enhance the
quality of its implementation.

7. How to Implement Responsiveness to Community Values

The options for implementing responsiveness to community values to be considered here will be:

- Judges simply disciplining themselves to reason from shared community
  values;

- Judges using community values as evidence of moral truth (within a
  Dworkinian framework, for example);

- An entrenched Bill of Values and Rights;

- A non-entrenched Bill of Values and Rights subject to parliamentary
  amendment; and

- A Bill of Values and Rights subject to amendment by periodic
  constitutional conventions.

The straightforward option for implementing judicial responsiveness to
community values would be simply for judges to discipline themselves to reason from values that empirical research shows to be consensually shared in
the Australian community, just as they discipline themselves to reason from
the law. Michael Smith has suggested a Dworkinian option of both pursuing
fit with existing law and making the body of law as a whole as justified as
possible:

> The task of judges is to make new decisions that make the law as a whole
> morally justifiable, and they appeal to community values because the fact
> that a value is embraced by a community is a useful bit of evidence to use in
> support of the claim that the value is correct.... Given that judges must jus-
> tify their appeals to moral principle ... judges need to be aware of the distinc-
> tion between community values and community attitudes, they need to be
> aware of why appeals to community values will provide better evidence of
> moral truth than community attitudes, and they therefore need to have avail-
> able current data showing what the community's values are.[62]

To facilitate this, the kind of research discussed in Section 3 could be updated
on a larger national sample. Moreover, and critically, wording of a number of
the values would need to be modified so that they more concisely connect
with concepts in Australian law.

The most sweeping response would be to entrench a Bill of Values and
Rights in a way that was informed by research within the values paradigm. In
addition to the political difficulty of accomplishing the bipartisan and interstate support to carry a referendum for an entrenched Bill, an argument
against entrenched values (to which judges would be required to attend in interpreting the law) is that this would entrench the values of this generation.

---

62 Personal communication from Smith, M, commenting on this article.

An intermediate response would be for a non-entrenched Bill of Values and Rights.[63] Such a Bill could be up-dated from time to time by the parliament. One could take greater risks with it than with an entrenched Bill. If judges applied the values unwisely or autocratically, then parliament could change the Bill. Hence, a non-entrenched Bill of Values and Rights would have a judicial accountability advantage over an entrenched Bill, and an inter-generational flexibility advantage. At the same time, a non-entrenched Bill would absolve judges of the responsibility for selecting the values that should influence their deliberations, and for contracting the research leading to this selection. Another possible advantage of parliament voting on a list of values is that parliament, after due deliberation, might conclude that certain values which are not subject to extensive community consensus should nevertheless be included in the Bill. Because parliament is accountable to the people through election, it is proper for it to require judges to attend to values rejected by significant numbers of citizens — for example, values below the line in Table 1. Non-elected judges, however, cannot so properly foist values on the community that a substantial proportion of the community rejects.

A response intermediate between an entrenched and a non-entrenched Bill of Values and Rights subject to parliamentary amendment could be a constitutional convention every 10 years, for example, to consider amendments.[64]

8.   *A Republican Bill of Values and Rights?*

The entrenchment question is one on which there is merit in being open-minded at this stage of the national discussion, as is the question of whether a period of judicial development of the jurisprudence of Australian community values would be superior to a rush to any kind of Bill. However, I should like to put on the agenda of the rights debate the alternative of creating a distinctively Australian institution called a Bill of Values and Rights as a response to the distinctively Australian debate about the jurisprudence of community values to which I have sought to contribute.

How would the values in such a Bill be different from the rights? Under a republican conception of a Bill of Values and Rights, the rights would be derived from the values. By republican lights, as Pettit and I have argued, rights should only be enshrined in law when doing so, and only when doing so, will have good consequences in terms of republican values.[65] The philosophical difference between values and rights is that values are targets while rights are constraints.

Consider one value from Table 1: "THE PURSUIT OF KNOWLEDGE". This is defined as a target; knowledge is something worth maximising. However, the value can be used to define a constraint as well as a target — free primary education guaranteed to all citizens, for example. The latter right is a constraint, meaning that we are required to choose one particular option which

---

63   For a discussion of the issues with a Bill of Rights and Freedoms not being entrenched, see Queensland Electoral and Administrative Review Commission, *Report on Review of the Preservation and Enhancement of Individuals' Rights and Freedoms* (1993) Electoral and Administrative Review Commission, Brisbane.

64   I am indebted to Cheryl Saunders for drawing this option to my attention.

65   Above n61; Pettit, P, "The Consequentialist Can Recognise Rights" (1988) 38 *Philos Q* 42.

exemplifies the value of knowledge and that option constrains us to guarantee free primary education. We can multiply the examples; "GREATER ECONOMIC EQUALITY" is a target we should pursue; the right to state support during periods of unemployment is a constraint we should honour.

According to the republican theory of justice elaborated by Pettit and me elsewhere, a considerable number of legal, social, economic and political rights can and should be grounded in republican values.[66] Contests about how to balance different values, in turn, can be decided against the yardstick of a master value — republican liberty. The mix of values that should be pursued, according to this view, is that mix which will best advance republican liberty. Republican liberty is the condition where citizens can make choices about their own lives under guarantees of freedom from coercion by those with greater power. This is liberty as a citizenship status of security against unchecked or arbitrary power. It is freedom of choice with domination held in check, a freedom that can therefore be enhanced by state intervention to check domination. This freedom as non-domination is contrasted to freedom as simply non-interference.

Hence, a republican Bill of Values and Rights could define:

1.   A set of rights to be honoured, even in the face of a statute directing otherwise;

2.   A set of fundamental values (that justify the above rights) upon which the interpretations of a court should only trench in the face of an "unambiguous and unmistakable expression of intention" by the legislature;[67] and

3.   A privileging of liberty, defined in a republican way, as a yardstick against which to assess trade-offs between different values.

These three elements are separable. It is possible to have only (1) (a Bill of Rights), only (1) and (2) (a Bill of Values and Rights), or all three (a republican Bill of Values and Rights). For a republican, the first and second options could both amount to progress. Indeed, my own view is that pushing for the third option would be premature and a political mistake, pushing the republican agenda beyond the point where it has been clearly thought through, let alone debated. While Pettit and I feel we have thought through the implications of a republican yardstick for trading values in the limited domain of criminal justice,[68] I harbour doubts about its more general applicability, doubts that have to be the topic for another, longer article. Yet, so long as democratic institutions are put in place that allow space for dialogue about how to trade values against one another, republicans have their fora for arguing against classical negative liberty and for trade-offs that find more favour against the yardstick of republican liberty.

---

66   Ibid.
67   See text accompanying n42.
68   Above n61.

9. *Conclusion*

Most scholars assume that public opinion is so fickle and divided as to provide a foundation of sand for judicial deliberation. This article has sought to show that this is true if by public opinion we mean community attitudes, but false if we mean community values. There are a set of values that enjoy near-universal support in the Australian community. Values such as health, peace, freedom and equality of opportunity, and some dozens of others enjoy robust community support across samples, and for different question wording. Most citizens are able to justify most of their attitudes and political choices in terms of this finite set of values. Values do not change dramatically from year to year in the way that attitudes to political parties, or to the punishment of criminals, sometimes do. Large value shifts do occur, such as the shift Inglehart has documented from materialist to post-materialist values, but these occur across decades or centuries rather than years.[69] Moreover, the shift from materialist to post-materialist values is typical in that it does not involve an outright rejection of materialist values such as "ECONOMIC PROSPERITY"; it simply means post-materialist values such as "PRESERVING THE NATURAL ENVIRONMENT" have acquired a relatively higher priority in comparison to the materialist values. An exception here is that perhaps "MAN'S DOMINATION OF NATURE" once was a consensus value in Australia; Section 3 shows it is no longer.

The most profound reason for a separation of powers with an independent, unelected judiciary is that the judges are given the backbone to stand firm against public opinion when it threatens the rule of law and community values (which include the rule of law). The vision of democracy here is not one of direct rule by the people. Rule by public opinion of the day is particularly dangerous in a world where control of the means of forming public opinion is concentrated in few hands; a busy world in which most citizens do not have time to talk with each other or to think deeply about most questions of public opinion. The vision of democracy here is a republican one, one based on the ballot box and on deliberation by an executive, a legislature, and a judiciary. The depth of democracy in a republic depends on the quality of that deliberation — its openness to participation and input from citizens, to plural and conflicting perspectives. In addition, I have contended, it depends on the level of commitment in the democracy to explaining how conflicts are resolved in terms of values shared by the people. The parliament's laws; the people's values; the judges' reasoning (where all are enriched by active institutions of civil society). A circle of accountability that is closed by the people's vote to change a parliament.

---

69   Inglehart, R, *Culture Shift in Advanced Industrial Society* (1990).

[12]
On Speaking Softly and Carrying Big Sticks: Neglected Dimensions of a Republican Separation of Powers†

I *The Concentration of Private Power*

A. TOWARDS THE 'PURE DOCTRINE' OF THE SEPARATION OF POWERS

The separation of powers may be the most central idea in the theory of institutional design. Yet this has only been true of thinking about public institutions. This paper extends the relevance of the doctrine into thinking about checking the power of private institutions. The practice of separating powers dates at least from the Code of Hammurabi[1] when laws were carved in literal stone that would constrain the actions not only of subjects but also of the king. There follows a more or less cumulative history of separations of powers that we see sedimented in the institutions of contemporary Western democracies. Among the important moments in this history were the mixed Spartan Constitution,[2] the Roman Senate and Justinian's Code,[3] Magna Carta,[4] the jury, the growth of universities

† I owe a debt to four different intellectual communities within the Australian National University that have shaped my thinking in this paper. Parts of the paper have been presented to seminars of the Economics Program and the Social Political Theory Group of the Research School of Social Sciences. From the former group, I am particularly grateful for Bruce Chapman's criticisms on the economic analysis of law. From the latter, I am particularly indebted to Philip Pettit's ideas on republican institutional design. Third, I have been stimulated by the group of scholars within the Law Program in RSSS interested in the separation of powers – Sir Anthony Mason, Christine Parker, Fiona Wheeler, John Williams, & Leslie Zines. Fourth, I thankfully acknowledge the large group of scholars of regulatory institutions from across ANU whose work is cited in the paper, particularly Stephen Bottomley. Finally, my thanks to Tonia Vincent for her relentless research assistance. Part VII of the paper relies heavily on things I learned with and from Brent Fisse during our fieldwork together. Thanks also to Colin Scott & Peter Grabosky for helpful comments.

1 W.F. Leemans, *Legal and Administrative Documents of the Time of Hammurabi and Samsuiluna (Mainly from Lagaba)* (Leiden: J.E. Brill, 1960).

2 W.B. Gwyn, *The Meaning of the Separation of Powers* (The Hague: Martinus Nijhof, 1965) at 88 [hereinafter *Meaning*].

3 Justinian, *The Digest of Roman Law: Theft, Rapine, Damage and Insult*, trans. and ed. C.F. Kolbert (Harmondsworth: Penguin Books, 1983). .

4 A. Pallister, *Magna Carta: The Heritage of Liberty* (Oxford: Clarendon Press, 1971); W.I. Jennings, *Magna Carta and Its Influence in the World Today* (London: HMSO, 1965).

as accumulators and communicators of knowledge that become progressively more independent of church and state, the rise of judicial independence, and bicameral parliaments.

Notwithstanding the important contributions of Locke[5] and other enlightenment scholars,[6] the practice of separation of powers was ahead of the theory until Montesquieu published *The Spirit of the Laws*.[7] The richest development of these ideas flowed from the debates between the federalists[8] and anti-federalists[9] in the drafting of the US Constitution. The political philosophy of both the federalists and anti-federalists was republican. Philip Pettit has been the primary inspiration in a program of work at the Australian National University to excavate the foundations of the republican approach to the checking of power as a commitment to freedom as non-domination.[10] In that work, checking power under a rule of law designed to minimize the capacity of others to exercise arbitrary power over us is seen as the keystone of the freedom republicans cherish.

While the republican theorizing and Constitution-writing of the late eighteenth century clarified thinking about the separation of powers, its legacy was also to narrow vigilance to the checking of state power. What Vile characterises as the 'pure doctrine' of the separation of powers illustrates

It is essential for the establishment and maintenance of political liberty that the government be divided into three branches or departments, the legislature, the executive and the judiciary. To each of these three branches there is a corresponding identifiable function of government, legislative, executive or judicial. Each branch of government must be confined to the exercise of its own function and not allowed to encroach upon the functions of other branches. Furthermore, the persons who compose these three agencies of government must be kept separate and distinct , no individual being allowed to be at the same time a member of more than one branch. In this way each of the branches will be a

---

5 J. Locke, *Two Treatises of Government* (Cambridge: Cambridge University Press, 1960).
6 For example, James Harrington & John Milton on mixed government. See M.J.C. Vile, *Constitutionalism and Separation of Powers* (Oxford: Clarendon Press, 1963) at 29–30.
7 C. de Secondat Montesquieu, *The Spirit of the Laws*, trans, and ed. A.M. Cohler, B.C. Miller & H.S. (Cambridge: Cambridge University Press, 1989).
8 A. Hamilton, J. Madison & J. Jay, *The Federalist Papers* (New York: Mentor Books, 1961).
9 R. Ketcham, ed., *The Anti-Federalist Papers and the Constitutional Convention Debates* (New York: Mentor Books, 1986).
10 P. Pettit, *Republicanism: A Theory of Freedom and Government* (Oxford: Oxford University Press, 1997); J. Braithwaite & P. Pettit, *Not Just Desserts: A Republican Theory of Criminal Justice* (Oxford: Oxford University Press, 1990); S. Bronitt & G. Williams, 'Political Freedom as an Outlaw: Republican Theory and Political Protest' (1996) 18 A.L.R. 289.

check to the others and no single group of people will be able to control the machinery of the State.[11]

B. BEYOND THE PURE DOCTRINE

The autocrat of the state was seen as the threat to our freedom. As a result, when we think of the separation of powers today, we think of separations among these branches of the state – the legislature, the executive, and the judiciary. Yet equally important in the history of the separation of powers has been the separation of church and state. More important in terms of contemporary effects is the separation of business and the state. Today, the largest fifty transnational corporations all have greater resources, stronger political connections in the world system, more practical coercive capabilities, and more sophisticated private policing technology than most of the world's states.[12] The technology that monitors all our financial transactions, the trace of our movements about the city as we make them, the actual things we do in the most private spaces of the metropolis are captured on video not by the state tyrant that George Orwell feared,[13] but by private repositories of power. The legacy of the republican tradition is obsession with the powers of state police in societies with twice as many private as public police.[14] In nations like Australia, a Rupert Murdoch has more influence over the Prime Minister and Cabinet than any member of the judiciary. Moreover, that is only a tiny part of Rupert Murdoch's power compared to the influence he has in the United States, China, and beyond. Through influence in a number of states, such private actors sometimes shape global regulatory regimes in ways that make the citizens of all states subservient to them.[15]

11 Vile, supra note 6. Distinguishing these three branches is no simple matter, as Sir Anthony Mason explains '[t]he lesson of history is that the separation of doctrine serves a valuable purpose in providing safeguards against the emergence of arbitrary or totalitarian power. The lesson of experience is that the division of powers is artificial and confusing because the three powers of government do not lend themselves to definition in a way that leads readily to a classification of functions (Anthony Mason, 'A New Perspective on the Separation of Powers,' *Reshaping Australian Institutions: Australian National University Public Lecture*, Lecture 1, 25 July 1996 at 5).

12 R.J. Barnet & R.E. Muller, *Global Reach: The Power of the Multinational Corporations* (New York: Simon and Schuster, 1974); R.J. Barnet & J. Cavanagh, *Global Dreams: Imperial Corporations and the New World Order* (New York: Simon and Schuster, 1994).

13 G. Orwell, *1984* (New York: Harcourt, Brace, Jovanovich, 1949).

14 For the seminal collection on the privatization of policing, see C.D. Shearing & P.C. Stenning, eds., *Private Policing. Sage Criminal Justice System Annuals*, vol. 23 (Beverly Hills: Sage, 1987). Also see C.D. Shearing & P.C. Stenning, 'Modern Private Security: Its Growth and Implications,' *Crime and Justice: An Annual Review of Research*, vol. 3, eds., M. Tonry & N. Morris (Chicago: University of Chicago Press, 1981).

15 For example, Peter Drahos and I are documenting the influence of 16 chief executives of American companies in reshaping the world intellectual property order

Today, therefore, the separation of business and state has an importance that the separation of church and state and separation of powers within the state once had. Even more neglected in the scholarly literature, however, is the separation of powers within business. The major exception is the vast literature on national antitrust and the breaking of global cartels such as OPEC.[16] If the reason why we take the separation of powers seriously is the republican concern to protect liberty from domination by concentrations of power, then separation of private power must be of equal importance today to state power. One objective of this paper is to help redress this imbalance in the separation of powers literature by focusing primarily on separations of private power. I will show that the different perspective I develop on the separation of private powers is relevant to public power as well.

The way the need for a separation of powers is reconceptualized in this paper is in terms of certain deep practical difficulties in monitoring and deterring abuse of power. I will show why attempts to deter abuse of power often rebound, making things worse for citizens who suffer the abuse of power. Then I will show how innovative separations of powers can ameliorate this problem. Using research on corporate regulation and self-regulation, I will suggest that the most innovative practice is decades ahead of theory in this matter.

An aspiration of the paper is to make a minor contribution to republican political theory. Two ideals under that theory are the separation of powers and dialogic democracy, 'deliberation in governance in order to shape as well as balance interests (as opposed to deal making between prepolitical interests).'[17] Hitherto, these have been regarded as separate desiderata, albeit ones that can both be justified in terms of the promotion of freedom as non-domination.[18] A contribution of this paper will be to show how the separation of powers nurtures the possibility of dialogic decision making.

C. PLAN OF THE PAPER

The next section (Part II) clarifies the reconceptualization of the separation of powers that will be sought in this paper and the method by which we will seek it. Part III reviews an increasingly coherent body of theory and data on why attempts to deter abuse of power with countervailing

---

through the GATT. For a preliminary product of this work, see P. Drahos, 'Global Property Rights in Information: The Story of TRIPS at the GATT' (1995) 13 Prometheus. 6; P. Drahos, 'Information Feudalism in the Information Society' (1995) 11 The Information Society. 209.

16 See, for example, R.D Blair & D.L. Kaserman, *Antitrust Economics* (Irwin: Homewood, 1985); D.W. Carlton & J.M. Perloff, *Modern Industrial Organization* (Scott Foresman: Illinois, 1990); D. Dewey, *The Antitrust Experiment in America* (Columbia University Press: New York, 1990).

17 C. Sunstein, 'Beyond the Republican Revival' (1988) 97 Yale L.J. 1539.

18 P. Pettit, supra note 10.

power evoke defiance and counter-control. Part IV shows why weak sanctions, especially dialogic ones, generally do better than strong sanctions directed against those who abuse power. Part V shows that those weak sanctions are least likely to work when directed against those who actually benefit from the abuse of power; they are more likely to work when directed against non-beneficiaries of the abuse who have preventative capabilities. Part VI shows that plural separations of power both within and between the public and private sectors create the conditions in which dialogic mechanisms to control abuse of power can flourish. Part VII explains what separation of powers means within the private sector, while Part VIII sketches some implications of the analysis for the economic efficiency of the separation of powers. The conclusion, Part IX, is that a plural republican separation of powers is the midwife of deliberative democracy wherein dialogue is more important than deterrence to the control of abuse of power. Dialogic responsibility among powers with richly pluralized separations means that abuse of power is checked through the process of soft targets simply being persuaded or shamed by discussion into accepting accountability for putting things right. Republican dialogue itself is also concluded to be the best guarantee we can hope for to protect us against economically inefficient ways of transacting the separation of powers.

II *The Concept of the Separation of Powers*

A. ON METHOD

The method in this paper is not to analyze the history of the idea of the separation of powers. Rather it is to move inductively toward a reconceptualization of the idea from (1) an understanding of contemporary practices of separating private and public powers, and (2) from the revelations of empirical social science about the difficulties of deterring abuse of power with countervailing power. At the same time, the method is to move deductively from a republican political theory to a proposed reshaping of the doctrine of separation of powers.

An analysis of the history of the idea of the separation of powers is of less use to making such a contribution to the theory of institutional design than the abductive[19] analysis of practice employed here because of the limited theoretical coherence of the distinctions that have been made in the great historical contests between the competing, yet related,

---

19 Abduction means shuttling backwards and forwards between induction and deduction. See T.J. Scheff, *Microsociology: Discourse, Emotion and Social Structure* (Chicago: University of Chicago Press, 1990).

310 UNIVERSITY OF TORONTO LAW JOURNAL

ideas of the separation of powers, mixed government, balanced government, and checks and balances. A mixing or balancing of powers logically entails a separation of powers;[20] yet these labels in the history are
attached to distinctive and competing concrete programs of institutional
reform, and indeed to very different reform programs in different
nations. Moreover, as M.J.C. Vile showed,[21] the competing reform
programs of the separation of powers, mixed and balanced government,
and checks and balances have all left their traces in the complex constitutional theories that are the contemporary inheritance of these contests.

B. FROM SPARTA TO MADISONIAN SEPARATIONS OF PRIVATE POWERS
Mixed government is the oldest idea, figuring in the writing of Aristotle
and Plato and justified in terms of securing moderation rather than
excess in government and avoiding arbitrary rule.[22] The mix in Sparta
was between the powers of dual kings (replicated in recent times by
transnational corporations such as Philips which have had dual CEOs), a
Council of Elders and Ephors elected by lot.[23] During the transition from
feudalism to capitalism, the reform program of mixed government
involved the king or queen, the lords and the male bourgeoisie sharing
power so that no single power would predominate. 'The importance of
the ancient theory of mixed government ... is its insistence upon the
necessity for a number of separate branches of government if arbitrary
rule is to be avoided.'[24] It was not based on a separation of the functions
proper to each branch, as each branch was expected to check the
arbitrary power of other branches by getting involved in all aspects of
government. The mid-seventeenth-century theory of the balanced
Constitution was a hybrid of mixed government between king, lords, and
commoners, and some division of functions among them.[25] Then in the
late seventeenth century, the American anti-federalists embraced a purist
conception of the separation of powers which mapped onto a strict
division of the functions of executive, legislative, and judicial branches.[26]

20 You cannot 'mix' or 'balance' powers that are unified; they must be separated first.
21 Vile, supra note 6.
22 Plato, *Laws, II, The Dialogues of Plato*, vol. 72, 3rd ed., trans. B. Jowett, (Oxford:
    Clarendon Press, 1892).
23 Vile, supra note 6 at 35.
24 Ibid. at 36.
25 Ibid. at 39–40, 98–101.
26 B. Manin, 'Checks, Balances and Boundaries: The Separation of Powers in the
    Constitutional Debate of 1787,' *The Invention of the Modern Republic*, ed. B. Fontana
    (Cambridge: Cambridge University Press, 1994).

ON SPEAKING SOFTLY AND CARRYING STICKS 311

The contemporary republican reconceptualization of the separation of powers I will advance has it that the ancients were wise to see the objective of mixed government as the checking of arbitrary power.[27] Historically contingent judgments are then needed about whether arbitrary power will be better checked by associating more or less clearly separated functions with the powers that different branches of governance exercise. Neither a purist commitment to dividing power as strictly as possible among branches which do not interfere in each other's functions nor a purist commitment to empowering all branches to be equally involved in all functions of government will prove attractive if one's objective is the republican one of checking arbitrary power.[28] Sometimes we will need a strong state to exercise countervailing power against strong private interests, or vice versa. Sometimes we will want to constrain one branch from a kind of interference in the governance of another branch which would completely compromise the latter's capacity for independent action.

International relations theorists of balance of power have provided more useful formulations for consequentialist republicans who must reject such purisms. For example, Hans Morgenthau conceptualizes 'balance of power' as 'allowing the different elements to pursue their opposing tendencies up to the point where the tendency of one is not so strong as to overcome the tendency of the others, but strong enough to prevent the others from overcoming its own.'[29] While this is useful, Morgenthau is even more myopic than Montesquieu in the powers he sees as contesting the balance. They are unitary nation states, while for Montesquieu they are limited to the legislative, executive and judicial branches of states. Closer to the position I will reach here is Madison's in Federalist No. 10 that more rather than fewer factions in a republic provide better protection against domination of our liberty by one faction because of 'the greater security afforded by a greater variety of parties, against the event of any one party being able to outnumber and oppress the rest.'[30] Madison also made passing reference to the importance of separating private powers, 'where the constant aim is to divide and arrange the several offices in such a way that each may be a check on the other.'[31]

27 See further P. Pettit, supra note 10.
28 Ibid.
29 H. Morgenthau, *Politics Among Nations*, 5th ed. (New York: Alfred A. Knopf, 1973) at 169.
30 J. Madison, A. Hamilton & J. Jay, supra note 9 at 128. See also 'Federalist No. 51' at 321.
31 Ibid. at 320.

312 UNIVERSITY OF TORONTO LAW JOURNAL

Contrary to Montesquieu, my conclusion will be that it is better to have many unclear separations of public and private powers than a few clear ones. The republican canvas Madison sought to paint was more a Jackson Pollock than a Mondrian. The canvas I will splash will be one where private powers will need to be granted some autonomy from state powers and vice versa, yet where private power is able to check public power and vice versa. It will be a canvas where powers are separated between the private and the public, within the public and within the private sphere, where separations are many and transcend private-public divides. The ideal is of enough independence for one branch of private, public, or hybrid governance for it to be able to make its best contribution to advancing republican freedom without being prevented from doing so by the domination of some other branch. The ideal is also of enough interdependence for many branches to be able to check the power of one branch from dominating others. I will argue for the ideal of many semi-autonomous powers[32] recursively checking one another rather than a few autonomous branches of governance. The more richly plural the separations into semi-autonomous powers, the more the dependence of each power on many other guardians of power will secure their independence from domination by one power.

Just as this conception of separations of powers in the modern world is pluralist about the variety of branches of private and public power that should be involved in pursuing and checking power, so we should be pluralist about what we mean by the nature of the power that is separated. Both Madison and I are loose in the way we switch between talking about the power of factions, of parties, of 'the multiplicity of interests,' 'the multiplicity of sects,'[33] of branches of governance, of guardians. Many different kinds of power can be exercised by many different kinds of individual and collective actors. Some of the separated powers will be the power of one actor to impose their will on others,[34] some will be the power to write rules which the writer has no power to impose,[35] some will be Lukes' second face of power as a capacity to keep items off the agenda without a need for any imposition of will,[36] some will be a Latourian capacity to enrol others to one's projects without directly imposing one's

32 On the notion of semi-autonomy in law, see S. Falk Moore, *Law as Process: An Anthropological Approach* (London: Routledge & Kegan Paul, 1978).
33 J. Madison, A. Hamilton & J. Jay, supra note 9 at 321.
34 This is a classic Dahlian conception of power. See R.A. Dahl, 'The Concept of Power' (1957) 2 Behavioral Science. 201.
35 On this distinction, see S. Clegg, *Power, Rule and Domination* (London: Routledge & Kegan Paul, 1975) at 67–75.
36 S. Lukes, *Power: A Radical View* (London: Macmillan, 1974).

ON SPEAKING SOFTLY AND CARRYING STICKS 313

will on the object of control,[37] some will be a Gramscian hegemony which constitutes individuals who cannot recognize that they are being dominated,[38] some will be Foucauldian disciplinary networks partially advanced through the practices of agents rather than intended or willed as acts of power,[39] some will be Foucauldian shepherds governing and caring for their flock.[40] Normatively, what republicans of my stripe want preserved is freedom as non-domination; in different contexts different types of power exercised by plural agents of power will do that job best. So one wants such plural separations of disparate modalities of private and public power as will maximize freedom as non-domination. None of this is particularly novel; it is simply a somewhat radicalising extension of tendencies that can be found in the writings of James Madison. There is, however, novelty in the analysis of speaking softly and carrying sticks that is my reason for pushing far with this pluralising of Madison.

There are a number of reasons why Madison and other advocates of the separation of powers found the doctrine attractive. There is the desire to limit the damage that one all-powerful bad ruler can do, to expand the diversity of perspectives that have influence in politics, to foster deliberative democracy by requiring one branch of governance to persuade another that it has exercised its power wisely, to constrain the rule of men by the rule of law, to empower those who might otherwise be powerless. This essay will not systematically evaluate the desirability or feasibility of these rationales for the separation of powers. The analysis will be limited to a fresh perspective on just one rationale for the separation of powers, albeit what republicans should regard as the most fundamental one[41] – checking abuse of power.

Before we can reach the point of understanding why pluralities of checks is the reconceptualization of the separation of powers we need for the contemporary world, we must begin with an understanding of the empirical literature on why efforts to check abuse of power so often backfire.

37 B. Latour, 'The Powers of Association,' ed. J. Law, *Power, Action and Belief: A New Sociology of Knowledge? Sociological Review Monograph 32* (London: Routledge & Kegan Paul, 1986).

38 A. Gramsci, *Selections from the Prison Notebooks of Antonio Gramsci*, trans. and ed. Q. Hoare & G.N. Smith (London, Lawrence & Wishart, 1971).

39 M. Foucault, *Discipline and Punish: The Birth of the Prison* (Pantheon: New York, 1977).

40 B. Hindess, *Discourses of Power: From Hobbes to Foucault* (Oxford: Blackwell, 1996).

41 It is the most important one for those who, like me, share Pettit's view that the most fundamental value in the design of political institutions is the assurance of freedom as non-domination (P. Pettit, supra note 10).

III *Why Big Sticks Rebound*

A. DETERRENCE FAILURE

The starting point for reaching the conclusions promised in the Introduction is to abstract from what we have learned empirically about the way the regulation of private power works, or rather why it so regularly fails to work. The republican idea of checking power with countervailing power is often read as a deterrence model for controlling abuse of power. Indeed, deterrence will have an important place in the conclusion ultimately reached in the present analysis.[42]

This section will explain first why deterrence often does not work well, drawing on research about emotion and rationality. Then we will see that deterrence often backfires and explain why deterrence has this capacity to defeat its own objectives. In subsequent sections, the argument will be that if we understand these problems properly, the separation of powers will prove relevant to their amelioration.

The discipline that has grappled most systematically with why deterrence does not work well is criminology. People almost universally value their lives. So it is surprising that introducing capital punishment is not shown to significantly reduce the crime rate, nor does abolishing the death penalty increase it.[43] It is surprising that building more prisons and locking up more people in them for longer periods, tougher sentencing, does not have predictable effects in reducing the crime rate.[44] Even the

42 Abuse of power might of course be controlled by rewards rather than sanctions. Rewards are not as seriously considered as deterrence in this role because giving even more resources to the rich and powerful for doing what it should be their citizenship obligation to do is unappealing to republicans. While rewards should be taken more seriously than they are in the theory and practice of checking power, some of the empirical limitations of control by deterrence will also be found to apply to control by reward.

43 W.C Bailey & R.D. Peterson, 'Murder, Capital Punishment and Deterrence – A Review of the Evidence and an Examination of Police Killings' (1994) 50 Journal of Social Issues. 53; J.K. Cochrane, M.B. Chamlin & M. Seth, 'Deterrence Brutalization – An Impact Assessment of Oklahoma Return to Capital-Punishment' (1994) 32 Criminology. 107; B. Forst, 'Capital Punishment and Deterrence: Conflicting Evidence?' (1983) 74 Journal of Criminal Law and Criminology. 927; T. Sellin, *The Penalty of Death* (Beverly Hills: Sage, 1980); Schuessler, 'The Deterrent Influence of the Death Penalty' (1952) 284 Annals of the Academy of Political and Social Sciences. 54; R. Hood, *The Death Penalty: A World Wide Survey* (Oxford: Oxford University Press, 1989).

44 A. Blumstein, J. Cohen & D. Nagin, eds. *Deterrence and Incapacitation: Estimating the Effects of Criminal Sanctions on Crime Rates* (Washington, DC: National Academy of Sciences, 1978). J.P. Gibbs, *Crime, Punishment and Deterrence* (New York: Elsevier, 1975); E.A. Fattah, 'Deterrence: A Review of the Literature,' (1977) 19 Canadian Journal of Criminology. 1; P.J. Cook, 'Research in Criminal Deterrence: Laying the Groundwork for the Second Decade,' *Crime and Justice: An Annual Review of Research,*

ON SPEAKING SOFTLY AND CARRYING STICKS 315

optimists about imprisonment do not conclude it has large effects.[45] It is surprising that we can experimentally double or halve the number of police patrol cars in neighbourhoods, without the experimental areas experiencing changes in crime rates in comparison to control neighbourhoods.[46] It is surprising that people who perceive the expected severity of punishment for committing a crime to be high are not more likely to refrain from crime than people who expect the severity of punishment from committing a crime to be low.[47] The US, with a death penalty that

vol. 2, eds. N. Morris & M. Tonry (1980) at 211. The latter review and an update soon to be published in the same series by Daniel Nagin ('Criminal Deterrence Research: A Review of the Evidence and a Research Agenda for the Outset of the 21st Century') are more optimistic about the existence of a deterrent effect. Nagin concludes that 'evidence for a substantial deterrent is much firmer than it was fifteen years ago.' With research on the deterrent effect of imprisonment Nagin concludes that the most recent study (S.D. Levitt, 'The Effect of Prison Population Size on Crime Rates: Evidence from Prison Overcrowding Litigation' (1996) 111 Quarterly Journal of Economics. 319) is both the most methodologically advanced and shows the biggest crime-reduction effect of any of these studies. However, there may not be a significant deterrent effect even in Levitt's study because Nagin reports that the estimated reduction in crime from imprisonment is 'not much larger than rates of offending of incarcerated populations reported in various studies of the incapacitation impacts' (thereby leaving little residual deterrent impact after the effect of the offenders' being off the street is taken into account).

45 James Q. Wilson, 'Crime and Public Policy,' *Crime*, eds. J.Q. Wilson & J. Petersilia (San Francisco: ICS Press, 1995) at 489.

46 D.H. Bayley, *Police for the Future* (New York: Oxford University Press, 1994). The classic study here, the Kansas City Preventive Patrol Experiment is not without its methodological problems as Lawrence Sherman & David Weisburd have shown. Sherman & Weisburd show, moreover, that increased police activity targeted on known hot spots, as opposed to random patrol as in the Kansas City experiment, can have a significant effect on crime. L. Sherman & D. Weisburd, 'General Deterrent Effects of Police Patrol in Crime "Hot Spots": A Randomized, Controlled Trial' (1995) 12 Justice Quarterly. 625–49. For the original study see G. Kelling *et al., The Kansas City Preventive Patrol Experiment: A Summary Report* (Washington, DC: Police Foundation, 1974).

47 While this is mostly the result in the following studies, the expected certainty of punishment is also in the majority found to have an effect, at least in some contexts. G.P. Waldo & T.G. Chiricos, 'Perceived Penal Sanction and Self-reported Criminality: A Neglected Approach to Deterrence Research' (1972) 19 Social Problems. 522; W.C. Bailey & R.P. Lot, 'Crime, Punishment and Personality: An Analysis of the Deterrence Question' (1976) 67 Journal of Criminal Law and Criminology. 99; R.E. Kraut, 'Deterrent and Definitional Influences on Shoplifting' (1976) 23 Social Problems. 358; M. Silberman, 'Towards a Theory of Criminal Deterrence' (1976) 41 American Sociological Review. 442; M.W. Spicer & S.B. Lundstedt, 'Understanding Tax Evasion' (1976) 31 Public Finance. 295; J. Teevan, Jr., 'Deterrent Effects of Punishment: Subject Measures Continued' (1976) 18 Cdn. Jo. Corr. 152; J. Teevan, Jr., 'Subjective Perceptions of Deterrence (Continued)' (1976) 13 Journal of Research in Crime and Delinquency. 155; J. Teevan, Jr., 'Deterrent Effects of Punishment for Breaking and Entering and Theft,' *Law Reform Commission of Canada, Fear of Punishment*

316 UNIVERSITY OF TORONTO LAW JOURNAL

other developed nations do not have, with more private and public police than they, with imprisonment rates several times higher than the OECD average, has not the lowest crime rates, but the highest of any of the wealthy nations. How can this be so?

B. EMOTION AND DEFIANCE

One reason is that the protection we get from many of the worst crimes is not bound up with calculative deliberation. For most of the people who

(Ottawa: Law Reform Commission, 1976); L.S. Anderson, T.G. Chiricos & G.P. Waldo, 'Formal and Informal Sanctions: A Comparison of Deterrent Effects' (1977) 25 Social Problems. 103; R.F. Meier & Weldon T. Johnson, 'Deterrence as Social Control: The Legal and Extra-legal Production of Conformity' (1977) 42 American Sociological Review. 292; W. Minor, 'A Deterrence Control Theory of Crime,' *Theory in Criminology: Contemporary Views*, ed. R. Meier (Beverly Hills: Sage, 1977); L. Cohen, 'Sanction Threats and Violation Behavior: An Inquiry into Perceptual Variation,' *Quantitative Studies in Criminology*, ed. C.F. Welford (Beverly Hills: Sage, 1978); G.F. Jensen & M. Erickson, 'The Social Meaning of Sanctions,' *Crime, Law and Sanction: Theoretical Perspectives*, eds. M. Krohn & R. Akers (Beverly Hills: Sage, 1978); R. Mason & L. D. Calvin, 'A Study of Admitted Income Tax Evasion' (1978) 13 Law and Soc'y Rev. 73; K.E. Waerneryd & B. Walerud, 'Taxes and Economic Behavior – Some Interview Data an Tax Evasion in Sweden' (1982) 2 Journal of Economic Psychology. 187; R.L. Akers *et al.*, 'Social Learning and Deviant Behavior: A Specific Test of a General Theory' (1979) 44 American Sociological Review. 635; H.G. Grasmick & G.J. Bryjak, 'The Deterrent Effect of Perceived Severity of Punishment' (1980) 59 Social Forces. 471; R.F. Meier, 'Jurisdictional Differences in Deterring Marijuana Use' (1982) 12 Journal of Drug Issues. 51; R. Paternoster *et al.*, 'Estimating Perceptual Stability and Deterrent Effects: The Role of Perceived Legal Punishment in the Inhibition of Criminal Involvement' (1983) 74 Journal of Criminal Law and Criminology. 270; R. Paternoster *et al.*, 'Perceived Risk and Social Control: Do Sanctions Really Deter?' (1983) 17 Law and Soc'y Rev. 457; D.M. Bishop, 'Legal and Extralegal Barriers to Delinquency: A Panel Analysis' (1984) 22 Criminology. 403; F.P. Williams III, 'Deterrence and Social Control: Rethinking the Relationship' (1985) 13 Journal of Crim. Just. 141; K.A. Kinsey, 'Theories and Models of Tax Cheating' (1986) 18 Criminal Justice Abstracts. 403; R. Paternoster & L. Iovanni, 'The Deterrent Effect of Perceived Severity: A Re-examination' (1986) 64 Social Forces. 751; I. Piliavin *et al.*, 'Crime, Deterrence and Rational Choice' (1986) 51 American Sociological Review. 101; S. Klepper & D. Nagin, 'The Deterrent Effect of Perceived Certainty and Severity of Punishment Revisited' (1989) 27 Criminology. 721; S. Klepper & D. Nagin, 'Tax Compliance and Perceptions of the Risk of Detection and Criminal Prosecution' (1989) 23 Law and Soc'y Rev. 209; H.G. Grasmick & R. Bursik, 'Conscience, Significant Others and Rational Choice: Extending the Deterrence Model' (1990) 24 Law and Society Review. 837; S.R. Burkett & E.L. Jensen, 'Conventional Ties, Peer Influence and the Fear of Apprehension: A Study of Adolescent Marijuana Use' (1975) 16 Sociological Quarterly. 522; C.R. Tittle, Sanctions and Social Deviance (New York: Preager, 1980); K. Williams & R. Hawkins, 'The Meaning of Arrest for Wife Assault' (1989) 27 Criminology. 163; S. Simpson, 'Corporate Crime Deterrence and Corporate Control Policies: Views from the Inside,' *White-Collar Crime Reconsidered*, eds. K. Schlegel & D. Weisburd (Boston: Northeastern University Press, 1992).

caused us problems last week, we did not deal with those problems by killing them. Our refraining from murder was not because we weighed up the benefits against the probability of detection and likely punishment; it was because murder was right off our deliberative agenda; murder was simply unthinkable to us as a way of solving our problems. It is understanding what constitutes that unthinkableness that is the key to crime prevention. Whether the penalty for murder is death or something else is mostly quite unimportant to that understanding.

Moreover, when murder does become thinkable, it often does so in a way that is not rationally deliberative in a way the deterrence model assumes. It sometimes becomes thinkable in the context of emotions temporarily hijacking those more calculative processes in the brain on which deterrence depends.[48] This emotional short-circuiting of rational calculation in our brain had survival value in the history of our species. The emotion of anger sends blood rushing to our hands so we are ready to fight, to grasp a weapon. The emotion of fear sends blood to our feet so we are ready to flee. The emotion of lust sends blood rushing to a place in between. The short circuit gives our bodies the capacity to exploit windows of opportunity to attack, defend, flee, procreate before the opportunity has passed.

In the contemporary world, as opposed to the world of our biological creation, the means of risk management and procreation are institutionalized in ways that make more doubtful the survival value of a brain that is liable to have its faculties for rational deliberation pre-empted by emotion. So the plight of modern humans is to experience regular regret for things we do during those moments when the emotions hijack the brain. For most of us, this is a weekly occurrence, for some a daily one. It does not take something as drastic as a man attacking us with a spear for threat to trigger anger; the brain makes connections of lower-level threats like an angry voice to fire up our anger. This is why emotional defiance to regulatory threats is relevant not only to 'crimes of passion' like murder. Overbearing threats by a government official can engender emotional defiance to what economists would expect to be rational business compliance with regulatory laws. Toni Makkai and I examined compliance by chief executives of 410 Australian nursing homes with 31 regulatory standards. We found that the subjective expected level of punishment did not predict compliance in any of a variety of more simple and more complex multivariate models we were able to

---

48 For a readily digestible account, if neurophysiologically dubious in parts, of this phenomenon see D. Goleman, *Emotional Intelligence* (New York: Bantam Books, 1995).

construct.[49] Diagram 1 shows, however, that this result conceals the fact that there were contexts where deterrence worked and other contexts where it not only failed to work, but where there was a counter-deterrent effect. A scale to measure the psychological trait of the emotionality of the chief executive was the only variable we could find which specified when the deterrence model would work and when it would not. When managers were low on emotionality, they responded to perceived increases in threat in a 'cold and calculating' way. But the CEOs who were high on emotionality responded to escalated threats by getting mad rather than by ceasing to be bad. In Diagram 1 if deterrence simply failed for high emotionality managers, the high emotionality line would be flat. In fact it slopes downwards, meaning that for emotional managers, the stronger the deterrent threat, the less compliance. Deterrence fails as a policy not so much because it is irrelevant (though it is for many) but because the gains from contexts where it works are cancelled by the losses from contexts where it backfires.

The most concentrated research effort criminology has seen was on the deterrence of domestic violence.[50] It tends to bear out a similar picture. In a first randomized experiment, Sherman and Berk[51] found that arrested domestic violence offenders were less likely to re-offend than those dealt with less punitively. This study had a major effect on public policy. However, subsequent experiments found no net effect of arrest in reducing violence. Again, this overall result concealed the fact that for employed men arrest reduced subsequent violence, while for unemployed men it escalated violence. Sherman interprets this as a result of underclass men who have experienced repeated stigmatizing and unfair experiences with the criminal justice system responding with anger and defiance when they are arrested. Unfortunately, while there are fewer unemployed than employed men in most communities, the violence-escalation effect of arrest for the unemployed was about twice the violence-reduction effect among the employed, giving a nil result overall in most of the studies. How to interpret the various methodological weaknesses of these studies is riddled with controversy.[52] What is clear,

---

49 J. Braithwaite & T. Makkai, 'Testing an Expected Utility Model of Corporate Deterrence' (1991) 25 Law and Soc'y Rev. 7 [hereinafter 'Testing']; Toni Makkai & John Braithwaite, 'The Dialectics of Corporate Deterrence' (1994) 31 J. of Res. Crime & Del. 347 [hereinafter 'Dialectics'].

50 For a review of the research effort by its most central participant, see L. Sherman, *Policing Domestic Violence* (New York: Free Press, 1992).

51 L.W. Sherman & R.A. Berk 'The Specific Deterrent Effect of Arrest for Domestic Assault' (1984) 49 American Sociological Review. 261.

52 See E. Stanko 'Policing Domestic Violence: Dilemmas and Contradictions' (1995) Austl. & N.Z. J. Crim. Criminology, Special Supplementary Issue. 31.

Diagram 1
Effect of interaction between emotionality and deterrence on compliance with the law[53]

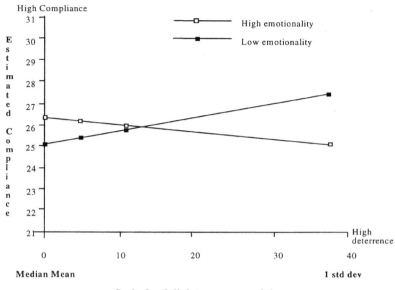

Scale for full deterrence model

however, is that never in my lifetime are we likely to see such a large investment of public money in systematic randomized tests at multiple sites of a deterrence hypothesis. If we are not likely ever to get better data than this, at least we need to settle on the conclusion that it is problematic to claim that deterrence is more likely to produce negative than positive effects on those who abuse power.

C. COGNITIONS OF STIGMA AND PROCEDURAL INJUSTICE

Moreover, on the same nursing home compliance data set as in Diagram 1, Sherman's approach to interpreting positive and negative effects of deterrence receives support. It was found that nursing home inspectors with a highly stigmatizing approach to law-breakers reduced compliance by 39 per cent in Diagram 2, while inspectors with a reintegrative shaming philosophy for securing compliance improved compliance in the two years following their inspection by the same amount. With reintegrative shaming, the non-compliant act is disapproved, while those responsible

53 Ibid.

Diagram 2

Mean improvement in compliance for nursing homes where inspectors used high disapproval and high reintegration styles; high disapproval and low reintegration styles; low disapproval and high reintegration styles (N=129; F-Value=3.58; p=.03)

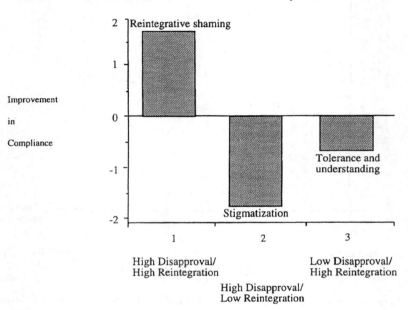

are treated with respect as responsible citizens. With stigmatization, they are shamed disrespectfully, labelled as bad people who have done the bad act. Inspectors who one might call captured, inspectors who were 'nice,' tolerant, and understanding of law-breakers, also made things worse, though the deterioration in compliance following their inspection was less than with the stigmatizing inspectors.

Sherman's invocation of the literature showing that compliance is more likely when actors perceive regulation to be procedurally fair suggests that the reasons big sticks rebound are to be found in the psychology of cognition as well as the psychology of emotion.[54] More

54 See T. Tyler, *Why People Obey the Law?* (New Haven: Yale University Press, 1990). A.E. Lind & T. Tyler, *The Social Psychology of Procedural Justice* (New York: Plenum Press, 1988). For the nursing home data discussed in Diagrams 1 and 2, only one of the standard facets of procedural justice – process control – had a significant effect in improving compliance, see T. Makkai & J. Braithwaite, 'Procedural Justice and Regulatory Compliance' (1996) 20(1) L. & Human Beh. 83.

ON SPEAKING SOFTLY AND CARRYING STICKS 321

police can increase crime if police are systematically procedurally unfair or stigmatizing in the way they deal with an underclass; more police can reduce crime if they are procedurally fair and reintegrative in their policing. When we increase the number of police, one reason we do not generally achieve a measurable reduction in crime is that we put on the beat a mixture of extra stigmatizing police who make things worse and extra fair, and reintegrative police who make things better.

The cognitive mechanisms that produce a 'reactance' against threat have now been the subject of an enormous experimental research effort. This work shows how foolish it is to follow the institutional design advice of Hobbes[55] and Hume[56] of preparing for the worst – assuming that people are knaves. Unfortunately, when we treat people as knaves they are more likely to become knaves. The less salient and powerful the control technique used to secure compliance, the more likely that internalization of the virtue of compliance will occur. Experimental research on children and college students demonstrates the counter-productive effect salient rewards and punishments can have: long-term internalization of values like altruism and resistance to temptation are inhibited when they view their action as caused by a reward or punishment.[57]

Over 50 studies examining the effect of extrinsic incentives on later intrinsic motivation indicate that inducements that are often perceived as controlling (e.g., tangible rewards, surveillance, deadlines), depending on the manner in which they are administered, reduce feelings of self-determination and undermine subsequent motivation in a wide variety of achievement-related activities after the reward is removed.[58]

These findings seem to be of fairly general import, being supported in domains including moral behaviour, altruism, personal interaction, aggressive behaviour, and resistance to temptation.[59] Just as strong

55 T. Hobbes, *De Cive* (New York: Appleton-Century-Crofts, 1949).
56 D. Hume 'Of the Independency of Parliament,' *Essays, Moral, Political and Literary*, vol. 1 (Oxford: Oxford University Press, 1963).
57 M.R. Lepper, 'Dissonance, Self-Perception and Honesty in Children' (1973) 25 Journal of Personality and Social Psychology. 65; M.R. Lepper & D. Greene, *The Hidden Costs of Reward* (Hillsdale, NJ: Erlbaum, 1978); T. Dix & J.E. Grusec, 'Parental Influence Techniques: An Attributional Analysis' (1983) 54 Child Development. 645; M.L. Hoffman, 'Affective and Cognitive Processes in Moral Internalization,' *Social Cognition and Social Development*, eds. E.T. Higgins, D.N. Rubble & W.W. Hartup (New York: Cambridge University Press, 1983).
58 A.K. Boggiano *et al.*, 'Use of the Maximal-Operant Principle to Motivate Children's Intrinsic Interest' (1987) 53 Journal of Personality and Social Psychology. 866.
59 M.R. Lepper, supra note 57; R.A. Dienstbier *et al.*, 'An Emotion-Attribution Approach to Moral Behavior: Interfacing Cognitive and Avoidance Theories of Moral Develop-

322 UNIVERSITY OF TORONTO LAW JOURNAL

external incentives retard internalization, using reasoning in preference to power-assertion tends to promote it.[60]

D. REACTANCE

Such findings are an important part of an empirical grounding for why republicans should have a preference for dialogue over coercion as a means of checking power. Brehm and Brehm[61] constructed a theory of psychological reactance on the basis of the kinds of studies we have been discussing. Diagram 3 shows that the net effect of deterrent threats[62] is the sum of a deterrence effect and a reactance effect. Diagram 3 also shows that reactance is least when we seek to restrict freedom to do something that is not very important to us, greatest when the freedom subjected to control is something the regulated actor deeply cares about. Hence, if freedom to park our car where we want is not an especially important freedom, the way we react to the size of parking fines will be rather like the left-hand panel in Diagram 3. The net effect of threat on compliance will be close to the prediction of a crude rational actor model. If freedom of religion is a vitally important freedom to Christians, then throwing more Christians to the lions may only strengthen their commitment to martyrdom, adding rather than detracting from the growth of Christianity, as in the right-hand panel of Diagram 3.

For republicans, the pattern of empirical results summarized in Diagram 3 has an ominous implication. Countervailing threats to check

---

ment' (1975) 82 Psychological Review. 229; T. Dix & J.E. Grusec, 'Parental Influence Techniques: An Attributional Analysis' (1983) 54 Child Development. 645; A.K. Boggiano *et al.*, 'Use of the Maximal-Operant Principle to Motivate Children's Intrinsic Interest,' ibid.

60 J.A. Cheyne & R.H. Walters, 'Intensity of Punishment, Timing of Punishment, and Cognitive Structure as Determinants of Response Inhibition' (1969) 7 Journal of Experimental Child Psychology. 231; R.D. Parke, 'Effectiveness of Punishment as an Interaction of Intensity, Timing, Agent Nurturance and Cognitive Structuring' (1969) 40 Child Development. 213; M.L. Hoffman, 'Moral Development,' *Carmichael's Manual of Child Psychology*, ed. P.H. Mussen (New York: Wiley, 1970); D.Baumrind, 'The Development of Instrumental Competence Through Socialization,' *Minnesota Symposium of Motivation*, vol. 7, ed. A.D. Pick (Minneapolis: University of Minnesota Press, 1973); C.Z. Zahn-Waxler, M.R. Radke-Yarrow & R.A. King, 'Child Rearing and Children's Prosocial Initiations Towards Victims in Distress' (1979) 50 Child Development. 319.

61 Ibid.

62 The theory posits the same form of relationship as in Diagram 3 for reactance to rewards as to punishments. However, the data suggest that reactance to punishment is stronger than to rewards. See S.S. Brehm & J.W. Brehm, *Psychological Reactance: A Theory of Freedom and Control* (New York: Academic Press, 1981) at 229–46.

Diagram 3
The interactive effects of force and importance of freedom[63]

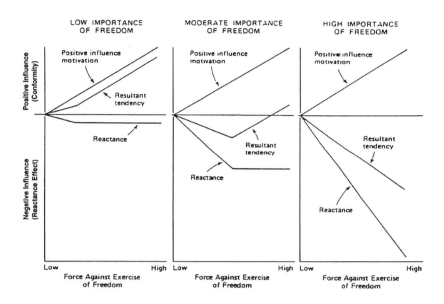

the power of tyrants will work well when it is a power the tyrant cares little about. But try to check the power of a tyrant to enslave his people (when he sees that enslavement as central to his power), try to force a patriarch to desist from family violence when domination of family is a prerogative of utmost importance, then one confronts maximum defiance.

At the same time, we will find an encouraging republican implication of the pattern of results in Diagram 3. If deterrence works well (without reactance) for freedoms that actors do not care deeply about, what we can do about organizational abuse of power is target the actors within the organization who care least about the freedom being deterred. In the next section we will find that such deterrable soft targets with the capacity to prevent abuse of power can usually be uncovered by processes of dialogic regulation.

Empirical research about how big sticks rebound has been much more manageable (and amenable to random assignment) in relatively micro-

63 S.S. Brehm & J.W. Brehm, *Psychological Reactance: A Theory of Freedom and Control*, ibid. at 60.

contexts, such as families and nursing homes. Yet there are now the beginnings of an historical scholarship applying the theoretical framework to how stigmatization and punitiveness that is perceived as unjust can threaten violence between nations, indeed how it can risk global tyranny.[64] The way Hitler exploited the humiliation of the German people at Versailles is the most thoroughly researched instance of this kind of macro-reactance.[65]

E. RATIONAL COUNTER-DETERRENCE

At all the levels we have discussed – individuals, families, small organizations like nursing homes, transnational corporations and states which are major powers – the conclusion is that simple rational choice models of compliance do not work especially well because empirical results sum contexts where rational threats are productive, non-productive, and counter-productive. In addition to reactance effects that have emotional and cognitive dimensions not captured by rational choice models (rage, defiance, perceived procedural injustice, stigmatization, devaluation of the intrinsic virtue of compliance) the stronger deterrents are, the more rational actors will find countermeasures that effectively undermine the deterrents. Hence, in Diagram 3, we need to discount the rational deterrence effect not only by the reactance effect, but also by measures which rationally subvert the deterrent effect. These grow with the size of the deterrent because the more severe the deterrents, the more reason regulated actors have to invest in counter-deterrence. And of course, the more powerful the regulated actors are, the more capacity they have to mobilize counter-deterrence. An unemployed person convicted of a crime is relatively powerless to do anything to duck the stigma, while a transnational corporation convicted of crime can hire a public relations firm to convince people through full-page counter-publicity that what it did was, all things considered, in the public interest, and that the prosecution was vindictive.[66]

More fundamentally, TNCs (transnational corporations) have a well-documented capacity to organize their affairs so that no one can be

64 T.J. Scheff, *Bloody Revenge: Emotions, Nationalism and War* (Boulder, CO: Westview Press, 1994); T.J. Scheff & S. Retzinger, Shame, Violence and Social Structure (Lexington: Lexington Books, 1991). J. Braithwaite, 'Thinking About the Structural Context of International Dispute Resolution,' *Whose New World Order: What Role for the United Nations?*, eds. M.R. Bustelo & P. Alston (Sydney: Federation Press, 1991).
65 A. Offer, 'Going to War in 1914: A Matter of Honour?' Paper to Australian War Memorial Conference (1994). See also ibid.
66 For the most systematic empirical investigation of corporate counter-publicity, see B. Fisse & J. Braithwaite, *The Impact of Publicity on Corporate Offenders* (Albany, NY: State University of New York Press, 1983) [hereinafter *Impact*].

called to account.[67] The larger and more powerful the organization, the more inherently complex and hard to prove are their abuses of power. But more than that, complexity is something powerful actors are able to contrive into their affairs. This includes organizational complexity as to who is responsible for what, jurisdictional complexity as to the nation in which each element of the offence occurs, complexity of the accounts and complexity that repeat corporate players have been able to contrive into the law on previous occasions when they have 'played for rules' rather than played for outcomes. The more punitive a regulatory regime is, the more worthwhile it is for TNCs to have 'vice-presidents responsible for going to jail.'[68] Lines of responsibility and reporting are drawn in the organization so that if someone has to be a scapegoat for the crimes of the CEO, it will be the vice-president responsible for going to jail. The latter was promoted to vice-president on the basis of assuming this risk. After a period of faithful service in the role, they would be moved sideways to a safe vice-presidency. Again, the empirical nature of rational contriving of sophisticated counter-deterrents is ominous for republicans. The more powerful the corporate or state actor, the greater the capability for putting countermeasures in place; the more credible is the checking of power, the more reason tyrants have for counter-deterrence.

F. THE DETERRENCE TRAP

This connects to one final problem. Precisely when the stakes are highest with an abuse of power, the regulator is likely to fall into a 'deterrence trap.'[69] Because of the inherent and contrived complexity associated with the biggest abuses of organizational power, probabilities of both detection and conviction fall. Imagine, for example, that the risks of conviction for insider trading are only one in a hundred for a corporate stock market player who can afford quality legal advice. (In fact, in Australia they had been zero until recently when the first private actor was convicted of this crime.) Imagine that the average returns to insider trading

---

67 This is one of the rationales for corporate/enterprise liability. If there is only individual liability, the corporation can simply set up the kinds of liability avoidance mechanisms discussed here. See Fisse & Braithwaite, *Corporations, Crime and Accountability* (Cambridge: Cambridge University Press, 1993) [hereinafter *Corporations*].

68 These were executives I discovered and interviewed in my research on corporate crime in the pharmaceutical industry. J. Braithwaite, *Corporate Crime in the Pharmaceutical Industry* (London: Routledge & Kegan Paul, 1984) [hereinafter *Pharmaceutical*].

69 This concept was coined by Coffee. J.C. Coffee, Jr., 'No Soul to Damn, No Body to Kick: An Unscandalized Essay on the Problem of Corporate Punishment' (1981) 79 Mich. L. Rev. 413.

are a million dollars. Under a crude expected utility model, it will then be rational for the average insider trader to continue unless the penalty exceeds 100 million dollars. That would be a large enough penalty to bankrupt many medium-sized companies, leaving innocent workers unemployed, creditors unpaid, communities deprived of their financial base. This is what is required to deter the average insider trader under these crude assumptions. But the criminal law cannot be designed to deal simply with the average case. It should be designed so it can deter the worst cases, which, with sophisticated corporate crime, involve not millions, but billions. Here the deterrence trap seems inescapably deep. These problems are further compounded with public sector abuse of power. The public trading enterprise may have some capital or assets that can be seized, but with a purely administrative agency, the compensatory or deterrent resources that can be accessed are limited to the savings of culpable public servants. Beyond that point, innocent citizens are taxed for compensation payouts to other innocent citizens (the victims) and for organizational deterrent payouts, which are a practical irrelevance to the individual beneficiaries of the crimes.

In Parts IV and V, I will advance two counter-intuitive strategies for beating the emotional and cognitive reactance, the rational countermeasures and the deterrence traps that make legal checks on abuse of power difficult at best, counter-productive at worst:

1. Replace narrow, formal and strongly punitive responsibility (the 'find the crook' strategy) with broad, informal, weak sanctions;
2. Separate enforcement targeting from identification of the actor who benefits from the abuse of power.

Part VII will show that at the macro level of the polity, these strategies depend on plural separations of powers both within and between the public and private sectors.

IV *The Strength of Weak Sanctions*

A. OVERDETERMINATION AND SOFT TARGETS

These two strategies for beating reactance rely on an obvious fact about the abuse of power: the more serious the abuse, the more likely it is that many people will be involved. The most egregious abuses of power arise when whole armies, police forces, bureaucracies, or transnational corporations can be mobilized to prosecute the exploitative conduct at issue. Brent Fisse and I have concluded from our various empirical studies that a feature of corporate crime is that it is over-determined, as the philosophers say, by the acts and omissions of many individuals, organizations, and sub-units of organizations.[70] While only a small number of people may be involved in committing a corporate crime, our empirical work shows that a much larger number usually have the power to prevent it. These people vary in the degree they care about the freedom being regulated and, therefore, in their susceptibility to reactance. The data here relate only to corporate crime, but it is plausible that the same feature is true of non-criminal abuses of power.

It may be that rational dollar-maximizing actors need a fine of 100 million dollars if they are to be deterred from insider trading from which they benefit. But they, the beneficiary(ies) of the crime, are not the only potential deterrence targets. They may have a boss; their boss may have a boss who is in a position to stop the misconduct. They may have a variety of subordinates who can prevent the wrongdoing by exposing the crime. A secretary, for example, who is privy to information, could do the 'whistle blowing' that lands their employer in jail for major frauds.[71] Then there are auditors, law firms, consultants, investment bankers, suppliers, other organizations upstream and downstream who know what is going on in the criminal organization.[72] Hence, Fisse and Braithwaite concluded

In a complex corporate offence there can be three types of actors who bear some level of responsibility for the wrongdoing or capacity to prevent the wrongdoing:

1. hard targets who cannot be deterred by maximum penalties provided in the law;
2. vulnerable targets who can be deterred by maximum penalties; and
3. soft targets who can be deterred by shame, by the mere exposure of the fact that they have failed to meet some responsibility they bear, even if that is not a matter of criminal responsibility.[73]

70 B. Fisse & J. Braithwaite, *Corporations*, supra note 67.
71 Among the empirical studies of fraud that have documented the secretary blowing the whistle on the boss is J. Braithwaite, *Pharmaceutical*, supra note 68.
72 Often, they get to know as a result of explicit auditing practices that put them in a better position to regulate malpractice than any government regulator. For example, in analysing the implications of the chemical industry's Responsible Care program, Neil Gunningham explains that 'Dow insists on conducting an audit before it agrees to supply a new customer with hazardous material, and routinely audits its distributors. The audit involves a team visiting the distributor's operations to examine handling, transportation, storage and terminating techniques and prescribing improvements aimed at achieving environmental standards far in advance of current regulatory requirements. Many large chemical manufacturers go further....' N. Gunningham, 'From Adversarialism to Partnership? ISO 14000 and Regulation.' Paper to Australian Centre for Environmental Law, Australian National University Conference on ISO 14000 (Canberra, 1996).
73 B. Fisse & J. Braithwaite, *Corporations*, supra note 67 at 220.

B. THE SOFT TARGET AT SOLOMONS

Let me now illustrate the practical way regulators can escape the deterrence trap with a case from my own experience as a Commissioner with Australia's national antitrust and consumer protection agency, the Trade Practices Commission.[74] Solomons Carpets ran advertisements claiming that certain carpets were on sale for up to 40 dollars per metre off the normal price. This representation was false. The Commission had difficulty deciding what action to take on this alleged breach of its act. It was a less serious matter than others that were putting demands on its scarce litigation resources.

The Commission decided to offer Solomons an administrative settlement which included voluntary compensation for consumers in an amount exceeding the criminal fine that was likely should they be convicted. The facts of the matter made it fairly unlikely that any court would order compensation for consumers, but likely that a modest fine would be imposed. All the Commissioners felt that Solomons would reject the administrative settlement because it would be cheaper for them to face the consequences of litigation. Moreover, Solomons management seemed tough nuts, treating the Commission as if it were bluffing on the threat of criminal enforcement. The Commissioners (including me) turned out to be wrong in assuming that such decisions are necessarily made by companies according to a deterrence cost-benefit calculus. Unknown to the Commission at the time, there was also a soft target within the company, namely the Chairman of the Board, the retired patriarch of this family company. For him, as a responsible businessman, it made sense to accept the Commission's argument that resources should be spent on correcting the problem for the benefit of consumers rather than on litigation and fines.

The Chairman of the Board was dismayed at the prospects of allegations of criminality against his company and was concerned for its reputation. He was also angry with his chief executive for allowing the situation to arise and for indulging in such a marketing practice. The CEO, like his underlings, had proved a hard target, determined to tough it out. The chairman sought the resignation of his chief executive and instructed the remaining senior management to cooperate with an administrative settlement that included the following seven requirements:

1. compensation to consumers (legal advisers on both sides were of the opinion that the amount was considerably in excess of what was likely to be ordered by a court);

74 This case and the insurance cases are based on the account in ibid. at c. 7.

2. a voluntary investigation report to be conducted by a mutually agreed law firm to identify the persons and defective procedures that were responsible for the misleading advertising;
3. discipline of these employees and remediation of those defective procedures;
4. a voluntary Trade Practices education and compliance program within the firm and among its franchises directed at remedying the problems identified in the self-investigation report on an ongoing basis and at improving Trade Practices compliance more generally;
5. an industry-wide national Trade Practices education campaign funded by Solomons to get its competitors to also improve their compliance with regard to advertising of carpets;
6. auditing and annual certification of completion of the agreed compliance programs by an agreed outside law firm at Solomons' expense;
7. a press release from the Commission advising the community of all of the above and of the conduct by Solomons that initially triggered the investigation (The press release attracted significant coverage in most major Australian newspapers.).

In addition, although it was not part of the deed of agreement, Solomons volunteered to conduct an evaluation study of the improvement (or absence thereof) in compliance with the Act by its competitors as a result of the industry-wide education campaign that it funded.

C. THE ACCOUNTABILITY MODEL

Solomons was a watershed case for the Commission. The next major cases dealt with in this way were the largest consumer protection cases ever handled in Australia, one involving a settlement of at least 50 million and possibly 100 million dollars. The most egregious involved misrepresentations in selling insurance on remote Aboriginal communities. Top and middle management of the insurance companies met with Aboriginal victims and Aboriginal Community Councils to discuss the harm they had done and how it might be repaired. Some, but not all, of these insurance executives were soft targets who came away from these encounters deeply ashamed of what their company had done. They agreed to extraordinary penance, in some cases well beyond what the law would have required. In one case, the company's self-investigation report led to a rather punitive outcome – eighty employees, some of them senior managers, were dismissed.

Many subsequent cases were handled through a process of working up the organization until a soft management target was found who would trigger a dialogic process of responsive reform among those below the soft target. Brent Fisse and I developed this strategy into an Accountability Model that seeks to mobilize corporate private justice systems to hold responsible all who are responsible (generally at sub-criminal levels of responsibility).[75] While holding the axe of criminal enforcement over an organization's head, the company is required, generally with an independent law firm, to produce a self-investigation report identifying all the persons and procedures responsible for the wrongdoing, and proposing remedies. Again, the idea is that some of the persons identified as having a responsibility under this process will be soft targets who will initiate responsive processes of reform, recompense, and prevention for the future.

D. GENERALIZED RESTORATIVE JUSTICE AND SOFT TARGETS

These Australian corporate crime cases are at the leading edge of what is now a global social movement for restorative justice as an alternative to punitive justice.[76] The Accountability Model might have less force in relation to simpler corporate wrongdoings, which are less over-determined by the causative and preventive capabilities of many hands and minds. However, the same restorative justice ideas are being found to have relevance to crimes that involve even the lowest-level abuses of power by individuals, such as the abuse of the power to drive a motor vehicle (by doing so when drunk). My colleagues Lawrence Sherman and Heather Strang are conducting an experiment in which drunk driving offenders are randomly assigned to court versus a restorative justice conference. In the conference, representatives of the neighbourhood,

---

75 Ibid.
76 Restorative justice has even made inroads in some of the most punitive societies in the world, including South Africa (where thousands of juvenile offenders were being sentenced to flogging annually until Mr. Mandela took over), Singapore (where a preliminary evaluation has concluded that a restorative conferencing program based on the theory of reintegrative shaming has reduced reoffending (W.Y. Chan, 'Family Conferencing in the Juvenile Justice Process: Survey on the Impact of Family Conferencing on Juvenile Offenders and their Families,' *Subordinate Courts Statistics and Planning Unit Research Bulletin 3* [1996]; L.L. Hsien, 'Family Conferencing Good for Young Delinquents: Report,' *IMAGE Database* [1996]), and the United States where the Assistant Attorney General has lauded the fact that 'innovative efforts are under way to 'reinvent' the justice system itself. 'Restorative' – or community – justice experimentation is taking place in jurisdictions across the country.... Community justice is also being incorporated into community policing programs...like the program in Australia that replaces formal prosecution with a 'family group conference' designed to shame the offender and explain the full impact of the crime on the victim and the community' (L. Robertson, 'Linking Community-Based Initiatives and Community Justice: The Office of Justice Programs' [August 1996] National Institute of Justice Journal. 6).

ON SPEAKING SOFTLY AND CARRYING STICKS 331

where the offence occurred, have the opportunity to express their concerns about letting their children cross the streets when drivers are on the road in this condition. A video message to the offender from a woman who has lost members of her family at the hands of a drink driver is played and discussed. Loved ones, drinking mates, and friends from work express their support for the offender and her commitment to responsible citizenship. They also become key players in suggesting ideas for a restorative plan of action. This may include an apology, compensation for any victims, and community service. But it may also include preventive agreements that draw on the capacity of many hands to prevent. Drinking mates may sign a designated driver agreement. Bar staff at the drinker's pub may undertake to call a taxi when the offender has had too much to drink. Uncle Harry may undertake to ensure that the car is always left in the garage on Friday and Saturday nights. Even with an offence as seemingly solitary as drunk driving, often there are many with preventive capabilities who can be rendered responsible for mobilizing those capabilities through a restorative justice dialogue. While reactance may be strong with the young, male drunk driver – who is a 'petrol head,' proud of his capacity to hold his drink – there may be no reactance from any of the other targets at a restorative justice conference. Indeed, when there is a collective reaction of non-reactance, we observe this to calm the anger of a young offender.

Common garden varieties of juvenile crime are even more collective, proffering softer targets than drink driving.[77] Hence recent work has shown that dialogic, 'whole school' approaches to confronting bullying have reduced bullying in the seminal Norwegian study, by 50 per cent.[78] Most juvenile crime is a collective phenomenon. This points up another limitation of the punishment model. By locking up some members of a juvenile gang or a drug distribution network, we can cause the group to recruit replacements from law-abiding peer groups.[79] The more we move toward more serious abuses of power involving more complex organizational forms (from school-yard bullies to motorcycle gangs to the Mafia)

---

77 See F.E. Zimring 'Kids, Groups and Crime: Some Implications of a Well-Known Secret' (1981) 72 J. Crim. L. & Criminal. 867.

78 D.P Farrington, 'Understanding and Preventing Bullying,' *Crime and Justice: Annual Review of Research*, vol. 17, ed. M. Tonry (Chicago: University of Chicago Press, 1993); D. Olweus, 'Annotation: Bullying at School: Basic Facts and Effects of a School Based Intervention Program' (1994) 35 Journal of Child Psychology and Psychiatry. 1171; D. Pepler *et al.*, 'A School-Based Anti-Bullying Intervention: Preliminary Evaluation,' *Understanding and Managing Bullyin*, ed. D. Tattum (London: Heinemann, 1993).

79 A.J. Reiss, Jr., 'Understanding Changes in Crime Rates,' *Indicators of Crime and Criminal Justice: Quantitative Studies*, eds. S.E. Feinberg & A.J. Reiss (Washington, DC: US Government Printing Office, 1980).

the more force in this analysis of the limits of deterrence and the over-determined causative and preventive capability of multiple actors. Of course, some might say that the code of silence makes everyone a 'vice-president responsible for going to jail' in the Mafia. No soft targets here? Prosecutorial experience proves this not to be the case. Even in the most systematically ruthless and disciplined criminal organizations – the Colombian drug cartels, for example – there are defectors who are sick of the killing and insecurity, who would like to retire like normal 70 year olds, who are sufficiently ashamed of what they have done to not want this life for their children.[80] The fact is that such soft targets will do deals, particularly if they are allowed to pass on to their children the parts of their ill-gotten wealth that are invested in law-abiding businesses, that will enable them to lead the respectable and secure life the criminal has been denied.

Unfortunately, systematic empirical testing of whether restorative justice works better than punitive justice is more possible with juvenile bullying, young adult violence, property crime, and drunk driving, where we are randomly assigning hundreds of cases to the two kinds of justice. There are not enough detected cases of the biggest abuses of power[81] for quantitative empirical work that compares outcomes.

In one domain of corporate lawbreaking, regulation of the quality of care of nursing home residents, systematic quantitative work on a sample of 410 organizations has been possible. In that domain, as discussed earlier, Toni Makkai and I failed to find support for a simple deterrence hypothesis.[82] However, we did find support for the effectiveness in increasing compliance of a dialogic approach to regulation based on the proffering of trust,[83] praise and the nurturing of pride in corporate social responsibilities,[84] and reintegrative shaming.[85] The way Australian nursing home regulation works is that at the end of an inspection, a meeting occurs between the inspection team and the home's management team.

---

80 See, for example, W.L. Rensselaer III, 'Colombia's Cocaine Syndicates,' *War on Drugs: Studies in the Failure of US Narcotics Policy*, eds. A. McCoy & A. Block (Boulder, CO: Westview, 1992).

81 Cases like the billion dollar frauds of the Bank of Credit and Commerce International which Fisse and I have used to argue the comparative advantage of the Accountability Model. B. Fisse & J. Braithwaite, *Corporations*, supra note 67 at 222–7.

82 J. Braithwaite & T. Makkai, 'Testing,' supra note 49; T. Makkai & J. Braithwaite, 'Dialectics,' supra note 49.

83 J. Braithwaite & T. Makkai, 'Trust and Compliance' (1994) 4 Policing and Society. 1.

84 T. Makkai & J. Braithwaite, 'Praise, Pride and Corporate Compliance' (1993) 21 Int'l J. Soc. L. 73.

85 T. Makkai & J. Braithwaite, 'Reintegrative Shaming and Compliance with Regulatory Standards' (1994) 32 Criminology. 361.

ON SPEAKING SOFTLY AND CARRYING STICKS 333

The owner, or a representative of the Board in the case of a church or charitable home, is invited, as are representatives of the Residents' Committee. It is a meeting of the separate powers of the state, owners, managers, workers, and consumers. A dialogue proceeds for about an hour on the positive things that have been accomplished, what the problems are, and who will take responsibility for what needs to be done. In this process, most participants turn out to be soft targets, wanting to put their responsible self forward, volunteering action plans to put right what has been found wrong. The best evidence we have from our systematic research on this regulatory regime is that it succeeds moderately well in improving compliance with the law and tackling the many very troubling kinds of abuses of power that occur in nursing homes.[86]

At the same time, it is clear from our data that there are cases where dialogic regulation fails – where the hardest of targets are in charge, dominating and intimidating softer targets who work under them. Empirical experience gives good reasons for assuming that even the worst of corporate malefactors have a public-regarding self that can be appealed to.[87] However, when trust is tried and found to be misplaced, there is a need to escalate to deterrence as a regulatory strategy. When deterrence fails – because of reactance, a deterrence trap, or simply because non-compliance is caused by managerial incompetence rather than rational calculation of costs and benefits – then there is a need to move higher up an enforcement pyramid to an incapacitative strategy. Incapacitation can mean withdrawing or suspending a licence for a nursing home that has proved impregnable to both persuasion and deterrence.

Hence, there are increasingly solid empirical grounds for suspecting that we can often reduce abuse of power by replacing narrow, formal, and strongly punitive responsibility with broad, informal, weak sanctions – by making the many dialogically responsible instead of the few criminally responsible. By dialogically responsible I mean responsible for participating in a dialogue, listening, being open to accountability for failings and to suggestions for remedying those failings. The theory I have advanced is that this is more likely when there are many actors with causative or preventative capability with respect to that abuse.[88] Where we

---

86 J. Braithwaite *et al.*, *Raising the Standard: Resident Centred Nursing Home Regulation in Australia* (Canberra: Australian Government Publishing Service, 1993).

87 See I. Ayres & J. Braithwaite, *Responsive Regulation: Transcending the Deregulation Debate* (New York: Oxford University Press, 1992) at c. 2 [hereinafter *Responsive*].

88 Christine Parker in commenting on this correctly, I think, adumbrates that 'the Braithwaite argument is that there almost always are many with that capacity because we all live in a community wherein many individuals can pull strings of informal control and evoke bonds of responsibility.'

can engage all of those actors in moral reasoning and problem-solving dialogue, the more of them there are, the more likely that one or more will be a soft target. When even only one player with causative responsibility or with a powerful preventative capability turns, empirical experience shows that many other actors who had hitherto been ruthlessly exploitative suddenly find a public-regarding self that becomes surprisingly engaged with a constructive process of righting the wrong. For example, Fisse and Braithwaite's interviews at Lockheed following the foreign bribery scandals of the seventies showed that once Lockheed's auditors, Arthur Young, put their responsible corporate self forward by refusing to certify the Lockheed Annual Report, other senior managers switched to responsiveness, to public-regarding deliberation, and corporate reform.[89] As a result of this domino-effect of public-regarding deliberation, Lockheed became, in the words of Boulton, 'a born again corporation.'[90] This case also instantiates the second mechanism for beating reactance, which is about the strategic significance of gatekeepers like auditors in a separation of private powers that renders dialogic social control feasible.

V *Separating Enforcement Targeting from the Actor who Benefits from the Abuse*

A. TARGETING GATEKEEPERS

In the Lockheed example, within the company's separation of powers, Arthur Young was a gatekeeper.[91] By refusing to let Lockheed's Annual Report through the gate it guarded, Arthur Young brought Lockheed's bribery of defence ministers and heads of state to an end, not to mention the careers of the company's Chairman and President. Large corporations have many different kinds of gatekeepers, such as the general counsel, environmental auditors, underwriters, insurers, board audit or ethics committees, and occupational health and safety committees. Each has the power to open and close gates that give the organization access to things it wants.

A gatekeeper like Arthur Young surely had an interest in doing Lockheed's bidding so it could keep the company's account. Yet Arthur Young was much more deterrable than Lockheed itself, which benefited so directly from the bribery (as did Lockheed's senior managers). Arthur Young, as a non-beneficiary of the bribes, had less to lose from stopping them; as a gatekeeper which was not responsible for paying bribes, but only for failing to detect them, it also had less to lose from the truth than

---

89 B. Fisse & J. Braithwaite, *Impact*, supra note 66 at 144.
90 D. Boulton, *The Grease Machine* (New York: Harper and Row, 1978) at 276.
91 See R.H. Kraakman, 'Corporate Liability Strategies and the Costs of Legal Controls' (1984) 93 Yale L.J. 857.

ON SPEAKING SOFTLY AND CARRYING STICKS 335

did those who were handing over the cash. Yet it had much to lose in reputational capital[92] as a gatekeeper of hundreds of other corporate clients if someone else revealed the truth. In this case, they were the comparatively soft target who felt compelled to sound an alarm that led to the demise of some of the hardest targets one could find in the world at that time – such as Prime Minister Tanaka of Japan.

Most people's intuition would be that we should design enforcement systems to target the beneficiaries of wrongdoing. They are the actors who make the criminal choice on the basis of the benefits of lawbreaking exceeding its costs. So from a simple rational choice perspective we should target increased costs of lawbreaking on them, the choosing criminals, not on their guardians. There is also a moral justification for this intuition: it is the criminal who deserves to pay for the crime.[93]

92 L. Lin, 'The Effectiveness of Outside Directors as a Corporate Governance Mechnism: Theories and Evidence' (1996) 90 North U. L. Rev. 898 [hereinafter 'Effectiveness'].

93 The moral argument has been brought into sharp relief in recent years by laws in many jurisdictions around the world requiring parents and guardians to pay for the damage from the juvenile crimes of their children. My own view is that such laws do perpetrate an intolerable injustice on the parents. Yet there is a difference between this hard-edged parental liability for the crime and exposing a parent to moral censure by concerned citizens for, say, allowing their child to wander the streets at any time of night. One reason that dialogic conferences often seem to work better as a means of controlling delinquency than criminal trials is that the parental gatekeeper is a softer target than the young offender. In New Zealand and Australian family group conferences for juvenile crime I have often observed the following scenario. The victim of the crime, aided by the victim's supporters, explain the suffering the crime has caused them. The offender, a tough with a hard shell, is unmoved. His emotional shell is a shield that protects him from shame directed at him. But when the victim sends a shaft of shame across the room, that shield deflects it so that it pierces like a spear through the heart of the mother of the offender, or the father, or sister, who sit beside him. One of them begins to sob. It then becomes the shame and the sadness of his sister that gets through the offender's hardened exterior. He internalizes the pain he has caused, experiences shame, and from then on is quite unable to sustain the delusion that he has done nothing wrong. Dialogic regulation does mean sharing responsibility for those we care about and feeling it deeply. That is something natural and human, in a way that making the sobbing sister pay the compensation to the victim is not. Dialogic regulation picks up the gatekeeper vulnerability analysis in a subtle and decent way rather than in the barbaric way of legal liability for parents. According to New Zealand Maori traditions of justice, Western justice is barbaric for allowing the offender to stand alone in the dock as an individual accused of a crime. Individuals, in their view, must take responsibility for their wrongdoing supported by those who love them, with those who love them sharing vicariously in that responsibility and voluntarily offering to help as best they can to right the wrong. The offender thereby is not alone, alienated, at risk of the pathology of individualized guilt that can eat away at a person. Rather, they are meant to feel the shame of letting their loved ones down, of causing them to share in this pain. Unlike Western guilt, this shame (whakama) can be readily transcended. As the shame of letting one's family down, it is

336 UNIVERSITY OF TORONTO LAW JOURNAL

B. TARGETING INSURERS AND SUPPLIERS

The most powerful empirical demonstration of the power of targeting gatekeepers rather than beneficiaries of the wrongdoing comes from the most global of regulatory problems – pollution from ships at sea. Ronald Mitchell has demonstrated how the International Convention for the Prevention of Pollution from Ships (MARPOL) was an utter failure.[94] Signatories were required under the convention to impose penalties for intentional oil spills. The most important targets – petroleum exporting nations – were committed not to enforcing these laws. Most nations simply did not care to invest in proving offences that were difficult to detect. It was only a few petroleum importing nations such as the US who took the requirement seriously. This simply meant that ships had to be a little careful to discharge pollution outside the territorial waters of these few countries. Non-compliance with the regime was the norm.

Then in 1980 the MARPOL regime was reformed in a way that Mitchell estimates has generated 98 per cent compliance.[95] This was a remarkable accomplishment given that the costs of compliance with the new regime were very high for ship owners, that predictions grounded in the economic analysis of regulation were for minimal compliance.[96] The key change was a move away from imposition of penalties on ships responsible for spills to an equipment sub-regime that enforced the installation of segregated ballast tanks and crude oil washing. One reason for the improvement was transparency; it is easy to check whether a tanker has segregated ballast tanks but hard to catch it actually discharging at sea. But the other critical factor was the role of third party enforcers (a) on whom ship operators are dependent, and (b) who have no economic interest in avoiding the considerable costs of the regulation. These third party enforcers are builders, classification societies and insurance

acquitted by forgiveness and restoration within that family. Forcing a family to accept liability directly to a victim obviously cuts totally across this philosophy. (For a more detailed exposition of the gatekeeper dynamic in restorative justice conferences, see J. Braithwaite & S. Mugford, 'Conditions of Successful Reintegration Ceremonies: Dealing With Juvenile Offenders' (1994) 34 Brit. J. Criminal. 139).

94 R. Mitchell, 'Intentional Oil Pollution of the Oceans,' *Institutions for the Earth: Sources of Effective International Environmental Protection*, eds. P.M. Haas, R.O. Keohane & M.A. Levy(Cambridge, MA: MIT Press, 1993); R. Mitchell, 'Regime Design Matters: International Oil Pollution and Treaty Compliance' (1994) 48 International Organization. 425; R. Mitchell, 'Compliance Theory: A Synthesis' 2 Receil. 327; R. Mitchell, *Intentional Oil Pollution at Sea: Environmental Policy and Treaty Compliance* (Cambridge, MA: MIT Press, 1994).

95 R. Mitchell, Intentional Oil Pollution at Sea: Environmental Policy and Treaty Compliance, ibid. at 270–1.

96 C. Okidi, Regional Control of Ocean Pollution: Legal and Institutional Problems and Prospects (Alphen aan den Rijn, Netherlands: Sijthoff & Noordhoff, 1978) at 34.

companies. Builders have no interest in building cheaper ships which will not get certification by international classification societies nominated by national governments. Classification societies have no interest in corrupting the standards they enforce, which are the whole reason for the generation of their income. Finally, insurers will not insure ships that have not been passed by a classification society acceptable to them because they have an interest in reducing the liabilities that might arise from oil spills.

The new MARPOL regime therefore achieves 98 per cent compliance in large part because the effective target of enforcement shifted from the ship operators who benefit from the pollution to builders, classification societies, and insurance companies who do not benefit from it. However, because the ship operators (and builders) are totally dependent on classification societies and insurers, they have no choice but to accept that the regime-compliant ships, which the classification societies have an interest in ensuring, are the only ones that get through the gate.

C. THE PLETHORA OF THIRD PARTY TARGETS

The best-known examples of separating enforcement targeting from the actor who benefits from the abuse is requiring employers to withhold tax from the taxable income of their employees, which they report; or banks to withhold and report tax on the interest earned by their customers. Little enforcement is needed against the employers and banks who withhold and report because they do not benefit from any under-reporting of income. Tax cheating is only a really major problem in those domains where it is impossible to harness such disinterested gatekeepers.

Peter Grabosky has initiated a program of work which continually discovers new species of third party enforcers of regulatory regimes – from volunteer divers who check compliance with South Australia's historic shipwrecks legislation to elected worker health and safety representatives.[97] Grabosky's work shows just how disparate are the possibilities for shifting enforcement targeting – from actors who benefit

97 P.N. Grabosky, 'Professional Advisors and White Collar Illegality. Towards Explaining and Excusing Professional Failure' (1990) 13 U. New So. Wales L.J. 1; P.N. Grabosky, 'Citizen Co-Production and Corruption Control' (1990) 5 Corruption and Reform. 125; P.N. Grabosky, 'Law Enforcement and the Citizen: Non-governmental Participants in Crime Prevention and Control' (1992) 2 Policing and Society. 249; P.N. Grabosky, 'Green Markets: The Environmental Regulation by the Private Sector' +(1994) 16 Law and Policy. 419; P.N. Grabosky Beyond the Regulatory State (1994) 27 Australian and New Zealand Journal of Criminology. 192; P.N. Grabosky, 'Counterproductive Regulation' (1995) 23 International Journal of the Sociology of Law. 347; P.N. Grabosky, 'Using Non-Governmental Resources to Foster Regulatory Compliance' (1995) 8 Governance. 527.

from the cheating to actors who do not but on whom the cheat depends for something critical to their welfare. This simple shift is capable of making headway with some of our seemingly most intractable regulatory problems.

Another colleague, Neil Gunningham, has long despaired about the way hazardous chemicals regulation succeeds in changing the practices of the top 20 chemicals transnationals, but barely touches thousands of little chemical companies who are too many, too unsophisticated, and too dispersed to be effectively supervised by state inspectors.[98] More recently, however, Gunningham has realized that most of these little chemical companies are vitally dependent on TNCs as suppliers, distributors, customers, or all three. This has led Gunningham to the insight that a private or public regulatory regime, which requires major companies to ensure not only that its own employees comply with the regulations but also that the upstream and downstream users and suppliers of its products comply, may massively increase the effectiveness of the regime.[99] The reason is that a TNC that supplies a little chemical company has much more regular contact with them than any government inspector, more intimate and technically sophisticated knowledge of where their bodies are buried, greater technical capacity to help them fix the problems, and has more leverage over them than the state.

D. BUILDING A THOUSAND GATES TO THE POWER OF CORRUPT OFFICIALS
Privatising public gatekeeping can be one way of separating powers so that enforcement can be targeted on an actor who does not benefit from the abuse of public power. Most national customs services have a lot of corruption. Both senior managers and street-level bureaucrats benefit enormously from bribes paid for turning a blind eye to the under- or over-invoicing of goods. The fact that public customs services have an organizational interest in continuing to sell favours creates a market opportunity for a private organization set up to 'sell trust.' This is just what the Swiss company, Societé Generale de Surveillance (SGS), set out to do when it took over the customs service of Indonesia and other developing countries. It persuades nations to sell large parts of their customs work to SGS through a reputation for incorruptibility that

98 See, for example, N. Gunningham, 'Environment, Self-Regulation and the Chemical Industry: Assuming Responsible Care' (1995) 17 Law and Policy. 57.
99 I rely here on personal communications with Gunningham at ANU seminars. Also seminally relevant here are the insights in Fiona Haines work on regulation in primary and secondary capitalist markets, see F. Haynes, 'The Show Must Go On: Organizational Responses to Traumatic Employee Fatalities Within Multiple Employer Worksites' (PhD Dissertation, University of Melbourne, 1996).

enables it to deliver huge savings to governments. A 1991 Press Statement of the Indonesian Minister of Finance claimed that SGS had saved his country 4.5 billion dollars US of foreign exchange between 1985 and 1990 and earned it 1 billion dollars US in extra duties and taxes. Because it is such testimonials that bring SGS business, SGS has a financial incentive to catch cheats and weed out corruption in its own ranks. A major corruption scandal that would strike everyone as quite normal in the customs service of a developing country might cause financial ruin for SGS. SGS sets up its inspection gates in the country of export (where superior intelligence on over- or under-invoicing is available) rather than in the importing country. It accomplishes this by having over a thousand scrupulously audited offices at all the world's key exporting sites. The company constrains itself from engaging in any manufacturing or in any trading or financial interests that would threaten its independence.

'Selling trust' is profitable, so operatives are well paid. As the company's Senior Vice President, J. Friedrich Sauerlander confessed to me, in an organization of 27 000 people, his internal security organization had uncovered 'some slip-ups.' But in all major ways, it had been possible to sustain an organization with an incentive structure to reward trust. The beneficiaries of the old breaches of trust were left where they were. But through building a thousand gates to their power on the other side of the world, and guarding those gates with SGS units that flourished in proportion to how much abuse of trust they stopped, targeting enforcement on the bad guys inside the gates became mostly redundant.

From Lockheed, to polluters from ships, to employers and banks withholding tax, to chemical companies, to outside (instead of inside) Directors targeted by public interest groups over corporate abuse of power,[100] to big adolescent boys exposed at family group conferences for assaulting their mothers and sisters,[101] we can see some promise in

---

100 The leading example here is the 'Corporate Campaign' against the J.P. Stevens company over their abusive labour practices. The top management team were very hard nuts here. But the campaign was able to so embarrass outside directors that they resigned from the board, a consequence which really did concern top management. See B. Fisse & J. Braithwaite, *Impact*, supra note 66 at c. 2.

101 Here an alternative target is an extended family with capacities to monitor, restrain, and shame the violent boy. See J. Braithwaite & K. Daly, 'Masculinities, Violence and Communitarian Control,' *Just Boys Doing Business*, eds. T. Newburn & E. Stanko (London: Routledge & Kegan Paul, 1994). Also see T. Lajeunesse, *Community Holistic Circle Healing: Hollow Water First Nation, Aboriginal Peoples Collection* (Canada: Supply and Services, 1993). G. Burford & J. Pennell, 'Family Group Decision Making: An Innovation in Child and Family Welfare,' *Child Welfare in Canada: Policy Implications*, eds. B. Galaway & J. Hudson (Toronto: Thompson Educational Publishing, 1995); G. Burford & J. Pennell, *Family Group Decision Making: New Roles for 'Old' Partners in*

340 UNIVERSITY OF TORONTO LAW JOURNAL

shifting enforcement targeting from actors who benefit from their abuse to actors who do not but on whom the abuser depends for something critical to their welfare.

VI *Separating Powers Within and Between the Public and Private Sectors*

A. SUMMARY SO FAR

This paper has shown that deterrence failure is a major impediment to effective regulation and made a case for two strategies that can beat reactance, the deterrence trap, and other sources of deterrence failure:

1. replace narrow, formal and strongly punitive responsibility (the 'find the crook' strategy) with broad, informal, weak sanctions (dialogic regulation);
2. separate enforcement targeting from identification of the actor who benefits from the wrongdoing.

At the macro level of the polity, the combination of (1) and (2) means dialogic regulation combined with robust separations of powers both within and between the public and private sectors. The number of third party enforcement targets is greater to the extent that we have richer, more plural, separations of powers in a polity. For example, under a plural separation of powers, the media baron who sells editorial support and biased reporting to a politician in return for the promise of a television licence might in a more effective republic than the one in which we live have their power checked by

- courts of law;
- a statutorily independent broadcasting authority that allocates licences only to fit and proper persons and has the capacity to investigate in cases of non-compliance;[102]
- industry association self-regulatory bodies;[103]
- the Press Council;[104]
- corporate charters of editorial independence;[105]

Resolving Family Violence. Implementation Report Summary (Newfoundland: Family Group Decision Making Project, 1995).

102 Broadcasting Services Act (Cth.) (1992).

103 In Australia, the Federation of Australian Radio Broadcasters and the Federation of Australian Commercial Television Broadcasters are important.

104 P. O'Malley, 'Regulating Contradictions: The Australian Press Council and the Dispersal of Social Control' (1987) 21 Law and Society Review. 83.

105 John Fairfax Publications Proprietary Limited, Charter of Editorial Independence, adopted by the Board of Directors on 12 March, 1992.

ON SPEAKING SOFTLY AND CARRYING STICKS 341

- a vigilant journalists association that requires its members to comply with a journalists' code of ethics;[106]
- parliamentary oversight committees that investigate abuses of power by the executive, and other (separate) committees that check diligent performance of the duties of independent regulators;
- public interest groups that are granted standing to lodge complaints to all of the foregoing institutions;
- audit committees of boards of directors (all of whom are outside Directors) with a remit to adjudicate complaints against management for ethical abuses;
- corporate ombudsmen with public reporting capabilities;[107]
- ethical investment funds with an investigative capacity they can use to put activist shareholders on notice about such abuses of power in media corporations.

Separations of powers both within and between the private and public sectors are important to controlling such abuses of power, as is counter-vailing power from institutions of civil society that muddy any simple public-private divide. Moreover, the more potential targets of third party enforcement such separations of powers throw up, the better the chance that one of them will be a soft target with such leverage over the abuser of power that the simple device of a regulatory dialogue will move that third party to use their leverage to stop the abuse, trigger internal reforms to prevent recurrence, and trigger the private justice system of the organization to discipline those responsible for the abuse.

Thus, the richer and more plural the separations of powers in a polity, the less we have to rely on narrow, formal, strongly punitive regulation targeted on the beneficiaries of abuse of power. The more we can rely on a regulatory dialogue wherein an appeal is made to the sense of social responsibility of all actors with a capacity to prevent the wrongdoing, the more persuasion can replace punishment. Reasons for this are that the more hands powers are separated into (a) the more likely that one of those actors with power to prevent will be a soft target, and (b) the more third parties there will be who do not benefit from the abuse themselves

---

106 In Australia, journalists comply with the Australian Journalists Association Section of the Media, Entertainment and Arts Alliance (formerly the Australian Journalists Association) Code of Ethics (1996).

107 Among the companies that have or have had ombudsmen are the *Washington Post*, General Electric, Dow Chemical, and American Airlines. J. Braithwaite, 'Taking Responsibility Seriously: Corporate Compliance Systems,' *Corrigible Corporations and Unruly Law*, eds. B. Fisse & P.A. French (San Antonio: Trinity University Press, 1985) at 46.

but who hold power over the abuser. Put another way, the more plural the separations of powers (a) the more overdetermined is the capacity to prevent abuse; and (b) the more cases there are of disjuncture between an interest in the abuse and a capacity to prevent it.

B. PLURAL PRIVATE SEPARATIONS; PLURAL PUBLIC SEPARATIONS

This paper seeks to correct the bias of the republican tradition toward a focus on separations of *public* powers. Yet the arguments advanced are as relevant to abuse of power by the police as they are to a private media organization. The head of state who rigs electoral boundaries is a hard target because nothing is more important to her career than the election outcome. Citizens who ask a judge to overturn the head of state's electoral rigging approach a softer target because the judge does not benefit from the election result. The traditional separation of powers between executive government and judiciary can deliver the benefits revealed in our analysis of private sector disjunctions between interest and preventive power.

At the same time that our novel rationale for the separation of powers shows traditional republican thinking about the separation of powers in the public sphere to be somewhat impoverished, its impoverishment arises from the fact that it is not as plural as it might be. Three (executive, legislature, judiciary) is not a very big plurality. Moreover, antifederalist separations of powers (in some pre-revolutionary US state constitutions) aspired to avoid the concentration of power (as did its private sector analogue in anti-monopoly law) by having the executive responsible for X, the legislature for Y, the judiciary for Z. In the most uncharitable reading of this arrangement, each branch is left alone to abuse power without too much interference within its own sphere from the other branches of government; a strict separation of powers simply assures that the sphere of each is not too broad. This would be uncharitable, however, because in all of the early US state governments, while each branch had spheres of independence from the other branches, they also had spheres where their power was checked by the other branches of government.[108]

---

108 M.S. Flaherty, 'The Most Dangerous Branch' (1996) 105 Yale L.J. 1725. Yet, late in his career, no lesser a republican figure than Jefferson (much influenced by John Taylor's, *An Inquiry into the Principles and Policy of the Government of the United States*, 1814 [New Haven: Yale University Press, 1950]) became an advocate of a total separation of the powers of three branches, rejecting the dominant view of John Adams and the Federalists that there should be some overlapping so there could be mutual checking of power. For Taylor, 'Instead of balancing power, we divide it, and make it responsible' (by which he and Jefferson meant the three branches all must be responsible to the people by direct election) (ibid. at 88). See Vile, supra note 6 at

ON SPEAKING SOFTLY AND CARRYING STICKS 343

Even so, the reconceptualization of the rationale for the separation of powers in this paper implies that in debates on the separation of public powers, attention is needed not just to assurance of the independence of honest judges from corrupt parliamentarians and corrupt executive governments (and vice versa). Attention is also needed to making corrupt, self-serving, nepotistic judges who flout the rule of law; patrimonial parliamentarians; and evil executives each vulnerable to the power of the other branches. One of the problems we must confront if we are to make progress with some of our tougher problems, like police corruption, is how to deal with pleas that any encroachment on the independence of the police will take us back to a world where the police lock up whomsoever the executive government tells them is a troublemaker. How do we get universities that are fearless in undertaking research of which the state disapproves, yet that do not use this independence to deflect responsiveness to a community which sees it as dominated by venal godfathers of disciplines of less value than other neglected spheres of scholarship?

The answer proposed is to have a police force and a university that are sufficiently autonomous from state power, business power, church power, media power, and the power of professions like law not to be dominated by them. Part of their resilience to any single source of domination will come from their very dependence on all those sources of power. We need a police that is vulnerable to publicly reported surveys of citizen satisfaction with the respect police show for rights,[109] to meetings of the Police-Aboriginal Liaison Committee, to meetings of the Police-Gay Liaison Committee, to meetings with local businesses concerned about break-ins at their factories, to meetings of local Neighbourhood Watch groups, to criticisms made at family group conferences that the police officer involved was unnecessarily rough, to the Ombudsman, to Parliamentary Committees, to Royal Commissions to investigate matters of extraordinary malfeasance, to a free and fearless press, to the Council for Civil Liberties, to the judiciary, and yes, vulnerable to an executive government that will sack the Commissioner if there is reasonable

163–70. The late eighteenth-century French constitutions also rejected the idea of checks and balances in favour of a strict separation of powers, at least until the lessons of Robespierre and Napoleon Bonaparte had been learnt. These were lessons about the fragility, adversarialism, and vulnerability to tyrannical coup d'état of purist democratarian separations of powers, see Vile, supra note 6 at 198–9. Madison had foreseen that the best way to preserve the separation of powers was 'by so contriving the interior structure of government as that its several constituent parts may, by their mutual relations, be the means of keeping each other in their proper places' (A. Hamilton, J. Madison & J. Jay, supra note 9 at 318–9, see also at 302–18.)

109 J. Braithwaite, 'Good and Bad Police Services and How to Pick Them,' Policing Australia, eds. P. Moir & H. Eijkman (Melbourne: Macmillan, 1992).

suspicion that she is corrupt. After 200 years of ugly tyranny in nations with beautiful constitutions, it is no longer persuasive to suggest that a separation of state powers will ensure that the government 'will be controlled by itself.'[110]

In other words, a police service that is enmeshed in many webs of dependency will be vulnerable to the many when it corruptly does the bidding of the one. This, I suspect, is the way of resolving the dilemma of independence for different branches of government versus checking of power between branches of government. Checking of power between branches of government is not enough. The republican should want a world where different branches of business, public, and civil society power are all checking each other. While the broad principles are clear here, the nuts and bolts of checks and balances, of independence and interdependence, require contextual deliberation for any given source of power. Clearly, there must be some sorts of power against which a police service must be protected by law ('Arrest this man or we will cut your budget.'). Republican theory of the sort Philip Pettit and I endorse[111] requires detailed empirical investigation of the different ways of organizing independence and interdependence so as to discover a set of institutional arrangements most likely to maximize freedom as non-domination. At least the principle of separating powers so that there are enough actors with the independence and preventative capacity so that one of them can be moved by dialogue to stop the abuse is clear enough.

In the public arena, the literature on separation of powers bequeaths to us a variety of reasonably well-understood heads of public power that might be separated – different houses of parliament, levels of government in a federation, lower versus appellate courts, administrative appeals tribunals, and so on. While it is a tricky business to put together or tinker with a robust public architecture of powers, at least we have some sense of the elements we might play with. In contrast, the separation of private powers is comparatively under-researched. Here most readers will need some elementary sense of what might be involved in separating private powers. The next section is a preliminary foray into what might be at issue.

VII *How to Separate Powers in the Private Sector*

A. POWERS OF SHAREHOLDERS, DIRECTORS, MANAGERS

The law review literature on corporate governance has a deal of useful guidance on accomplishing separations of powers in the private sector,

---

110 A. Hamilton, J. Madison & J. Jay, supra note 9 at 323 (James Madison).
111 P. Pettit, supra note 10; J. Braithwaite & P. Pettit, supra note 10.

but not useful enough. The concentration tends to be on the separate powers of shareholders, directors, and managers.[112] Important separation of powers issues are at stake here; such as whether a majority of members of the board of directors of a public company should be 'unrelated directors,'[113] meaning that they have no business dealings with, nor a management position in, the company; whether the nominating committee for the appointment of new directors should have no management directors on it;[114] whether it should be forbidden for the CEO to be Chairman of the Board;[115] whether there should be a bicameral board with a supervisory board as in Germany, France, the Netherlands, and Indonesia;[116] and generally how to give outside directors a role more than that of the CEO's 'pet rocks.'[117] There is certainly merit from a republican point of view in engendering shareholder democracy, encouraging activist shareholders to call management to account,[118] securing representation for minority shareholders on the board, and effective monitoring of the board by institutional shareholders.[119] When the New York Stock Exchange first required a Board Audit Committee of non-Executive Directors as a condition of listing on the exchange in 1977,[120] this was an important step for the separation of private powers. It has spread to many parts of the world. Long before that, in 1862, a more important step was requiring companies as a matter of law to be audited by a pro-

112 M.A. Eisenberg, 'Legal Models of Management Structure in the Modern Corporation: Officers, Directors, and Accountants' (1975) 63 Cal. L.R. 363; K.A. Kirwan, 'The Use and Abuse of Power – The Supreme Court and Separation of Powers' (1995) 537 Annals of the American Academy of Political and Social Science. 76; B.H. Siegan, 'Separation of Powers and Economic Liberties' (1995) 70 Notre Dame L. Rev. 415; M. Hardt, 'The Non-Equivalence of Accounting Separation and Structure Separation as Regulatory Devices' (1995) 19 Telecommunications Policy. 69.

113 Toronto Stock Exchange Committee on Public Governance in Canada, *'Where Were the Directors?' Guidelines for Improving Corporate Governance in Canada* (Toronto: Toronto Stock Exchange Committee on Public Governance in Canada, 1994) at 4.

114 Ibid. at 4–5.

115 Ibid. at 41.; S. Bottomley, 'From Contractualism to Constitutionalism: A Framework for Corporate Governance' (draft paper) [hereinafter 'Contractualism.']

116 S. Turnbull, 'Governance Flaws and Remedies,' Corporate Directors' diploma Course, University of New England, Topic 7.2 (Armisdale, NSW: University of New England, 1993).

117 GM outside directors are reported as having had a 'pet rock' self-image in L. Lin, 'Effectiveness,' supra note 92 at 898, notes 246, 940.

118 A. Fraser, 'Reinventing Aristocracy: Corporate Governance in the Civil Constitution of a Modern Republican Society' (unpublished manuscript).

119 G.P. Stapledon, *Institutional Shareholders and Corporate Governance* (Oxford: Clarendon Press, 1996); S. Bottomley, 'Contractualism,' supra note 115.

120 L. Loss, *Fundamentals of Securities Regulation* (Boston & Toronto: Little Brown & Company, 1983) at 484.

fessionally certified auditor.[121] This is the well-understood end of the separation of private powers. Useful literatures already exist on how to make these separations work better: how to improve shareholder accountability, restructure Directors' duties, bring board audit committees to life, and improve the performance and independence of auditors. The emphasis on separation of powers between management and the two other branches of corporate governance neglects the main game, however, which is separation within management. With private power, moreso even than with public power, the power in the hands of the other branches of governance is extremely modest compared with the concentration of power in the executive.

B. AUDIT AND AUDIT OF AUDIT

The most important steps toward separating powers within management have involved internalising the outside audit by setting up internal reporting of audit-based accountability. This has not been restricted to financial auditing. In private companies today, environmental audit, safety audit, audits of compliance with the US Foreign Corrupt Practices Act (introduced after the Lockheed scandal), antitrust audit, and the like, are common.[122] During the past decade, there has been a US-based movement to partially integrate these functions under the rubric of legal audit.[123]

Companies like Exxon have long had a functional equivalent of such an internal audit of the auditors. Instead of doing it under the auspices of a legal audit by the general counsel, from 1973 Exxon used the office of the Controller, a vice president at corporate headquarters in New York. Brent Fisse and I investigated the internal auditing of Exxon fifteen years ago following the payment of 46 million dollars US in bribes in Italy, more minor payoffs in Thailand, the Dominican Republic, Indonesia and Japan and the improper recording of political donations in Australia as legal fees.[124] By 1981 there were no fewer than 400 internal auditors working for Exxon. These were by no means all financial auditors; they included engineers, for example, who would work on teams with the

---

121 The English Registered Companies Act of 1862. See G.R. Brown, 'Changing Audit Objectives and Techniques' (October 1962) The Accounting Review. 696 at 697; D.J. Fraser & M.E. Aiken, *Stettler's System Based Audits* (Sydney: Prentice Hall, 1981) at 12–3; R. Tomasic & S. Bottomley, *Corporations Law in Australia* (Sydney: Federation Press, 1995) at 15–17.

122 For example, T. Lamond & I. Watt, *Environmental Management and Audit Manual* (Sydney: CCH Australia, 1996).

123 L.M. Brown & A.O. Kandel, *The Legal Audit: Corporate Internal Investigation* (New York: Clark, Boardman, Callaghan, 1990). The journals Preventive Law Reporter and Corporate Conduct Quarterly are devoted to this topic.

124 B. Fisse & J. Braithwaite, *Impact*, supra note 66 at c. 15.

ON SPEAKING SOFTLY AND CARRYING STICKS 347

accountants to ensure that the company's environmental policies were being implemented in all subsidiaries.

Auditors in each Exxon subsidiary reported directly to their chief executive, but they also had a dotted line reporting relationship up to the Controller in New York. It was the latter who decided the size of each auditor's workforce. Auditors were therefore not tied to the purse strings of those whom they were auditing. Auditors could also bypass the Controller in circumstances where people in the Controller's office might be part of a cover-up. Indeed, the most lowly local auditor who detected, say, an improper bookkeeping practice, was required to ensure that this was reported through the general auditor to the audit committee of the Board in New York. A former Exxon general auditor, Ted Kline, explained:

> Say, for example – I was an auditor and uncovered something that was unsavory or should have been reported and told my supervisor and he said to let it go. Well, auditors are briefed that their obligations do not end there. The employee who makes the report knows that his supervisor should report it up the line and that if his supervisor does not, the auditor must. He cannot seek sanctuary, so to speak, just by saying, 'It was not my job. I told my boss and that was it....' Much to the consternation, I guess, of some employees perhaps who would say, 'Surely the Company does not want me to put this in writing'; and the answer is 'yes.' We want it to be put in writing, exactly what happened, and we will send it right up to New York to the board audit committee. There is no other way we know that we can get the message across that we are very serious about this.[125]

Auditors have a responsibility to report on matters that are not within their area of direct responsibility. For example, auditors in most companies who discovered a letter suggestive of a price fixing conspiracy would regard this as none of their business. An effectively working separation of corporate powers tackles such a perception, as the same former Exxon general auditor explains:

> When an auditor reaches a situation where he needs to question whether we have violated antitrust laws, then he needs to go to the Law Department in order to ascertain that. Most of our auditors are not lawyers and they are not qualified to find out whether we have committed a violation. When he does contact the Law Department he makes a record of the fact that this was turned over to the Law Department and he sends word up through audit channels to New York that he has turned over a situation to the Law Department. The Law Department then sends up through the Law Department channels the fact that they are handling the situation, so the New York Law Department knows that it is

---

125 W. Clifford & J. Braithwaite, *Cost Effective Business Regulation* (Canberra: Australian Institute of Criminology, 1981) at 30.

not being covered up down in the individual territory someplace. Anything having to do with antitrust is both a complicated and very delicate matter so we make sure it is carried up through the Law Department. We do not let an auditor walk out on a limb and carry something all the way to the board audit committee and then the lawyers shrug their shoulders and say that it is not an antitrust violation at all. That is the way we handle things when we are not sure it is a law violation.[126]

At the heart of Exxon's auditing system was a marrying of independence and interdependence designed to deliver an effective intra-corporate separation of powers. The former general auditor explained the key concepts as follows

First – the well known segregation of duties and responsibilities such that no single function, department or employee will have exclusive knowledge, authority or control over any significant transaction or group of transactions;

Second – the proper documentation of transactions and business events;

Third – the systematic and thoughtful supervision in documented reviews of managers and other employees' work;

Fourth – the timely preparation of records, reports and reviews;

Fifth – control measures designed in such a way that they are responsive to the nature and degree of risk and exposure....;

Sixth – the various aspects of control should not be so interdependent that a serious deficiency in any one would make other controls also ineffective.[127]

The separation of powers became explicit when the full Board of directors annually received the report of the board audit committee on compliance with Exxon's rather encompassing Business Ethics Policy. At the same meeting, independent reports on the same subject were received from the company's external auditors, the auditor general, the controller, the general counsel, and the CEO.

The globalization of business has enabled new separations of powers, new answers to the question of 'Who audits the auditors?' At Exxon, IBM, and in many leading US and European pharmaceutical companies, the auditors from one country regularly audit the auditors from another; regional office auditors audit the auditors of national subsidiaries, and a national auditor or the Asian regional auditors may audit the head office auditing group in New York. Arranging guardianship in a circle is an advance on the hierarchical organization of guardianship that historically allowed companies like Lockheed and Exxon to rot, like fish, from the head down. In the hierarchical organization on the left side of Diagram 4, the only guarantee against corruption by an nth order guardian is an

126 Ibid. at 34.
127 Ibid. at 24–5.

Diagram 4
Formal models of hierarchical and republican conceptions of trust

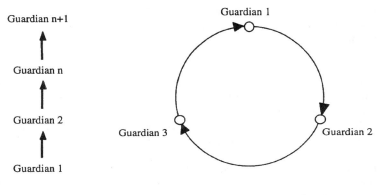

| Heirarchical fiduciary conception of guardianship | Republican conception of guardianship |

n+1th order guardian; if the guardian at the top of the hierarchy is corrupt, then all assurance against abuse of power by the system collapses. Yet guardianship which is organized in a circle is still a reasonably closed system, even when the circle includes external auditors and an Ethics Committee of outside directors.

C. ENTERING THE CIRCLE WITH OUTSIDE POWER

Progress to bring into the circle utterly outside watchdogs, who do not depend on the corporation for an income, is slow in the world of corporate governance and restricted to rather special domains of accountability. In Australia, consumer movement nominees on the Banking Ombudsman Council have access to the consumer complaint records of private banks and have a public reporting responsibility.

The most widespread accomplishments in widening the circle of guardianship to give total outsiders a window to examine the audit performance of companies have arisen under the European Union's EMAS (Eco-Management and Audit Scheme).[128] These are voluntary standards, yet with considerable force in a world where many major purchasers (particularly state purchasers) and some insurers require

---

128 Council Regulation (EEC) No. 1836/93 (29 June 1993) Allowing Voluntary Participation by Companies in the Industrial Sector in a Community Eco-Management Audit Scheme, Official Journal of the European Community L 168/1 (10.7.1993).

EMAS certification from companies in environmentally high-risk industries. EMAS requires companies to demonstrate continuous improvement in environmental impact and product stewardship to an outside environmental auditor. The report of that outside auditor is generally public and therefore can be examined by green groups on the lookout for environmental scandals.

There is a much longer history of empowerment of constituencies internal to the corporation, which have very different interests from management, and affiliations to power bases outside the organization. The leading example here is elected union health and safety representatives who report both to the management, who pays them, and the union, which legitimates them.[129] Rights of access to safety data are often negotiated as a matter of contract between the union and the employer,[130] or as a matter of public law. These rights of access are sometimes checked by union-employed safety inspectors who conduct inspections of workplaces independently of state inspectors. In the case of large unions like the US United Mine Workers these can be many dozens in number.[131] A comparison of high-accident and low-accident coal mines by Pfeifer, Stefanski, and Grether found that both safety directors and miners in mines with low accident rates reported that in the low-accident mines the union put greater pressure on management for safety through bargaining and dialogue.[132] In Australian coal mines, elected worker inspectors do an independent check of a mine before a shift starts to double-check the assessment of company safety staff that levels of methane and other fundamental concerns are under control. Their assessment of the safety of the workplace is written in a record book at the entrance to the mine, which is available to all workers and to government safety inspectors. Union inspectors have a legal right to prevent or stop work at a mine on safety grounds until such time as a government safety inspector can get out to the mine to adjudicate whether the safety stoppage is justified. This is quite an impressive separation of private powers that has existed in the British Empire for more than a century

---

129 See N. Gunningham, *Safeguarding the Worker: The Role of Law* (Sydney: Law Book Company, 1984).

130 J. Braithwaite, *To Punish or Persuade: Enforcement of Coal Mine Safety* (Albany: State University of New York Press, 1985) at 8 [hereinafter *Punish*].

131 Ibid. at 8.

132 M.C. Pfeifer, Jr., J.L. Stefanski & C.B. Grether, *Psychological, Behavioral and Organizational Factors Affecting Coal Miner Safety and Health* (Columbia, MD: Westinghouse Behavioral Services Center, 1976); see also D.R Biggins, M. Phillips & P. O'Sullivan, 'Benefits of Worker Participation in Health and safety' (1991) 4 Labour and Industry. 138.

and that can also be seen in mine safety auditing in Japan, the United States, France, Romania, and Poland.[133]

While the union is an independent external agent of certain categories of employees for certain types of problems, professions are more general external agents. A corporate circle of accountability is less closed to the extent that a general counsel who is in it feels an allegiance to the ethics of the legal profession that approaches in strength allegiance to the corporation, an accountant who feels ethical responsibility to the accountancy profession, and so on. Western nations are witnessing a proliferation of new professionalisms relevant to penetration of corporate accountability by allegiances to values from outside the company. These include emerging professionalism in environmental auditing, occupational health and safety, the Society of Consumer Affairs Professionals in Business, pharmacology (especially important in the pharmaceutical industry), and now in Australia even an Association of Compliance Professionals, and internationally a Regulatory Affairs Professionals Society.

D. REPORTING ARCHITECTURE TO SECURE TRANSPARENCY AND INDEPENDENCE
As the earlier comments about the Exxon system imply, reporting relationships are critical to an effective separation of corporate powers. Checking of power cannot work without a transparency that renders abuses in one area visible to another sphere of power. A recurrent abuse in the pharmaceutical industry occurs when the production manager of a plant, who is paid performance bonuses and promoted on the basis of getting product out of the plant, overrules a finding of her quality control manager that a batch of drugs does not m+eet specifications.[134] The chances of a batch of drugs that just fails to meet specs causing side effects that would be sheeted home to this failure are slight, while the payment of the production manager's bonus may be a certainty, but only so long as she gets the batch at issue out on time. Hence, the incentive of the manager to break the law.

A simple solution to this problem was adopted by some of the more quality-conscious TNCs in the 1970s, and has now been mandated in the laws of a number of countries. This is that a production manager is not allowed to overrule a quality-control judgment on a batch of drugs. It can only be done over the signature of the CEO. The effect is to make the perverse incentives the firm creates for the production manager to break the law transparent. Another effect is to taint the CEO and people who advise her with knowledge (the reverse of a vice president responsible for

133 J. Braithwaite, *Punish*, supra note 130 at 9–10.
134 J. Braithwaite, *Pharmaceutical*, supra note 68 at c. 3.

going to jail policy). The final effect is to strengthen the hand of quality-control management against the normally more senior production managers. CEOs in practice are extremely reluctant to overrule quality-control recommendations because the cost of redoing one batch of drugs is a comparatively minor matter to them, and is perhaps a good way of sending a message to production managers to improve their performance on quality. Yet the prospect of a batch causing a fatality, however remote, could also be fatal for the CEO, as could the CEO tolerating a culture of sloppiness about quality. This then is an example of how clever reporting architecture assures the separation of powers between quality control and production, prompts the need for dialogue on a quality culture that tolerates no errors on pharmaceutical specifications, and shifts decision making following the dialogue from a hard target with incentives to abuse power (the production manager) to soft targets, with incentives to uphold the law (the CEO and the quality-control manager).

In a more generalized way, the post-scandal reporting policies Brent Fisse and I discovered at Exxon were exemplary in the way they ensured, if implemented,[135] that the soft targets in the company, who could be moved by ethical dialogue, got to know about the temptations to which hardened crooks within Exxon were succumbing.

As the Controller explained to us, effective control means having an organization full of 'antennas.' All units of the organization had a responsibility not only to report confirmed violations of the 'Business Ethics Policy' but also 'probable violations.' 'Probable violations' were defined by corporate policy as 'situations where the facts available indicate that a violation probably occurred, even though there was insufficient information for a definite determination.'[136] Hence, a matter could not be sat upon on the strength of being 'under investigation.' However, an obligation to report 'probable violations' is a less potent protection than a responsibility to report 'suspected violations' as well.

When a violation is reported, there is an obligation on the part of the recipient of the report to send back a determination as to whether a violation has occurred, and if it has, what remedial and/or disciplinary action is to be taken. Thus, the junior auditor who reports an offence and hears back nothing about it knows that his or her report has been blocked or sat on somewhere. She then must use the safety valve channel direct to the board audit committee.

---

135 We have no data on how rigorously these policies were implemented throughout this massive organization, though we have some doubts. On the other hand, we are confident they were policies that top management took seriously at the time of our research in the early eighties.

136 Exxon Corporation, *Australian Compliance Professionals Association* (New York: Exxon, 1978).

If she does not, she is in breach of the Business Ethics Policy for failing to ensure that the problem gets either resolved or put before the board ethics committee. Many companies have policies requiring the reporting of ethics violations, but not many have policies that oblige the reporter to assure that the report is not blocked. This is important because one thing we know about criminal corporations is that they are expert at structuring communication blockages into the organization to protect top management from the taint of knowledge. This had been true when Exxon was paying off politicians around the world during the seventies. We cited memos from this era with statements like '[d]etailed knowledge could be embarrassing to the Chief Executive at some occasion on the witness stand.'

E. THE STRATEGIES

The strategies of generic importance for separating private powers we have discussed are

1. better securing the separation of the powers of the three major branches of corporate governance – shareholders, directors, and managers;
2. better separating powers within management – quality and production, environment and production, for example;
3. expanding audit capabilities to a range of areas beyond finance – safety, antitrust, ethics, for example;
4. professionalizing audit so that internal auditors have an external professional allegiance to balance corporate loyalty;
5. abandoning hierarchies of accountability in favour of circles of accountability so that auditors audit auditors, ensuring that someone guards the guardians;
6. allowing outsiders with interests different from corporate interests into the circle of accountability – unions into safety management circles, consumer group representatives into consumer complaint handling circles, greens into environmental circles by mandated public reporting of corporate environmental objectives, and public reporting of audits of whether the objectives are attained;
7. guaranteeing transparency and tainting soft targets with knowledge by institutionalizing a safety valve reporting route direct to a board audit committee, a corporate ombudsman, or both;
8. in domains where serious abuse of power is at risk, independent reports on compliance to the board audit committee from separate powers – line management, legal, audit, unions;
9. obligations on all employees to report suspected violations of law and violations of all corporate policies that involve an abuse of corporate

354 UNIVERSITY OF TORONTO LAW JOURNAL

power (e.g., corporate ethics and environmental policies). Obligations to report the suspected violations direct to the board when the employee does not receive back a written report that the matter has been satisfactorily resolved. Failure to meet this obligation being itself an ethical breach that colleagues have an ethical obligation to report.

For each of these strategies there is a debate to have about whether they should be mandated by the state, left to business or professional self-regulation or seen as demands that social movements should seek to extract directly from private power. These debates will not be engaged here.

VIII *Separation of Powers and Efficiency*

A. TWO CONCERNS
Since the decline of communism and fascism, not many of us believe that totalitarianism is more economically efficient than democracy with checks and balances.[137] This is not to deny that there are trade-offs between the virtues of checking power and the inefficiency of doing so. Sometimes there are significant economic costs that we are happy to bear when constitutional courts hold up decisions of executive governments. On the other hand, economists are more convinced than ever that a strict separation of powers between the central bank and other branches of government,[138] and political independence for the authority that enforces anti-monopoly law, are essential for economic efficiency.

We must consider, however, whether the reconceptualized rationale for a public-private separation of powers I have articulated raises a spectre of new inefficiencies which we may not happily bear. One worry arises from the separation of enforcement targeting from the actor who benefits from the abuse of power. According to the economic analysis of law, regulatory enforcement should be designed so as to deliver an optimal level of attainment of a regulatory objective. Pursuit of perfect compliance with, say, environmental law is an error. We should set sanctions at a level where inefficient non-compliance will always be

---

137 Advocates of the separation of powers such as Jefferson have always been concerned to separate powers in such a way as to allow the executive government to get on with governing. See W.G Gwyn, *Meaning*, supra note 2 at 33–5, 58, 118–20. For my own account of why a rich republican democracy is likely to be more economically efficient than totalitarianism, see, J. Braithwaite, 'Institutionalizing Distrust: Enculturating Trust,' *Trust and Democratic Governance*, eds. M. Levi & V. Braithwaite (New York: Russel Sage Foundation, 1997).

138 O. Issing, *Central Bank Independence and Monetary Stability* (London: Institute of Economic Affairs, 1993).

deterred. But when the economic benefits of non-compliance exceed the environment costs reflected in a fine the firm is willing to pay, we should want it to break the law. Economic welfare will be enhanced when it pays the fine to compensate for the environmental damage and goes ahead with the benefits of the economic activity. This kind of analysis is based on a variety of assumptions that prove to be false in regulatory practice – as a result of vice presidents responsible for going to jail bearing costs, while presidents get benefits without costs, and other complications.

The most basic complication is that managers routinely have little idea of the costs and benefits of regulatory compliance. A study of nursing home regulatory compliance, by Makkai and Braithwaite,[139] found, for example, that while the dominant models in the economic analysis of law assume that the relationship between the expected cost of compliance and compliance is monotonic, it is non-monotonic (a curve with a turning point). The models assume that expected costs are determined by actual costs, whereas only 19 per cent of the variance in expected costs was explained by actual costs. Some of the limits of economic models in this case were explained by CEOs who were 'disengagers.' The behaviour of disengagers was to be understood not in terms of rational game playing but in terms of dropping out of the regulatory game. The disengagers were in the regulatory system but not of it and certainly not economically calculative about it. Makkai and Braithwaite show that the fit of economic models can be improved by adding attitudes of managerial disengagement to the models. What all this means is that if we use under-specified pure economic models to determine the optimum level of penalties to ensure that rational actors, who bear both the costs and benefits, make choices that maximize welfare, we will fail to do so. Economic models with a grain of truth and a gram of falsity will prescribe major under-compliance or over-compliance most of the time.

But let us assume there are some contexts where the assumptions of economic models of law are not false. The worry is that by shifting enforcement on to gatekeepers who do not care about the benefits of the polluting activity, who care only about the costs of sanctions, compliance will be secured in circumstances where compliance is inefficient. We will get over-compliance. This worry also exists in domains where false economic models have set levels of standards and penalties for their breach that cause over-compliance even before cost-bearing is separated from benefit-taking.

---

139 T. Makkai & J. Braithwaite, 'The Limits of the Economic Analysis of Regulation: An Empirical Case and Case for Empiricism' (1993) 15 Law and Policy. 271.

Another worry about the rather radical separation of powers in the US system of government is that it nurtures fiscal irresponsibility. For example, when there is a clear need to reduce the deficit by increasing taxes or cutting spending, very often this does not happen. It is a kind of mismanagement the Americans are more able to live with than other nations because of the many other sources of resilience in their economy. When failure to cut a deficit occurs in the face of a transparent need to do so, the political tradition is for the President to blame the Congress, the Congress the President. A system of mutual irresponsibility, if we paint it in the worst light.

Separations of powers can induce economic inefficiencies, either from over-compliance or from mutual fiscal irresponsibility. But there is a common solution to these two problems and it is a republican one. Both types of inefficiency arise from an adversarial approach to how regulation should work in the first case, and to how politics should work in the second. Concerns about over-compliance and mutual irresponsibility are ameliorated to the extent that we can replace adversarialism which fortifies self-regarding interests with dialogue that redefines interests in a public-regarding way.

B. OVERCOMPLIANCE

In the form of regulation described in this paper and elsewhere in the work of new regulation scholars,[140] actors discuss regulatory problems in a way that is not totally self-regarding. In the conferences following nursing home inspections, the discourse is public-regarding on all sides. Of course there is underlying self-interest. But it is inconceivable that a nursing home manager would dismiss a plea to reduce the pain of a resident by suggesting that she did not care about the pain, only about the costs. The more genuine the dialogue, the more seriously management internalizes the concerns of the residents; the more seriously residents and regulators internalize the concerns of management. Under such a regime of other-regarding actors negotiating outcomes with recourse to sanctions only when good faith breaks down, any conception of an economically optimal level of regulatory sanctions makes no sense.

The hope for avoiding over-compliance rejects the spurious quantification of the economic analysis of law in favour of a negotiated search for win-win solutions based on a regulatory culture wherein actors

---

140 E. Bardach & R. Kagan, *Going by the Book: The Problem of Regulatory Unreasonableness* (Philadelphia: Temple University Press, 1982); V. Braithwaite, *Games of Engagement: Postures within the Regulatory Community* (forthcoming); V. Braithwaite *et al.*, 'Regulatory Styles, Motivational Postures and Nursing Home Compliance' (1994) 16(4) Law and Policy. 363; E. Meidinger, 'Regulatory Culture: A Theoretical Outline' (1987) 9 Law and Policy. 353.

are seen as virtuous when they take seriously not only their own concerns but the concerns of others, including the concerns of business about over-compliance. Empirically, it often happens that nursing home managers do speak up when they fear over-compliance – regulatory demands which deliver small benefits at such a high cost that if only some of those dollars could be spent elsewhere in the home, both sides would be better off. Indeed, it is common for regulators and residents to speak up about shifting resources from over-compliance here to under-compliance there. Republican regulatory institutions foster the creative search for optimality through sharing ideas and mutual identification with the interests of the other. The mutuality that engenders this creativity is destroyed by the adversarialism of deterrent-based regulation and, indeed, by the game-playing of tax-incentive-based regulation.[141]

In the day-to-day work of little regulatory decisions on the ground, dialogue in which all actors empathize with concerns about one another's costs and benefits is the most practical protection we can suggest against over- and under-compliance. Going after 'soft targets' would be a dangerous strategy if it were not embedded in a plural dialogue among actors with different spins on costs and benefits. More precisely, it would be a contingently dangerous threat to the efficiency of a regulatory regime – depending on whether the economic analysis underpinning it was misspecified in a way that caused under- or over-compliance. Contextual dialogue among hard and soft targets moves the soft targets more than the hard, yet in a way that has the soft targets listen to the point of view of the hard targets. The irony in our observations of nursing home regulation is that this kind a dialogue about regulatory costs actually generates some contextual data about costs to replace the ill-informed 'gut feels' that managers have about regulatory costs when subjected to traditional command and control directed at the beneficiaries of cheating.

C. FISCAL IRRESPONSIBILITY

To the extent that the game of American politics is totally adversarial and politically self-interested, parties will simply manoeuvre to make the other party impose unpopular taxes or spending cuts while avoiding doing so themselves. Fortunately, American political life does attenuate adversarial self-interest through dialogic mechanisms. The President meets with Congressional leaders to discuss public-regarding solutions to gridlock in

---

141 In as-yet-unpublished data on US nursing home regulation, Toni Makkai, Valerie Braithwaite, Dianne Gibson, and I will document perverse ritualism of limited or no benefit to residents in nursing homes where extra Medicaid payments accrue to homes that perform better on performance indicators. An example is wheeling in residents who are sound asleep to be present at an activities program when the performance indicator is the number of residents present at activities programs.

circumstances where the press and the people stand ready to condemn both sides if they do not manifest a more public-regarding approach to the dilemma. To the extent that the democracy succeeds in being dialogic in this way in the President's office and in the media debate, the admitted economic inefficiency from the separation of powers is attenuated.

Considering the problem from the opposite direction, cabinet government in British parliamentary systems more or less solves the mutual irresponsibility problem. Cabinet is of the parliament and effectively controls it (or hands over to a new cabinet if it cannot). If a tough budget is needed, cabinet does in practice bear responsibility at the next election if the electorate perceives it as failing to have done what was needed. But the cost is that the budget is the creation only of the parties represented in cabinet to the exclusion of other interests represented in the legislature. A less republican concentration of power than in the American case. Again one remedy to this concentration is a dialogic one. Citizen groups have their pre-budget submissions tabled not before cabinet but before parliament. Perhaps they should be allowed to address the parliament on them. Then members of parliament from all parties have an opportunity to discuss these submissions together with Treasury forecasts relevant to the budget before the budget is framed. An alternative during the early years of the Hawke-Keating government (1983–1996) in Australia was that pre-budget submissions would be discussed by the Economic Planning Advisory Council. As a member of this council representing community and consumer groups, my job was to argue with the Prime Minister, Treasurer, and other members of the Cabinet and bureaucracy about the pre-budget submissions from that consumer-community group perspective. More importantly perhaps, the Council included state Premiers from parties other than that represented in Federal cabinet. In the private dialogue of the Council meeting, the Premiers were not performing for the media, not seeking to score points against the other party. Rather they seemed to seize a genuine opportunity to listen to the thinking of the Prime Minister and to seek to sway it through public-regarding reasoning.

Either way, the checking of power that seems most valuable is dialogic. Adversarial politics in the glare of the television cameras is good for getting the issues before the people. Efficient economic resolution of those issues depends, however, on the quality of the economic dialogue in a democracy. Be the concern about economically inefficient outcomes articulated in an American or an Australian political context, in the context of framing budgets or implementing regulation, republicans are on the economic high ground because of their commitment to institutionalizing dialogue that can transcend the deepest inefficiencies. These are, at root, the outcome of self-serving adversarialism.

Bruce Chapman has raised a quite different economists' worry about stability. This is the 'danger in having an overlapping separation of powers with many sources of decision-making for the stability of any final organizational choice? One can certainly imagine that the plurality of interests might lead to a range of different and decisive coalitions (a bit like the voting paradox) cycling over a rich but unstable array of possible choices.'[142] The first reply is that the deeper worry is impoverished but stable choice – the economic choices of Breznev's Soviet Union or Marcos's Philippines. The fundamental protection against pathological policy instability for the republican is constitutional conventions that guarantee all the separated powers a legitimate voice in the deliberations, followed by a constitutional method for settling the matter until such time as new circumstances can be shown to prevail.

Charles Sabel[143] sees 'the central dilemma' of economic growth as 'reconciling the demands of learning with the demands of monitoring.' The dilemma is that economic actors need to trust each other to learn by sharing know-how. At the same time, they must distrust each other by monitoring that the gains from the shared know-how are shared in the agreed way. Sabel views economic success as flowing from the design of discursive institutions that make discussion of know-how inextricable from discussion of apportioning gains or losses. Mutual dependence can resolve the paralysing fear of deceit by allowing both scrutiny and learning to be natural consequences of a joint enterprise. A fusion of identities (as we see in families even moreso than in work groups) means that untrustworthiness by one member causes other members to share the shame of the breach of trust while all share the joy of others' learning. Both learning and monitoring are products of discursive problem-solving and partial fusing of identities in joint ventures.[144] As in the public sector, so within the private sector, therefore, the inefficiencies from separations of power that risk uncoupling the demands of learning from the demands of monitoring are best resolved by the mutuality and deliberation commended by the republican ideal of governance.

---

142 Editor's comments on an earlier version of this paper.

143 C. Sabel, 'Learning by Monitoring: The Institutions of Economic Development,' *The Handbook of Economic Sociology*, eds. N.J. Smelser & R. Swedburg, (Princeton: Princeton University Press, 1986) at 137.

144 See also W. Powell, 'Trust-Based Forms of Governance,' *Trust in Organizations: Frontiers of Theory and Research*, eds. R.M. Kramer & T.R. Tyler (Beverly Hills: Sage, 1996).

360 UNIVERSITY OF TORONTO LAW JOURNAL

IX *Conclusion*

A standard rationale for the separation of powers is deterring abuse of power with countervailing power. Deterring abuse of power, be it private or public, is not something we are good at. Problems like police corruption, dumping hazardous wastes and corporate fraud seem to bounce back after each wave of scandal and reform.[145] An increasingly coherent theoretical and empirical literature can now make sense of why deterring the abuse of power so often backfires. Emotive defiance, cognitions of stigma and procedural injustice, psychological reactance, the deterrence trap, and rational countermeasures are among the reasons big sticks often rebound. We have seen that all of these mechanisms apply to powerful actors; several of them have more force with powerful than powerless actors. Reactance and rational countermeasures are greatest with the powers the powerful care most about, which generally means the commanding heights of their power.

It has been argued that solutions to these problems are to

1. replace narrow, formal and strongly punitive responsibility with broad, informal, weak sanctions;
2. separate enforcement targeting from identification of the actor who benefits from the abuse.

Together 1 and 2 imply: (a) strong separations of powers within and between both the public and private sectors, combined with (b) another republican regulative ideal – problem-solving dialogue. The richer and more plural the separation of powers, the more over-determined will be the capacity to detect and prevent abuse of power. The more actors there are with this preventive capability, the more likely some of them will be soft targets who can be persuaded to check abuse of power by simple and cheap discursive appeals to their virtue. The more institutions for the control of abuse of power are based on moral reasoning rather than deterrence, the more public-regarding actors with preventive capability will there be.

Deterrence is certainly needed when dialogue fails to control abuse of power, as is incapacitation when deterrence fails.[146] But the more we can succeed in keeping deterrence and incapacitation in the background, the better the prospect that the separation of powers will check abuse of power through moral suasion and the better the chance that it will do so in a way that enhances rather than hampers economic efficiency.

---

145 See L. Sherman, *Scandal and Reform* (Berkeley: University of California Press, 1978).
146 I. Ayres & J. Braithwaite, *Responsive,* supra note 87.

An interesting implication of this for republican political theory is that the separation of powers and dialogic appeals to the virtue of citizens are not just separate republican ideals. The separation of powers creates a world where dialogue can displace sanctioning as the dominant means of regulating abuse of power. These republican prescriptions are not only coherent in the sense that both the separation of powers and dialogic reconstitution of interests help secure freedom as non-domination. Deliberative democracy is also causally dependent on the separation of powers.

We have shown that if appeals to the virtue of soft strategic targets is to work, the form this separation of powers must take is much more plural than the traditional separation of legislature, executive, and judiciary. The more richly plural the separations of public and private powers, the more the dependence of each fiduciary on many other fiduciaries will secure their independence from domination by any one of them.

This theory of republicanism amounts to a rejection of the radical Jeffersonianism of strict separation of powers that became influential in the early nineteenth century, that is represented in the French Constitution of 1795.[147] Simply dividing power and making it directly accountable to the electorate, preventing judges from meddling in the affairs of the legislature and vice versa, was a romantic theory even then, one that was bound to give birth to adversarial struggles for control that would deliver a Napoleon Bonaparte. The romantic theory of this century has been that antitrust law could democratize the new private power.[148] A pragmatic republicanism for the burgeoning private power of the twenty-first century will give more emphasis to the checking of power part of the republican ideal; it will pluralize the separations of powers, while rejecting any aspiration that each divided power be fully independent. Many semi-autonomous powers recursively checking one another[149] rather than a few autonomous branches of governance. This means rejecting the status quo of the separation of powers, rejecting radical Jeffersonianism, and creatively radicalizing Madison for a world where new and disturbing concentrations of private power continually emerge.

147 See note 109.
148 Maximizing the breaking up of private power through antitrust law that creates inefficiently small firms is politically unsustainable in a world of intense international competition. Even if one could do it, why would one want to? In some senses, it is easier for state and civil society to demand the kinds of separations of powers and dialogic justice discussed in this article from one profitable large firm than from a dozen small struggling firms. A conception of the separation of powers as simply dividing or breaking up concentrations of power is neither attractive nor realistic in the contemporary world.
149 See Diagram 4.

PART IV

Restorative Justice

[13]
Shame and Modernity

If shaming is crucial to crime control, then is not the task of controlling crime hopeless in modern urbanized societies? It is argued here that any such pessimism must be qualified by a broader understanding of shame in human history. First, the article considers the arguments of Elias that shame became more important in the affect structure of citizens with the demise of feudalism. Elias did not consider the movement away from shame and towards brutal punishment in crime control directed at the lower classes in the seventeenth and eighteenth centuries. This period culminated in a demonstration of the failure of stigmatization and punitive excess, opening the way for reintegrative ideals to gather support in the Victorian era and beyond. Finally, drawing on Goffman, it is argued that there are some neglected ways in which shaming can have more power in the city than in the village. Overall, there is no structural inevitability about the impotence of shaming in industrialized societies; there is no inexorable march with modernization towards a society where shaming does not count.

My recent book, *Crime, Shame and Reintegration* (Braithwaite 1989) advances the theory that nations with low crime rates, and periods of history where crime is more effectively controlled, are those where shaming has the greatest social power. For shaming to attain its maximum effectiveness, it must be of a reintegrative sort, avoiding stigmatization. Stigmatization is shaming which creates outcasts, where 'criminal' becomes a master status trait that drives out all other identities, shaming where bonds of respect with the offender are not sustained. Reintegrative shaming, in contrast, is disapproval dispensed within an ongoing relationship with the offender based on respect, shaming which focuses on the evil of the deed rather than on the offender as an irremediably evil person, where degradation ceremonies are followed by ceremonies to decertify deviance, where forgiveness, apology, and repentance are culturally important. The

I would like to thank an anonymous reviewer and particularly thank Susanne Karstedt and David Garland who provided enormously valuable assistance in improving this manuscript.

key contention, which I will not defend here, is that societies where shaming of criminal conduct is both potent and reintegrative are societies with low crime rates.

Most of us refrain most of the time from crimes like murder not from any rational calculation of the costs of incarceration or the costs of the electric chair, but because murder is simply off our deliberative agenda as something to calculate about. Murder is unthinkable as a way of solving our problems of daily living. The key to crime prevention is to understand what constitutes this unthinkableness. My answer is reintegrative shaming rather than stigmatization. Stigmatization can be counter-productive through increasing the attractions for outcasts of criminal subcultures. What criminal subcultures do is provide symbolic resources that render the unthinkable thinkable.

Urbanization is posited in the theory as one of the structural variables that enfeeble the communitarianism that makes shaming possible. At the same time, I am anxious to qualify any excessive structural determinism about this by emphasizing the low crime rates of Tokyo and by pointing to the growing power of reintegrative shaming and the declining crime rates in the Victorian era, a period of unprecedented urbanization (Braithwaite 1989: 111–18). Cynics about the significance of the theory latch on to the urbanization and industrialization question. Whenever I present a seminar on *Crime, Shame and Reintegration*, a member of the audience always asks something like the following: 'Yes, I accept that the nature of shaming is important to understanding why there are such vast differences between societies in crime rates. But the practical implications of your theory for dealing with crime are small. They amount to a plea to turn back the clock from *Gesellschaft* to *Gemeinschaft* [Tönnies 1887], from urban back to folk society [Redfield, 1947]. But urbanization and industrialization are facts that cannot be reversed; there is no practical import to a theory that amounts to a romantic plea for a bygone communitarian era.' The purpose of this article is to suggest that standard comment reflects a simplistic understanding of shame in human history. The understanding I will squeeze into the next few pages will be only slightly more complex and limited to Western history, even though I suspect a more interesting treatment could be given by reflecting on Japanese, Chinese, or Australian Aboriginal history. Limited though it will be, I hope it will be an advance on the way criminologists are wont to think historically about shame.

First, I will consider Norbert Elias's account of the rise of shame in Western history. Then I will argue that Elias did not take account of some important historical reversals in the influence of shame; and that he also ignored the way social control based on violence rather than shame escalated in dealings with the lower classes just as the prominence of shaming in upper-class social relations increased. To highlight the theme that there is no unidirectional historical trend either towards or away from shame-based social control with modernization, it is shown how the nature of interdependencies in modern urban social relations can actually increase rather than decrease our exposure to shame.

The Civilizing Process

The most important work on shame in Western history is Norbert Elias's two volumes on *The Civilizing Process*. This was published in German in 1939, with the first volume appearing in English in 1978, the second in 1982. I confess I had not read this work

SHAME AND MODERNITY

when I wrote *Crime, Shame and Reintegration*. This was a pity because Elias's analysis of shame has some resonances with mine, and Elias accomplishes his analysis with a broader historical sweep than I dared contemplate.

Elias sees shame as in the ascendent rather than declining during the last 700 years. Two related structural changes were important in the rise of shaming as the predominant form of social control: the growth of the state as a monopolist of physical force, and the proliferation of a more elaborate division of labour. The process is strategically illustrated by the transformation of the nobility from a class of knights into a class of courtiers as physical force was progressively monopolized by a monarch. The monopolization of force created pacified social spaces. Prior to this pacification, with violence an unavoidable and everyday event, 'a strong and continuous moderation of drives and affects is neither necessary, possible nor useful' (Elias 1982: 236). In the feudal era characterized by a warrior upper class not only the warriors themselves, but all people, were threatened continually by acts of physical violence. The members of the warrior upper class enjoyed an extraordinary freedom in living out their feelings and passions through uninhibited satisfaction of sexual pleasure and gratification of vengeful impulses through acts of torture and dismemberment. This is consistent with the evidence we have on the extraordinarily high levels of homicide in the middle ages (Gurr 1980: 44). The evidence suggests a substantial downward trend in violent crime in England from the thirteenth century extending well into the twentieth century, a trend Gurr (1984: 295–353) attributes in part to strengthening internal controls against violence (see also Garland 1990: 233–4). During the sixteenth century, according to Elias, unrestrained passion became less a source of power and more an impediment to it. The affective make-up of the nobility changes as warriors became courtiers (whence 'courtesy'), peddling influence at the court of a monarch who monopolized force. As La Bruyère wrote: 'Life at court is a serious melancholy game, which requires of us that we arrange our pieces and our batteries, have a plan, follow it, foil that of our adversary, sometimes take risks and play on impulse. And after all our measures and mediations are in check, sometimes checkmate' (quoted in Elias, 1982: 270).

Gradually the sword became less important than words and intrigue in competing for career success. This happened because the court of an absolute monarch was a social formation in which a great many people were continuously dependent on one another. Elias likens the court to a stock exchange, where the value of each individual is continually being formed and assessed. The most important determinants of this value are 'the favour he enjoys with the king, the influence he has with other mighty ones, his importance in the play of courtly cliques'. In this subtle game of building value in a diplomatic market, 'physical force and direct affective outbursts are prohibited and a threat to existence' (Elias 1982: 271). What is demanded of each participant is self-control and exact knowledge of every other player with whom he is interdependent. A loss of affective control can devalue courtly opinion, threatening his whole position at court: 'A man who knows the court is master of his gestures, of his eyes and his expression; he is deep, impenetrable. He dissimulates the bad turns he does, smiles at his enemies, suppresses his ill-temper, disguises his passions, disavows his heart, acts against his feelings' (Elias 1982: 272). Elias illustrates how the affective structure of the warrior class was doomed through cases of bold and brave knights like the Duke of Montmorency being defeated by consummate courtiers such as Richelieu (Elias 1982:

3

279). The role of the court and its associated institutions in dismantling the violent apparatus of feudalism remained influential for many centuries, even in England where the court waned earlier than on the continent as the pre-eminent site for politicking. The eighteenth-century reign of Beau Nash at the quasi-court of Bath civilized country squires by hastening the disappearance of the sword as the proper adornment of a gentleman's thigh; as a result, the settling of disagreements with cold steel became increasingly infrequent (Trevelyan 1985: 385). Similarly, among humbler males, stabbing was replaced by the 'civilized' rules of fair play of the boxing ring. Even the boxing ring came to be viewed as uncivilized in early Victorian times, and withered away, only to be revived in the twentieth century, as Trevelyan (1973: 504) quaintly put it, as a 'largely American' preoccupation, 'tempered with gloves'.

The 'civilizing' effect of courtly life was not as profound and all-embracing as that of later bourgeois society. The only interdependencies that mattered for the courtier and the court lady were those involving their peers and superiors at court. Elias uses etiquette texts and other sources to show how they felt no shame at the gaze or disapproval of their inferiors. 'To receive inferiors when getting up and being dressed was for a whole period a matter of course. And it shows exactly the same stage of the shame-feeling when Voltaire's mistress, the Marquise de Châtelet, shows herself naked to her servant while bathing in a way that casts him into confusion, and then with total unconcern scolds him because he is not pouring in the hot water properly' (Elias 1978: 138). However, Duerr's two-volume study (1988a,b) calls into question the way Elias has used historical materials on this and other questions (see also van Krieken, 1989). Duerr (1988a: 242–52) contends that in fact the record suggests that the Marquise de Châtelet's behaviour in the passage quoted above was no common behaviour and therefore worth mentioning. Books on manners at court on which Elias relied were written with the moralistic intent of revealing the *lack* of manners at court and therefore were prone to exaggeration (Garland 1990: 230).[1] Bourgeois society, according to Elias, set in motion a lasting transformation of the situation where superordinates need not care about shame in the eyes of subordinates. Gradually interdependencies with subordinate capitalists, professionals, workers, and consumers (customers who are allowed to be 'always right' according to the mythology of capitalism even if they are social inferiors) mean that it becomes possible for the upper classes to be shamed by their inferiors.

State formation, by creating a large zone of pacification, enables networks of transport, money, and trade to expand in conditions of physical safety. Thus, the absolutist central court not only constitutes its own interdependencies but also enables the constitution of a new set of bourgeois interdependencies. Both forms of interdependency have the effect of increasing the centrality of shame as a form of social control: 'As the interdependence of men increases with the increasing division of labour, everyone becomes increasingly dependent on everyone else, those of high social rank on those socially inferior and weaker. The latter become so much the equals of the former that they, the socially superior, feel shame even before their inferiors' (Elias 1978: 138). While Elias identifies an interesting trend toward the democratizing of shame, he overstates it. Today, shame remains class-structured in important ways and is profoundly gendered. White-collar workers will shamelessly indulge inconsiderate

---

[1] I am indebted to Susanna Karstedt for drawing this to my attention.

SHAME AND MODERNITY

behaviour in the gaze of their secretary that they would never indulge in the presence of their boss.

Elias's longer time horizon makes a fascinating contrast with the analysis of community from the vantage of the shorter time-frame typically grasped by post-war criminologists. The latter bemoan the increased criminality which is a consequence of a loss of community, of a world where we care less about what others think of us. Perhaps it is partly because Elias writes from a vantage point which predates the short-term postwar rise in crime rates in the West that he can see the long-term growth in interdependency, shame, and the disciplining of violent impulses. Elias sees the skills needed to negotiate travel on roadways as an interesting model of what is needed to survive in a world of interdependencies within a complex division of labour. This need is for self-regulation which has been constituted by shame:

One should think of the country roads of a simple warrior society with a barter economy, uneven, unmetalled, exposed to damage from wind and rain. With a few exceptions, there is very little traffic; the main danger which man here represents for other men is an attack by soldiers or thieves. When people look around them, scanning the trees and hills or the road itself, they do so primarily because they must always be prepared for armed attack, and only secondarily because they have to avoid collision. Life on the main roads of this society demands a constant readiness to fight, and free play of the emotions in defence of one's life or possessions from physical attack. Traffic on the main roads of a big city in the complex society of our time demands a quite different moulding of the psychological apparatus. Here the danger of physical attack is minimal. Cars are rushing in all directions; pedestrians and cyclists are trying to thread their way through the melee of cars; policemen stand at the main crossroads to regulate the traffic with varying success. But this external control is founded on the assumption that every individual is himself regulating his behaviour with the utmost exactitude in accordance with the necessities of this network. The chief danger that people here represent for others results from someone in this bustle losing his self-control. A constant and highly differentiated regulation of one's own behaviour is needed for the individual to steer his way through the traffic. If the strain of such constant self-control becomes too much for an individual, this is enough to put himself and others in mortal danger. (Elias 1982: 233–4)

For Elias, shame as the feared experience which generates this self-control is not distinguished from guilt (see also Scheff 1990: 17). What we talk of today as guilt is, I think rightly, conceived as shame where the original sources of the shame in social interaction have been forgotten or suppressed:

Shame takes on its particular coloration from the fact that the person feeling it has done or is about to do something through which he comes into contradiction with people to whom he is bound in one form or another, and with himself, with the sector of his consciousness by which he controls himself. The conflict expressed in shame-fear is not merely a conflict of the individual with prevalent social opinion; the individual's behaviour has brought him into conflict with the part of himself that represents this social opinion. (Elias 1982: 292)

According to Elias, the transformation of the affect structure of the nobility from the knightly to the courtly structure based on shame commenced in the sixteenth century and continued through the seventeenth and eighteenth centuries. In the eighteenth and nineteenth centuries this affect structure spread, transformed in important respects, to the bourgeoisie and later to all classes in Western societies. The more the

5

nobility sought to distinguish their 'civilized' manners and affect from those of the lower orders, the more incentive status-conscious members of the bourgeoisie had to model *civilité*. But more fundamentally, the bourgeoisie found themselves entwined in an even more complex set of interdependencies than the nobility: for them, to an even greater extent, the skills they needed for success were sensitivity to the disapproval of others, internalization of norms, and finesse in communicating disapproval to others. Just as the capitalist division of labour renders the bourgeoisie dependent on their inferiors, so that disapproval from below begins to matter to them, equally the nobility becomes economically dependent on the bourgeoisie. By the nineteenth century shame is a more democratic emotion.

The affect structure of the upper class colonizes the lower while the lower models the upper. But there is a two-way interpenetration of the structure of affect between classes. For example, Elias talks of upper-class penetration of the middle class with a code of manners and middle-class penetration of the upper class with a code of morals. He talks of affect control in the United States being more influentially shaped by the middle class than in England. However, Elias has remarkably little to say about how shame-based affect control is transmitted one step further down to the working class. Ultimately, of course, all classes travel on the complex road systems of contemporary cities which, for survival, require internalization and affect control. It might be pointed out, however, that it is young working-class males—the fraction of the population where control of aggression fails most often—who are most of those killed on our roads (Willett 1964). Elias does point out that with the success of capitalism, the working class accrues more disposable income, and therefore the upper class becomes more economically dependent on it. By the twentieth century chains of interdependency reach right down to the working class. He might also have said that the rise of trade unions and working-class influence in political parties increased downward dependency. He might have hypothesized that the working class would want to copy the *civilité* of higher classes in its quest for higher status, though this hardly seems as convincing as it is when the juxtaposition is between the rising bourgeoisie and the nobility. The fact that it is not so convincing is perhaps why Elias does not draw out this part of the argument. To build on the historical understanding we can obtain from Elias, we must think more critically about shaming and the working class. I attempt to tackle this problem in the next section.

In doing so, it will become clear that Elias exaggerated the extent to which shame and interdependency were democratized. While Elias (1978: 186) says that 'The civilizing process does not follow a straight line,' his theory remains one of more or less unilinear evolutionism. But the civilizing of violence has certainly not been all onwards and upwards—witness the subsequent butchering of Elias's family at Auschwitz and Breslau. Yet the claim that Elias's thesis is undermined by the Holocaust should not be made casually, because Elias was clear that violence does not disappear with civilization. Rather, violence is stored up 'behind the scenes', in prisons and military arsenals, ready to be unleashed in an emergency (Garland 1990: 223). But late modernity has not kept violence behind the scenes; most homes have violent events visible on their television screens every night of the year. Duerr correctly points out that late modernity has involved a frontal assault on shame wherein everything—nakedness, sex, violence, rage, fidelity—is turned into a consumer item. The commodification of the body, sexuality, and violence has probably weakened the threshold of shame in

6

SHAME AND MODERNITY

relation to them (Duerr 1988*b*: 260). A rising divorce rate is another outcome of the displacement of a sacred view of fidelity with a commodified view; when marriage becomes just another consumer choice, this in turn has implications for the power of family shaming. Perhaps most critically, as Scheff has pointed out, during the twentieth century we became ashamed to be ashamed in certain ways and the very word shame atrophied in our vocabulary (Scheff 1990: 16). Half a century after Elias wrote, the withering of many types of shame has significantly reversed the most fundamental unilinear trend in his theory. Moreover, I will suggest that while shame may have been the 'success story' described by Elias in the context of upper-class social relations, shame failed dismally during the seventeenth and eighteenth centuries in its extension to the lower classes. Moreover, to suggest that the violence of the criminal justice system was 'behind the scenes' seems a ruling-class perspective. One might argue that the brutality of the criminal justice system was displayed on front stage for the lower classes, and intentionally so.

Criminal Justice as Class Control in the Seventeenth and Eighteenth Centuries

As trade expanded in the zones pacified by the new state monopolies of force, towns and cities grew. There congregated in these urban spaces dispossessed persons with no means of subsistence. Many survived by crime. The creation of such visible concentrations of criminal poor motivated an escalation of the punitiveness of the criminal justice system as an instrument of class control. The feudal criminal justice system had been much less punitive, and more concerned with ironing out disputes between equals (Weisser 1979: 100). But with the rise of the central state criminal justice began to become more punitive and more concerned with class control. In the sixteenth century, fining and banishment, which had been the staple feudal punishments, were progressively overtaken by corporal punishments as the predominant sanctions—flogging, mutilation, and even execution (Weisser 1979: 100–1; on the escalation of schoolroom corporal punishment at the same time, see Stone 1977: 163–5). This shift was probably connected to the practical problems of enforcement associated with criminalizing reintegration: in seventeenth-century Amsterdam, for example, 'infraction of banishment' (the crime of reintegration) was one of the more common offences the courts had to deal with (Spierenburg 1984: 130–1).

But it was in the late seventeenth century and throughout the eighteenth that the problem of crime was most visibly identified as a growing urban lower-class problem that required suppression with maximum brutality. In England during this period the number of offences punishable by death increased from fifty to more than 200 (Weisser 1979: 138–9; Foucault 1977; see also Beattie 1984). A particularly crucial escalation was the Black Acts (Thompson 1975) which, in addition to extending the scope of the death penalty, removed procedural protections such as trial by jury for many (lower-class) offences. In Holland as well, the period 1650–1750 saw an intensification of scaffold punishment (Spierenburg 1984: 176–7). The repeal of the Black Acts in 1823 occurred near a turning-point away from two centuries of the most brutal regime of criminal justice as class warfare. During these two centuries, there was limited pretence of *civilité* in dealings with the lower classes (though see Spierenburg (1984: 191–265) on growing ruling-class repugnance and shame at the sight of the awful violence meted out). Reintegrative shaming may have been replacing outbursts of violence and passion

7

in the royal court, in bourgeois society, and in relations between the two, but for the lower classes these were the two centuries of their most brutal physical torture and their most vituperous stigmatization. In the eighteenth century, in France as well as England, the Enlightenment of critics of brutality and torture in the criminal justice system and the supporters of some steps towards equality before the law—Beccaria in Italy, Montesquieu and Voltaire in France, Howard in England—started to become influential in the criminal justice debate. Torture was abolished by law in most of Europe late in the eighteenth century (Spierenburg 1984: 190). Prisons, according to the reformers, were to be used in preference to corporal and capital punishment, and prisons were to be places of correction. The lower classes should be saved, reclaimed, and rehabilitated instead of bowed and brutalized.

According to Foucault (1977) the ideological shift away from horrific degradation ceremonies to signify the evil of the criminal, to inscribe the power of the monarch on the offending body, occurred because this signification began to backfire. The public spectacle of corporal and capital punishment in the seventeenth and eighteenth centuries was all about shame, but clearly stigmatization rather than reintegrative shaming. Any reintegration for those who repented would be left to the Almighty after the twisted body of the felon expired. Shame was made explicit by hanging placards around the necks of those subjected to the public humiliation of torture. They were also forced to proclaim the blackness of their crimes and of themselves. The eighteenth-century French murderer Jean-Dominique Langlade was required to consecrate his torture by saying: 'Listen to my horrible, infamous and lamentable deed, committed in the city of Avignon, where the memory of me is excretable, for having inhumanly violated the sacred rights of friendship' (Foucault 1977: 66). Yet this stigmatization frequently did not go according to plan. Instead of forced repentance, victims often attacked the barbarity of the judge and the executioner, the injustice of the king. When this happened, the crowd often cheered, in some cases even being moved to turn on the executioner by physical attack or hurling projectiles (see also Hay 1975: 67–8).

In these executions, which ought to show only the terrorizing power of the prince, there was a whole aspect of the carnival, in which rules were inverted, authority mocked and criminals transformed into heroes. The shame was turned round; the courage, like the tears and cries of the condemned, caused offence only to the law. Fielding notes with regret: 'To unite the ideas of death and shame is not so easy as may be imagined . . . I will appeal to any man who hath seen an execution, or a procession to an execution; let him tell me. When he hath beheld a poor wretch, bound in a cart, just on the verge of eternity, all pale and trembling with his approaching fate, whether the idea of shame hath ever intruded on his mind? Much less will the bold daring rogue, who glories in his present condition, inspire the beholder with any such sensation.' (Foucault 1977: 61).

Executions became occasions for expressions of solidarity with petty property offenders, ceremonies which educated the masses to see the criminal justice system for what it was—an instrument of terror designed to pacify the lower classes (but see Spierenburg 1984: 92–109). As a victim of class injustice, of tyranny and excess, the condemned felon could now be celebrated as a hero: 'Against the law, against the rich, the powerful, the magistrates, the constabulary or the watch, against taxes and their collectors, he appeared to wage a struggle with which one too . easily identified'

SHAME AND MODERNITY

(Foucault 1977: 67).[2] In England at the same time juries were refusing to convict for minor offences that would lead to the gallows (Trevelyan 1973: 348).

This was a dramatic historical affirmation of the thesis that stigmatization can engender subcultures of resistance to the law.[3] So there was a retreat from the barbarism against the lower classes that had risen at the very time that *civilité* was rising among the upper classes. Reintegrative policies were put on the agenda for extension to the lower classes. Foucault saw two alternatives emerging in the eighteenth century. One was the reintegrative option of criminal justice practices which requalify guilty individuals as citizens. The other was the project of a prison institution which was a coercive technology of power to train, to discipline the body. Neither vision secured victory in the struggle that ensued between these two ideologies: to this day prison policy continues to be contested between defenders respectively of a rehabilitative and of a coercive disciplinary ideal.

What is clear is that the ideal of the body as a text on which torture inscribes the power of the sovereign was defeated and that reintegrative ideals gained momentum. Branding was abolished in Holland by a law of 1854 (Spierenburg 1984: 199) and disappeared throughout Europe by the mid-nineteenth century. Garland (1985) disagrees with Foucault on the timing of such changes, at least for Britain. While seeing some tendencies in the earlier Victorian period for the dominant ideology to shift from despising and outcasting criminals to pitying and reclaiming them, Garland suggests that the most decisive changes in this direction occurred between 1895 and 1914 (see also Forsythe 1991). In England, as in most Western nations, in 1930 one could look back on a century of falling crime, of rising optimism about reintegrating criminals and the criminal classes, and on dramatic reductions in the brutality of the criminal justice system. Stigmatic and outcasting forms of punishment such as flogging and transportation had disappeared and capital punishment had all but disappeared. The imprisonment rate per 100,000 population was one-seventh of its level of 100 years earlier (Ramsay 1982).

I will move on now to discuss how the Victorian era may have laid the foundations not only for a triumph of shame, but also perhaps for a triumph of the policy of integration over the policy of casting out. Those developments continued in the Edwardian period, but were sharply reversed later in the twentieth century, when shame was for the most part excised from our vocabulary (Scheff 1988; Lynd 1958), when the steadily growing influence of the rehabilitative ideal was halted and then reversed as we set about building and filling coercive prisons again. The classicism which preceded late Victorian optimism about the reclaimability of criminals was revived in a neo-classical penology—retribution or 'just deserts' was back.

The broad historical pattern seems consistent with the theory of reintegrative shaming. For several centuries prior to the nineteenth century, the West relied on social control that was brutally punitive. The punishment was public and coupled with

---

[2] See also Foucault's (1977: 260–3) account of the later demise of the chain gang in the same terms. Chain gangs would sing songs celebrating their deviance; their trudging journeys through the streets of the city were ceremonies no longer of shame but of defiance. So they came to be transported in enclosed carriages.

[3] Indeed, in the record of micro-encounters of seventeenth-century punishment as well, one can find evidence for the stigmatization hypothesis. In 1653 as Gillis Nicaes left an Amsterdam scaffold after being whipped and branded, he loudly exclaimed: 'Of course I won't be good now, but will do wrong a hundred times more' (Spierenburg 1984: 64). For verbalizing this truth, the magistrates had him whipped again.

shame, but the shame was highly stigmatic—humiliating, degrading, and outcasting (Beattie 1984; Spierenburg 1984).[4] Under this punitive–stigmatic system, the level of violence in society was much higher than today (Gurr 1980, 1984; Beattie 1984; Stone 1977: 93–102). During the nineteenth century and well into the twentieth, the system became less punitive and the shaming more reintegrative—and crime rates fell sharply (Braithwaite 1989: 111–14). But by the late twentieth century we had seen both a general weakening of shaming and some shift with neo-classicism back to stigmatic and away from reintegrative shaming; and from the 1960s onwards, crime rates rose again (Braithwaite 1989: 49).

In the 1920s one might have looked back on the Victorian period as an ongoing contest between two visions of how to deal with the dangerous classes: reclaim them, or discipline and segregate tham (clear them out of slums that are intolerably close to respectable areas). And perhaps the integrative vision finally got the upper hand. Stedman Jones has described this battle between the policies of integrating and outcasting:

Historians have generally discussed this question in a rather one-sided and teleological manner. Looking forward to the creation of the welfare state, they have concentrated upon proposals for old-age pensions, free education, free school meals, subsidized housing, and national insurance. They have virtually ignored parallel proposals to segregate the casual poor, to establish detention centres for 'loafers', to separate pauper children from 'degenerate' parents or to ship the 'residuum' overseas. Yet, for contemporaries, both sort of proposals composed parts of a single debate. (Stedman Jones 1984: 313–14)

The Victorian era might be conceived as one when the policies of outcasting were gradually replaced by integrative policies, first in the form of private charities which attempted to make the poor reputable and deserving through the supervision of 'lady rent collectors' and others, and finally by the integrative ideology of the embryonic welfare state. Concomitantly, criminal justice policies became more humane and integrative.

At the micro level of the family we can see the culmination of a reintegrative shift even more clearly than at the macro level. Stearns and Stearns (1986: 241) see the predominant norms of child-rearing in the seventeenth century as will-breaking techniques and the indulgence of anger by parents. By the Victorian period this had changed dramatically (Thompson 1988: 127–8, 134). Children were now to be viewed as objects of loving tenderness; anger and violence in family relations became matters for shame. 'Family manuals began to include specific injunctions against anger, as part of a larger emphasis on affection and on the mutuality of obligations among family members' (Stearns and Stearns 1986: 29). Lawrence Stone, in his monumental study, *The Family, Sex and Marriage in England, 1500–1800*, concludes that it is wrong to see a unilinear historical shift from *Gemeinschaft* to *Gesellschaft* during the period he examines (Stone 1977: 660). This is because between 1500 and 1800 the family became in important ways less of a *Gesellschaft* institution with an impersonal contractual, coercive

---

[4] 'The Elizabethan village was a place filled with malice and hatred, its only unifying bond being the occasional episode of mass hysteria, which temporarily bound together the majority in order to harry and persecute the local witch' (Stone 1977: 98).

SHAME AND MODERNITY

quality to its ordering and more of a *Gemeinschaft* institution, closely knit by bonds of love.

This creation of a family where social control is based on what, in my theoretical terms, would be called reintegrative shaming is well documented from records of upper-class family life. However, it is not so clear what was happening within working-class families. Also, there were clear gender differences in upper-class families, with daughters being socialized to unconditional control of anger to secure family harmony, while boys were taught to channel their anger, restraining it to outside those channels: 'According to the founder of the [US] National Congress of Mothers, while girls should be trained to prepare a tranquil home and face problems cheerfully, boys should simply be trained in righteous indignation' (Stearns and Stearns 1986: 76). Women, both privately in their family roles (Howe 1976) and publicly through their roles in the caring professions (particularly social work), were in the vanguard of shifts towards reintegrative modalities of social control.

Critics who say that the notion of reintegrative shaming is one that could only work in pre-industrial-revolution villages therefore miss an important point. More families in the twentieth-century city exhibit loving socialization practices based on the socially integrative fostering of pride in doing right and shame at doing wrong, compared with seventeenth-century life where families relied more on will-breaking techniques and violent punishment (Beattie 1984: 41–3; Stone 1977: 6–7). Here it is critical to remember that the theory posits that shaming will be most powerful within proximate groups (particularly families) where the conditions of communitarianism are maximally satisfied, where interdependency is so strong that family members care deeply about approval and disapproval. Hence it could be that while the capacity of the local church congregation to shame effectively has declined since the seventeenth century, the capacity of families to do so has increased (even after allowing for the possibility of some postwar slippage in this capacity). Yet even this interpretation must be treated with some scepticism. Though churches shame less than they used to in the pre-industrial village, progressively since the Inquisition the church has taken the teachings of Christ more seriously and shamed less stigmatically and more reintegratively.

Garland (1985) sees Victorian social policy as oriented towards integrating the deserving poor into the mainstream of British life, while Victorian prisons were institutions which segregated the undeserving poor, separating the disreputable from the respectable working class. The 1834 Poor Law Report was clear that there was a 'small disreputable minority, whose resentment was not to be feared, and whose favour was of no value' (Checkland 1974: 216; see also Foucault 1971). But this moral divide was increasingly contested, especially in the late nineteenth and early twentieth centuries, as prison reformers argued that the goal of social policy should always be to reclaim, to rehabilitate even the most disreputable.

But if policies of reintegrative shaming did get the upper hand by the end of the Victorian era through the rise of institutions like the Sunday School, the loving family, and the profession of social work (Wilson and Herrnstein 1985: 432; Thompson 1988), they did not keep it. While clear legacies of them exist today in welfare state policies, community corrections, and community policing, exclusionary and stigmatic criminal justice policies have staged a comeback. There has been a shift from moralizing to punitive social control, at least in social control directed against working-class criminals: when business regulatory agencies deal with white-collar criminals, their

11

preferred strategy continues to be social control by moral suasion (Hawkins 1983; Grabosky and Braithwaite 1986). Nevertheless, the point remains that there has been neither a continuous historical decline nor a continuously rising ascendancy of shaming. There were the trends Elias identified of shifts within and between the nobility and the bourgeoisie from control mediated by physical coercion to control mediated by shaming; but Elias was inattentive to the fact that at the same time control of the lower classes by shame collapsed as physical coercion escalated. Yet in the century to the depression of 1930 there were important integrative changes as the upper classes became more dependent on and afraid of the working classes. The 'reputable' working class was certainly integrated into the mainstream of Victorian propriety. And it became more acceptable to argue that even the disreputable poor should be subject to inclusionary rather than exclusionary social control. Certainly the welfare state has left us with a working class which is no longer a 'dangerous' outcast class from polite society. The emergent interdependency discussed by Elias among the upper classes has been somewhat extended to the lower classes. And it is reasonable to posit that when relationships between two classes shift from stigmatization to interdependency, inter-class shaming is more likely to be heeded.

It is just that as these changes occurred we began to lose faith and interest in shaming and dialogue as methods of social control, and our enthusiasm for economistic and coercive social control rekindled. Shame was *declassé* within the increasingly popular libertarian vision of the citizen freely choosing in a market for commodities where punishment was just another commodity. It became a tolerated idea that we have a right to break the law so long as we pay the price in punishment. While the coercion of the *ancien régime* was coupled with shame, modern coercion is uncoupled from shame to a considerable degree (Braithwaite 1989: 59–61). So the potentialities of shame for good and ill are less exploited.

Interdependency in a Complex Urban Society

In *Crime, Shame and Reintegration* I argue that shaming affects us most when we are shamed by people who matter to us. It follows that people enmeshed in many interdependent relationships with others are exposed to more sources of effective shaming. Contrary to the common view, there has been no unilinear movement away from interdependency across the past millenium. Trevelyan (1985: 317) makes this comment about life in seventeenth-century England:

Men and women were widely scattered through the island, thrown back upon themselves during frequent hours of solitude and isolation; each had space to grow, like the spreading oak tree alone in the field, without troubling too much to conform to any conventional pattern. It was 'every man in his humour'. The typical economic life of the time, as conducted by yeoman, farmer, and small craftsman, left the individual more unfettered and self-dependent than he had been in the corporate life of medieval burgher and serf, or has become in our own day under great capitalist and labour combinations.

The contention is often made that in a complex urban society citizens are isolated, while in a village they were traditionally enmeshed in powerful interdependencies. This is both true and false. At the level of geographical neighbourhood it is true. In the village we are much more vulnerable to shame by our neighbours than in the city.

SHAME AND MODERNITY

However, in terms of their total sets of interdependencies twentieth-century city-dwellers have many more interdependencies than fifteenth-century villagers for the reasons outlined by Elias, even if they have fewer interdependencies than nineteenth-century city-dwellers. The contemporary city-dweller may have a set of colleagues at work, in her trade union, among members of his golf club, among drinking associates whom he meets at the same pub, among members of a professional association, the parents and citizens' committee for her daughter's school, not to mention a geographic-ally extended family, where many of these significant others can mobilize potent disapproval. There are actually more interdependencies in the nineteenth- and twentieth-century city; it is just that they are not geographically segregated within a community. If I think of my own place in the division of labour, it becomes clear that some of the actors in the best position to shame me are professional colleagues who live as far away from me on this planet as it is possible to live. I care more about the approval of Gilbert Geis than I care about the approval of my nextdoor neighbour.[5] No matter how exotic my interests are, in the city those interests can become a basis for constructing communities. Moreover, many of the new interdependencies that started as privileges of the wealthy have spread throughout the class structure. Most importantly, the school progressively expanded from being a set of interdependencies reserved for a select group of ruling-class families to universality. Sporting clubs, once solely the preserve of the rich, today have large numbers of working-class members.

One of the mythologies of late modernity is that capitalism runs on formal controls to the exclusion of the informal. The fact is that at the very centre of capitalism what you have on Wall Street, in Tokyo, and in the City of London is a surprisingly communitarian culture of capital. This is illustrated in Burrough and Helyar's (1991) rich ethnography of the greatest takeover of them all—the battle for RJR Nabisco. The following passage shows, through the agency of Henry Kravis, the investment banker who won the takeover battle, the importance of ceremonies of reintegration in the Wall Street investment community:

Wall Street is a small place, and in the interests of harmony Kravis wasted no time healing wounds inflicted during the fight. He made peace with Peter Cohen at a summit in February and actually hired Tom Hill to investigate the possible takeover of Northwest Airlines. . . . Kravis also moved to smooth relations with Linda Robinson. Soon after the Gerstner episode, Linda took a message that Kravis had called. She ignored it. Within days she received a small ceramic doghouse with a cute note from Kravis, suggesting he was in the Robinsons' doghouse. Linda Robinson waited a few days, then sent Kravis a twenty-pound bag of dog food. All was forgiven. She and Kravis still own 'Trillion'.

Fees, of course, went infinitely further toward soothing Wall Street's wounds . . . Kravis even spread the largesse to those whose feelings he might have bruised. Geoff Boisi's Goldman Sachs got the job of auctioning Del Monte, while Felix Rohatyn's Lazard Freres did the same for the company's stake in ESPN. (Burrough and Helyar 1991: 508)

These may be vulgar modalities of reintegration; yet they are practical means of nurturing vulgar communities. A standard observation in the business culture litera-ture is that the City of London is much more communitarian than New York (e.g.

---

[5] Moreover, this concern to enjoy approval and avoid disapproval seems to prevent crime. In criminology we do not seem to have a major problem of scholars seeking rapid career advancement by fraudulently fabricating data, a problem at least one other discipline has in a very serious way (Braithwaite 1984: ch. 3).

13

Wechsberg 1966: 41; Coleman 1990: 109). Indeed, a large part of the theme of Michael Clarke's (1986) classic work on the City is that a shift to more formal regulatory control was needed there because Wall Street cowboys and dirty diggers did not quite understand that they were being allowed into a gentlemen's club 'where a word is as good as a contract'.

Admittedly, it is easier to cut oneself off from disapproval by some of these non-geographical communities of modernity (by simply withdrawing from them) than it is to cut oneself off from the disapproval of fellow villagers. But the reverse is also sometimes true. One cannot withdraw from the disapproval of one's international professional community by moving house; to do that one must learn a new career.

Modern communications interact with the division of labour to expand our interdependencies further. Business deals that decades ago were done by correspondence are today negotiated face to face; air travel means that business is transacted with an intimacy and exposure to interpersonal reproach that were once not possible.[6] Communications are also important to explaining how exotic interest-based communities that could not exist in the past are created in the modern city. If my consuming recreational interest is in breeding blue canaries, there is a chance in a large city with an efficient transport system that I will form interdependencies that will be very important to me within an association of canary breeders.

There are actually various sides to the effect on shame of this proliferation of roles. On the one hand, as Duerr (1988a: 10) points out, in pre-modern societies, because people were confronted with the *whole* person rather than (as today) *fragments* of the personality, the consequences of a blackened reputation could be total. It should be noted, however, that this point has maximum force with respect to the costs of stigmatization. It has less force concerning the power of reintegrative shaming, which means, by definition, that a person's whole self is accepted as good; it is just a part of their conduct which is disapproved as bad. For those of us who believe that stigmatization tends to be counterproductive, it is not a very telling point that the consequences of stigmatization are more terrible in the village than in the city. On the other hand, it is a telling point that stigmatization will be less likely in the village because the understanding villagers have of the complex totality of their neighbours renders them less susceptible to the stereotypical outcasting of deviants that is normal in the metropolis (Braithwaite 1989: 88). Finally, it strikes me as a rather open empirical question whether reintegrative shaming by a single group on which we depend for everything will be more or less powerful than reintegrative shaming by many groups on each of which we depend for some important subset of our needs.

Today's enormous proliferation of roles in fact makes us vulnerable to shame in a way that is peculiar to a world of such role proliferation. We all experience the minor embarrassment of coming into contact with others who know us in different roles—the former Sunday School teacher from whom we purchase condoms in a pharmacy, the appointment with a doctor married to a colleague at work, the inhibition we feel at enjoying an intimate meal with our spouse in a restaurant when some of our students are seated at the adjoining table. Goffman (1956) has explained how we minimize these minor embarrassments by strategies to match audience segregation to role segregation. The result is that 'those before whom he plays out one of his roles will not be the

---

[6] I am grateful to Mike Miller for this point.

SHAME AND MODERNITY

individuals before whom he plays out another, allowing him to be a different person in each role without discrediting the other' (Goffman 1956: 269).

However, Benson (1989) showed through his interviews with convicted white-collar criminals that one of the consequences of a criminal conviction is that audience segregation cannot be sustained. The worst side of the offender's business or professional self is exposed to people to whom he normally presents his churchgoing self, his golf-playing self, his fatherly self. Precisely because we make ourselves comfortable in a role-segregated world by partitioning audiences in a way that enables us to present radically different selves to those different audiences, our shame can be many-sided and more unmanageable in a role-segregated world. In the village society, there is limited segregation of audiences. Our neighbours will have seen most of the sides to our personality. When the worst of one side of that personality is exposed, it is not such a shock. The segmented self is therefore a double-edged sword. It affords us day-to-day protection from shame as we move around groups with different values; but it leaves us very vulnerable when an act of wrongdoing becomes so public as to become known to all these groups. The latter vulnerability has maximum force with the shaming of crime, because this is the most public institutionalization of shaming that we have.

To understand how shame can be either more or less powerful in a complex industrialized society, we must understand the implications of this role segregation. Shaming can be the more powerful, as we have seen, when we care about how our actions in one of our roles will be thought of by those who know us in other roles. But shaming will be less powerful when we immerse ourselves in one role, cutting ourselves off from caring about how we are viewed through the lenses of other role relationships. And there is an important standard way in which this cutting off occurs. It is stigmatization.

Assume I am a used car dealer and used car dealing is what matters to me more than anything else. If I am stigmatized as shady in my church, my club, and my extended family simply because I am a used car dealer, then I may cope with this by cutting myself off from those interdependencies. I may retreat into a stigmatized subculture of used car dealers. If I am a young black gang member who is stigmatized in all my other relationships as a gang member, I am likely to cut myself off from those relationships. In fact I may do more than cut myself off from caring about what my teachers and family think of me; out of resentment at the way they stigmatize me, I may seek to do exactly the opposite to that which they would approve. In short, stigmatization not only cuts away the heightened exposure to shame we have in a structurally differentiated world, it can create criminal subcultures where shame resides in *complying* with the law. I have argued the importance of stigmatization in fostering criminal subculture formation at greater length in *Crime, Shame and Reintegration*. Here I wish only to make the point that there is no structural inevitability about the impotence of shaming in an urbanized industrial society. Tokyo is testimony to that. And so are Japanese, Chinese, and Jewish communities within the most violent of American cities. Even in New York City the best protection that citizens get is not from the police but from loving families who dispense disapproval effectively. There is no inexorable historical march with modernization towards a society where shaming works less well. As a society becomes more role-differentiated, the potential for effective shaming increases in important ways, but so does the potential for stigmatization that cuts off effective shaming. In the industrial city, there is more potential than in the village for

15

subcultures isolated from and opposed to the cultural mainstream to be sustained. This, needless to say, is a source of good, vital, and creative things that come of urban life, as well as brutal, destructive, and exploitative things.

But a community that gives up on shaming cannot make the political choice to mobilize against the brutal and exploitative. It also relinquishes its capacity to restrain those who would trample the rights of citizens who wish to be deviant in ways that do no harm to others (Braithwaite forthcoming). In a community where there is no pride in respecting the rights of others, no shame in trampling on the rights of others, rights will afford protection only on those extremely rare occasions when rich people assert them in the courts. This, at least, is the contention of *Crime, Shame and Reintegration*.

Conclusion

Before the seventeenth century, before the time when an embryonic parliamentary democracy such as England could become a major power, the view across the globe was that despotism was the key to efficiency and economic might. 'Freedom was a luxury to be enjoyed by small communities like the Cantons of Switzerland and the Seven Provinces of Holland' (Trevelyan 1985: 72). In the twentieth century we suffer from a similar simple-minded view with regard to informal social control. Many politicians believe that informal control is a luxury only small communities can deploy to secure the dominion of their citizens. In large industrialized nations, there is no choice but to give up on communitarianism and sacrifice our freedom to a strong centralized system of formal social control.

The objective of this article has been no more than to dispute this pessimism about the role of community in contemporary mass societies. We actually know very little about the history of shame in the West, let alone elsewhere. However, we do know enough to reject the proposition of a unidirectional trend away from the efficacy of shame as societies modernize. And we know that some of the most important types of criminal offending are more shameful today than they were in earlier, even recent, historical periods. We rightly lament the contemporary shamelessness of corporate environmental criminals and of men who assault their wives. And we rightly identify these crimes as having deep structural and cultural roots in exploitive and patriarchal ideologies. But we know that business executives are more vulnerable to shame for environmental crimes today than they were just twenty-five years ago, before the rise of the environmental movement (McAllister 1991). And we know that, limited as the power of feminist shaming has been, the following description of the shamelessness of male violence in fifteenth-century England could not be regarded as an accurate description of the contemporary situation (see also Beattie 1984: 41–3): 'Wife-beating was a recognised right of man, and was practised without shame by high as well as low. Similarly, the daughter who refused to marry the gentleman of her parents' choice was liable to be locked up, beaten, and flung about the room, without any shock being inflicted upon public opinion' (Trevelyan 1985: 196). Whether beating of wives and daughters is more or less common today is hard to say. But we can say that such beatings attract more shame. A ducking-stool for the disciplining of nagging wives could not be installed in an English town in 1992. Because this would be shameful in the late twentieth century, brutal men discipline their wives secretly, away from the disapproving gaze of others.

16

SHAME 'AND MODERNITY

It is no simple matter to prescribe the political struggle for an urban republic in which public disapproval penetrates the private domains of those who do violence to other human beings, without also destroying privacy rights. But it would be a tragedy if we were dissuaded from such a struggle by the view that social disapproval was something we left behind on the farm.

REFERENCES

BEATTIE, J. M. (1984), 'Violence and Society in Early Modern England', in A. Doobar and E. Greenspan, eds., *Perspectives in Criminal Law*. Amora: Canada Law Book Co.

BENSON, M. L. (1989), 'Emotions and Adjudication: A Study of Status Degradation Among White-Collar Criminals', unpublished paper, Dept. of Sociology, University of Tennessee.

BRAITHWAITE, J. (1989), *Crime, Shame and Reintegration*. Melbourne: Oxford University Press.

—— (forthcoming), 'Inequality and Republican Criminology', in John Hagan and Ruth Petersen, eds., *Crime and Inequality*. Stanford: Stanford University Press.

BURROUGH, B., and HELYAR, J. (1991), *Barbarians at the Gate: The Fall of RJR Nabisco*. New York: Harper.

CHECKLAND, S. G., ed. (1974), *The Poor Law Report of 1834*. Harmondsworth: Penguin.

CLARKE, M. (1986), *Regulating the City: Competition, Scandal and Reform*. Milton Keynes: Open University Press.

COLEMAN, J. S. (1990), *Foundations of Social Theory*. Cambridge, Mass.: Harvard University Press.

DUERR, H. P. (1988*a*), *Nacktheit und Scham: Der Mythos Vom Zivilisationsprozess, Band 1*. Frankfurt: Suhrkamp.

—— (1988*b*), *Intimät: Der Mythos Vom Zivilisationsprozess, Band 2*. Frankfurt: Suhrkamp.

ELIAS, N. (1978), *The Civilizing Process: The History of Manners*, trans. Edmund Jephcott. Oxford: Blackwell.

—— (1982), *State. Formation and Civilization: The Civilizing Process*, trans. Edmund Jephcott. Oxford: Blackwell.

FORSYTHE, W. 1991. *Penal Discipline, Reformatory Projects and the English Prison Commission, 1895–1939*. Exeter: University of Exeter Press.

FOUCAULT. M. 1971. *Madness and Civilization*. New York: Mentor Books.

—— (1977), *Discipline and Punish: The Birth of the Prison*. London: Allen Lane.

GARLAND, D. 1985. *Punishment and Welfare*. Aldershot: Gower.

—— (1990), *Punishment and Modern Society*. Chicago: University of Chicago Press.

GOFFMAN, E. 1956. 'Embarrassment and Social Organization', *American Journal of Sociology*, 62: 264–71.

GRABOSKY, P., and BRAITHWAITE, J. (1986), *Of Manners Gentle: Enforcement Strategies of Australian Regulatory Agencies*. Melbourne: Oxford University Press.

GURR, E. R. 1980. 'Development and Decay: Their Impact on Public Order in Western History', in James A. Inciardi and Charles E. Faupel, eds., *History and Crime*. Beverly Hills: Sage.

—— (1984), 'Historical Trends in Violent Crime: A Critical Review of the Evidence', in M. Tonry and N. Morris, eds., *Crime and Justice*, vol. 3. Chicago: University of Chicago Press.

HAWKINS, K. (1984), *Environment and Enforcement: Regulation and the Social Definition of Pollution*. Oxford: Clarendon Press.

17

HAY, D. (1975), 'Property, Authority and the Criminal Law', in D. Hay, P. Linebaugh, J. G. Rule, E. P. Thompson, and C. Winslow, eds., *Albion's Fatal Tree*. London: Allen Lane.

HOWE, D. (1976), 'Victorian Culture in America', in D. Howe, ed., *Victorian America*. Philadelphia: University of Pennsylvania Press.

LYND, H. M. (1958), *On Shame and the Search for Identity*. London: Routledge and Kegan Paul.

MCALLISTER, I. (1991), *Community Attitudes to the Environment, Forests and Forest Management in Australia*. Canberra: Resources Assessment Commission.

RAMSAY, M. (1982). 'Two Centuries of Imprisonment', *Home Office Research Bulletin* 17: 39–41.

REDFIELD, R. (1947), 'The Folk Society', *American Journal of Sociology*, 52: 293–308.

SCHEFF, T. J. (1988), 'Shame and Conformity: The Deference-Emotion System', *American Sociological Review*, 53: 395–406.

—— (1990), *Microsociology: Discourse, Emotion and Social Structure*. Chicago: University of Chicago Press.

SPIERENBURG, P. (1984), *The Spectacle of Suffering*. Cambridge: Cambridge University Press.

STEARNS, C. Z., and STEARNS, P. N. (1986), *Anger: The Struggle for Emotional Control in America's History*. Chicago: University of Chicago Press.

STEDMAN, JONES, G. (1984), *Outcast London: A Study in the Relationships Between Classes in Victorian Society*. Harmondsworth: Penguin.

STONE, L. (1977), *The Family, Sex and Marriage in England, 1500–1800*. London: Weidenfeld and Nicolson.

THOMPSON, E. P. (1975), *Whigs and Hunters*. London: Allen Lane.

THOMPSON, F. M. L. (1988), *The Rise of Respectable Society: A Social History of Victorian Britain, 1830–1900*. Cambridge, Mass.: Harvard University Press.

TÖNNIES, F. (1887), *Community and Society*. New York: Harper and Row.

TREVELYAN, G. M. (1973), *English Social History: Chaucer to Queen Victoria*. London: Book Club Associates.

—— (1985), *A Shortened History of England*. Harmondsworth: Penguin.

VAN KRIEKEN, R. (1989), 'Violence, Self-Discipline and Modernity: Beyond the Civilizing Process', *The Sociological Review*, 37: 193–218.

WECHSBERG, J. (1966), *The Merchant Bankers*. Boston: Little, Brown.

WEISSER, M. R. (1979), *Crime and Punishment in Early Modern Europe*. Brighton: Harvester.

WILLETT, T. C. (1964), *Criminal on the Road: A Study of Serious Motoring Offences and Those Who Commit Them*. London: Tavistock.

WILSON, J. Q. and HERRNSTEIN, R. (1985), *Crime and Human Nature*. New York: Simon and Schuster.

18

[14]
Conditions of Successful Reintegration Ceremonies

Shifting criminal justice practices away from stigmatization and toward reintegration is no small challenge. The innovation of community conferences in New Zealand and Australia has two structural features that are conducive to reintegrative shaming: (a) selection of the people who respect and care most about the offender as conference participants (conducing to reintegration); and (b) confrontation with victims (conducing to shaming). Observation of some failures and successes of these conferences in reintegrating both offenders and victims is used to hypothesize 14 conditions of successful reintegration ceremonies.

The spectre of failure haunts modern criminology and penology. Deep down many feel what some say openly—that 'nothing works': that despite decades of study and debate, we are no nearer deterrence than we ever were and/or that more 'humane' forms of treatment are mere masquerades concealing a descent into Kafaesque bureaucracy where offenders suffer a slow and silent suffocation of the soul. Worse still, we fear that even when something does work, it is seen to do so only in the eyes of certain professionals, while 'outside' the system ordinary citizens are left without a role or voice in the criminal justice process.

This paper takes a different view. Rejecting the pessimism that pervades discussions about crime and punishment, it offers an optimistic view of at least one area—the punishment of juvenile offenders. It argues that it is possible to develop practices that 'work'—both in the sense of reducing recidivism and reintegrating offenders into a wider web of community ties and support and, at the same time, in giving victims a 'voice' in a fashion that is both satisfying and also socially productive. Further, it links a theory (reintegrative shaming) and a practice (the reintegration ceremony) which explain how to understand and how to implement this success.

While there are elements that are quite distinctive about both the theory and practice of reintegrative shaming, there is also a great deal in common with the theory and practice of 'making amends' (Wright 1982); restorative justice (Cragg 1992; Galaway and Hudson 1990; Zehr 1990); reconciliation (Dignan 1992; Marshall 1985; Umbreit 1985); peacemaking (Pepinsky and Quinney 1991); redress (de Haan 1990) and feminist abolitionism (Meima 1990). We differ from abolitionists, however, in believing that it is right to shame certain kinds of conduct as criminal in certain contexts.

The rest of the paper has two sections. The second section outlines some fieldwork

We would like to thank John McDonald, Gabrielle Maxwell, David Moore, Jane Mugford, Terry O'Connell, and Clifford Shearing for the stimulation and critique they provided in developing the ideas in this paper.

which we have undertaken to examine such ceremonies, makes a relatively brief series of arguments which connect the theory of reintegrative shaming to the seminal paper by Garfinkel on degradation ceremonies and outlines how the latter must be transformed to cover reintegration ceremonies. The major point of this section is a specification of the conditions for successful reintegration ceremonies. The third and longer section follows the logic of such ceremonies, illustrating each point with material derived from the fieldwork and offering comments about policy and implementation.

Background to the Argument: Reintegrative Shaming in Theory and Practice

The theory of reintegrative shaming (Braithwaite 1989, 1993) has been offered as a way of achieving two major aims. First, to recast criminological findings in a more coherent and productive fashion. Secondly, to offer a practical basis for a principled reform of criminal justice practices. Central to the endeavour is an understanding of the relationship between crime and social control which argues for the shaming of criminal *acts* and the subsequent reintegration of deviant *actors* once suitable redress and apology have been made. It is argued that societies that have low rates of common types of crime (such as Japan) rely more upon this type of social control, working hard at reforming the deviant through reconstructing his or her social ties. Conversely, high crime societies (such as the US) rely upon stigmatization, thus doing little to prevent cycles of re-offending.

This theory has clear practical implications and people involved in various reform programmes have drawn on it in various ways—sometimes as an inspiration for reform blueprints (see e.g., Howard and Purches 1992; Mugford and Mugford 1991, 1992; O'Connell and Moore 1992), often as a way to articulate what they are trying to achieve and give it a sharper focus. Some, such as the New Zealand Maoris, have comprehended and applied the principles of the theory for hundreds of years (Hazlehurst 1985). Where we have heard of or been involved in programmes, we have sought to carry out some limited fieldwork which would help us to understand both what is practically possible and how we might refine our ideas.

This paper utilizes such ongoing fieldwork, specifically observations of community conferences for 23 juvenile offenders in Auckland, New Zealand, and Wagga Wagga, Australia. In New Zealand, these conferences are called family group conferences. While there are differences between the approaches adopted in the two cities, both involve diverting young offenders from court and keeping them out of exclusionary juvenile institutions. Both programmes subscribe to the philosophy of reintegrative shaming as outlined above. Shame and shaming is commonly used in both programmes to describe what is going on; reintegration is commonly used in Wagga, while healing is more commonly used in Auckland for this aspect of the process. The approach in both cities involves assembling in a room the offender and supporters of the offender (usually the nuclear family, often aunts, uncles, grandparents, sometimes neighbours, counsellors, even a teacher or football coach) along with the victim of the crime (and supporters of the victim, usually from their nuclear family) under the supervision of a co-ordinator—a police sergeant in Wagga, a youth justice co-ordinator from the Department of Social Welfare in Auckland. Auckland conferences usually only have single offenders, but can have multiple victims in the room. Wagga conferences often bring together multiple offenders who were involved jointly in the same offences with

CONDITIONS OF SUCCESSFUL REINTEGRATION CEREMONIES

multiple victims. In the conferences we observed, the number of people in the room ranged from five to 30. More systematic data from New Zealand puts the average attendance at nine (Maxwell and Morris 1993: 74). At both sites, the offender(s) plays an important role in describing the nature of the offence(s). The psychological, social, and economic consequences of the offence—for victims, offenders, and others—are elicited in discussions guided by the co-ordinator. Disapproval, often emotional disapproval, is usually communicated by victims, and often by victim supporters and family members of the offender. At the same time, the professional who co-ordinates the conference strives to bring out support for and forgiveness towards the offender from participants in the conference.

A striking common feature of both locations is that the formal properties of the cautioning conference have come to take on a ceremonial or ritual character, based partly upon 'common sense', itself expanded and tempered by experiences of what does and does not seem to work well. With varying degrees of accomplishment, co-ordinators have developed procedures designed to ensure that the potential for shaming and reintegration of offenders is realized in practice. In so doing, they have effectively invented the reintegration ceremony, even if that is not what they would always call it. In this ceremony, identities are in a social crucible. The vision that an offender holds of himself as a 'tough guy' or that victims have of him as a 'mindless hooligan' are challenged, altered, and recreated (for example, as a 'good lad who has strayed into bad ways').

Viewing these events as a reintegration ceremony recalls the seminal contribution of Harold Garfinkel (1956) on 'Conditions of Successful Degradation Ceremonies'. Perhaps the same kind of social structures and socio-psychological processes he analyses in that paper are at work here, but in different combination and directed to different ends? Posing the problem that way has been a productive way for us to organize our views of reintegration ceremonies and so we choose to use the Garfinkel approach as a way of outlining this rather different set of events.

By degradation ceremonies, Garfinkel meant communicative work that names an actor as an 'outsider', that transforms an individual's total identity into an identity 'lower in the group's scheme of social types' (1956: 420). Most criminal trials are good examples of status degradation ceremonies and this view of them became a central idea in the sociology of deviance, especially among labelling theorists (see Becker 1963; Schur 1973). For Erikson (1962: 311), for example, this communicative work constitutes 'a sharp rite of transition at once moving him out of his normal position in society and transferring him into a distinctive deviant role'. Moreover, Erikson continues, an '. . . important feature of these ceremonies in our culture is that they are almost irreversible' (1962: 311).

Such a view, however, is simplistic, exaggerated, and overly deterministic (Braithwaite 1989). Most people who go into mental hospitals come out of them; many alcoholics give up drinking; most marijuana users stop being users at some point in their lives, usually permanently; most kids labelled as delinquents never go to jail as adults. Labelling theorists did useful empirical work, but their work was myopic, exclusively focused on 'front-end' processes that certify deviance. Above all, they envisaged individuals as having 'total identities'. We suggest that by employing instead the notion of multiple identities one can recast the interest in transformation ceremonies, asking questions as much about ceremonies to decertify deviance as to certify it.

While degradation ceremonies are about the sequence disapproval–degradation–exclusion, reintegration ceremonies are about the sequence disapproval–non-degradation–inclusion. In a reintegration ceremony, disapproval of a bad act is communicated while sustaining the identity of the actor as good. Shame is transmitted within a continuum of respect for the wrongdoer. Repair work is directed at ensuring that a deviant identity (one of the actor's multiple identities) does not become a master status trait that overwhelms other identities. Communicative work is directed at sustaining identities like daughter, student, promising footballer, in preference to creating 'master' identities like delinquent.

Considerable analytic and policy implications follow this refocusing from degradation to reintegration. Indeed, we suggest that the implication is a redesign of everything about contemporary criminal justice systems and everything about the labelling theory critique of those institutions. To achieve this, however, it is necessary to show where one must transcend earlier accounts. As a first step, we juxtapose in Table 1 Garfinkel's conditions of successful degradation ceremonies with our own conditions of successful ceremonies of reintegration. These latter were condensed from our observations and cast in a form that allows comparison and contrast. Eight of the conditions we specify for reintegration ceremonies involve presenting a deliberate twist on Garfinkel's conditions. The other six are based on observations and discussions and, we feel, address some of the theoretical neglects of the ethnomethodological tradition.

Reintegration Ceremonies in Practice

In this section, we outline each of the 14 conditions identified in Table 1. For each one, we provide a detailed discussion, drawing on our field work observations.

(1) The event, but not the perpetrator, is removed from the realm of its everyday character and is defined as irresponsible, wrong, a crime

Courtroom ceremonies tend to degradation rather than reintegration—that is, they remove both event *and* perpetrator from the everyday domain in just the way suggested by Garfinkel. This is because the production-line technocracy and discourse of legalism makes it easy for the offender to sustain psychological barriers against shame for acts that the court defines as wrongful. It is hard for a person who we do not know or respect, who speaks a strange legal language, who forces us into a relationship of feigned respect by making us stand when she walks into the room, to touch our soul. Thus event and perpetrator remain united. One casts out both or neither. So the denunciation of the judge may degrade the offender, but the process is so incomprehensible, such a blur, that all the judge usually accomplishes is some authoritative outcasting.

In contrast to formal courtrooms, community conferences in New Zealand and Wagga are held in less formal spaces. Conference co-ordinators purposively assemble actors with the best chance of persuading the offender of the irresponsibility of a criminal act. Close kin are prime candidates for commanding the respect that enables such persuasion, but with homeless or abused children the challenge is to discover who

CONDITIONS OF SUCCESSFUL REINTEGRATION CEREMONIES

TABLE 1

Conditions of successful degradation ceremonies	Conditions of successful reintegration ceremonies
1. Both event and perpetrator must be removed from the realm of their everyday character and be made to stand as 'out of the ordinary'.	1. The event, *but not the perpetrator*, is removed from the realm of its everyday character and is defined as irresponsible, wrong, a crime.
2. Both event and perpetrator must be placed within a scheme of preferences that shows the following properties:	2. Event and perpetrator must be uncoupled rather than defined as instances of a profane uniformity. The self of the perpetrator is sustained as sacred rather than profane. This is accomplished by comprehending: (a) how essentially good people have a pluralistic self that accounts for their occasional lapse into profane acts; and (b) that the profane act of a perpetrator occurs in a social context for which many actors may bear some shared responsibility. Collective as well as individual shame must be brought into the open and confronted.
(a) The preferences must not be for event A over event B, but for event of *type* A over event of *type* B. The same typing must be accomplished for the perpetrator. Event and perpetrator must be defined as instances of a uniformity and must be treated as a uniformity throughout the work of the denunciation.	
(b) The witnesses must appreciate the characteristics of the typed person and event by referring the type to a dialectical counterpart. Ideally, the witnesses should not be able to contemplate the features of the denounced person without reference to the counter-conception, as the profanity of an occurrence or a desire or a character trait, for example, is clarified by the references it bears to its opposite, the sacred.	
3. The denouncer must so identify himself to the witnesses that during the denunciation they regard him not as a private but as a publicly known person.	3. Co-ordinators must identify themselves with all private parties—perpetrators, their families, victims, witnesses—as well as being identified with the public interest in upholding the law.
4. The denouncer must make the dignity of the supra-personal values of the tribe salient and accessible to view, and his denunciation must be delivered in their name.	4. Denunciation must be both by and in the name of victims and in the name of supra-personal values enshrined in the law.
5. The denouncer must arrange to be invested with the right to speak in the name of these ultimate values. The success of the denunciation will be undermined if, for his authority to denounce, the denouncer invokes the personal interests that he may have acquired by virtue of the wrong done to him or someone else.	5. Non-authoritative actors (victims, offenders, offenders' families) must be empowered with process control. The power of actors normally authorized to issue denunciations on behalf of the public interest (e.g., judges) must be decentred.
6. The denouncer must get himself so defined by the witnesses that they locate him as a supporter of these values.	6. The perpetrator must be so defined by all the participants (particularly by the perpetrator himself) that he is located as a supporter of both the supra-personal values enshrined in the law and the private interests of victims.
7. Not only must the denouncer fix his distance from the person being denounced, but the witnesses must be made to experience their distance from him also.	7. Distance between each participant and the other participants must be closed; empathy among all participants must be enhanced; opportunities must be provided for perpetrators and victims to show (unexpected) generosity toward each other.
8. Finally, the denounced person must be ritually separated from a place in the legitimate order, i.e., he must be defined as standing at a place opposed to it. He must be placed 'outside', he must be made 'strange'.	8. The separation of the denounced person must be terminated by rituals of inclusion that place him, even physically, inside rather than outside.
	9. The separation of the victim, any fear or shame of victims, must be terminated by rituals of reintegration.
	10. Means must be supplied to intervene against power imbalances that inhibit either shaming or reintegration, or both.
	11. Ceremony design must be flexible and culturally plural, so that participants exercise their process control constrained by only very broad procedural requirements.
	12. Reintegration agreements must be followed through to ensure that they are enacted.
	13. When a single reintegration ceremony fails, ceremony after ceremony must be scheduled, never giving up, until success is achieved.
	14. The ceremony must be justified by a politically resonant discourse.

the child does respect.[1] Perhaps there is an uncle who he feels sticks up for him, a football coach he admires, a grandmother he adores. The uncle, the football coach, and the grandmother must then be urged to attend. Normally, they are flattered to be told that they have been nominated as one of the few human beings this young person still respects. So they come. They come when the appeal to them is 'to support and help the young person to take responsibility for what they have done'. Thus the setting and the ceremonial character seek to 'hold' the offender while allowing separation from the offence.

Victims play a crucial role in this, for they are in a unique position to communicate the irresponsibility of the *act*. Much delinquency is casual and thoughtless (O'Connor and Sweetapple 1988: 117–18). The offenders who thought all they had done was to take 50 dollars from the house of a faceless person find that person is a vulnerable elderly woman who did without something significant because of the loss of the money. They learn that as a result of the break-in she now feels insecure in her own home, as does her next door neighbour. Both have invested in new security locks and are afraid to go out in the street alone because they have come to view the neighbourhood as a dangerous place. Collateral damage from victimization is normal rather than exceptional and co-ordinators become expert at drawing it out of victims and victim supporters. Techniques of neutralization (Sykes and Matza 1957) that may originally have been employed, such as '. . . I am unemployed and poor while the householder is employed and rich' are seriously challenged when confronted by the elderly victim. Sometimes this shocks the offender. Other times it does not. Many of the worst offenders have developed a capacity to cut themselves off from the shame for exploiting other human beings. They deploy a variety of barriers against feeling responsibility. But what does not affect the offender directly may affect those who have come to support her. The shaft of shame fired by the victim in the direction of the offender might go right over the offender's head, yet it might pierce like a spear through the heart of the offender's mother, sitting behind him. It is very common for offenders' mothers to start to sob when victims describe their suffering or loss. So while display of the victim's suffering may fail to hit its intended mark, the anguish of the offender's mother during the ceremony may succeed in bringing home to the offender the need to confront rather than deny an act of irresponsibility.

Indeed, in our observations mothers often seize the ceremony of the occasion to make eloquent and moving speeches that they have long wanted to make to their child:

I imagine life as a family living in a valley and the children gradually start to venture out from the family house in the valley. Eventually they have to climb up the mountain to get out of the valley. That mountain is adolescence. At the top of the mountain is a job. When they have that they can walk gently down the other side of the mountain into life. But there's another way they can go. They can decide not to climb the path up the mountain but to wander in the easier paths out into the valley. But those paths, while they are easier, lead to greater and greater

---

[1] A common cynicism when we have spoken to American audiences about these ideas has been that it sounds like a good idea for sweet, sheep-loving New Zealanders, with their intact families, but that it could never work in the face of the family disintegration of American slums. This is an odd perspective, given the empirical reality in New Zealand that Youth Aid Officers saw 'poor family support/background' as the most important factor *in favour of* opting for referral of a case to a family group conference rather than some other disposition (Maxwell and Morris 1993: 60–1). Moreover, in practice, 14 per cent of young people processed in family group conferences do not live with their families, compared to 4 per cent of those processed by informal police diversion (Maxwell and Morris 1993: 64, 66).

CONDITIONS OF SUCCESSFUL REINTEGRATION CEREMONIES

darkness. I'm concerned that my little boy took one of those paths and I'm losing him into the darkness.

Co-ordinators work at bringing out collateral damage. Parents are asked: 'How did this episode affect the family?' Offenders are asked: 'How did mum and dad feel about it?' Typically, the offender will admit that their kin were 'pretty upset'. In Wagga, the co-ordinator then routinely asks why and in a large proportion of cases, young people will say something to the effect that the parents care about them or love them. This is the main chance the reintegrative co-ordinator is looking for. Once this is uttered, the co-ordinator returns to this again and again as a theme of what is being learnt from the conference. In the wrap-up, he will reaffirm that 'Jim has learned that his mum and dad care a lot, that his Uncle Bob wants to help . . .' This is not to deny that this strategy of reintegration can be mismanaged:

Co-ordinator: 'James, why are your parents upset?'
James: [Silence]
Co-ordinator: 'Do you think it's because they care about you?'
James: 'Don't know.'

Another way this path to reintegration can be derailed is when the parents indulge in outcasting attacks on their child. Co-ordinators sometimes manage this problem by intervening to divert stigmatization before it gets into full swing:

Mother: 'He used to be a good boy until then.'
Co-ordinator interrupts: 'And he still is a good boy. No one here thinks we're dealing with a bad kid. He's a good kid who made a mistake and I hope he knows now that that's what we all think of him.'

Even when serious stigmatic attacks are launched, the communal character of the encounter creates the possibility of reintegrative amelioration. The worst stigmatic attack we observed arose when the mother of a 14-year-old girl arrived at the conference. She told the co-ordinator that she was unhappy to be here. Then when she saw her daughter, who preceded her to the conference, she said: 'I'll kill you, you little bitch.' A few minutes into the conference, the mother jumped up from her seat, shouting: 'This is a load of rubbish.' Then pointing angrily at her shaking daughter, she said: 'She should be punished.' Then she stormed out. These events might have created a degradation sub-ceremony of great magnitude. Instead, the other participants in the room were transformed by it and developed a quite different direction. Victim supporters who had arrived at the conference very angry at the offender were now sorry for her and wanted to help. They learnt she was a street kid and their anger turned against a mother who could abandon her daughter like this. This dramatic example highlights two common processes seen in the conferences—the alteration of perspectives and the generation of social support. We believe these processes occur for two reasons:

1. the more serious the delinquency of the young offender, the more likely it is to come out that she has had to endure some rather terrible life circumstances. Rather than rely on stereotypes they see the offender as a whole person (a point we return to later); *and*

2. participants at the conference have been invited on the basis of their capacity to be supportive to either the offender or the victim. Being supportive people placed in a social context where supportive behaviour is expected and socially approved, they often react to stigmatic attacks with gestures of reintegration.

Even as they use stigmatic terms, ordinary citizens understand the concept of communicating contempt for the deed simultaneously with respect for the young person. An adult member of the Maori community caused tears to trickle down the cheeks of a huge, tough 15-year-old with the following speech:

Stealing cars. You've got no brains, boy . . . But I've got respect for you. I've got a soft spot for you. I've been to see you play football. I went because I care about you. You're a brilliant footballer, boy. That shows you have the ability to knuckle down and apply yourself to something more sensible than stealing cars . . . We're not giving up on you.

(2) Event and perpetrator must be uncoupled rather than defined as instances of a profane uniformity. The self of the perpetrator is sustained as sacred rather than profane. This is accomplished by comprehending: (a) how essentially good people have a pluralistic self that accounts for their occasional lapse into profane acts; and (b) that the profane act of a perpetrator occurs in a social context for which many actors may bear some shared responsibility. Collective as well as individual shame must be brought out into the open and confronted

In speaking of degradation ceremonies, Garfinkel (1956: 422) says: 'Any sense of accident, coincidence, indeterminism, chance or momentary occurrence must not merely be minimised. Ideally, such measures should be inconceivable; at least they should be made false.' There must be no escape, no loophole. Rather, degradation insists upon fitting an identity of total deviant with a single, coherent set of motives into a black and white scheme of things. In contrast, a condition of successful reintegration ceremonies is that they leave open multiple interpretations of responsibility while refusing to allow the offender to deny personal responsibility entirely. In degradation ceremonies, the suppression of a range of motives and the insistence upon one account of responsibility allow the criminal to maintain (at least in her own eyes) an identity for herself as 'criminal as victim', to dwell on the irresponsibility of others or of circumstances. When the crime is constructed as the bad act of a good person, uncoupling event and perpetrator, a well-rounded discussion of the multiple account-abilities for the crime does not threaten the ceremony as an exercise in community disapproval. The strategy is to focus on problem rather than person, and on the group finding solutions to the problem. The family, particularly in the New Zealand model, is held accountable for coming up with a plan of action, which is then ratified by the whole group. The collective shame and collective responsibility of the family need not detract from individual responsibility for the crime nor from community respons-ibilities, such as to provide rewarding employment and schooling for young people. Yet the collective assumption of responsibility moves the ceremony beyond a permanent preoccupation with the responsibility of the individual that might stall at the point of stigmatization and the adoption of a delinquent identity. The practical task of designing a plan of action is a way of putting the shame behind the offender, of moving from a shaming phase to a reintegration phase. Agreement on the action plan can be an

146

CONDITIONS OF SUCCESSFUL REINTEGRATION CEREMONIES

even more ceremonial decertification of the deviance of the offender through institutionalizing a signing ceremony where offender, family, and police put their signatures side by side on the agreement. In signing such an agreement, the responsible, reintegrated self of the offender distances itself from the shamed behaviour. The sacredness of the self is sustained through its own attack upon and transcendence of the profane act. Similarly, the collectivity of the family acknowledges its shame and takes collective responsibility for problem solving in a way that transcends its collective shame.

(3) Co-ordinators must identify themselves with all private parties—perpetrators, their families, victims, witnesses—as well as being identified with the public interest in upholding the law

Garfinkel's third condition of successful degradation ceremonies is that the denouncer must claim more than a private role but must communicate degradation in the name of an [imaginary, unified, and static] public. This condition is explicitly incorporated into Western criminal law, wherein the police and the judge in a criminal trial are legally defined as fiduciaries of public rather than private interests. In community conferences, this totalizing fiction is put aside. Co-ordinators have responsibilities to, and identify with, a plurality of interests. Reintegration and consensus on an agreement is quite unlikely unless the co-ordinator identifies with and respects all the interests in the room. Outside interests will put the agreement at risk unless the co-ordinator also speaks up on behalf of any public interest beyond the set of private interests assembled for the conference. This sounds demanding, perhaps even impossible. How can so many interests be juggled and a workable outcome reached? Our answer is simple—in practice consensus is reached more than 90 per cent of the time at both research sites and in most of these cases the consensus is implemented (Maxwell and Morris 1993: 121).[2]

(4) Denunciation must be both by and in the name of victims and in the name of supra-personal values enshrined in the law

For Garfinkel, degradation ceremonies are enacted in the name of the supra-personal values of the tribe. We have seen that successful reintegration requires confronting the private hurts and losses from the crime as well. A key condition for the success of reintegration ceremonies is to get the victim to turn up. Where victims are institutions (like schools), this means getting victim representatives to turn up (e.g., the principal, elected student representatives). Blagg (1986) has discussed the greater problems of making reparation meaningful with impersonal victims. Victim or victim representative attendance has been nearly universally achieved in Wagga, but in New Zealand the success rate has been under 50 per cent (Maxwell and Morris 1993: 79), though there is reason to suspect that the latter disappointing statistic has been improving in more recent times in New Zealand.[3] Some will be surprised at the near-universal

---

[2] See, however, the discussion of professionally manipulated consensus under point (5) and in the conclusion to this article.

[3] The main reason for non-attendance for victims in New Zealand was simply their not being invited, followed by being invited at a time unsuitable to them (Maxwell and Morris 1993: 79), a result of poor understanding of the philosophy of the reform by conference co-ordinators, heavy workload, and practical difficulties, such as the police failing to pass on the victim's address. Only 6 per cent of victims said they did not want to meet the offender (Morris *et al.*, in press).

success in Wagga and the recent higher success in New Zealand in getting victims along to conferences. But when the co-ordinator issues a combined appeal to private interest, public virtue (playing your part in getting this young person back on track) and citizen empowerment, the appeal is rather persuasive. In the words of Senior Sergeant Terry O'Connell—the key actor in adopting and developing the programme at Wagga—the key is to 'make the victim feel important and they will come'. And important they are: in New Zealand victims can effectively veto any agreement reached at the conference, but only if they actually attend and listen to the arguments. Even in conventional dyadic victim–offender reconciliation programmes in a non-communitarian society such as the United States, victim interest in participation is quite high (Weitekamp 1989: 82; Galaway 1985: 626; Galaway and Hudson 1975: 359; Novack *et al.* 1980; Galaway *et al.* 1980). Some of this may be sheer curiosity to meet the person who 'did it'.

When the victim and victim supporters turn up, of course, there remains the possibility that private hurts and losses will not be fully communicated to the offender. Sometimes the victim says that they suffered no real loss. For example, at one conference we attended, the victim said that the car stolen for a joy ride was found as soon as he noticed it to be missing and he could detect no damage. Here the co-ordinator must reiterate the public interest in being able to assume that one can park a car somewhere without constant worry that it might be stolen. Pointing out that '. . . it was a lucky thing for you and Mr X [the victim] on this occasion' reinforces responsibility in the absence of specific private harm. Furthermore, in stressing the public as well as the private view of a crime, if the absence of private harm means that there is no direct compensation to be paid or worked for, conferences will usually agree to some community service work for the offender. Often there will be both private compensation and community work, signifying both the private and the public harm. The gesture of restoration to both community and victim, even if it is modest in comparison to the enormity of the crime, enables the offender to seize back pride and reassume a law-respecting, other-respecting, and self-respecting identity.

(5) Non-authoritative actors (victims, offenders, offenders' families) must be empowered with process control. The power of actors normally authorized to issue denunciations on behalf of the public interest (e.g., judges) must be decentred

Degradation ceremonies for Garfinkel are about privileging authoritative actors with the right to denounce the profane on behalf of the tribe. Judges, for example, silence the denunciations of victims or pleas for mercy from relatives. Their role in the courtroom is simply as evidentiary fodder for the legal digestive system. They must stick to the facts and suppress their opinions. Consequently, they often emerge from the experience deeply dissatisfied with their day in court. For victims and their supporters, this often means they scream ineffectively for more blood. But it makes no difference when the system responds to such people by giving them more and more blood, because the blood-lust is not the source of the problem; it is an unfocused cry from disempowered citizens who have been denied a voice.

Reintegration ceremonies have a [dimly recognized] political value because, when well managed, they deliver victim satisfaction that the courts can never deliver. In

CONDITIONS OF SUCCESSFUL REINTEGRATION CEREMONIES

Wagga, a standard question to the victims is: 'What do you want out of this meeting here today?' The responses are in sharp contrast to the cries for 'more punishment' heard on the steps of more conventional courts. Offered empowerment in the way we have suggested, victims commonly say that they do not want the offender punished; they do not want vengeance; they want the young offender to learn from his mistake and get his life back in order. Very often they say they want compensation for their loss. Even here, however, it is suprising how often victims waive just claims for compensation out of consideration for the need for an indigent teenager to be unencumbered in making a fresh start.

Clifford Shearing attended two of the Wagga conferences with us. Struck by the readiness of victims not to insist on compensation claims but to press instead for signs of remorse and willingness to reform, Shearing said, '. . . they all wanted to win the battle for his [the offender's] soul[4] rather than his money'.

How can we make sense of outcomes that are so at odds with preconceptions of vengeful victims? In fact, even in traditional stigmatic punishment systems, victims are not as vengeful as popular preconceptions suggest (Weitekamp 1989: 83–4; Heinze and Kerstetter 1981; Shapland, Willmore, and Duff 1985; Kigin and Novack 1980; Youth Justice Coalition 1990: 52–4). Citizens seem extremely punitive and supportive of degradation ceremonies when asked their views in public opinion surveys. Distance, a stereotyped offender, and a simplification of evil conduce to public support for degradation ceremonies. But the closer people get to the complexities of particular cases, the less punitive they get (Ashworth 1986: 118; Doob and Roberts 1983, 1988). As we noted earlier, the reality of the meeting between victim, offender, and others tends to undermine stereotyping. Instead, immediacy, a particular known offender and a complex grasp of all the situational pressures at work conduce to public support for reintegration.

Some reconciliations at family group conferences are quite remarkable. The most extraordinary case we know of involved a young man guilty of aggravated assault with a firearm on a woman who ran a lotto shop. The offender locked the woman at gunpoint in the back of her shop while he robbed her of over $1,000. When the time for the conference came, she was mad, after blood. Yet after considerable discussion, part of the plan of action, fully agreed to by the victim, involved the victim housing the offender while he did some community work for her family! This is not an isolated case, although it involves the most dramatic shift of which we became aware. Occasionally, victims make job offers to unemployed offenders at conferences.

Unresolved fury and victim dissatisfaction is, of course, the stuff of unsuccessful reintegration ceremonies. An important recent New Zealand evaluation shows that failure as a result of such dissatisfaction remains (Maxwell and Morris 1993: 119). In fact over a third of victims who attended conferences said they felt worse after the conference, a result of insufficient attention to victim reintegration (see point (9) below).

It is not only victims who can benefit from the empowerment that arises from having cases dealt with in this non-traditional setting. Offenders and offenders' families are also very much empowered when community conferences work well. Maxwell and Morris (1993: 110) found that New Zealand conferences work better at empowering

---

[4] An allusion to Rose (1990) and his discussion of 'governing the soul'.

parents than offenders.[5] This is probably true in Wagga as well, though the Wagga approach rejects the Auckland tendency to give the arresting police officer the first opportunity to explain the incident of concern. Instead, the young person, rather than police or parents, are always given the first opportunity to describe in their own words what has brought them to the conference. We see this Wagga practice of temporally privileging the accounts of the young persons as a desirable way of seeking to empower them in the dialogue. For all parties, success is predicated upon a significant degree of agency. On the other hand, when agency is denied the ceremonies fail. Then there is the pretence of empowerment, with families and offenders being manipulated into agreements that are developed by the police or youth justice co-ordinators, an outcome that is not uncommon (Maxwell and Morris 1993: 112). There can be little real experience of shame when apology and remedial measures are forced on the offender and his family rather than initiated by them. Empowerment is crucial to reintegration, while manipulation makes instead for degradation.

(6) The perpetrator must be so defined by all the participants (particularly by the perpetrator himself) that he is located as a supporter of both the supra-personal values enshrined in the law and the private interests of victims

This condition of successful reintegration is accomplished by having the offender's responsible self disassociate itself from the irresponsible self. Apology is the standard device for accomplishing this, as Goffman pointed out:

An apology is a gesture through which an individual splits himself into two parts, the part that is guilty of an offence and the part that disassociates itself from the delict and affirms a belief in the offended rule (1971: 113).

At all the conferences we attended, the offenders offered an apology.[6] Often they agreed to follow up with a letter of apology or a visit to apologize again to the victim and other members of the family. Often there was also apology to parents, teachers, even the police. A common feature of successful reintegration ceremonies can be a rallying of the support of loved ones behind the disassociation of self created by a genuine apology. After one moving and tearful statement by a Maori offender in Auckland, for example, elders offered congratulatory speeches on the fine apology he had given to his parents.

The verbal apology can be accompanied by physical acts. The most common physical accompaniment to apology is the handshake. Female victims sometimes hug young offenders, an especially moving gesture when it reaches across a racial divide. In Maori conferences,[7] kissing on the cheek, nose pressing and hugging occur among

---

[5] This is not to downplay the wonderful successes with offender empowerment that can and do occur within the New Zealand process: 'I felt safe because my whanau [extended family] were there with me. I would have felt like stink if I had to face it on my own. My auntie explained it so I understood. It was good that she allowed me to take a role' (young person quoted in Maxwell and Morris 1993: 78).

[6] In this regard, we were somewhat surprised by Maxwell and Morris's (1993: 93) finding that an apology was formally recorded as offered in only 70 per cent of their sample of conferences. We wondered if all of the more informal means of apology (including backstage apology) were counted in this result.

[7] With Samoan conferences, it is common for offenders to apologize on their knees, a degrading form of apology in Western eyes, but perhaps not so when the cultural context is to elevate the offender quickly, embracing his restored identity. That is, for the Samoan, the kneeling may represent part of a reintegrative sequence rather than signifying degradation.

various of the participants (even visiting sociologists!). Ritual bodily contact is not the only form of physical act to accompany apology. Other common acts include the handing over of compensation or the offer of a beverage. In a recreation of the theme that commensalism celebrates solidarity, successful ceremonies have ended with victim and offender families arranging to have dinner together after the conference.

Despite the manifestly successful effect of apology, it is not something encouraged by court rooms. Criminal trials tend to leave criminal identities untouched by attacks from responsible, law-abiding, or caring identities. Indeed, degradation tends to harden them. It is not a major challenge in identity management for a tough guy to sustain this identity during a criminal trial. The challenge is more difficult in an open dialogue among the different parties assembled for a community conference. Usually, there are some things that the police know about the offender's conduct that his parents do not know and there are vulnerabilities the parents know that the police do not. The traditional criminal process enables the offender to sustain different kinds of stories and even different identities with parents and police. Conferences can expose these multiple selves to the partitioned audiences for which these selves are differentially displayed. Out of one conference, Wagga parents learned that their teenage son had punched a 14-year-old girl in the face; then the police learned that the boy had beaten his mother before, once with a broom; then everyone learned that he had also hit other girls. There are some lies that the offender can live in the eyes of the police; others in the eyes of his parents; but many of them cannot stand in the face of a dialogue among all three that also enjoins victims.

All this is not to deny that apology, even the sincerest apology, can be secured without challenging a delinquent identity that remains dominant over a law-abiding identity. In one case, a 14-year-old girl acknowledged that the effect of stealing a cheque from the mail-box of an elderly woman had been 'awful' for the victim and she apologized with feeling. But when it came to the action plan, she was intransigently against the idea of returning to school: 'No. I don't like school.' Even a modest proposition from the group for community service work of 20 hours over four weeks was bitterly resisted: 'It's too much time. I want to be a normal street kid and if you're a street kid you need time to be on the street. That would take up too much of my time.' Nothing was going to interrupt her career path as a street kid! This is a familiar theme in literature on identity maintenance from writers associated with labelling and similar perspectives. There comes a point where a change which seems both possible and advantageous in the immediate context is resisted because of the degree of commitment to a path and the consequent 'side bets' (Becker 1960) that an individual has made in following that path.

Interestingly, however, our empirical observations match the general case we made earlier: namely, that while such commitment to deviance is possible, it is also rare. The norm is strongly towards the reversibility rather than irreversibility of the deviant identity and, as in the case just described, in contrast to the labelling claim, irreversibility seems more connected to the individual commitment to an identity (agency) than to structural features that prevent reversion. No doubt, the matter of commitment is not exhausted by these brief comments. We might suppose that as adults get older, deviant identities might become more encrusted and harder to change (and hence shaming and reintegration less relevant). For some people such a process probably occurs. But as data on the relationship between age and deviance shows

(Hirschi and Gottfredson 1983; Youth Justice Coalition 1990: 22–3) reversion from deviant to mainstream identities is the norm with progressing age. Thus the idea that shaming and reintegration ceremonies are valuable only for the young is not well founded. Indeed, preliminary qualitative evidence indicates that it may be extremely valuable for individuals well into middle age.[8]

(7) Distance between each participant and the other participants must be closed; empathy among all participants must be enhanced; opportunities must be provided for perpetrators and victims to show (unexpected) generosity toward each other

At the start of conferences, victims and offenders, victim supporters, and offender supporters tend to work hard at avoiding eye contact. By contrast, at the end of a successful reintegration ceremony, participants are looking each other in the eye. Reintegration ceremonies succeed when one side makes an early gesture of self-blame or self-deprecation. In one case, an offender wrote a long letter of apology to the victim before the conference was convened. At another conference, a mix-up by the police resulted in the victim being advised of the wrong date for the conference. Despite this, she came within 15 minutes of a 'phone call at 6 p.m. in the middle of preparing for dinner guests'. The conference co-ordinator said that she agreed to drop everything to come 'if it would help the boys'. 'What do you think of that?' said the co-ordinator. 'She's a nice lady', said one of the offenders. 'And I bet you were frightened to go out from your own house after this', added the mother of another offender.

In many cases, the offender's family does not wait for their offspring to come under attack from the victim. They pre-emptively launch the attack themselves in terms so strong that the victim can be moved to enjoin that the family '[Not] be too hard on the boy. We all make mistakes.' Self-deprecating gestures from either side can facilitate reintegration, which is powerfully facilitated by exchanges such as:

Victim: 'It was partly my fault. I shouldn't have left it unlocked.'

Offender: 'No that's not your fault. You shouldn't have to lock it. We're the only ones who should be blamed.'

A common strategy of all parties for seeking to elicit empathy from others is to refer to how they may suffer these problems themselves in another phase of their own life cycle. Offender's uncle to offender: 'In a few years you will be a father and have to growl at your boys.' Co-ordinator to victims: 'You were once parents of teenagers yourselves.'

---

[8] In Australia, we have been experimenting with reintegrative conferences with white-collar crime, cases that illustrate the problem of victim shame. A recent case has involved action by the Trade Practices Commission against a number of Australia's largest insurance companies in what have been the biggest consumer protection cases in Australian history. The victims were Aborigines in remote communities who were sold (generally) useless insurance and investment policies as a result of a variety of shocking misrepresentations, even the misrepresentation that the Aborigine would be sent to jail if he did not sign the policy. Victims sometimes escaped through the back door when the government man in the white shirt arrived to interview them, fearing that *they* had done something wrong. Many shook and cried throughout their interviews. They felt shame at losing the little money their families had. The apologies issued by company chief executives at highly publicized press conferences were about communicating the message that it was the company who had to face 'the same job' (as Aborigines put it). Moreover, full compensation with 15 per cent compound interest would acquit the shame victims felt as providers. In addition, insurance company top management were required to attend negotiation conferences at Wujal Wujal, where they faced their victims, apologized to them and lived the life conditions of their victims, sleeping on mattresses on concrete floors, eating tinned food, during several days of negotiation. For more details on this and other cases of corporate shaming praxis, see Fisse and Braithwaite (1993) and Braithwaite (1992).

CONDITIONS OF SUCCESSFUL REINTEGRATION CEREMONIES

One case we attended involved a father and son who had a stormy relationship. A Maori elder counselled the father that he should put his arm around his boy more often, advice the father conceded that he needed to take. The father was a harsh and tough man, once a famous rugby forward with a reputation as an enforcer. The attempt of a Maori police officer to elicit empathy in these difficult circumstances was both innovative and effective, since tears began to stream down the face of the young offender, who up to this point had managed the impression of being a young tough:

Policeman: 'Look what you have done to your father and mother. If your father hit you, you'd stay hit. You wouldn't be getting up. But he hasn't.' [Offender gasps, his chest heaving with unnatural struggling for air]. 'I was always angry and bitter at my father. He was a hard man.'

Uncle interjects: 'Yes, he'd hit you first, then ask questions afterwards.'

Policeman continues: 'Then he died. Then I realised how I loved and missed the old bastard. Don't wait till your father dies, Mark.'

At this point the mother buried her head in her lap with quiet sobbing. Then the father and then the son cried, by which point all in the room had tears in our eyes. How impressive an accomplishment this was—eliciting such empathy for a father about whom it was clearly difficult to say anything laudatory. Taken out of context, it does not seem a very positive thing to say about a father that he has refrained from ironing out his son. But for a son who himself was enmeshed in the culture of rugby and who knew his father's history of ironing out a great number of other human beings, the tribute was deeply moving.

(8) The separation of denounced persons must be terminated by rituals of inclusion that place them, even physically, inside rather than outside

Already we have mentioned a number of rituals of inclusion: apology and its acceptance, handshaking, the putting of signatures side by side on an agreement, and so on. In a traditional Samoan context, this is taken further. Following an assault, the Matai, or head of the extended family unit of the offender, will kneel on a mat outside the house of the victim family until he is invited in and forgiven. Sometimes that will take days. There may be something to learn from the Samoans here on the conditions of successful reintegration ceremonies, namely the provision of a spatio-temporal dimension to the imperative for reintegration. For how long should I continue to avoid eye contact with this person who still kneels in front of me? When do I conclude it by embracing him in forgiveness? The sheer physicality of his remorse makes ignoring him indefinitely a rather limited third option. The ceremony is driven by a spatial imperative. Indeed, most successful ceremonies in our own society specify place (e.g., a church, a presentation dais) and a time when it is appropriate and fitting to carry out that ceremony. Moreover, in moving individuals through space and time, those movements are not haphazard—they fit the messages of transformation or reaffirmation that the ceremony seeks to convey.

In Wagga, the spatial arrangement that is employed to convey both the unity of the community and yet the tension between victim and offender, is a horseshoe seating arrangement. At one end of the horseshoe sits the offender(s) with her family(ies) sitting in the row behind. At the other end sits the victim(s) with his family(ies) sitting in the row behind him. The horseshoe symbolizes the tension of the meeting, part of one community but at widely separated points on this matter. Moreover, movements within the space can and do occur, such as when people cross the central space to shake hands at certain moments. These are culturally contingent matters; offending boys are commonly made to sit on the floor during Polynesian conferences, a temporary obeisance that seems culturally appropriate to them rather than debasing. Sometimes they are asked to come out and stand at the front for their formal apology, after which they return to their seat in a circle. In each of these, the physical space is used constructively to convey important messages. And, as we shall see later, the separation of the overall space into front and backstage areas also has its uses.

The symbolic meanings signified by space rarely surface in the discursive consciousness of the participants (or so we presume) but the successful use of space is not predicated upon that level of reflection. In all probability, more still could be done with the symbolic use of space in such ceremonies—one could take this even further by placing offenders alone in the centre of the horseshoe for the first stage of the conference, though one might worry about this intimidating them into silence. These are matters that require more detailed exploration, but note here merely that there is a fine line between artifice and artificiality.

The temporal dimension of the ceremony is also important. The phases in a successful ceremony are clearly visible in the way that participants comport themselves and a 'winding down' is often discernible. Indeed, the phased structure is not dissimilar to that described by Bales (1950) in his work on interaction process analysis. As Bales argued there, the social group that has formed to handle a particular risk (in this case for the ceremony) comes to develop a bounded process of its own, marking its phases with different styles of comportment and mood. Although breaks in the meeting are rarely used in Wagga,[9] one could conceivably have a coffee break once there had been good progress toward a settlement during which the protagonists could physically mix; after the break, offender families could come back side by side with their children to present their plan of action. Certainly, such activities are used to mark the end of the formal ceremony and handle transitions back to the 'outside world' and at such moments drinking together, whether coffee or—as might be appropriate in other contexts, alcohol—serves to mark that transition (Gusfield 1987; cf. also Bott 1987; Hazan 1987).

It is also important to note here that the physical act of handing over money as compensation or a bunch of flowers (as happened in one case) creates a strong imperative for an apology–forgiveness interaction sequence. Most English-speaking people find it normal to cancel grudges at the moment of a physical act of compensating wrongdoing by uttering the word 'sorry'. Faced with such an utterance, only unusual victims resist the imperative to return a word of forgiveness, to 'let bygones by bygones', or at least to show acceptance, thanks, or understanding.

Regrettably the common legal processes of a gesellschaft society sanitize such physical moments out of transactions. They are, in the Weberian sense, 'disenchanted'. With the loss of that enchantment they lose also powerful opportunities for transformations of self and context. Rational actor models of the world notwithstanding, successful

---

[9] In New Zealand, it is usual to have a break in the proceedings during which the offender's family meets on its own to prepare a plan of action.

CONDITIONS OF SUCCESSFUL REINTEGRATION CEREMONIES

practice of justice is not merely a technical-rational action. When restitution is reduced to 'the cheque is in the mail' (likely put there by the clerk of the court) matters of deep moral concern have been reduced to mere money, to the ubiquitous question 'how much?' (Simmel 1978). In contrast, successful reintegration ceremonies put reintegrative physicality back into the process. In so doing they transcend the merely rational to speak to vital concerns of human conscience.

(9) The separation of the victim, any fear or shame experienced by victims, must be terminated by rituals of reintegration

The objective of reintegrating offenders is advanced by reintegrating victims; the objective of reintegrating victims is advanced by reintegrating offenders.[10] Victims are invisible in Garfinkel's model, but our thesis is that effective reintegration ceremonies are victim-centred, a centrality described under conditions (3), (4), and (5). Victims often suffer from bypassed shame (Scheff and Retzinger 1991) and bypassed fear. The girl who is sexually assaulted by a young man often feels that the incident says something about the respect in which she is held by males. She feels devalued to have been treated with such disrespect (Murphy and Hampton 1989). One way to rehabilitate her self-respect is a ceremonial show of community respect for her. Apology from the man who disrespected her is the most powerful way of resuscitating this self-esteem and community shaming of the disrespecting behaviour is also powerful affirmation of the respect for her as a person.

Victims often continue to be afraid after a crime and at an apparently irrational level. When a break-in causes a victim to feel insecure in her home, it is good for this fear to be openly expressed. For one thing, there is practical advice the police are usually able to give that can leave the victim both safer and feeling more assured of being safe.

In one Wagga conference involving teenage lads who inflicted a terrifying assault on a much younger boy and girl, the boys offered to come around to the home of the victim family to apologize more formally to all members of the family. The young girl looked afraid and said that she did not want them coming near her home. So it was decided they would apologize in writing. But from that point on in the conference, the cautioning sergeant highlighted the fact that there was no particular meaning to the choice of these two children as victims. It was a one-off incident that could have happened to anyone. At the end of the conference, the sergeant ushered the offenders and their supporters out, asking the victim family to stay behind. Then he asked the children if they now felt assured that these boys would not come after them again. He asked them what they thought of the boys and they said that the conference had put it all behind them now. They felt more sorry for the boys than afraid of them. The mother said later that she had come to see them as frightened little boys. This interpretation

---

[10] In practice, the Wagga process has been more oriented from the outset to reintegrating victims than the New Zealand process. Many New Zealand co-ordinators, interpreting literally a clause in the New Zealand Children, Young Persons and Their Families Act, have been reluctant to allow victim supporters to attend the conference. There has been a lot of learning in New Zealand on this question, but in some parts there is still a fear of the vindictiveness of victims and, more particularly, of victim supporters. If victims are to be reintegrated, however, caring supporters are a necessary ingredient. Our strongest criticism of the New Zealand reform effort has been the half-hearted commitment to victim reintegration in many quarters.

was confirmed by a minister of religion who met with the family immediately after the conference.

Note here the importance of two smaller backstage conferences after the formal conference—a further instance of the significance of space referred to earlier. Backstage conferences can do some reintegrative work for both offenders and victims that cannot be accomplished front stage. Every conference we have attended broke up into some important little backstage meetings after the main conference. At times, the reintegrative work that happened after the conference was more significant than that transacted within it. A boy who maintained a defiant demeanour throughout the conference shed a tear when his uncle put his arm around him after the conference (his identity as nephew allows him to cry, but not the identity he must maintain in the face of his mates). A mother confesses that she does not believe she can get her daughter to attend the agreed community work and another uncle volunteers to 'make sure she gets there'. Backstage intimacy can allow some masks to be removed that actors feel impelled to sustain during the conference proper. A practical implication is not to rush the exit from the theatre.

(10) Means must be supplied to intervene against power imbalances that inhibit either shaming or reintegration, or both

Of the various criticisms we have heard raised about the ceremonial process that we are describing in this paper, one of the most common concerns the imbalance of power in society and the way that this must spill over into, and hence structure in negative ways, the reintegration process. How, they ask, can this process disassociate itself from wider matters of class, race, patriarchy, and age stratification? If such disassociation does not occur, how can the ceremony act other than to reproduce that same patterning of ageism, class, race, and patriarchy? The risk is obvious. The ethnomethodologists of the 1960s, among whom Garfinkel is counted, were rightly condemned by the marxists of the 1970s (Taylor, Walton, and Young 1973) for inattentiveness to issues of power. By using Garfinkel's work as a starting point might we not fall into the same trap, blithely praising a ceremony whose deeper realities are much darker than we sense? Are the ceremonies of reintegration we are discussing capable of intervening against power imbalances in any serious way?

Our answer to this falls into several parts, and these parts relate to what we have seen in our observational work.

First, in no sense is intervention to deal with individual offences the most important thing we can do to respond constructively to the crime problem: attacking deeper structures of inequality is more important (Polk 1992; Braithwaite 1991, 1993). But let us not underestimate how important a basis of inequality criminal justice oppression is to (say) Aboriginal Australians. The structure of laws and the daily routines of the police and the courts contribute mightily to that oppression. Thus, to alter the police-court process is an important step, even if it is not a sufficient step. Indeed the very history of the Antipodean conferences we are discussing here begins with Maori frustration with the way the Western state disempowered them through the criminal justice system (Report of the Ministerial Advisory Committee 1986). These reforms 'came from below' and were explicitly understood by Maori protagonists to introduce

CONDITIONS OF SUCCESSFUL REINTEGRATION CEREMONIES

communitarian reintegrative features into a system that lacked them and which stigmatized their young people in destructive ways. In this sense, if in no other, we advocate the reintegration ceremonies because they are valuable in the eyes of most of those who are involved in them.[11]

Our second point is more theoretical. At the core of the criticism about power imbalances undermining the ceremony is a failure to think through the precise nature of the ceremony. The current of mainstream sociology that has dealt with ritual and ceremony has principally been conservative and functionally oriented (Cheal 1988). As a result, the tendency has been to emphasize static, system-integrative, and totalizing aspects of rituals over dynamic aspects, multiple identities, and social change. But that shortcoming is a feature of the theory, not the ceremony. If commentators associate conservatism with ceremony for this reason, they do so out of habit rather than evidence. There are dynamic features to these ceremonies which emphasize agency and social freedom (within obvious bounds) not merely totalizing conformity. No doubt, there are meanings which ceremonies permit and others they do not and no doubt some of those privilegings and silencings may be problematic. But we dispute that they can be 'read off' in advance.

Third and last, the criticism implies that anyone who pursues the course we describe here is utopian—class, race, and patriarchy are so ingrained in 'the system', it can be said that the system can never transcend them. Perhaps. But our view is quite different. We see that the existing 'system'—which is not particularly systematic in that it lacks unity, coherence, and direction—is racked with problems arising from differences in power which we can identify as 'class, race, and patriarchy'. But we go on to argue that if so, this identifies the places where we need to work relentlessly for change. Moreover, we suggest that our observations of such ceremonies indicate that while power imbalances remain ineradicably within what we describe, they also provide a greater space in which people can be agents than the existing processes. More voices are heard, saying more things than in conventional courts and that is a positive thing. Concrete examples may help to make the point.

It is an empirical question whether powerful outside voices are likely to be raised in a conference or a court against a father who dominates his daughter. Here we observe that the condition of the successful reintegration ceremony is that the co-ordinator act on this fact of domination by asking the daughter *who she would like* to be there to stick up for her against her father.

The philosophy of the New Zealand reforms (Children, Young Persons and Their Families Act 1989) is that when families are in deep trouble, a social worker from the state is not likely to be the best person to straighten out their problems (Maxwell and Morris 1993). However big a mess the family is in, the best hope for solving the problem of families resides within the families themselves and their immediate communities of intimate support. What the state can do is empower families with resources: offer to pay to bring Auntie Edna from another city for the conference (as they do in New Zealand), offer to pay for a smorgasbord of life skills, job training, remedial education, anger control courses, but with *the power of choice from that*

---

[11] In New Zealand, 53 per cent of the offenders processed through family group conferences are Maori (Maxwell and Morris 1993: 69). On Maori perceptions of the value of the reforms, see n. 13 below.

smorgasbord resting entirely with the young offender and her support group.[12] Processes like this do offer a redress of power imbalances centred upon race, albeit not completely. In New Zealand, where the Maori community contribute half the cases processed by the New Zealand juvenile justice system, conferences offer an important redress in a criminal justice system that is otherwise not a peripheral but a central source of their disempowerment. The same point can be made about racial minorities in all the English-speaking countries. It is a small blow against black oppression when the white father of the victim of a brutal assault offers to go with the family of the Aboriginal offender to argue the reversal of a decision to expel him from school because of the assault. Conferences will never usher in revolutionary changes; they do, however, give little people chances to strike little blows against oppression.

The possibilities for improving the position of women within criminal justice processes also seem to us to be quite promising. This is illustrated by the Wagga case mentioned earlier of the mother who was being beaten by her son. Court-based criminal justice systematically obscures the fact that in Australia we have a massive problem of son–mother violence. Domestic violence is constructed in the literature as spouse abuse because mothers keep the problems with their sons submerged, blaming themselves, refusing to complain against their own children. If the Wagga case discussed earlier had gone to court, it is most unlikely that the assault on the girl would have led on to a discussion of the wider problem of the assault on the mother and other females. The family group conference approach enabled community confrontation of this 15-year-old boy with the problem of his violence at an early enough age for such a confrontation to make a difference. But most mothers and sisters are unlikely to co-operate in a stigmatic or punitive vilification of their young son or brother. Ceremonies must be perceived as reintegrative, directed not only at getting the boy to take responsibility for his actions but also at supporting and helping him, before most mothers and sisters will break the silence.

We could add that the economic prospects of offenders, which are often very dim, are not always neglected in these conferences. While this is not a widespread feature, sometimes the unemployed are helped to find jobs; sometimes the homeless are found homes; often the school dropouts are assisted in getting back to school or into some alternative kind of technical training or educational development. Clearly there are many more important fronts on which to struggle for a more just economic system than through family group conferences, but these conferences are at worst not deepening the problems that the young offenders face.

In short, while the reintegration ceremonies we write of here do not overcome inequalities, they can be and are sensitive to them and do what they can to allow for and/or redress some of those inequalities. In so doing, they create spaces for agency and voice; they return conflicts that are 'stolen' by state professionals to ordinary citizens (Christie 1977). This, we think, is a progressive move. The structural feature of successful conferences that we hypothesize to be most critical here is proactive empowerment of the most vulnerable participants—offenders and victims—with the choice of caring advocates, who may be more powerful than themselves, to exercise countervailing power against whoever they see as their oppressors.

---

[12] With the weak welfare states that exist in both Australia and New Zealand, the range of such choices effectively available to young people, in most localities but particularly in rural localities, is very poor (Maxwell and Morris 1993: 180).

CONDITIONS OF SUCCESSFUL REINTEGRATION CEREMONIES

(11) Ceremony design must be flexible and culturally plural, so that participants exercise their process control constrained by only very broad procedural requirements

We should be pluralist enough to see that a good process for Maoris will not necessarily be a good process for Europeans, or even for some Maoris who say they don't believe in 'too much shit about the Maori way' (Maxwell and Morris 1993: 126).[13] At the same time, we should not be so culturally relativist as to reject the possibility of Europeans learning something worthwhile from Maori practice. Family group conferences are essentially a Maori idea, but the idea has been very favourably received by white communities in New Zealand and Australia, Australian Aboriginal communities, and Pacific Islander communities living in New Zealand. The reason is the flexibility built into the approach. Because Samoan participants have genuine process control, they can choose to encourage kneeling in front of the victim. Maori communities can choose to break the tension during proceedings by singing a song, something Westerners would find a rather odd thing to do on such an occasion. Maori conferences often signify the sacredness of the public interests involved (conditions 3 and 4) by opening and closing the conference with a (reintegrative) prayer.

Every conference we have attended has been completely different from every other conference. Indeed, flexibility and participant control of the process are the reasons why this strategy can succeed in a multicultural metropolis like Auckland. This is not a communitarian strategy for the nineteenth century village, but for the twenty-first century city. Flexible process, participant control—these are keys to delivering the legal pluralism necessary for the metropolis. Another key is that this is an individual-centred communitarianism, giving it a practical edge for constructing community in an individualistic society. The authors of this paper choose not to attend Neighbourhood Watch meetings, because the appeal of community obligation is not sufficient to motivate our participation. In contrast, if one of us were asked to attend a family group conference on the basis that either a victim or an offender from our neighbourhood or family had nominated us as a person who could lend support, we would go. We would be flattered to have been nominated by the individual. This is what we mean by the practical appeal of individual-centred communitarianism. Helping an individual is more motivating to citizens than abstractions such as 'contributing to making your neighbourhood safer'.

While the reintegrative strategy is firmly grounded in the theory of legal pluralism, certain basic procedural rules cannot be trumped. The most important of these is that if the offender denies committing the alleged offences, she has the right to terminate the

---

[13] While it is easy to find Maoris who resist the notion that there is a lot of point in turning back the clock to a pre-European society and others who see family group conferences as a corruption and debasement of Maori traditions by the Western justice system, we suspect the predominant Maori reaction is as expressed by the Maori researchers on the Maxwell and Morris project in the following quote—accepting the need for mutual accommodation between Maori and Western justice systems, especially when victims and offenders come from different cultures:

'We feel that the Act for the most part is an excellent piece of legislation which promises exciting possibilities for the future. When the processes outlined in the Act were observed, Maori families were indeed empowered and able to take an active part in decisions concerning their young people. It is not difficult to see the beneficial influences that the Act may eventually exert on wider Maori, Polynesian and Pakeha society. Maori society could gain immensely from legislation that acknowledges and strengthens the hapu and tribal structures and their place in decisions regarding the wellbeing of young people and [from legislation] that provides them with an opportunity to contribute to any reparation and to support those offended against. The same scenario would apply to Pacific Island peoples. Pakeha society would also benefit from a process which acknowledges the family and gives redress to victims' (Maxwell and Morris 1993: 187).

conference, demanding that the facts be tried in a court of law. She does not have to plead guilty. The conference can proceed only if she chooses 'not to deny' charges made by the police. Some of the more informal ground rules that co-ordinators enforce, such as 'no name calling' and 'no badgering of the young person' have the effect of tipping the balance against degrading discourse in favour of reintegrative dialogue. What such basic procedural rules do is constitute a generally acceptable framework within which a plurality of dialogic forms can flourish (see Habermas 1986).

Given a commitment to flexibility and participant empowerment, one central concern is the prospect of standardization and routinization. It would be easy for ceremonies to be converted into Foucauldian 'discipline', extending the net of state control. Disturbing signs of this as a future trend can be discerned, for example in the near-automatic tendency of some state officials at New Zealand conferences to suggest a curfew as part of the plan of action. Families can and do argue against their children being put on a rigid curfew, suggesting that a degree of participant control of the process is prevailing against pressures for standardized response, but the routinization of the suggestion without apparent consideration of case details implies a standardizing tendency. Similarly, after a training conference for co-ordinators in Wagga that we attended with Clifford Shearing and Jane Mugford, they expressed concern to us that some of the contributions to the training by local social workers and psychologists undercut the shifts away from stigmatization and toward community empowerment. The tendency there was to speak and reason in abstract categories such as 'problem youth' in a way that, taken seriously, would erode the agency and voice of participants in favour of the imposition of control by 'experts'.

These tendencies notwithstanding, our view is that, at present, the family group conferences do not extend the net of state control (see also Moore 1992), but rather extend the net of community control, partly at the expense of state control, partly at the expense of doing something about problems that were previously ignored (such as mother-bashing by sons).[14] Conferences can be used by communities to co-opt state power (formalism harnessed to empower informalism) (Braithwaite and Daly, in press); or they can be used by state authorities to expand their net of coercion by capturing informal community control (as in the net-widening critique). The contingent potential for both these developments and for the re-emergence of professionalized routinization need to be kept in mind in planning the expansion of such programmes.

(12) Reintegration agreements must be followed through to ensure that they are enacted

In the early days of the family group conferences in both New Zealand and Wagga, there was poor follow-up to ensure that agreements reached at the conference were implemented. Now more systematic procedures are in place in New Zealand to ensure, for example, that where monetary compensation is involved, victims do receive it. For a sample of 203 family group conferences held in 1990, Maxwell and Morris (1993: 102) found that in 59 per cent of cases agreements were completely implemented within three to four months and partly completed in a further 28 per cent of cases, leaving only

---

[14] Maxwell and Morris's (1993: 176) New Zealand data support this interpretation. They find that the result of the New Zealand reforms is fewer children going to court, fewer receiving custodial penalties, but more children whose delinquency was previously ignored altogether or discharged by the court experiencing moderate interventions such as formal apology, compensation, and community service decided through family group conferences or police diversion.

CONDITIONS OF SUCCESSFUL REINTEGRATION CEREMONIES

13 per cent of cases in which the tasks were largely uncompleted in this time frame—a very good result. At Wagga, young offenders and their families are invited to at least one follow-up workshop to close out the process. Families have an opportunity to swap notes at the workshop on the difficulties they have faced in implementing their plan of action. The Wagga police also see a reintegrative rationale for the workshop in helping families to overcome their shame by working with other families in the same situation. It is possible that this interpretation is right, as illustrated by the following passage from our fieldwork notes:

Of the three offenders [in this particular case] George was the one who seemed totally unmoved by what the victim and his family said at the conference. George's mother got together with mothers of George's friends who had also been in trouble, to talk about their problems. One of the mothers said that her boy had been sexually assaulted and that was one thing that upset him. Later George's mother said to George that he has not had it so tough as John, who had been sexually assaulted. George said nothing. Later, he called his mother back, broke down and said he had been sexually assaulted too (by the same person, we assume). George's mother now dates the assault as marking the time since which George had been getting into trouble. Her social construction of George is no longer as a boy who went bad. Now it is of a boy who was good, who went through a bad time as a result of a sexual assault, and who is now coming to terms with what happened to him and is coming out of it—a 'good boy' again.

Implementation of agreements from family group conferences is more effective than with court ordered compensation largely because the compensation is a collective obligation entered into by voluntary collective agreement.[15] Moreover, the co-ordinator will often secure the nomination of a relative who will be responsible for ensuring that the offender complies with the terms of the agreement. Dr Gabrielle Maxwell has made the same point about completion of community work orders: 'The community work projects that work are the ones the family comes up with itself.'

(13) When a single reintegration ceremony fails, ceremony after ceremony must be scheduled, never giving up, until success is achieved

Traditional criminal justice processes paint themselves into a corner because of two imperatives: the desire to give kids another chance; notwithstanding this, the desire to signal that 'the system is tough and next time you will not be so lucky'. These two imperatives intersect with the empirical reality that young offenders offend a lot during their years of peak offending. Most will come through this peak period within two or three years if the criminal justice system does not make things worse by degradation ceremonies (such as institutionalization). The two imperatives and the empirical pattern of offending intersect to cause the criminal justice system to do exactly what its

[15] As an aside, it is worth noting here the implications for the justice model which provides a critique of family group conferences as inferior to courts. Courts, according to this critique, provide singular, consistent justice, in contrast to the plural, inconsistent justice of conferences. It is an interesting empirical question whether in practice, as opposed to theory, courts do deliver more just sanctioning when compensation, fines, and community service ordered by the court are defied in the majority of cases. It is not inconceivable that even though there is greater inequity in the sanctions ordered by group conferences, in the sanctions actually implemented there is greater equity for the group conference than for the court process.

practitioners know is the worst thing to do, that is, set up a self-defeating chain of events:

Conviction 1:   'Take this as a warning.'
Conviction 2:   'I'll give you a second chance. But this is your last chance.'
Conviction 3:   'With regret, I must say that you have already been given your last chance.'

The policy in New Zealand is to avoid this slippery slope. While some cases in the juvenile justice system continue to slide down it, most do not and since 1988 the rate of institutionalization of young offenders has dropped by more than half (Maxwell and Morris 1993: 176), possibly by 75 per cent (McDonald and Ireland 1990: 16). Now, most detected offences are judged not to warrant the cost of convening a family group conference, and informal warnings to juveniles on the spot or at the police station remain the predominant response for very minor offences (Maxwell and Morris 1993: 53). Taking no action beyond a formal letter of warning from the police is also common (Maxwell and Morris 1993: 59). Visits by the police to the offender's home to arrange informally for reparation and apology to the victim occur in a quarter of non-arrest cases (Maxwell and Morris 1993: 53). Only if these steps are insufficient is a full conference arranged.

In addition to these informal pre-conference measures, some New Zealand young offenders have been through six or seven formal conferences for different offences. The New Zealand Police Association, which strongly supports the family group conference strategy for most offenders, has reservations about repeated use of the approach on 'hardened' offenders. They illustrated the problem with examples such as this:

Ngaruawahia reports that a 16 year old youth had a Family Group Conference on 26 June 1990 for three offences, another on 10 July for six offences, another on 20 July 1990 for two offences, Youth Court hearing on 24 July 1990, another Family Group Conference on 14 February 1991 for two offences. The youth committed suicide at Weymouth Boys Home in April 1991 (New Zealand Police Association 1991: 19).

Of course, such a case seems a 'failure'. But what kind of failure is it? We can think of three ways of categorizing it: (a) a failure of the family group conference; (b) the likely failure of any approach with the most difficult cases; or (c) the failure of giving up on the family group conference in favour of the court-institutionalization route. The implication of the passage is that this is a failure of type (a), but we suspect that it is better understood as type (b) and/or (c).

Of course, it would be naïve to expect that a one- or two-hour conference can normally turn around the problems of a lifetime. In any case, the theory of the conference is not really that what is said at the conference will change lives in an instant and irreversible way—a conference is a social activity, not a genie from a bottle. Rather the hope for the conference is that it will be a catalyst for community problem solving. Viewed in this way, when there is re-offending after a conference, it is to some extent the community that has failed. The failure of the conference was in not catalysing the right sort of community support for the offender. If the failure is not inherent to the conference process, but is a failure in the community catalysis of the intervention, then one conference after another, each time seeking to catalyse community support in a different way, or with different invitees, makes sense.

CONDITIONS OF SUCCESSFUL REINTEGRATION CEREMONIES

To achieve a successful reintegration ceremony, then, it is necessary that co-ordinators must never give up, that they act as if there is always a reason for the failure of the last intervention *other than* the irretrievable badness of the offender. Even if the offender dies before the community succeeds in preventing his offending, by trying again and again with reintegrative approaches, the co-ordinator believes that she has at least refrained from accelerating his criminal career path during the time he lived. The typical criminal career is a useful touchstone, here. Knowing the pattern typical of some offenders, it is *dis*abling to conceive success in terms of stopping offending. At the same time, it is *en*abling to define success as a downward shift in the slope of a criminal career path and failure as allowing an upward shift. Unless the offences are extreme,[16] it is always better to keep plugging away with a strategy that neither succeeds nor fails than to escalate to one that fails. At least the former does no harm.

Is there a practical way of implementing the attitude of never giving up? Below is an example of how the police might react to the first eight detected offences of a career criminal under a reintegrative strategy.

First offence: Boy warned by the police on the street for a minor offence. 'If I catch you at this again, I'll be in touch with your parents about it.'

Second offence: Same type of minor offence on the street results in a formal letter of warning and a visit to the family home to discuss the warning.

Third offence: Family group conference. Still a fairly minor offence, so no elaborate follow-up or detailed plan of action, just the reintegrative shaming of the offender and calling on the offender and the family to take responsibility for the problem in their own way. For the over-whelming majority of such minor offenders, this is the last the juvenile justice system will see of them, so any more detailed intervention is wasteful overkill.

Fourth offence: Second family group conference. More rigorous conference. What did the participants do, or fail to do, after the last conference? More detailed plan of action to respond to this analysis of the problem. Designation of offender supporters to monitor and report on imple-mentation. Follow-up by co-ordinator to report back to participants on implementation. Modest quantum of community work.

Fifth offence: Third family group conference. Escalation of shaming of offender: 'You gave undertakings to your family at the last conference that you have broken in the most thoughtless way. You breached the trust your parents put in you with that agreement.' Redesign the plan of action. This time, secure a more solemn oath to the parents. Follow through. More community work.

Sixth offence: Fourth family group conference. New invitees. The smorgasbord of intervention options that the family group can choose (life skills or work skills courses, remedial education, church-run programmes, anger control courses, regular meetings with the school counsellor,

---

[16] There will be rare cases where the offender is so dangerous that escalation to institutionalization is inevitable and necessary. We have no dispute with such a course of action in those cases.

outward bound, drug rehabilitation programmes, etc.) is put before them in a different way. 'We chose the wrong option before. That was our mistake. But we believe in the caring side of you that your family sees so often, so eventually you will find with them the right option to assist you to consider the hurt you cause to victims like Mrs Smith and to consider your own future.' Keep up the shaming, this time focused on the particular circumstances of Mrs Smith. Work for Mrs Smith.

Seventh offence: Fifth family group conference. Try again basic strategy of fourth conference with a different victim, different participants, and a different way of presenting the smorgasbord of intervention options.

Eighth offence: Sixth family group conference. Change tack. Eventually come back to the fact that the offender is still responsible for this particular criminal act, but lead off with collective self-blame: 'As a group, your parents, your sister, grandfather and aunt, your teacher, Mrs Brown, who has such a soft spot for you, and me as the co-ordinator of this conference, we all feel responsible that we have let you down. We haven't listened to you well enough to come up with the right ways to help you. We need you to tell us where we have gone wrong.' Various other options can follow, such as one family member after another coming along prepared to give a speech on the mistakes they have made in the course of the saga. A search could be initiated by the family to find some new participants in the conference to add fresh perspectives, even asking another couple to become 'god-parents'. An option on the co-ordinator's side could be to bring in a consultant professional of some sort with new ideas to participate in the conference.

Obviously, it gets very difficult to keep coming up with new angles, to keep projecting faith in the essential goodness of the offender, to persist with the never-give-up ideology. The relentless optimism that successful reintegration enjoins may eventually surrender in the face of a natural human pessimism. We saw one stigmatizing conference for an offender (his fourth) which exemplified this surrender. During this encounter, the exasperated co-ordinator described the offender as a 'Yahoo'. Before inviting the offender to give his side of the story, he turned to the family and asked them what they thought was wrong with the boy. He said: 'The responsibility is the parents, not ours. I don't care. The Department doesn't care. We can just send it on to court.' The Youth Advocate said that she saw the key question as being whether 'his friends were bad or he was the bad one'. She supported the interpretation of the police that escalation to institutionalization was the track the boy was heading down. The police, the co-ordinator and the youth advocate had given up and everything they said gave the impression that they had given up on him. Even when the boy apologized, the co-ordinator evinced utter cynicism when he retorted dismissively, 'That's what you said last time.' This was a fully fledged degradation ceremony rather than an attempt at reintegration.

Pessimism is a natural human reaction to repeated misfortune and eventually the most determined commitment to 'never giving up on the offender' may succumb to it.

CONDITIONS OF SUCCESSFUL REINTEGRATION CEREMONIES

But a tenacious commitment to the ideology of never giving up will allow co-ordinators to cling to it for the fourth conference after the failure of the third. A slightly more tenacious commitment allows optimism to survive the fifth conference into the sixth. At each stage, more and more offenders drop off never to return, their criminal careers coming to an end without being inflicted with degradation ceremonies. Very few offenders indeed will make it through to a sixth conference. If we can hold out with optimism until then, the criminal justice system will have been transformed to a 99 per cent reintegrative institution. That can hardly be a bad outcome.

True disciples of reintegration, including ourselves, take the injunction to never give up on offenders to the absolute extreme. Even when a criminal career has continued to the point of the offender being the most powerful organized criminal in the country, the best hope for dealing with him is conceived as persuading him to convert his illegitimate capital into a legitimate business, giving his children a better future, a more respectable future, than the shame of his criminal empire. Going further still, as we have illustrated earlier (see n. 8 above), we think even the top management of certain Australian insurance companies are best negotiated with reintegratively! In the extraordinary cases where offenders are such a danger to the community that incarceration is defensible, we should not give up on pushing for reintegration, even though the degradation ceremony of confinement makes this maximally difficult.

(14) The ceremony must be justified by a politically resonant discourse

Shaming and reintegration are terms that we think have merit (that we will not defend here) in the discourse of criminological theory. These days, they have surprising currency among the police and community of Wagga. But in New Zealand, the terms that have more currency are, respectively, young offenders and their families 'taking responsibility' and 'healing'. The discourse of responsibility and healing may have more popular political appeal than that of shame and reintegration, as evidenced by the wide political support it has attracted in New Zealand and the growing support throughout Australia (Interim Report of the Select Committee on the Juvenile Justice System 1992; Tate 1992).

Much more crucial to this political and media support has been the marketing of this reintegration strategy as victim-centred and family-centred. It is a progressive reform that calls the hand of conservative politicians. They are forever claiming that victims are the forgotten people of the criminal justice system and bemoaning the declining importance of the family in contemporary society. Here is a reform that empowers victims and at the same time values and empowers families. Such a reform puts conservatives in a vulnerable position when they seek to oppose it.

Moreover, conservatives have also found in Australia and New Zealand that they cannot count on their allegedly 'natural allies' in law and order campaigns, the police. The Australian and New Zealand Police Federation carried a resolution at its 1991 conference supporting the New Zealand juvenile justice reforms. In New Zealand, 91 per cent of the time, police report that they are satisfied with the outcomes of the conferences in which they participate, a higher level than for youth justice co-ordinators (86 per cent), parents (85 per cent), offenders (84 per cent) and victims (48 per cent) (Morris and Maxwell 1992). Perhaps this should not surprise us. The approach appeals to the common sense of police. On balance, it cuts their paperwork and economizes on criminal justice system resources; they often feel empowered by the capacity the conference gives them to make practical suggestions to the family on what might be done about the problem (an opportunity they are rarely given by courts); they like to treat victims with the decency that they believe courts deny them (in particular, they like to see victims actually getting compensation); and they find that the programme builds goodwill toward the police in communities that are empowered through the process. Most critically, they find participation in community conferences more interesting, challenging, and satisfying work than typing up charges and sitting around in courthouses for cases that are rushed through in a matter of minutes. This is by no means a universal police reaction. But we can certainly say that the strongest support for these reintegrative programmes in Australia has come from the police. While New Zealand reform was Maori-driven, the Australian reform is being police-driven.

Finally, the political appeal of the process is that it can be advocated in the discourse of fiscal restraint. In New Zealand, one of the most conservative governments in the Western world liked a reform that helped the budget deficit by allowing them to sell most of the institutions for juvenile offenders in the country. We were told that the Department of Social Welfare alone estimated that in 1991, they saved $6 million as a result of the reform. In this area of criminal justice, youth justice co-ordinators not only do the job more effectively than judges in court, they are cheaper than judges. By the same token, youth justice advocates are cheaper than prosecutors and public defenders. At all levels of the criminal justice system there are savings—not always massive savings, but rarely trivial.[17]

At the same time, reintegration ceremonies offer an attractive political package for a reforming politician. Presented properly, it can satisfy the otherwise incompatible imperatives of keeping the police and the finance ministry happy at the same time. It can even put the victims movement and liberally minded criminal justice reformers—who so often seem diametrically opposed—together on the same platform of support.

Conclusion

A useful way of thinking about ceremonies for dealing with rule breakers is in terms of the ratio of stigmatic to reintegrative meanings during the ceremony. When that ratio is high, we have a degradation ceremony; when low, a reintegration ceremony. There are few, if any, actors who are perfectly faithful to the theory of reintegrative shaming during such ceremonies. Typically, messages are mixed, as with the Maori participant quoted above: 'You've got no brains, boy (stigmatization) . . . But I've got respect for you (reintegration) . . .' There are many actors like this one who communicate shame while also sustaining a high ratio of reintegrative to stigmatizing meanings. The subtleties in the ways shaming and reintegration are mixed by practical human communicators are myriad. We noted one police sergeant who addressed male offenders by their names whenever he was engaging them in responsibility talk, but

---

[17] Against this view, economists might say that we should cost the (considerable) time involved in the attendance of victims and supporters, for example. If we calculated these costs, perhaps there would be no savings. But why should we make a negative entry for victims in the economic calculus when the fact is that the reform increases utility for victims? To enter the costs would make sense only if we could value the benefits. And if we did that, then no doubt the system we describe would again show a better balance sheet.

CONDITIONS OF SUCCESSFUL REINTEGRATION CEREMONIES

who called them 'mate' whenever he switched to reintegrative talk. When we pointed out this observation and asked him whether he was aware of the pattern, the sergeant told us it was a conscious communication strategy.

In Giddens's (1984) terms, many actors have practical but not discursive consciousness of the idea of reintegration; some actors, like this sergeant, have both. A feasible objective is to increase the proportion of actors who are conscious of the virtues of reintegration. This is not best achieved by lectures from theoretical criminology texts, but from telling stories (Shearing and Ericson 1991) and simple homilies such as that of one police constable: 'Just because we sometimes do stupid things; that does not mean we are a stupid person.' It could be that if there is a key principle of successful reintegration ceremonies, it is that there should not be too many principles. Training of co-ordinators should be kept simple, leaving them wide discretion to implement flexibly a few broad principles.

Stigma cannot be rooted out of confrontations between people who are angry and affronted by acts of rule breaking. But the ratio of stigmatization to reintegration can be shifted substantially by story-based training methods that focus on a few core principles—empower the victim, respect and support the offender while condemning his act, engage the offender's supporters. Just by having a process that is more victim-centred, problem-centred, and community-oriented, rather than centred on the offender and his pathologies, we institute a logic that produces less stigmatization and more reintegration. Obversely, the offender-centred logic of the courtroom or the psychiatrist's couch institutionalizes stigmatization.

One of the inevitable problems is that the stigmatizing, disempowering professional knowledges of the court and consultancy rooms penetrate the reintegration ceremony. Most depressingly, this was observed in New Zealand with the role of certain youth advocates, private lawyers contracted by the state to watch out for the rights of young offenders during conferences. Sometimes they 'earn their fee' by taking charge, telling the family what sort of action plan will satisfy the police and the courts. Or worse, we see 'the practice of law as a confidence game' (Blumberg 1967) where advocate, co-ordinator and police conspire to settle a practical deal among the professionals, then sell that deal to the conference participants, a deal that in at least one case seemed to us a sell-out of both the offender and the victim.

We commented earlier about the observations made by Clifford Shearing and Jane Mugford after a Wagga training session. Their point was that the reform process must create a new knowledge, a citizen knowledge, otherwise the old professional knowledges would colonize the spaces in the programme. We agree—hence the importance of the simple principles outlined above and the importance of the central involvement of local police–citizen consultative committees and other community groups in guiding reform. At the same time, however, we think the professional knowledges also include the seeds of their own reform. Reintegrative concepts have a major place in psychological and particularly social work discourse. These can be brought to the fore through reforms such as we are seeing in New Zealand and Wagga. While the youth advocates were criticized by a number of people we spoke to in New Zealand for importing professional control into family group conferences, some of these critics also pointed out how many advocates had changed their legalistic habits to accommodate the communitarian ideology of the conferences. Finally, there can be no doubt that these reforms are part of wider changes in police knowledges in Australia and New Zealand—away from 'lock-'em-up' law enforcement and toward community policing. None the less, at the crucial middle management levels, the old punitive knowledges of policing continue to predominate and must be confronted by reasoned cases based on the success of alternative practices. Reformers can't lock professional knowledges out of the process. Hence, reformers must be engaged with police education, counter-colonizing that area with reintegrative ideas.[18]

There are no criminal justice utopias to be found, just better and worse directions to head in.[19] The New Zealand Maori have shown a direction for making reintegration ceremonies work in multicultural metropolises such as Auckland, a city that faces deeper problems of recession, homelessness, and gang violence than many cities in Western Europe. Implementation of these ideas by the white New Zealand authorities has been riddled with imperfection—re-professionalization, patriarchy, ritualistic proceduralism that loses sight of objectives, and inappropriate net-widening. The important thing, however, is that the general direction of change is away from these pathologies; it is deprofessionalizing, empowering of women, oriented to flexible community problem-solving and, for the most part, narrowing nets of state control (Maxwell and Morris 1993: 25, 134, 136, but see 128, 176; on net-narrowing at Wagga see Moore 1992; O'Connell 1992). Most critically, it shows that the conditions of successful reintegration ceremonies that criminologists identify when in high theory mode can be given practical content for implementation by police and citizens.

As both Max Scheler and Garfinkel point out: 'There is no society that does not provide in the very features of its organisation the conditions sufficient for inducing shame.' (Garfinkel 1956: 420). The question is what sort of balance societies will have between degradation ceremonies as a 'secular form of communion' and reintegration ceremonies as a rather different communion. Garfinkel showed that there was a practical programme of communication tactics that will get the work of status degradation done. We hope to have shown that equally there is a practical programme of communication tactics that can accomplish reintegration.

REFERENCES

ASHWORTH, A. (1986), 'Punishment and Compensation: Victims, Offenders and the State', *Oxford Journal of Legal Studies*, 6: 86–122.

BALES, R. (1950), *Interaction Process Analysis*. Cambridge: Addison Wesley.

BECKER, H. S. (1960), 'Notes on the concept of commitment', *American Journal of Sociology*, 66: 32–40.

—— (1963), *Outsiders: Studies in the Sociology of Deviance*. New York: Free Press.

BLUMBERG, A. S. (1967), 'The Practice of Law as a Confidence Game: Organizational Cooptation of a Profession', *Law and Society Review*, 1: 15–39.

---

[18] Something the senior author has been actively engaged with since 1986 as a member of the NSW Police Education Advisory Council.

[19] There is no persuasive evidence that the reforms we have described actually work in reducing delinquency. That would require random allocation experiments. We can say that official statistics do not support the conclusion that they are failing. Crime rates in Wagga Wagga seem to have fallen since the juvenile justice reforms were introduced. In New Zealand, juvenile crime rates were falling slightly before the Children, Young Persons and Their Families Act 1989 was passed, and continued to fall slightly after its introduction (Maxwell and Morris 1993: 45).

CONDITIONS OF SUCCESSFUL REINTEGRATION CEREMONIES

BLAGG, H. (1985), 'Reparation and Justice for Juveniles: The Corby Experience', *British Journal of Criminology*, 25: 267–79.

BOTT, E. (1987), 'The Kava Ceremonial as a Dream Structure', in M. Douglas, ed., *Constructive Drinking: Perspectives on Drinking from Anthropology*. Cambridge: Cambridge University Press, pp. 182–204.

BRAITHWAITE, J. (1989), *Crime, Shame and Reintegration*. Cambridge: Cambridge University Press.

—— (1991), 'Poverty, Power, White-Collar Crime and the Paradoxes of Criminological Theory', *Australian and New Zealand Journal of Criminology*, 24: 40–58.

—— (1992), 'Corporate Crime and Republican Criminological Praxis', Paper to Queens University Conference on Corporate Ethics, Law and the State, Kingston.

—— (1993), 'Inequality and Republican Criminology', in John Hagan and Ruth Peterson, eds, *Crime and Inequality*. Palo Alto: Stanford University Press.

BRAITHWAITE, J., and DALY, K. (in press), 'Masculinities, Violence and Communitarian Control', in T. Newburn and B. Stanko, eds, *Just Boys Doing Business? Men, Masculinity and Crime*. London: Routledge.

CHEAL, D. (1988), 'The Postmodern Origins of Ritual', *Journal for the Theory of Social Behaviour*, 18: 269–90.

CHRISTIE, N. (1977), 'Conflict as Property', *British Journal of Criminology*, 17: 1–26.

CRAGG, W. (1992), *The Practice of Punishment: Towards a Theory of Restorative Justice*. London: Routledge.

DE HAAN, W. (1990), *The Politics of Redress: Crime, Punishment and Penal Abolition*. London: Unwin Hyman.

DIGNAN, J. (1992), 'Repairing the Damage: Can Reparation Work in the Service of Diversion?', *British Journal of Criminology*, 32: 453–72.

DOOB, A., and ROBERTS, J. (1983), *Sentencing: An Analysis of the Public's View of Sentencing. A Report to the Department of Justice, Canada*. Department of Justice: Canada.

—— (1988), 'Public Attitudes towards Sentencing in Canada', in N. Walker and M. Hough, eds, *Public Attitudes to Sentencing*. Aldershot: Gower.

ERIKSON, K. T. (1962), 'Notes on the Sociology of Deviance', *Social Problems*, 9: 307–14.

FISSE, B., and BRAITHWAITE, J. (1993), *Corporations, Crime and Accountability*. Sydney: Cambridge University Press.

GALAWAY, B. (1985), 'Victim-Participation in the Penal Corrective process', *Victimology*, 10: 617–30.

GALAWAY, B., and HUDSON, J. (1975), 'Issues in the Correctional Implementation of Restitution to Victims of Crime', in J. Hudson and B. Galaway, eds, *Considering the Victim*. Springfield, IL: Charles C. Thomas.

—— (1990), *Criminal Justice, Restitution and Reconciliation*. Monsey, NY: Criminal Justice Press.

GALAWAY, B., HENZEL, M., RAMSEY, G., and WANYAMA, B. (1980), 'Victims and Delinquents in the Tulsa Juvenile Court', *Federal Probation*, 44: 42–8.

GARFINKEL, H. (1956), 'Conditions of Successful Degradation Ceremonies', *American Journal of Sociology*, 61: 420–4.

GIDDENS, A. (1984), *The Constitution of Society*. Berkeley, CA: University of California Press.

GOFFMAN, E. (1971), *Relations in Public*. New York: Basic Books.

GUSFIELD, J. R. (1987), 'Passage to Play: Rituals of Drink in American Society', in M. Douglas, ed., *Constructive Drinking: Perspectives on Drinking from Anthropology*. Cambridge: Cambridge University Press, pp. 73–90.

169

HABERMAS, J. (1986), 'Law as Medium and Law as Institution', in Gunther Teubner, ed., *Dilemmas of Law in the Welfare State*. Berlin: Walter de Gruyter.

HAZAN, H. (1987), 'Holding Time Still with Cups of Tea', in M. Douglas, ed., *Constructive Drinking: Perspectives on Drinking from Anthropology*. Cambridge: Cambridge University Press, pp. 205–19.

HAZLEHURST, K. (1985), 'Community Care/Community Responsibility: Community Participation in Criminal Justice Administration in New Zealand', in K. Hazlehurst, ed., *Justice Programs for Aboriginal and Other Indigenous Communities*. Canberra: Australian Institute of Criminology.

HEINZ, A., and KERSTETTER, W. (1981), 'Pretrial Settlement Conference: Evaluation of a Reform in Plea Bargaining', in B. Galaway and J. Hudson, eds, *Perspectives on Crime Victims*. St. Louis, MO: Mosby.

HIRSCHI, T., and GOTTFREDSON, M. (1983), 'Age and the Explanation of Crime', *American Journal of Sociology*, 89: 552–84.

HOWARD, B., and PURCHES, L. (1992), 'A Discussion of the Police Family Group Conferences and the Follow-Up Program (Stage 2) in the Wagga Wagga Juvenile Cautioning Process', *Rural Society*, 2: 20–3.

Interim Report of the Select Committee on the Juvenile Justice System (1992). Adelaide: Parliament of South Australia.

KIGIN, R., and NOVACK, S. (1980), 'A Rural Restitution Program for Juvenile Offenders and Victims', in J. Hudson and B. Galaway, eds, *Victims, Offenders and Alternative Sanctions*. Lexington, MA: Lexington Books.

MARSHALL, T. F. (1985), *Alternatives to Criminal Courts*. Aldershot: Gower.

MAXWELL, G. M., and MORRIS, A. (1993), *Family Victims and Culture: Youth Justice in New Zealand*. Wellington: Institute of Criminology, Victoria University of Wellington.

McDONALD, J., and IRELAND, S. (1990), *Can It be Done Another Way?* Sydney: New South Wales Police Service.

MEIMA, M. (1990), 'Sexual Violence, Criminal Law and Abolitionism', in B. Rolston and M. Tomlinson, eds, *Gender, Sexuality and Social Control*. Bristol: European Group for the Study of Deviance and Social Control.

MOORE, D. B. (1992), 'Facing the Consequences. Conferences and Juvenile Justice', *National Conference on Juvenile Justice*. Canberra: Australian Institute of Criminology.

MORRIS, A., and MAXWELL, G. (1992), 'Juvenile Justice in New Zealand: A New Paradigm', *Australian and New Zealand Journal of Criminology*, 26: 72–90.

MORRIS, A., MAXWELL, G., and ROBERTSON, J. P. (in press), 'Giving Victims a Voice: A New Zealand Experiment', *Howard Journal of Criminology*.

MUGFORD, J., and MUGFORD, S. (1991), 'Shame and Reintegration in the Punishment and Deterrence of Spouse Abuse'. Paper presented to the American Society of Criminology Conference, San Francisco, 20 November.

—— (1992), 'Policing Domestic Violence), in P. Moir and H. Eijckman, eds, *Policing Australia: Old Issues, New Perspectives*. Melbourne: MacMillan, pp. 321–83.

MURPHY, J. G., and HAMPTON, J. (1989), *Forgiveness and Mercy*. New York: Cambridge.

New Zealand Police Association (1991), Submission to the Review of the Children, Young Persons and their Families Act 1989. Wellington: New Zealand Police Association.

NOVACK, S., GALAWAY, B., and HUDSON, J. (1980), 'Victim and Offender Perceptions of the Fairness of Restitution and Community-Service Sanctions', in J. Hudson and B. Galaway, eds, *Victims, Offenders and Alternative Sanctions*. Lexington, MA: Lexington Books.

CONDITIONS OF SUCCESSFUL REINTEGRATION CEREMONIES

O'CONNELL, T. (1992), 'It May Be the Way to Go', *National Conference on Juvenile Justice*. Canberra: Australian Institute of Criminology.

O'CONNELL, T. and MOORE, D. (1992), 'Wagga Juvenile Cautioning Process: The General Applicability of Family Group Conferences for Juvenile Offenders and their Victims', *Rural Society*, 2: 16–19.

O'CONNOR, I., and SWEETAPPLE, P. (1988), *Children in Justice*. Sydney: Longman-Cheshire.

PEPINSKY, H. E., and QUINNEY, R. (eds) (1991) *Criminology as Peacemaking*. Bloomington: Indiana University Press.

POLK, K. (1992), 'Jobs not Jails: A New Agenda for Youth', *National Conference on Juvenile Justice*. Canberra: Australian Institute of Criminology.

Report of the Ministerial Advisory Committee on a Maori Perspective for the Department of Social Welfare (1986), *Puao-Te-Ata-Tu* (day break). Wellington, New Zealand: Department of Social Welfare.

ROSE, N. (1990), *Governing the Soul: Shaping the Private Self*. London: Routledge and Kegan Paul.

SCHEFF, T. J., and RETZINGER, S. M. (1991), *Emotions and Violence: Shame and Rage in Destructive Conflicts*. Lexington, MA: Lexington Books.

SCHUR, E. M. (1973), *Radical Non-Intervention: Rethinking the Delinquency Problem*. Englewood Cliffs, NJ: Prentice-Hall.

SHAPLAND, J., WILLMORE, J., and DUFF, P. (1985), *Victims in the Criminal Justice System*, Cambridge Studies in Criminology. Brookfield, VT: Gower.

SHEARING, C. D., and ERICSON, R. V. (1991), 'Towards a Figurative Conception of Action', *British Journal of Sociology*, 42: 481–506.

SIMMEL, G. (1978), *The Philosophy of Money*. London: Routledge.

SYKES, G., and MATZA, D. (1957), 'Techniques of Neutralization: A Theory of Delinquency', *American Sociological Review*, 22: 664–70.

TATE, SENATOR M. (1992), Opening Address, *National Conference on Juvenile Justice*. Canberra: Australian Institute of Criminology.

TAYLOR, I., WALTON, P., and YOUNG, J. (1973), *The New Criminology: For a Social Theory of Deviance*. London: Routledge and Kegan Paul.

UMBREIT, M. (1985), *Crime and Reconciliation: Creative Options for Victims and Offenders*. Nashville, TN: Abigton Press.

WEITEKAMP, E. (1989), Restitution: A New Paradigm of Criminal Justice or a New Way to Widen the System of Social Control? Unpublished Ph.D dissertation, University of Pennsylvania.

WRIGHT, M. (1982), *Making Good: Prisons, Punishment and Beyond*. London: Hutchinson.

Youth Justice Coalition (1990), *Kids in Justice: A Blueprint for the 90s*. Sydney: Law Foundation of New South Wales.

ZEHR, H. (1990), *Changing Lenses: A New Focus for Criminal Justice*. Scottdale, PA: Herald Press.

[15]
Restorative Justice
and a Better Future[1]

I WANT YOU TO IMAGINE two robbers. First, a teenager is arrested
in Halifax for a robbery. The police send him to court where he
is sentenced to six months incarceration. As a victim of child abuse,
he is both angry with the world and alienated from it. During his
period of confinement he acquires a heroin habit and suffers more
violence. He comes out more desperate and alienated than when
he went in, sustains his drug habit for the next twenty years by
stealing cars, burgles dozens of houses and pushes drugs to others
until he dies in a gutter, a death no one mourns. Probably someone
rather like that was arrested in Halifax today, perhaps more than
one.

Tomorrow another teenager, Sam, is arrested in Halifax for a
robbery. He is a composite of several Sams I have seen. The police
officer refers Sam to a facilitator who convenes a restorative justice
conference. When the facilitator asks about his parents, Sam says
he is homeless. His parents abused him and he hates them. Sam
refuses to cooperate with a conference if they attend. After talking
with the parents, the facilitator agrees that perhaps it is best not to
involve the parents. What about grandparents? No, they are dead.
Brothers and sisters? No, he hates his brothers too. Sam's older
sister, who was always kind to him, has long since left home. He
has no contact with her. Aunts and uncles? Not keen on them
either, because they would always put him down as the black
sheep of the family and stand by his parents. Uncle George was
the only one he ever had any time for, but he has not seen him for

[1]A longer version of this article will be appearing as "Restorative Justice" in *The
Oxford Handbook of Crime and Punishment,* ed. Michael Tonry (Oxford UP). My
thanks to Christine Baker and Heather Strang for helpful comments on an earlier
draft of this paper, and to Tonia Vincent for her insightful research assistance.

years. Teachers from school? Hates them all. Sam has dropped out.
They always treat him like dirt. The facilitator does not give up:
"No one ever treated you okay at school?" Well, the hockey coach
is the only one Sam can ever think of being fair to him. So the
hockey coach, Uncle George and older sister are tracked down by
the facilitator and invited to the conference along with the robbery
victim and her daughter, who comes along to support the victim
through the ordeal.

These six participants sit on chairs in a circle. The facilitator
starts by introducing everyone and reminding Sam that while he
has admitted to the robbery, he can change his plea at any time
during the conference and have the matter heard by a court. Sam is
asked to explain what happened in his own words. He mumbles
that he needed money to survive, saw the lady, knocked her over
and ran off with her purse. Uncle George is asked what he thinks
of this. He says that Sam used to be a good kid. But Sam had gone
off the rails. He had let his parents down so badly that they would
not even come today. "And now you have done this to this poor
lady. I never thought you would stoop to violence," continues Uncle
George, building into an angry tirade against the boy. The hockey
coach also says he is surprised that Sam could do something as
terrible as this. Sam was always a troublemaker at school. But he
could see a kindly side in Sam that left him shocked about the
violence. The sister is invited to enter the conversation, but the
facilitator moves on to the victim when Sam's sister seems too
emotional to speak.

The victim explains how much trouble she had to cancel the
credit cards in the purse, how she had no money for the shopping
she needed to do that day. Her daughter explains that the most
important consequence of the crime was that her mother is now
afraid to go out on her own. In particular, she is afraid that Sam is
stalking her, waiting to rob her again. Sam sneers at this and seems
callous throughout. His sister starts to sob. Concerned about how
distressed she is, the facilitator calls a brief adjournment so she can
comfort her, with help from Uncle George. During the break, the
sister reveals that she understands what Sam has been through.
She says she was abused by their parents as well. Uncle George
has never heard of this, is shocked, and not sure that he believes it.

When the conference reconvenes, Sam's sister speaks to him
with love and strength. Looking straight into his eyes, the first gaze

he could not avoid in the conference, she says that she knows exactly what he has been through with their parents. No details are spoken. But the victim seems to understand what is spoken of by the knowing communication between sister and brother. Tears rush down the old woman's cheeks and over a trembling mouth.

It is his sister's love that penetrates Sam's callous exterior. From then on he is emotionally engaged with the conference. He says he is sorry about what the victim has lost. He would like to pay it back, but has no money or job. He assures the victim he is not stalking her. She readily accepts this now and when questioned by the facilitator says now she thinks she will feel safe walking out alone. She wants her money back but says it will help her if they can talk about what to do to help Sam find a home and a job. Sam's sister says he can come and live in her house for a while. The hockey coach says he has some casual work that needs to be done, enough to pay Sam's debt to the victim and a bit more. If Sam does a good job, he will write him a reference for applications for permanent jobs. When the conference breaks up, the victim hugs Sam and tearfully wishes him good luck. He apologizes again. Uncle George quietly slips a hundred dollars to Sam's sister to defray the extra cost of having Sam in the house, and says he will be there for both of them if they need him.

Sam has a rocky life punctuated by several periods of unemployment. A year later he has to go through another conference after he steals a bicycle. But he finds work when he can, mostly stays out of trouble and lives to mourn at the funerals of Uncle George and his sister. The victim gets her money back and enjoys taking long walks alone. Both she and her daughter say that they feel enriched as a result of the conference, have a little more grace in their lives. I will return to the meanings of this story.

Institutional Collapse
Few sets of institutional arrangements created in the West since the industrial revolution have been as large a failure as the criminal justice system. In theory it administers just, proportionate corrections that deter. In practice, it fails to correct or deter, just as often making things worse as better. It is a criminal *injustice* system that systematically turns a blind eye to crimes of the powerful, while imprisonment remains the best-funded labour market program for the unemployed and indigenous peoples. It pretends to be equitable,

yet one offender may be sentenced to a year in a prison where he will be beaten on reception and then systematically bashed thereafter, raped, even infected with AIDS, while others serve twelve months in comparatively decent premises, especially if they are white-collar criminals. While I do believe that Canada's criminal justice system is more decent than ours in Australia, all western criminal justice systems are brutal, institutionally vengeful, and dishonest to their stated intentions. The interesting question is why are they such failures. Given that prisons are vicious and degrading places, you would expect fear of ending up in them would deter crime.

There are many reasons for the failures of the criminal justice system to prevent crime. I will give you just one, articulated in the terms of my theory in *Crime, Shame and Reintegration.*[2] The claim of this theory is that the societies that have the lowest crime rates are the societies that shame criminal conduct most effectively. There is an important difference between reintegrative shaming and stigmatization. While reintegrative shaming prevents crime, stigmatization is a kind of shaming that makes crime problems worse. Stigmatization is the kind of shaming that creates outcasts; it is disrespectful, humiliating. Stigmatization means treating criminals as evil people who have done evil acts. Reintegrative shaming means disapproving of the evil of the deed while treating the person as essentially good. Reintegrative shaming means strong disapproval of the act but doing so in a way that is respecting of the person. Once we understand this distinction, we can see why putting more police on the street can actually increase crime. More police can increase crime if they are systematically stigmatizing in the way they deal with citizens. More police can reduce crime if they are systematically reintegrative in the way they deal with citizens.

We can also understand why building more prisons could make the crime problem worse. Having more people in prison does deter some and incapacitates others from committing certain crimes, like bank robberies, because there are no banks inside the prison for them to rob, though there certainly are plenty of vulnerable people to rape and pillage. But because prisons stigmatize, they also make things worse for those who have criminal identities

---

[2]John Braithwaite, *Crime, Shame and Reintegration* (Cambridge: Cambridge UP, 1989).

affirmed by imprisonment, those whose stigmatization leads them to find solace in the society of the similarly outcast, those who are attracted into criminal subcultures, those who treat the prison as an educational institution for learning new skills for the illegitimate labour market. On this account, whether building more prisons reduces or increases the crime rate depends on whether the stigmatizing nature of a particular prison system does more to increase crime than its deterrent and incapacitative effects reduce it.

A lack of theoretical imagination among criminologists has been one underrated reason for the failure of the criminal justice system. Without theorizing why it fails, the debate has collapsed to a contest between those who want more of the same to make it work and those who advance the implausible position that it makes sense to stigmatize people first and later subject them to rehabilitation programs inside institutions. With juvenile justice in particular, the debate throughout the century has see-sawed between the justice model and the welfare model. See-sawing between retribution and rehabilitation has got us nowhere. If we are serious about a better future, we need to hop off this see-saw and strike out in search of a third model.

For me, that third model is restorative justice. During the past decade a number of different labels—reconciliation (Dignan,[3] Marshall,[4] Umbreit[5]), peacemaking (Pepinsky and Quinney[6]), redress (de Hann[7])—have described broadly similar intellectual currents. Philip Pettit and I have sought to argue for republican criminal justice (Braithwaite and Pettit,[8] Pettit with Braithwaite[9]). Yet the label that has secured by far the widest consent during the past

---

[3]J. Dignan, "Repairing the Damage: Can Reparation Work in the Service of Diversion?" *British Journal of Criminology* 32 (1992): 453–72.

[4]T.F. Marshall, *Alternatives to Criminal Courts* (Aldershot: Gower, 1985).

[5]M. Umbreit, *Crime and Reconciliation: Creative Options for Victims and Offenders* (Nashville, TN: Abigton Press, 1985).

[6]H.E. Pepinsky and R. Quinney, eds., *Criminology as Peacemaking* (Bloomington: Indiana UP, 1991).

[7]W. de Hann, *The Politics of Redress: Crime, Punishment and Penal Abolition* (London: Unwin and Hyman, 1990).

[8]John Braithwaite and Philip Pettit, *Not Just Deserts: A Republican Theory of Criminal Justice* (Oxford: Oxford UP, 1990).

[9]Philip Pettit with John Braithwaite, "Not Just Deserts Even in Sentencing," *Current Issues in Criminal Justice* 4 (1993): 225–39.

few years has been that employed by Zehr,[10] Galaway and Hudson,[11] Cragg,[12] Walgrave,[13] Bazemore,[14] Umbreit,[15] Consedine,[16] Peters and Aertsen,[17] Messmer and Otto,[18] Marshall,[19] McElrea,[20] McCold,[21]

---

[10]Howard Zehr, *Changing Lenses: A New Focus for Criminal Justice* (Scottdale, PA: Herald Press, 1990); Howard Zehr, "Retributive Justice, Restorative Justice," *New Perspectives on Crime and Justice: Occasional Papers of the MCC Canada Victim Offender Ministries Program and the MCC US Office of Criminal Justice*, issue 4, Sept. 1985.

[11]B. Galaway and J. Hudson, *Criminal Justice, Restitution and Reconciliation* (Monsey, NY: Criminal Justice Press, 1990); B. Galaway and J. Hudson, eds., *Restorative Justice: International Perspectives* (Monsey, NY: Criminal Justice Press, 1996).

[12]W. Cragg, *The Practice of Punishment: Towards a Theory of Restorative Justice* (London: Routledge, 1992).

[13]Lode Walgrave, "Restorative Justice for Juveniles: Just a Technique or a Fully Fledged Alternative?" *The Howard Journal* 34.3 (1995): 228–49; Lode Walgrave, "In Search of Limits to the Restorative Justice for Juveniles," unpublished paper presented to the International Congress on Criminology, Budapest, 23–27 Aug. 1993.

[14]G. Bazemore, *Balanced and Restorative Justice for Juvenile Offenders: An Overview of a New OJJDP Initiative* (Washington, DC: Office of Juvenile Justice and Delinquency Prevention, 1993).

[15]M. Umbreit, "Holding Juvenile Offenders Accountable: A Restorative Justice Perspective," *Juvenile and Family Court Journal* (Spring 1995): 31–42; M. Umbreit, *Victim Meets Offender: The Impact of Restorative Justice and Mediation* (Monsey, NY: Willow Tree Press, 1994); M. Umbreit, "Crime Victims Seeking Fairness, not Revenge: Towards Restorative Justice," *Federal Probation* 53.3: 52–57.

[16]Jim Consedine, *Restorative Justice: Healing the Effects of Crime* (Lyttleton, New Zealand: Ploughshares Publications, 1995).

[17]Tony Peters and Ivo Aertsen, "Restorative Justice: in Search of New Avenues in the Judicial Dealing with Crime: The Presentation of a Project of Mediation for Reparation," in C. Fijnaut et. al., eds., *Changes in Society, Crime and Criminal Justice in Europe* (Antwerp: Kluwer Law and Taxation Publishers, 1995).

[18]Heinz Messmer and Hans-Uwe Otto, "Restorative Justice: Steps on the Way Toward a Good Idea," in Heinz Messmer and Hans-Uwe Otto, eds., *Restorative Justice on Trial* (Dordrecht: Kluwer Academic Publishers, 1992).

[19]Tony Marshall, "Grassroots Initiatives Towards Restorative Justice: The New Paradigm?" unpublished paper for the Fullbright Colloquium, "Penal Theory and Penal Practice," University of Stirling, Sept. 1992.

[20]F.W.M. McElrea, "Restorative Justice—The New Zealand Youth Court: A Model for Development in Other Courts," *Journal of Judicial Administration* 4.1 (1994): 33–54.

[21]Paul McCold, "Restorative Justice and the Role of Community," unpublished paper presented to the Academy of Criminal Justice Sciences Annual Conference, Boston, March 1995.

Maxwell,[22] Carbonatto,[23] Crawford, Strong, Sargent, Souryal and Van Ness,[24] Denison,[25] Knopp,[26] Mackey,[27] Morrell,[28] Van Ness,[29] and Young[30]—restorative justice. It has become the slogan of a global social movement. For those of us who see constructive engagement with social movement politics as crucial for major change, labels that carry meaning for activists matter. In this spirit, I now wish that I had called reintegrative shaming, restorative shaming.

What Is Restorative Justice?

Restorative justice means restoring victims, a more victim-centred criminal justice system, as well as restoring offenders and restoring community. First, what does restoring victims mean? It means restoring the *property lost* or the *personal injury*, repairing the broken window or the broken teeth. It means restoring a *sense of security*. Even victims of property crimes such as burglary often suffer a loss of security when the private space of their home is violated. When the criminal justice system fails to leave women secure about walking alone at night, half the population is left unfree in a rather fundamental sense.

Victims suffer loss of dignity when someone violates their bodies or shows them the disrespect of taking things which are

---

[22]Gabrielle Maxwell, "Some Traditional Models of Restorative Justice from Canada, South Africa and Gaza," in McElrea, F.W.M., ed., *Rethinking Criminal Justice*, vol. 1: *Justice in the Community* (Auckland: Legal Research Foundation, 1995).

[23]H. Carbonatto, *Expanding Options for Spousal Abuse: The Use of Restorative Justice*, Occasional Papers in Criminology, New Series 4 (Wellington: Institute of Criminology, 1995).

[24]T. Crawford, K. Strong, K. Sargeant, C. Souryal and D. Van Ness, *Restorative Justice: Principles* (Washington, DC: Justice Fellowship, 1990).

[25]K. Denison, *Restorative Justice in Ourselves: New Perspectives on Crime and Justice* (Akron, PA: Mennonite Central Committee Office of Criminal Justice, 1991).

[26]F.H. Knopp, "Restorative Justice For Juvenile Sex Offenders," paper presented to the National Council of Juvenile and Family Court Judges, Lake Tahoe/Reno, 16 Nov. 1992.

[27]V. Mackey, *Restorative Justice: Towards Nonviolence* (Louisville, KY: Presbyterian Criminal Justice Program, 1990).

[28]V. Morrell, "Restorative Justice: An Overview," *Criminal Justice Quarterly* 5 (1993): 3–7.

[29]D. Van Ness, "New Wine and Old Wineskins: Four Challenges of Restorative Justice," *Criminal Law Forum* 4.2 (1993): 251–76.

[30]M. Young, *Restorative Community Justice: A Call to Action* (Washington, DC: National Organization for Victim Assistance, 1995).

precious to them. Sometimes this disrespectful treatment engenders victim shame: "He abused me rather than some other woman because I am trash," "She stole my dad's car because I was irresponsible to park it in such a risky place." Victim shame often triggers a shame-rage spiral wherein victims reciprocate indignity through vengeance or by their own criminal acts.

Disempowerment is part of the indignity of being a victim of crime. According to Pettit and Braithwaite's republican theory of criminal justice,[31] a wrong should not be defined as a crime unless it involves some domination of us that reduces our freedom to enjoy life as we choose. It follows that it is important to *restore any lost sense of empowerment* as a result of crime. This is particularly important where the victim suffers structurally systematic domination. For example, some of the most important restorative justice initiatives we have seen in Australia have involved some thousands of Aboriginal victims of consumer fraud by major insurance companies.[32] In these cases, victims from remote Aboriginal communities relished the power of being able to demand restoration and corporate reform from "white men in white shirts."

The way that western legal systems handle crime compounds the disempowerment that victims feel, first at the hands of offenders and then at the hands of a professional, remote justice system that eschews their participation. The lawyers, in the words of Nils Christie, "steal our conflict."[33] The western criminal justice system has, on balance, been corrosive of deliberative democracy, though the jury is one institution that has preserved a modicum of it. Restorative justice is deliberative justice; it is about people deliberating over the consequences of a crime, how to deal with them and prevent their recurrence. This contrasts with the professional justice of lawyers deciding which rules apply to a case and then constraining their deliberation within a technical discourse about that rule-application. So restorative justice restores the *deliberative control of justice by citizens*.

Restorative justice aims to *restore harmony based on a feeling that justice has been done*. Restoring harmony alone, while leaving

---

[31] *Not Just Deserts: A Republican Theory of Criminal Justice* (1990).
[32] See Brent Fisse and John Braithwaite, *Corporations, Crime and Accountability* (Cambridge: Cambridge UP, 1993) 218–23.
[33] Nils Christie, "Conflicts as Property," *British Journal of Criminology* 17 (1978): 1–15.

an underlying injustice to fester unaddressed, is not enough. "Restoring balance" is only acceptable as a restorative justice ideal if the "balance" between offender and victim that prevailed before the crime was a morally decent balance. There is no virtue in restoring the balance by having a woman pay for a loaf of bread she has stolen from a rich man to feed her children. Restoring harmony between victim and offender is only likely to be possible in such a context on the basis of a discussion of why the children are hungry and what should be done about the underlying injustice of their hunger.

Restorative justice cannot resolve the deep structural injustices that cause problems like hunger. But we must demand two things of restorative justice here. First, it must not make structural injustice worse (in the way, for example, that the Australian criminal justice system does by being an important cause of the unemployability and oppression of Aboriginal people). Indeed, we should hope from restorative justice for micro-measures that ameliorate macro-injustice where this is possible. Second, restorative justice should restore harmony with a remedy grounded in dialogue which takes account of underlying injustices. Restorative justice does not resolve the age-old questions of what should count as unjust outcomes. It is a more modest philosophy than that. It settles for the procedural requirement that the parties talk until they feel that harmony has been restored on the basis of a discussion of all the injustices they see as relevant to the case.

Finally, restorative justice aims to *restore social support.* Victims of crime need support from their loved ones during the process of requesting restoration. They sometimes need encouragement and support to engage with deliberation toward restoring harmony. Friends sometimes do blame the victim, or more commonly are frightened off by a victim going through an emotional trauma. Restorative justice aims to institutionalize the gathering around of friends during a time of crisis.

Restoring Offenders, Restoring Community
In most cases, a more limited range of types of restoration is relevant to offenders. Offenders have generally not suffered property loss or injury as a result of their own crime, though sometimes loss or injury is a cause of the crime. Dignity, however, is generally in need of repair after the shame associated with arrest. When there is

a victim who has been hurt, there is no dignity in denying that there is something to be ashamed about. Dignity is generally best restored by confronting the shame, accepting responsibility for the bad consequences suffered by the victim and apologizing with sincerity.[34] A task of restorative justice is to institutionalize such *restoration of dignity* for offenders.

The sense of insecurity and disempowerment of offenders is often an issue in their offending, and in discussion about what is to be done to prevent further offending. Violence by young men from racial minorities is sometimes connected to their feelings of being victims of racism. For offenders, *restoring a sense of security and empowerment* is often bound up with employment, the feeling of having a future, achieving some educational success, sporting success, indeed any kind of success.

Many patches are needed to sew the quilt of deliberative democracy. Criminal justice deliberation is not as important a patch as deliberation in the parliament, in trade unions, even in universities. But to the extent that restorative justice deliberation does lead ordinary citizens into serious democratic discussion about racism, unemployment, masculinist cultures in local schools and police accountability, it is not an unimportant element of a deliberatively rich democracy.

The mediation literature shows that satisfaction of complainants with the justice of the mediation is less important than the satisfaction of those who are complained against in achieving mutually beneficial outcomes.[35] Criminal subcultures are memory files that collect injustices.[36] Crime problems will continue to become deeply culturally embedded in western societies until we reinvent criminal justice as a process that restores a sense of procedural justice to offenders.[37]

Finally, Francis T. Cullen has suggested that there could be no better organizing concept for criminology than *social support*, given the large volume of evidence about the importance of social

[34]On this issue, especially the question of by-passed shame, see Tom Scheff and Suzanne Retzinger, *Emotions and Violence: Shame and Rage in Destructive Conflicts* (Lexington: Lexington Books, 1991).

[35]Dean G. Puritt, "Research Report: Process and Outcome in Community Mediation," *Negotiation Journal* Oct. 1995: 374.

[36]David Matza, *Delinquency and Drift* (New York: Wiley, 1964) 102.

[37]Tom Tyler, *Why People Obey the Law* (New Haven: Yale UP, 1990).

support for preventing crime.[38] The New Zealand Maori people see our justice system as barbaric because it requires the defendant to stand alone in the dock without social support. In Maori thinking, civilized justice requires the offender's loved ones to stand beside him during justice rituals, sharing the shame for what has happened. Hence the shame the offender feels is more the shame of letting his loved ones down than a western sense of individual guilt. The shame of letting loved ones down can be readily transcended by simple acts of forgiveness from those loved ones.

Restoring community is advanced by a proliferation of restorative justice rituals in which social support around specific victims and offenders is restored. At this micro level, restorative justice is an utterly bottom-up approach to restoring community. At a meso level, important elements of a restorative justice package are initiatives to foster community organization in schools, neighbourhoods, ethnic communities, churches, through professions and other NGOs who can deploy restorative justice in their self-regulatory practices. At a macro level, we must better design institutions of deliberative democracy so that concern about issues like unemployment and the effectiveness of labour market programs have a channel through which they can flow from discussions about local injustices up into national economic policy-making debate.

The Universality of Restorative Traditions
I have yet to discover a culture which does not have some deep-seated restorative traditions. Nor is there a culture without retributive traditions. Retributive traditions once had survival value. Cultures which were timid in fighting back were often wiped out by more determinedly violent cultures. In the contemporary world, as opposed to the world of our biological creation, retributive emotions have less survival value. Because risk management is institutionalized in this modern world, retributive emotions are more likely to get us into trouble than out of it, as individuals, groups and nations.

The message we might communicate to all cultures is that, in the world of the twenty-first century, you will find restorative traditions a more valuable resource than retributive traditions. Yet sadly, the hegemonic cultural forces in the contemporary world

---

[38]Francis T. Cullen, "Social Support as an Organizing Concept for Criminology: Presidential Address to the Academy of Criminal Justice Sciences," *Justice Quarterly* 11.4 (1994): 527–59.

communicate just the opposite message. Hollywood hammers the message that the way to deal with bad guys is through violence. Political leaders frequently hammer the same message. Yet many of our spiritual leaders are helping us to retrieve our restorative traditions—the Dalai Lama, for example. Archbishop Desmond Tutu in his Foreword to Jim Consedine's forthcoming new edition of *Restorative Justice*, correctly sees a "very ancient yet desperately needed truth" as underlying restorative justice processes, "rooted as they are in all indigenous cultures, including those of Africa." He sees his Truth and Reconciliation Commission as an example of restorative justice.

The restorative values I have been describing are cultural universals. All cultures value repair of damage to our persons and property, security, dignity, empowerment, deliberative democracy, harmony based on a sense of justice and social support. They are universals because they are all vital to our emotional survival as human beings and vital to the possibility of surviving without constant fear of violence. The world's great religions recognize that the desire to pursue these restorative justice values is universal, which is why some of our spiritual leaders are a hope against those political leaders who wish to rule through fear and by crushing deliberative democracy. Ultimately, those political leaders will find that they will have to reach an accommodation with the growing social movement for restorative justice, just as they must with the great religious movements they confront. Why? Because the evidence is now strong that ordinary citizens like restorative justice.[39] When the major political parties did their door-knocking during our last election in Canberra, they found that the thousands of citizens who had participated in a restorative justice conference mostly liked the justice they experienced.

---

[39]See, for example, Allison Morris and Gabrielle Maxwell, "Juvenile Justice in New Zealand: A New Paradigm," *Australian and New Zealand Journal of Criminology* 26 (1992): 72–90; Mary Hyndman, Margaret Thorsborne and Shirley Wood, *Community Accountability Conferencing: Trial Report* (Department of Education, Queensland, 1996); Tim Goodes, "Victims and Family Conferences: Juvenile Justice in South Australia," unpublished paper, 1995; David Moore with Lubica Forsaythe, *A New Approach to Juvenile Justice: An Evaluation of Family Conferencing in Wagga Wagga: A Report to the Criminology Research Council* (Wagga Wagga: The Centre for Rural Social Research, 1995); Donald Clairmont, "Alternative Justice Issues for Aboriginal Justice," unpublished paper, Atlantic Institute of Criminology, Nov. 1994.

It is true that the virtues restorative justice restores are viewed differently in different cultures and that opinion about the culturally appropriate ways of realizing them differ greatly. Hence, restorative justice must be a culturally diverse social movement that accommodates a rich plurality of strategies in pursuit of the truths it holds to be universal. It is about different cultures joining hands as they discover the profound commonalities of their experience of the human condition; it is about realizing the value of diversity, of preserving restorative traditions that work because they are embedded in a cultural past. Scientific criminology will never discover any universally best way of doing restorative justice. The best path is the path of cultural plurality in pursuit of culturally shared restorative values.

A Path to Culturally Plural Justice
A restorative research agenda to pursue this path has two elements:

1. *Culturally-specific investigation of how to save and revive the restorative justice practices that remain in all societies.*

2. *Culturally-specific investigation of how to transform state criminal justice both by making it more restorative and by rendering its abuses of power more vulnerable to restorative justice.*

On the first point, I doubt that neighbourhoods in our cities are replete with restorative justice practices that can be retrieved, though there are some. Yet in the more micro context of the nuclear family, the evidence is overwhelming from the metropolitan US that restorative justice is alive and well and that families who are more restorative are likely to have less delinquent children than families who are punitive and stigmatizing.[40]

Because families so often slip into stigmatization and brutalization of their difficult members, we need restorative justice institutionalized in a wider context that can engage and restore such families. In most societies, the wider contexts where the ethos and rituals of restorative justice are alive and ready to be piped into the wider streams of the society are schools, churches and remote indigenous communities. If it is hard to find restorative

---

[40]See the discussion of the evidence on this in Braithwaite, *Crime, Shame and Reintegration* 54–83.

justice in the disputing practices of our urban neighbourhoods, the experience of recent years has been that they are relatively easy to locate in urban schools.[41] This is because of the ethos of care and integration which is part of the western educational ideal (which, at its best, involves a total rejection of stigmatization) and because the interaction among the members of a school community tends to be more intense than the interaction among urban neighbours. Schools, like families, have actually become more restorative and less retributive than the brutal institutions of the nineteenth century. This is why we have seen very succesful restorative conferencing programs in contemporary schools.[42] We have also seen anti-bullying programs with what I would call a restorative ethos which have managed in some cases to halve bullying in schools.[43]

More of the momentum for the restorative justice movement has come from the world's churches than from any other quarter. Even in a nation like Indonesia where the state has such tyrannical power, the political imperative to allow some separation of church and state has left churches as enclaves where restorative traditions could survive. Religions like Islam and Christianity have strong retributive traditions as well, of course, though they have mostly been happy to leave it to the state to do the "dirty work" of temporal retribution.

When I spoke at a conference on restorative justice in Indonesia, I was struck in a conversation with three Indonesians— one Muslim, one Hindu and one Christian—that in ways I could not understand as an agnostic, each was drawing on a spirituality grounded in their religious experience to make sense of restorative justice. Similarly, I was moved by the spirituality of Cree approaches

---

[41]Mary Hyndman, Margaret Thorsborne and Shirley Wood, *Community Accountability Conferencing: Trial Report* (Department of Education, Queensland, 1996).

[42]Ibid.

[43]Dan Olweus, "Annotation: Bullying at School: Basic Facts and Effects of a School Based Intervention Program," *Journal of Child Psychology and Psychiatry* 35 (1994): 1171–90; David P. Farrington, "Understanding and Preventing Bullying," in M. Tonry, ed., *Crime and Justice: Annual Review of Research*, Vol. 17 (Chicago: U of Chicago P, 1993); John Pitts and Philip Smith, *Preventing School Bullying*, Police Research Group: Crime Detection and Prevention Series Paper 63 (London: Home Office, 1995); Debra J. Pepler, Wendy Craig, Suzanne Ziegler, and Alice Charach, "A School-based Antibullying Intervention," in Delwin Tattum, ed., *Understanding and Managing Bullying* (London: Heinemann, 1993).

to restorative justice when a number of Native Canadians visited Canberra this year. There is something important to learn about native North-American spirituality and how it enriches restorative justice.

Your Canadian indigenous communities are a cultural resource for the whole world. Because they have not been totally swamped by the justice codes of the West, they are a cultural resource, just as the biodiversity of your continent supplies the entire world a genetic resource. The very people who by virtue of their remoteness have succumbed least to the western justice model, who have been insulated from Hollywood a little more and for a little longer, the very people who are most backward in western eyes, are precisely those with the richest cultural resources from which the restorative justice movement can learn.

Important scholarly work is being done to unlock the cultural codes of restorative justice in your indigenous communities. "Healing circles," what a profound cultural code that is to unlock for the rest of the world.[44] How much we all have to learn from the experience of the Hollow Water community in dealing with an epidemic of child abuse through healing circles. Thérèse Lajeunesse's report on Hollow Water is already a wonderful resource for the world.[45] Joan Pennell and Gale Burford[46] have done a splendid job in their reports which document the conferences for dealing with family violence in Newfoundland, which are quite distinctive from, and doubtless superior to, the conferencing models we have applied in the southern hemisphere. I have already remonstrated with them about

---

[44]A.P. Melton, "Indigenous Justice Systems and Tribal Society," *Judicature* 79.3 (1995): 126–33; Four Worlds Development Project, *The Sacred Tree* (Alberta: Four Worlds Development Press, 1984).

[45]Thérèse Lajeunesse, *Community Holistic Circle Healing: Hollow Water First Nation* (Solicitor General: Ministry Secretariat, 1993).

[46]Gale Burford and Joan Pennell, *Family Group Decision Making: New Roles for 'Old' Partners in Resolving Family Violence* (St. John's: Memorial University of Newfoundland, 1995); Joan Pennell and Gale Burford, "Attending to Context: Family Group Decision Making in Canada," in J. Hudson et. al., eds., *Family Group Conferences: Perspectives on Policy and Practice* (Monsey, NY: Criminal Justice Press, 1994); Joan Pennell and Gale Burford, "Widening the Circle: Family Group Decision Making," *Journal of Child and Youth Care* 9.1: 1–11; Gale Burford and Joan Pennell, "Family Group Decision Making: An Innovation in Child and Family Welfare," in B. Galaway and J. Hudson, eds., *Child Welfare Systems: Canadian Research and Policy Implications* (forthcoming).

the need to pull all this illuminating research together into a book that can also have a massive effect internationally, as could a book on Hollow Water. So point one of the reform agenda of restorative justice is a research program to retrieve the restorative justice practices of not only native communities, but also of the schools and churches of dominant urban cultures. Scholars like Carol LaPrairie and Don Clairmont are among the Canadian scholars who are doing vital work in advancing point one of this agenda.

Point two of the agenda is to explore how to transform state criminal justice. In our multicultural cities I have said that we cannot rely on spontaneous ordering of justice in our neighbourhoods. There we must be more reliant on state reformers as catalysts of a new urban restorative justice. In our cities, where neighbourhood social support is least, where the loss from the statist takeover of disputing is most damaging, the gains that can be secured from restorative justice reform are greatest. When a police officer with a restorative justice ethos arrests a youth in a tightly knit rural community who lives in a loving family, who enjoys social support from a caring school and church, that police officer is not likely to do much better or worse by the child than a police officer who does not have a restorative justice ethos. Whatever the police do, the child's support network will probably sort the problem out so that serious reoffending does not occur. But when a metropolitan police officer with a restorative justice ethos arrests a homeless child like Sam, who hates parents who abused him, who has dropped out of school and is seemingly alone in the world, it is there that the restorative police officer can make a difference that will render him more effective in preventing crime than the retributive police officer. At least that is my hypothesis, one we can test empirically and are testing empirically.

In the alienated urban context where community is not spontaneously emergent in a satisfactory way, a criminal justice system aimed at restoration can construct a community of care around a specific offender or a specific victim who is in trouble. That is what the story of Sam is about. With the restorative justice conferences being convened in multicultural metropolises like Auckland, Adelaide, Sydney and Singapore, the selection principle as to who is invited to the conference is the opposite to that with a criminal trial. We invite to a criminal trial those who can inflict most damage on the other side. With a conference we invite those who might offer most support to their own side—Sam's sister, uncle and hockey coach, the victim's daughter.

In terms of the theory of reintegrative shaming, the rationale for who is invited to the conference is that the presence of supporters on the victim's side structures shame into the conference, the presence of supporters on the offender's side structures reintegration into the ritual. Conferences can be run in many different ways from the story of Sam's conference. Maori people in New Zealand tend to want to open and close their conferences with a prayer. The institutions of restorative justice we build in the city must be culturally plural, quite different from one community to another depending on the culture of the people involved. It is the empowerment principle of restorative justice that makes this possible—empowerment with process control.

From a restorative perspective, the important thing is that we have institutions in civil society which confront serious problems like violence rather than sweep them under the carpet, yet do so in a way that is neither retributive nor stigmatizing. Violence will not be effectively controlled by communities unless the shamefulness of violence is communicated. This does not mean that we need criminal justice institutions that set out to maximize shame. On the contrary, if we set out to do that we risk the creation of stigmatizing institutions.[47] All we need to do is nurture micro-institutions of deliberative democracy that allow citizens to discuss the consequences of criminal acts, who is responsible, who should put them right and how. Such deliberative processes naturally enable those responsible to confront and deal with the shame arising from what has happened. And if we get the invitation list right by inviting along people who enjoy maximum respect and trust on both the offender and victim side, then we maximize the chances that shame will be dealt with in a reintegrative way.

Decline and Revival in Restorative Traditions
The traditions of restorative justice that can be found in all the world's great cultures have been under attack during the past two centuries. Everywhere in the world, restorative ideals have suffered serious setbacks because of the globalization of the idea of a

---

[47]Suzanne Retzinger and Tom Scheff, "Strategy for Community Conferences: Emotions and Social Bonds," in B. Galaway and J. Hudson, eds., *Restorative Justice: International Perspectives* (Monsey, NY: Criminal Justice Press, 1996).

centralized state that takes central control of justice and rationalizes it into a punitive regime. Control of punishment strengthened the power and legitimacy of rulers.[48] So did control of mercy, the power of royal or presidential pardon. What rulers really wanted was the political power of controlling the police, the prisons and the courts. Yet abuse of that power proved at times such a threat to their legitimacy that they were forced by political opponents to institutionalize certain principles of fairness and consistency into the state system. Of course, the new democratic rulers were no more enthusiastic about returning justice to the people than were the tyrants they succeeded; the secret police continued to be important to combating organized threats to the state monopoly of violence, the regular police to disorganized threats. The pretence that the state punished crime in a consistent, politically even-handed way, was part of the legitimation for democratically centralized justice. Citizens continue to see this as a pretence. They realize that whatever the law says, the reality is one law for the rich, another for the poor; one set of rules for the politically connected, another for the powerless. Philip Pettit and I have sought to show that proportionality in practice is proportional punishment for the poor and impunity for the white-collar criminals.[49] Restorative justice, we contend, has a better chance of being made equitably available to rich and poor than just deserts.

While it is a myth that centralized state law enabled greater consistency and lesser partiality than community-based restorative justice, it is true that abuse of power always was and still is common in community justice, as Carol La Prairie's work shows for Canada.[50] And it is true that state oversight of restorative justice in the community can be a check on abuse of rights in local programs, local political dominations and those types of unequal treatment in local programs that are flagrantly unacceptable.[51] Equally it is true that restorative justice can be a check on abuse of rights by the

---

[48]See, for example, Michel Foucault, *Discipline and Punish: The Birth of the Prison*, trans. Alan Sheridan (London: Allen Lane, 1977).

[49]*Not Just Deserts: A Republican Theory of Criminal Justice*, ch. 9.

[50]Carol La Prairie, "Community Justice or Just Communities: Aboriginal Communities in Search of Justice," 1993.

[51]Jeremy Webber makes this point in the Canadian context: "the challenge is to reinvent aboriginal institutions so that they draw upon indigenous traditions and insights in a manner appropriate to the new situation. This may mean inventing checks to prevent abuse that were unnecessary two hundred years ago or which

central state. We see it in restorative justice conferences in Canberra when a mother asks during the conference that something be done about the police officers who continue to use excessive force in their dealings with her son, who continue to victimize her son for things done by others. The restorative justice ideal could not and should not be the romantic notion of shifting back to a world where state justice is replaced by local justice. Rather, it might be to use the existence of state traditions of rights, proportionality and rule of law as resources to check abuse of power in local justice and to use the revival of restorative traditions to check abuse of state power. In other words, restorative justice constitutionalized by the state can be the stuff of a republic with a richer separation of powers,[52] with less abuse of power, than could be obtained either under dispute resolution totally controlled by local politics or disputing totally dominated by the state.

The key elements of North Atlantic criminal justice that have globalized almost totally during the past two centuries are:

1. Central state control of criminal justice;

2. The idea of crime itself and that criminal law should be codified;

3. The idea that crimes are committed against the state (rather than the older ideas that they were committed against victims or God);

4. The idea of having a professionalized police who are granted a monopoly over the use of force in domestic conflicts;

5. The idea of moving away from compensation as the dominant way of dealing with crime by building a state prisons system to systematically segregate the good from the bad;

6. The idea that fundamental human rights should be protected during the criminal process.

---

existed in a very different form." See "Individuality, Equality and Difference: Justification for a Parallel System of Aboriginal Justice," in Robert Silverman and Marianne Nielsen, eds., *Aboriginal Peoples and Canadian Criminal Justice* (Toronto: Butterworths, 1992) 147.
[52]John Braithwaite, "On Speaking Softly and Carrying Sticks: Neglected Dimensions of a Republican Separation of Powers," unpublished paper, 1996.

Like abolitionists,[53] restorative justice theorists see most of these elements of the central state takeover of criminal justice as retrograde. However, unlike the most radical versions of abolitionism, restorative justice sees promise in preserving a state role as a watchdog of rights and concedes that for a tiny fraction of the people in our prisons it may actually be necessary to protect the community from them by incarceration. While restorative justice means treating many things we presently treat as crime simply as problems of living, restorative justice does not mean abolishing the concept of crime. In restorative justice rituals, being able to call wrongdoing a crime can be a powerful resource in persuading citizens to take responsibility, to pay compensation, to apologize, especially with corporate criminals who are not used to thinking of their exploitative conduct in that way.[54] Restorative justice does not mean abolishing the key elements of the state criminal justice system that has globalized so totally this century; it means shifting power from them to civil society, keeping key elements of the statist revolution but shifting power away from central institutions and checking the power that remains by the deliberative democracy from below that restorative justice enables.

So you see I have an analysis that is unfashionably universal. I believe that restorative justice will come to be a profoundly influential social movement throughout the world during the next century, first because it appeals to values that are shared universally by humanity, secondly because it responds to the defects of a centralized state criminal justice model that itself has totally globalized and utterly failed in every country where it gained the ascendancy. Everywhere it has failed, there are criminologists or lawyers within the state itself who are convinced of that failure. And given the global imperatives for states to be competitive by being fiscally frugal, large state expenditures that do not deliver on their objectives are vulnerable to social movements that claim they have an approach which will be cheaper, work better and be more popular with the people in the long run. Hence we should not be

---

[53]Herman Bianchi and Rene van Swaaningen, eds., *Abolitionism: Towards a Non-Repressive Approach to Crime* (Amsterdam: Free University Press, 1986); Nils Christie, *Limits to Pain* (Oxford: M. Robertson, 1982).

[54]See John Braithwaite, "Corporate Crime and Republican Criminological Praxis," in F. Pearce and L. Snider, eds., *Corporate Crime: Ethics, Law and the State* (Toronto: U of Toronto P, 1995).

surprised at the irony that some of the most savvy conservative governments in the world, who are most imbued with the imperatives for fiscal frugality, like New Zealand[55] and Singapore,[56] are early-movers in embracing the restorative justice movement against the grain of their traditional commitment to state punitiveness. In August of 1996, we even saw a US Assistant Attorney-General espousing a need to reinvent justice as restorative justice.[57]

While I am cautiously optimistic that the empirical evidence will continue to be encouraging about the efficacy and decency of restorative justice compared with retributive justice, the evidence is also clear that restorative justice often fails. Victims sometimes resent the time involved in deliberation; sometimes they experience heightened fear from meeting offenders; sometimes they are extremely vengeful, though more often I am moved by how forgiving they are when genuinely empowered with process control. We need quality research on when and why restorative justice fails and how to cover the weaknesses of restorative justice with complementary strengths of deterrence and incapaciation.[58]

---

[55]Gabrielle M. Maxwell and Allison Morris, *Family Participation, Cultural Diversity and Victim Involvement in Youth Justice: A New Zealand Experiment* (Wellington: Institute of Criminology, 1992): Allison Morris and Gabrielle M. Maxwell, "Juvenile Justice in New Zealand: A New Paradigm," *Australian and New Zealand Journal of Criminology* 26 (1993): 72–90.

[56]Lim Li Hsien, "Family Conferencing Good for Young Delinquents: Report," *Straits Times*, from IMAGE database, 6 March 1996; Wai Yin Chan, "Family Conferences in the Juvenile Justice Process: Survey on the Impact of Family Conferencing on Juvenile Offenders and Their Families," *Subordinate Courts Statistics and Planning Unit Research Bulletin* (Feb. 1996).

[57]"At the same time that communities across the country are mustering broad-based coalitions to tackle crime and youth justice, innovative efforts are under way to 'reinvent' the justice system itself. 'Restorative'—or community—justice experimentation is taking place in jurisdictions across the country .... Community justice is also being incorporated into community policing programs ... like the program in Australia that replaces formal prosecution with a 'family group conference' designed to shame the offender and explain the full impact of the crime on the victim and the community" (Laurie Robertson, "Linking Community-Based Initiatives and Community Justice: The Office of Justice Programs," *National Institute of Justice Journal* [Aug. 1996]: 6–7).

[58]John Braithwaite, "Beyond Positivism: Learning from Contextual Integrated Strategies," *Journal of Research in Crime and Delinquency* 30 (1993): 383–99.

Beyond Communitarianism Versus Individualism
Some criminologists in the West are critical of countries like
Singapore, Indonesia and Japan, where crime in the streets is not a
major problem, because they think individualism in these societies
is crushed by communitarianism or collective obligation. Their
prescription is that Asian societies need to shift the balance away
from communitarianism and allow greater individualism. I don't
find that a very attractive analysis.

Some Asian criminologists are critical of countries like the
US and Australia because they think these societies are excessively
individualistic, suffering much crime and incivility as a result.
According to this analysis, the West needs to shift the balance away
from individualism in favour of communitarianism, shift the balance
away from rights and toward collective responsibilities. I don't find
this a very attractive analysis either.

Both sides of this debate can do a better job of learning from
each other. We can aspire to a society that is strong on rights and
strong on responsibilities, that nurtures strong communities and
strong individuals. Indeed, in the good society strong communities
constitute strong individuals and vice versa. Our objective can be
to keep the benefits of the statist revolution at the same time as we
rediscover community-based justice. Community justice is often
oppressive of rights, often subjects the vulnerable to the domination
of local elites, subordinates women, can be procedurally unfair
and tends to neglect structural solutions. Mindful of this, we might
reframe the two challenges posed earlier in the paper:

*1. Helping indigenous community justice to learn from the virtues
of liberal statism—procedural fairness, rights, protecting the
vulnerable from domination.*

*2. Helping liberal state justice to learn from indigenous community
justice—learning the restorative community alternatives to
individualism.*

This reframed agenda resonates with the writing of Canadians such
as Donald Clairmont[59] and Marianne Nielsen, who writes that native

---

[59]Donald Clairmont, "Alternative Justice Issues for Aboriginal Justice," unpublished
paper, Atlantic Institute of Criminology, Nov. 1994.

communities "will have the opportunity of taking the best of the old, the best of the new and learning from others' mistakes so that they can design a system that may well turn into a flagship of social change."[60] Together these two questions ask how we save and revive traditional restorative justice practices in a way that helps them become procedurally fairer, in a way that respects fundamental human rights, that secures protection against domination. The liberal state can be a check on oppressive collectivism, just as bottom-up communitarianism can be a check on oppressive individualism. A healing circle can be a corrective to a justice system that can leave offenders and victims suicidally alone; a Charter of Rights and Freedoms a check on a tribal elder who imposes a violent tyranny on young people. The bringing together of these ideals is an old prescription—not just liberty, not just community, but liberté, égalité, fraternité. Competitive individualism has badly fractured this republican amalgam. The social movement for restorative justice does practical work to weld an amalgam that is relevant to the creation of contemporary urban multicultural republics. Day-to-day it is not sustained by romantic ideals in which I happen to believe, like deliberative democracy. They want to do it for Sam and for an old woman whom Sam pushed over one day. That is what enlists them to the social movement for restorative justice; in the process they are, I submit, enlisted into something of wider political significance.

---

[60]Marianne Nielsen, "Criminal Justice and Native Self-Government," in Robert Silverman and Marianne Nielsen, eds., *Aboriginal Peoples and Canadian Criminal Justice* (Toronto: Butterworths, 1992) 255.

Appendix

Further publications by John Braithwaite

Books

Inequality, Crime, and Public Policy, London and Boston, Routledge & Kegan Paul, 1979.

Prisons, Education and Work, Canberra and Brisbane, University of Queensland Press/ Australian Institute of Criminology, 1980.

with B. Fisse, *The Impact of Publicity on Corporate Offenders*, Albany, State University of New York Press, 1983.

Corporate Crime in the Pharmaceutical Industry, London and Boston, Routledge & Kegan Paul, 1984. (Japanese edition, Sanichi Shobo, 1992.)

with P. Grabosky, *Occupational Health and Safety Enforcement in Australia*, Canberra, Australian Institute of Criminology, 1985.

To Punish or Persuade: Enforcement of Coal Mine Safety, Albany, State University of New York Press, 1985.

with P. Grabosky, *Of Manners Gentle: Enforcement Strategies' of Australian Business Regulatory Agencies*, Melbourne, Oxford University Press, 1986.

Crime, Shame and Reintegration, Cambridge University Press, 1989.

with P. Pettit, *Not Just Deserts: A Republican Theory of Criminal Justice*, Oxford University Press, 1990.

with I. Ayres, *Responsive Regulation: Transcending the Deregulation Debate*, Oxford University Press, 1992.

with B. Fisse, *Corporations, Crime and Accountability*, Cambridge University Press, 1993.

with P. Drahos, *Global Business Regulation*, Cambridge University Press, 2000.

Edited Books

with P.R. Wilson (eds), *Two Faces of Deviance: Crimes of the Powerless and Powerful*, Brisbane, University of Queensland Press, 1978.

with P. Grabosky (eds) *Business Regulation and Australia's Future*, Canberra, Australian Institute of Criminology, 1993.

John Braithwaite

Refereed Journal Articles

1975

'Competitiveness in Schools and Delinquency', *Australian Journal of Social Issues*, 1975, 10, pp. 107–10.

'Population Growth and Crime', *Australian and New Zealand Journal of Criminology*, 1975, 8, pp. 57–61.

1976

with V.A. Braithwaite, P.R. Wilson and J.S. Western, 'The Validity of Charles Reich's Typology of Consciousness in Modern Society', *Journal of Social Psychology*, 1976, 99, pp. 241–9.

1978

with V.A. Braithwaite, 'An Exploratory Study of Delinquency and the Nature of Schooling', *Australian and New Zealand Journal of Sociology*, 1978, 14, pp. 25–31.

with H.G. Law, 'The Structure of Self-Reported Delinquency', *Applied Psychological Measurement*, 1978, 2, pp. 221–37.

1979

with M. Cass, 'Note on the Demographic Composition of Australian Police Forces and Prisons Services', *Australian and New Zealand Journal of Criminology*, 1979, 12, pp. 132–8.

with D. Biles, 'On Being Unemployed and Being a Victim of Crime', *Australian Journal of Social Issues*, 1979, 14, pp. 192–200.

'Transnational Corporations and Corruption: Toward Some International Solutions', *International Journal of the Sociology of Law*, 1979, 7, pp. 125–42.

with D. Biles and V. Braithwaite, 'The Mental Health of Victims of Crime', *International Journal of Offender Therapy and Comparative Criminology*, 1979, 23, pp. 129–34.

1980

'Inegalitarian Consequences of Egalitarian Reforms to Control Corporate Crime', *Temple Law Quarterly*, 1980, 53, pp. 1127–46.

with D. Biles, 'Crime Victimisation in Australia: A Comparison with the U.S.', *Journal of Crime and Justice*, 1980, 3, pp. 95–110.

with D. Biles, 'Overview of Findings from the First Australian National Crime Victims Survey', *Australian and New Zealand Journal of Criminology*, 1980, 13, pp. 41–51.

with D. Biles, 'Verifiability and Black's The Behaviour of Law', *American Sociological Review*, 1980, 45, pp. 334–8.

with V. Braithwaite, 'The Effect of Income Inequality and Social Democracy on Homicide: A Cross-National Comparison', *British Journal of Criminology*, 1980, 20, pp. 45–53.

'Merton's Theory of Crime and Differential Class Symbols of Success', *Crime and/et Justice*, 1980, 7/8, pp. 90–94.

with D. Biles, 'Women as Victims of Crime: Some Findings from the First Australian National Crime Victims Survey', *Australian Quarterly*, 1980, 52, pp. 329–39.

with D. Biles, Crime Victimisation Rates in Australian Cities, *Australian and New Zealand Journal of Sociology*, 1980, 16, pp. 79–85.

with D. Biles, The Police and Victims of Crime, *Australian Psychologist*, 1980, 14, pp. 345–55.

1981

with V. Braithwaite, Delinquency and the Question of Values, *International Journal of Offender Therapy and Comparative Criminology*, 1981, 25, pp. 273–89.

'The Myth of Social Class and Criminality' Reconsidered, *American Sociological Review*, 1981, 46, pp. 36–57. (Reprinted in J.F. Sheley (ed.) *Exploring Crime* , New York Wadworth Publishing Co, 1989.)

'The Limits of Economism in Controlling Harmful Corporate Conduct', *Law and Society Review*, 1981–82, 16, pp. 481–504.

1982

'Reply to Dr. Ernest van den Haag', *Journal of Criminal Law and Criminology*, 1982, 73, pp. 790–93.

Comment on 'The Criminal Law as a Threat System', *Journal of Criminal Law and Criminology*, 1982, 73, pp. 786–9.

'Challenging Just Deserts: Punishing White-Collar Criminals', *Journal of Criminal Law and Criminology*, 1982, 73, pp. 723–63.

'Enforced Self-Regulation: A New Strategy for Corporate Crime Control', *Michigan Law Review*, 1982, 80, pp. 1466–507.

with G. Geis, 'On Theory and Action for Corporate Crime Control', *Crime and Delinquency*, 1982, April, 292–314. (Reprinted in part as 'Stricter Penalties Would Reduce Corporate Crime', in *Crime and Criminals: Opposing Viewpoints*, 2nd ed. Edited by C. Debner, T. O'Neill and B. Szumski. St Paul: Greenhaven Press, 1984, pp. 115–19.)

with V. Braithwaite, Attitudes to Animal Suffering: An Exploratory Study, *International Journal for the Study of Animal Problems*, 1982, 3, pp. 42–9.

1983

with B. Fisse, Asbestos and Health: A Case of Informal Social Control, *Australian and New Zealand Journal of Criminology*, 1983, 16, pp. 67–80.

1984

'Prisons, Education and Work: One Step Forward, Two Steps Back', *Australian and New Zealand Journal of Criminology*, 1984, 17, pp. 49–57.

1985

'White Collar Crime', 1985, *Annual Review of Sociology*, 11, pp. 1–25. (Reprinted in G. Geis, R.F. Meier and L. Salinger (eds) *White-Collar Crime: Classic and Contemporary Views*, 3rd Edition, New York, Free Press, 1995 and D. Nelken (ed.), White Collar Crime, Aldershot, Dartmouth, 1994.)

with B. Fisse, 'Varieties of Responsibility and Organizational Crime', *Law and Policy*, 1985, 7, pp. 315–43. (Japanese translation in *National Business Law Journal*, 1988, No.409, 17–24; No. 411, 35–8; No. 413, 19–25.)

'Corporate Crime Research: Why Two Interviewers are Needed', *Sociology*, 1985, 19, pp. 136–8.

with S. Vale, 'Law Enforcement by Australian Consumer Affairs Agencies', *Australian and New Zealand Journal of Criminology*, 1985, 18, pp. 147–63.

1986

with P. Grabosky and D. Rickwood, Research Note: 'Corruption Allegations and Australian Business Regulation', *Australian and New Zealand Journal of Criminology*, 1986, 19, pp. 179–86.

'The Industries Assistance Commission Draft Report on Pharmaceutical Products', *Medical Journal of Australia*, 1986, 144, pp. 259–63.

1987

with P. Grabosky and J. Walker, 'An Enforcement Taxonomy of Regulatory Agencies', *Law and Policy*, 1987, 9, pp. 323–51.

'Negotiation Versus Litigation: Industry Regulation in Great Britain and the United States', *American Bar Foundation Research Journal*, 1987, 2, pp. 559–74.

with P. Grabosky and P. Wilson, 'The Myth of Community Tolerance Toward White-Collar Crime', *Australia and New Zealand Journal of Criminology*, 1987, 20, pp. 33–44.

Review Essay: 'The Mesomorphs Strike Back', *Australian and New Zealand Journal of Criminology*, 1987, 20, pp. 45–53.

with B. Fisse and G. Geis, 'Covert Facilitation and Crime: Restoring Balance to the Entrapment Debate', *Journal of Social Issues*, 1987, 43, pp. 5–42.

with B. Fisse and G. Geis, Overt Observations on Covert Facilitation: A Reply to the Commentators, *Journal of Social Issues*, 1987, 43, pp. 101–22.

1988

'White-Collar Crime, Competition and Capitalism: Comment on Coleman', *American Journal of Sociology*, 1988, 94, pp. 628–32.

with B. Fisse, 'The Allocation of Responsibility for Corporate Crime: Individualism, Collectivism and Accountability', *University of Sydney Law Review*, 1988, 11, pp. 468–513.

with B. Fisse, 'Preventive Law and Managerial Auditing', *Managerial Auditing Journal*, 1988, 3, pp. 17–20.

1989

'Criminological Theory and Organizational Crime', *Justice Quarterly*, 1989, 6, pp. 401–25. (Reprinted in D Nelken (ed.) *White Collar Crime*, Aldershot: Dartmouth, 1994.)

'The State of Criminology: Theoretical Decay or Renaissance', *Australian and New Zealand Journal of Criminology*, 1989, 22, pp. 129–35. (Reprinted in *Advances in Criminological Theory*, Vol. 2, 1990, pp. 155–66.)

1990

with J. Kelley, 'Public Opinion and the Death Penalty in Australia', *Justice Quarterly*, 1990, 7, pp. 501–36.

'Convergence in Models of Regulatory Strategy', *Current Issues in Criminal Justice*, 1990, 2, pp. 59–65.

with B. Fisse, 'On the Plausibility of Corporate Crime Theory', *Advances in Criminological Theory*, 1990, 2, pp. 15–38. (Reprinted in Japanese in *Kokushikan Law Review*, 1992, 15, pp. 149–77) and also Reprinted in G. Geis, R.F. Meier and L. Salinger eds *White-Collar Crime: Classic and Contemporary Views*, 3rd Edition, New York Free Press.

1991

with I. Ayres, 'Tripartism: Regulatory Capture and Empowerment', *Law and Social Inquiry*, 1991, 16, pp. 435–96.

with T. Makkai, 'Testing an Expected Utility Model of Corporate Deterrence', *Law and Society Review*, 1991, 25, pp. 7–40.

with T. Makkai, 'Criminological Theories and Regulatory Compliance', *Criminology*, 1991, 29, pp. 191–220.

'The Criminal Class and the Making and Breaking of Australia', *Australian and New Zealand Journal of Criminology*, 1991, 24, pp. 99–104.

'Poverty, Power, White-Collar Crime and the Paradoxes of Criminological Theory', *Australian and New Zealand Journal of Criminology*, 1991, 24, pp. 40–50. (Revised version reprinted in K. Schlegel and D. Weisburd (eds), *White Collar Crime Reconsidered, 1992*, Boston: Northeastern University Press.)

1992

with I. Ayres, 'Designing Responsive Regulatory Institutions', *The Responsive Community*, 1992, Summer, pp. 41–7.

'Reducing the Crime Problem: A Not So Dismal Criminology', *Australian and New Zealand Journal of Criminology, 1992*, 25, pp. 1–10.

with T. Makkai, 'In and Out of the Revolving Door: Making Sense of Regulatory Capture', *Journal of Public Policy*, 1992, pp. 12, pp. 61–78. (Reprinted in R. Baldwin, C. Scott and C. Hood (eds), *Regulation*. Oxford, 1998.)

with D. Gibson, V. Braithwaite and T. Makkai, 'Evaluating Quality of Care in Australian Nursing Homes', *Australian Journal on Ageing*, 11, 1992, pp. 3–9.

with I. Ayres, 'Partial Industry Regulation: A Monopsony Standard', *California Law Review*, 1992, 80, pp. 13–53.

with V. Braithwaite, D. Gibson and T. Makkai, 'Progress in Assessing the Quality of Australian Nursing Home Care', *Australian Journal of Public Health*, 1992, 16, pp. 89–97.

1993

with A. Jenkins, 'Profits, Pressure and Corporate Lawbreaking', *Crime, Law, and Social Change* 1993, 20, pp. 221–32.

with T. Makkai, 'The Limits of the Economic Analysis of Regulation', *Law and Policy*, 15, 1993, pp. 271–91.

with T. Makkai, 'Praise, Pride and Corporate Compliance', *International Journal of the Sociology of Law*, 21, 1993, pp. 73–91.

'Beyond Positivism: Learning from Contextual Integrated Strategies', *Journal of Research in Crime and Delinquency*, 1993, 30, pp. 383–99.

'Pride in Criminological Dissensus', *Law and Social Inquiry* 1993, 18, pp. 501–12.

'Transnational Regulation of the Pharmaceutical Industry', *The Annals of the American Academy of Political and Social Science, White-Collar Crime* 1993, 525, pp. 12–30. (Reprinted in G. Geis, R.F. Meier and L. Salinger eds *White-Collar Crime: Classic and Contemporary Views*, 3rd Edition, New York Free Press. Reprinted in N. Passas (ed.), *Transnational Crime*. Aldershot: Ashgate.)

'Shame and Modernity', *British Journal of Criminology*, 1993, 33, pp. 1–18. (Reprinted in Parker, David, Rosamund Dalziell and Iain Wright (eds) *Shame and the Modern Self*, Australian Scholarly Publishing, Melbourne, 1996.)

'Crime and the Average American: Review Essay', *Law and Society Review*, 1993, 27, pp. 215–31.

'Following the Money Trail to What Destination? An Introduction to the Symposium', *Alabama Law Review*, 1993, 44, pp. 657–68.

with J. Murphy, 'Clout and Internal Compliance Systems', *Corporate Conduct Quarterly*, 1993, 2, pp. 52–62.

with P. Pettit, 'Not Just Deserts Even in Sentencing', *Current Issues in Criminal Justice*, 1993, 4, pp. 225–39.

with T. Makkai, 'Can Resident-Centred Inspection of Nursing Homes Work with Very Sick Residents?' *Health Policy,* 24, 1993, pp. 19–33.

1994

with P. Pettit, 'Republican Criminology and Victim Advocacy', *Law and Society Review*, 28, 1994, pp. 765–76.

with T. Makkai, 'Trust and Compliance', *Policing and Society*, 4, 1994, pp. 1–12.

with T. Makkai, 'Reintegrative Shaming and Regulatory Compliance', *Criminology*, 32, 1994, pp. 361–85.

with T. Makkai, 'The Dialectics of Corporate Deterrence', *Journal of Research in Crime and Delinquency*, 31, 1994, pp. 347–73.

'A Sociology of Modeling and the Politics of Empowerment', *British Journal of Sociology*, 45, 1994, pp. 445–79.

'The Nursing Home Industry', in M. Tonry and A.J. Reiss (eds), Beyond the Law: Crime in Complex Organizations, *Crime and Justice: A Review of Research*, 18, 1994, pp. 11–54.

'Applying Some Lessons from Japanese and Maori Culture to the Reintegrative Shaming of Criminal Offenders', *Japanese Journal of Criminal Psychology*, 32, 1994, pp. 181–96.

with S. Mugford, 'Conditions of Successful Reintegration Ceremonies: Dealing with Juvenile Offenders', *British Journal of Criminology*, 34, 1994, pp. 139–71.

with V. Braithwaite, D. Gibson and T. Makkai, 'Regulatory Styles, Motivational Postures and Nursing Home Compliance', *Law and Policy*, 16, 1994, pp. 363–94.

with D. Chappell, 'The Job Compact and Crime', *Current Issues in Criminal Justice*, 5, 1994, pp. 295–300.

with P. Pettit, 'The Three Rs of Republican Sentencing', *Current Issues in Criminal Justice*, 5, 1994, pp. 318–25.

with D. Rickwood, 'Why Openness With Health Inspectors Pays', *Australian Journal of Public Health*, 18, 1994, pp. 165–70.

with P. Pettit 'Criminalization, Decriminalization and Republican Theory', *International Annals of Criminology*, 32 (1&2), 1994, pp. 61–80.

1995

'Community Values and Australian Jurisprudence', *Sydney Law Review*, 17, 1995, pp.351–72.

'Reply: Broadening Disciplines that Dull as Well as Sharpen', *Sydney Law Review*, 17, 1995.

with V. Braithwaite, 'The Politics of Legalism: Rules Versus Standards in Nursing-Home Regulation', *Social and Legal Studies*, 4, 1995, pp. 307–41.

1996

with T. Makkai, 'Procedural Justice and Regulatory Compliance', *Law and Human Behavior*, 1996, 20(1), pp. 83–98.

'Searching for Epistemologically Plural Criminology (And Finding Some)', *Australian and New Zealand Journal of Criminology*, 29(2), 1996, pp. 142–6.

1997

'Conferencing and Plurality', *British Journal of Criminology*, 1997, 37(4), pp. 502–6.

'Charles Tittle's *Control Balance* and criminological theory', *Theoretical Criminology*, 1997, 1(1), pp. 77–97.

'On Speaking Softly and Carrying Big Sticks: Neglected Dimensions of a Republication Separation of Powers', *University of Toronto Law Journal*, 1997, 47, pp. 305–61.

'Commentary: law, morality and restorative justice', *European Journal on Criminal Policy and Research*, 1997, 5(1), pp. 93–8.

1998

with C. Kapuscinski and B. Chapman, 'Unemployment and Crime: Towards Resolving the Paradox', *Journal of Quantitative Criminology*, 1998, 14(3), pp. 214–43.

'Regulation and Quality in Aged Care: A Cross-National Perspective', *Australasian Journal on Ageing*, 1998, 17(4), pp. 172–6.

'Education, Truth, Reconciliation: Comment on Scheff', *Revista Juridica Universidad de Puerto Rico*, 67(3), pp. 609–14.

1999

'Restorative Justice: Assessing Optimistic and Pessimistic Accounts', *Crime and Justice: A Review of Research*, 1999, 25, pp. 1–127.

with P. Drahos, 'Globalisation of Corporate Regulation and Corporate Citizenship', *Flinders Journal of Law Reform*, 1999, 3(1), pp. 33–74.

with L. Walgrave, 'Guilt, Shame and Restoration', *Justitiele Verkenningen*, 1999, 25(5), pp. 71–80.

'Accountability and Governance Under the New Regulatory State', *Australian Journal of Public Administration*, 1999, 58 (1), pp. 90–93.

'A Future Where Punishment is Marginalized: Realistic or Utopian?', *UCLA Law Review*, 1999, 46(6), 1727–50.

with P. Drahos, 'Ratcheting Up and Driving Down Global Regulatory Standards', *Development*, 1999, 42(2), pp. 109–14.

Chapters in Books and Published Conference Proceedings

1977

with P.R. Wilson, 'The School, Truancy and Delinquency', in P.R. Wilson (ed.), *Delinquency in Australia*, Brisbane, University of Queensland Press, 1977.

'Australian Delinquency: Research and Practical Considerations', in P.R. Wilson (ed.), *Delinquency in Australia*, Brisbane, University of Queensland Press, 1977.

1978

with B. Condon, 'On the Class Basis of Criminal Violence', in P.R. Wilson and J. Braithwaite (eds), *Two Faces of Deviance: Crimes of the Powerless and Powerful*, Brisbane, University of Queensland Press, 1978.

'An Exploratory Study of Used Car Fraud', in P.R. Wilson and J. Braithwaite (eds), *Two Faces of Deviance: Crimes of the Powerless and Powerful*, Brisbane, University of Queensland Press, 1978.

with P.R. Wilson, 'Pimps, Pervs and Power-Brokers', in P.R. Wilson and J. Braithwaite (eds), *Two Faces of Deviance: Crimes of the Powerless and Powerful*, Brisbane, University of Queensland Press, 1978.

'Unemployment and Crime: An Interpretation of the International Evidence', Proceedings of the Institute of Criminology No. 36, *Unemployment and Crime*, Sydney University Law School, 1978. (To be reprinted in M. Findlay (ed.) *Issues on Crime Control*.)

1980

'Political Economy of Punishment', in E.L. Wheelwright and K. Buckley (eds), *Essays in the Political Economy of Australian Capitalism*, Volume IV, Sydney, ANZ Books, 1980.

1982

'Paradoxes of Class Bias in Criminal Justice', in H. Pepinsky (ed.), *Breaking the Criminological Mold: New Premises, New Directions*, Beverly Hills, Sage, 1982.

with G. Geis, 'On Theory and Action for Corporate Crime Control', in G. Geis (ed.), *On White-Collar Crime*, Lexington, Mass., Lexington Books, 1982 (reprinted with modifications from Crime and Delinquency).

with D. Biles and R. Whitrod, 'Fear of Crime in Australia', in H.J. Schneider (ed.), *The Victim of International Perspective*, Berlin and New York, Walter de Gruyter, 1982. Translated into German as: 'Verbrechensfurcht in Australien', in H.J. Schneider (ed.) *Das Verbrechensopfer in der Strafrechtspflege*, Berlin, Walter de Gruyter, 1982.

1983

'A Clash of Criminological Imbeciles: The Great Crimes Commission Debate', in *A National Crimes Commission*, Proceedings of the Institute of Criminology, No.58, University of Sydney Law School, 1983.

1984

with D. Biles, 'Victims and Offenders: The Australian Experience, in Richard Block' (ed.), *Studies of Victimization*, Washington D.C., National Institute of Justice, 1984.

with B. Fisse, 'Sanctions Against Corporations: Dissolving the Monopoly of Fines', in R. Tomasic (ed.), *Business Regulation in Australia*, Sydney, CCH Australia, 1984.

1986

'Consumers as Victims of Corporate Crime', in E. Wheelwright (ed.), *Consumers, Transnational Corporations, and Development*; Volume VIII in the series Transnational Corporations in SE Asia, University of Sydney, Transnational Corporations Research Project, 1986.

'Taking Responsibility Seriously: Corporate Compliance Systems', in Brent Fisse and Peter French (eds), *Corrigible Corporations and Unruly Law*, San Antonio, Trinity University Press, 1986.

with Peter Grabosky, Corporate Crime and Governmental Response in Australia, in D. Chappell and P. Wilson (eds), *The Australian Criminal Justice System*, 3rd Edition, Sydney, Butterworths, 1986.

'Prison Industry: The Key Policy Dilemmas', in R. Schliemann (ed.), *Working: A Way to the Future*, Sydney, N.S.W. Department of Corrective Services, 1986.

'Retributivism, Punishment and Privilege', in W.B. Groves and G. Newman, (eds), *Punishment and Privilege*, New York, Harrow and Heston, 1986. (Reprinted in R.G. Kasinsky (ed.) *Crime, Oppression and Inequality*, Needham Heights, MA, Ginn Press.)

1987

with Brent Fisse, 'Self-Regulation and the Control of Corporate Crime', in C. Shearing and P. Stenning (eds), *Private Policing*, Vol.21, Crime and Justice System Annuals, Beverly Hills, Sage, 1987.

'Self-Regulation: Internal Compliance Strategies to Prevent Crime by Public Organizations', in P. Grabosky (ed.), *Government Illegality*, Canberra, Australian Institute of Criminology, 1987.

'From Bodgies and Widgies to J.R. Ewing: Beyond Folk Devils in Media Depiction of Crime', in *Media Effects on Attitudes to Crime*, Proceedings of the Institute of Criminology, No.72, University of Sydney Law School, 1987.

with B. Fisse, 'Corporate Offences: The Kepone Affair', in R. Weston (ed.), *Combatting Commercial Crime*, Sydney, Law Book Co., 1987.

with B. Fisse, The Pinto Papers, in M.D. Ermann and R.J. Lundman (eds), *Corporate and Governmental Deviance*, 3rd edition, New York, Oxford University Press, 1987.

1988

'Economic Policy: What the Electorate thinks', in J. Kelley and C. Bean (eds), *Australian Attitudes: Social and Political Analyses from the National Social Science Survey*. Sydney, Allen and Unwin, 1988.

'Crime in Australia', in J. Najman and J. Western (eds), *A Sociology of Australian Society*, Melbourne, Macmillan, 1988. Revised with K.M. Hazelhurst for the second edition, 1993.

with B. Fisse, 'Accountability and the Control of Corporate Crime: Making the Buck Stop', in M. Finlay and R. Hogg (eds) *Understanding Crime and Criminal Justice*, Sydney, Law Book Company, 1988.

'Regulatory Strategy and Animal Experimentation', in M. Rose (ed.), *Animal Experimentation: Ethical, Scientific and Legal Perspectives*, Sydney, University of New South Wales, 1988.

1989

with B. Fisse, 'Coke and Cancer at BHP', in P. Grabosky and A. Sutton (eds) *Stains on a White Collar*, Sydney, Federation Press, 1989.

1991

'Preface', in R. Scheff and S. Retzinger, *Shame, Violence and Social Structure*, Lexington: Lexington Books, 1991.

'Preface', in J.A. Sigler and J. Murphy (eds) *Corporate Lawbreaking and Interactive Corporate Compliance*, New York, Danorum Books, 1991.

'Thinking About the Structural Context of International Dispute Resolution', in M.R. Bustelo and P. Alston (eds) *Whose New World Order: What Role for the United Nations?* Sydney, Federation Press, 1991.

'Policies for an Era of Regulatory Flux', in B. Head and E. McCoy (eds) *Deregulation or Better Regulation*, Melbourne, Macmillan, 1991.

1992

'Good and Bad Police Services and How to Pick Them', in Peter Moir and Henk Eijkman (eds), *Policing Australia*, Melbourne: Macmillan, 1992.

'Penalties for White Collar Crime', in P. Grabosky (ed.), *Complex Commercial Fraud*, Canberra: Australian Institute of Criminology, 1992.

1993

'Responsive Business Regulatory Institutions', in C. Coady and C. Sampford (eds), *Business, Ethics and the Law*, Sydney: Federation Press, 1993. (Reprinted in Trade Practices Commission Bulletin No.77, 1994, pp. 2–8.)

'What Is to be Done about Criminal Justice?', in B. Brown and F. McElrea (eds) *The Yough Council in New Zealand: A New Model of Justice*, Auckland: Legal Research Foundation, 1993.

'Responsive Regulation for Australia', in P. Grabosky and J. Braithwaite (eds), *Business Regulation and Australia's Future*, Canberra: Australian Institute of Criminology, 1993.

'Juvenile Offending: New Theory and Practice', in L. Atkinson and S. Gerull (eds), National Conference on Juvenile Justice. Canberra: Australian Institute of Criminology, 1993.

with P. Grabosky, C. Shearing, 'Introduction', in P. Grabosky and J. Braithwaite (eds), *Business Regulation and Australia's Future*, Canberra: Australian Institute of Criminology, 1993.

1994

with K. Daly, 'Masculinities, Violence and Communitarian Control', in T. Newburn and B. Stanko (eds), *Just Boys Doing Business*, London: Routledge, 1994.

'Prospects for Win-Win International Rapprochement of Regulation in Organization for Economic Corporation and Development', in Organization for Economic Corporation and Development, *Regulatory Co-operation for an Interdependent World* Paris; OECD, 1994.

'Lessons for Regulatory Co-operation, in Organization for Economic Corporation and Development', *Regulatory Co-operation for an Interdependent World* Paris; OECD, 1994.

'Thinking Harder About Democratizing Social Control', in C. Alder and J. Wundersitz, (eds) *Family Conferencing and Juvenile Justice: The Way Forward or Misplaced Optimism?* Canberra: Australian Institute of Criminology, 1994.

'Regulation', in K Wiltshire (ed.) *Governance and Economic Efficiency*, Sydney: Committee for the Economic Development of Australia.

'Response to Nick Greiner and Catherine Walter', *Shaping Our Future: Proceedings of the National Strategies Conference*, Canberra, Economic Planning Advisory Council, 4, pp. 313–16, 1994.

1995

'Reintegrative Shaming, Republicanism and Policy', in H. Barlow (ed.), *Criminology and Public Policy: Putting Theory to Work*, Boulder: Westview Press, 1995.

'Resolving Crime in the Community: Restorative Justice Reforms in New Zealand and Australia', in C. Martin (ed.), *Resolving Crime in the Community Mediation in Criminal Justice*, London: Institute for the Study and Treatment of Delinquency, 1995.

'Globalisation of Regulation and Competition Policy, in Australian Federation of Consumer Organizations', *Competing Interests: Protecting the Public Interest in a Competitive Environment*, Canberra: AFCO, 1995.

'Inequality and Republican Criminology', in J. Hagan and R. Peterson (eds), *Crime and Inequality*, Palo Alto: Stanford University Press, 1995.

'Diversion, Reintegrative Shaming and Republican Criminology', in Günter Albrecht and Wolfgang Ludwig-Mayerhofer (eds), *Diversion and Informal Social Control*, Berlin: Walter de Gruyter, 1995, pp. 141–58.

'Sovereignty and Globalisation of Business Regulation', in Alston, P. and Chiam, M. (eds), *Treaty Making and Australia*. Sydney: The Federation Press, 1995, pp. 115–25.

'Restorative Justice', in F.W.M. McElrea (ed.), *Re-thinking Criminal Justice* vol 1. *Justice in the Community*. Auckland: Legal Research Foundation.

'Corporate Crime and Republication Criminological Praxis', in F. Pearce and L. Snider (eds), *Corporate Crime: Contemporary Debates*. Toronto: University of Toronto Press. 48–71. (Revised version in *Nikon University Comparative Law Journal* 11, 1994, pp. 123–50.)

1996

'Reintegrative Shaming', in J. Muncie, E. McLaughlin and M. Langan (eds), *Criminological Perspectives: A Reader*. Sage Publications in association with The Open University, London, 1996, pp. 432–8.

'Towards Criminology', in Kayleen M. Hazelburst, (ed.), *Crime and Justice: an Australian Textbook in Criminology*. Sydney: The Law Book Company Limited, 1996, pp. 1–12.

'Crime, Shame and Reintegration: Summary of the Theory', in Larry Siegal and Peter Cordella (eds), *Contemporary Criminological Theory*. Boston: Northeastern University Press, 1996, pp. 33–41.

'Shame and Modernity', in D. Parker, R. Dalziell and I. Wright (eds), *Shame and the Modern Self*. Melbourne: Australian Scholarly Publishing, 1996. 21–41. (Reprinted from *British Journal of Criminology*, 1996.)

1997

'Foreword', in A. Borowski and J. O'Connor (eds), *Juvenile Crime, Justice and Corrections*. Sydney: Longmans, 1997, pp. v–vii.

1998

'Reducing the Crime Problem: A Not So Dismal Criminology', in P. Walton and J. Young (eds), *The New Criminology Revisited*. New York: St Martin's Press, 1998, pp. 47–63. (Revised version of Braithwaite, 1992, Sir John Barry Memorial Lecture.)

'Shame and Repentance', in David Karp (ed.), *Repentance*. New York: Rowman and Littlefield, 1998.

'Institutionalizing Trust: Encultrating Distrust', in V. Braithwaite and M. Levi (eds), *Trust and Governance*, New York: Russell Sage, 1998, pp. 343–75.

'Restrative Justice', in M. Tonry (ed.), *Handbook of Crime and Punishment*, New York: Oxford University Press, 1998, pp. 323–44.

'Linking Crime and Prevention to Restorative Justice', in T. Wachtel (ed.), *Conferencing: A New Response to Wrongdoing*, Pipersville, Pennsylvania: Real Justice.

1999

with C. Parker, 'Restorative Justice is Republican Justice', in G. Bazemore and L. Walgrave (eds), *Restorative Juvenile Justice*. Palisades, New York: Criminal Justice Press, 1998.

Major Unrefereed Reports

with J.S. Western, P.R. Wilson, and K. Isles, 'Youth and Leisure: A Report to the YMCA', 1973.

with P.R. Wilson, G. Smith, and P. Hines, 'Prevention of Delinquency in New Planned Urban Environments', Report to the Criminology Research Council, 1974.

with P.R. Wilson, A. Guthrie and G. Smith, 'Truancy', Report to Australian Commission to Enquiry into Poverty, 1975.

with P.R. Wilson, and A. Guthrie, 'Latch-Key Children in Queensland', Report to Australian Commission of Enquiry into Poverty, 1975.

'A Public Opinion Poll Of Issues and Prospects for the 1977 State Election in Queensland', Commissioned by the Queensland Branch of the Australian Labor Party, 1977.

'Crime and the Abuse of Power in International Perspective'. An Australian Discussion Paper for the Sixth United Nations Congress on the Prevention of Crime and Treatment of Offenders, Canberra, Australian Govt. Publishing Service, 1979.

with W. Clifford, 'Cost-Effective Business Regulation: Views From the Australian Business Elite', Canberra, Australian Institute of Criminology, 1981.

with W. Clifford and J. Sandry (eds), *Regional Developments in Corrections: Proceedings of the Second Asian and Pacific Conference of Correctional Administrators, Bangkok 6–10 July*, 1981, Canberra, Australian Institute of Criminology, 1982.

with S. Vale and B. Fisse, 'The Role of Prosecution in Consumer Protection', Canberra, Australian Federation of Consumer Organisations, 1984.

with P. Grabosky and B. Fisse, 'Occupational Health and Safety Enforcement Guidelines: A Report to the Victorian Department of Labour', 1986.

with T. Makkai, V. Braithwaite, D. Gibson and D. Ermann, 'The Contribution of the Standards Monitoring Process to the Quality of Nursing Home Life: A Preliminary Report', Canberra, Department of Community Services and Health, 1990.

with V. Braithwaite, D. Gibson, M. Landau and T. Makkai, 'The Reliability and Validity of Nursing Home Standards', Canberra: Australian Government Publishing Service, 1992.

with T. Makkai, V. Braithwaite and D. Gibson, 'Raising the Standard: Resident Centred Nursing Home Regulation in Australia', Canberra: Australian Government Publishing Service, 1993.

'Improving Compliance: Strategies and Practical Applications in OECD Countries', Paris, OECD, 1993.

with L. Sherman, H. Strang, G. Barnes, M. Teh and N. Inkpen, 'Experiments in Restorative Policing', Canberra: Report to the National Police Research Unit, 1998.

with V. Braithwaite, 'Early Steps: Regulatory Strategy and Affirmative Action', Canberra: Report to the Department of Workplace Relations and Small Business, 1998.

Contributions to Policy Debates in Unrefereed Publications since 1984

'Tripartism in Public Administration: Is There a Role for Consumer and Community Groups?', *Canberra Bulletin of Public Administration*, October 1984.

'The Drug Pushers: How Corporations Create the Legal Drug Culture', *Australian Society*, May 1984, pp. 10–14.

'Safety Testing Fraud', *Consuming Interest*, March 1984.

J. Braithwaite, Yes, You Can Avoid Indirect Taxes, *Equity*, July 1985, 3, pp. 5–6.

'Dumping of Hazardous Products: The Australian Connection', *Multinational Monitor*, December/January 1985, pp. 21–2. (Reprinted in Rupert Journal, February 1985.)

with B. Fisse, 'Why Exposing Drug Dealers Won't Work', *Australian Society*, January 1985, pp. 21–3

with B. Fisse, Costigan: 'Publicity and Crime', *Reporter*, March 1985, 6, pp. 11–13.

'Bhopal: Never Again', *Consuming Interest*, March 1985.

'Privatisation, Deregulation and the Australian Community', *Canberra Bulletin of Public Administration*, 1986, 13, pp. 256–60.

'The Corrupt Industry', *New Internationalist*, November, 1986, pp. 19–20.

'IAC Drug's Proposal Means Open Season on Australian Consumers', *Consuming Interest*, June 1986, 2–4.

with P. Grabosky, 'Corporate Crime in Australia, *Trends and Issues in Crime and Criminal Justice, No.5*, 1987, Australian Institute of Criminology.

'Drug Evaluation', *Consuming Interest*, March 1988.

with B. Fisse, 'White-Collar Crime and Adverse Publicity', *The White Paper*, 1989, 3, pp. 12.

'Dangerous Simplifications', *Australian Society*, March 1991, pp. 32–3.

'Chance for Australia to Jump Off Deregulatory Bandwagon', *The Age*, 22 June 1990.

'Corporate Crime Becomes a Sick Joke for Australian Institutions', *Sydney Morning Herald*, 13 June 1991.

'Now for a Cease Fire and Back to the Blockade', *The Canberra Times*, 21 January 1991.

with V. Braithwaite, 'Impressions on the Nursing Home Industry in Three Countries', *NAHAT Network*, 13, July 1991, pp. 4–5.

'Passing the Buck for Corporate Crime', *Australian Society*, May 1991, 3–4.

'A New Order of Care for Aged Consumers', *HAI News*, April 1991, 1–11, Health Action International Penang.

with P. Grabosky, 'A Decade of Regulatory Ambivalence', *Consuming Interest*, April/May 1991, 14.

'Education and Training', *Police News*, 17 February 1992, pp. 4–5.

'Nursing Homes Crisis: Progress With Reform', *Consuming Interest*, May 1992, p. 4.

'Los Angeles and the Pathologies of Criminal Justice', *Criminology Australia*, 3, April 1992, pp. 2–5.

'Angels or Knaves? Assumptions Behind Business Regulation', *Res Publica*, 1992.

'Strengthening the Institutions of Civil Society and Social Development', Paper to the Australian National Consultative Committee for the World Summit for Social Development, 20 June 1994.

'Global Business Regulation, and The Sovereignty of Citizens', Occasional Paper 19, Social Sciences Research Centre and Department of Sociology, The University of Hong Kong. 22 pp, 1996.

with P. Drahos, 'The Smoking Gun Behind Intellectual Property', *Consuming Interest*, 1999, 28, 16–17.

Name Index